Contents

Notes on contributors   v

one   Introduction   I
           Ursula Apitzsch, Joanna Bornat and Prue Chamberlayne

Part One: Putting the subject into policy and practice   17

two   Biographical methods and social policy in European perspective 19
           Prue Chamberlayne

three   Balancing precarious work, entrepreneurship and a new   39
           gendered professionalism in migrant self-employment
           Ursula Apitzsch

four   Considerations on the biographical embeddedness of   57
           ethnic entrepreneurship
           Maria Kontos

five   Ethnic entrepreneurship as innovation   73
           Feiwel Kupferberg

Part Two: Subjectivity in context   91

six   The social subject in biographical interpretive methods: 93
           emotional, mute, creative, divided
           Andrew Cooper

seven   A socially and historically contextualised psychoanalytic   101
           perspective: Holocaust survival and suffering
           Daniel Bar-On

eight   Professional choices between private and state positions in   115
           Russia's transformation
           Victoria Semenova

nine   Maintaining a sense of individual autonomy under conditions   131
           of constraint: a study of East German managers
           Ulrike Nagel

Part Three: Self-awareness in research and practice   147

ten   Biographical reflections on the problem of changing violent   149
           men
           David Gadd

eleven   The biographical turn in health studies   165
           Wendy Rickard

twelve   Ethical aspects of biographical interviewing and analysis   181
           Kaja Kaźmierska

thirteen   Ghost writers: using biographical methods across languages   193
           Bogusia Temple

Part Four: Recognising trajectories of disempowerment   **203**

fourteen   'Bucking and kicking': race, gender and embodied resistance   205
in healthcare
Yasmin Gunaratnam

fifteen   Biography as empowering practice: lessons from research   221
Joanna Bornat and Jan Walmsley

sixteen   'It's in the way that you use it': biography as a tool in professional   237
social work
Riitta Kyllönen

seventeen   Interpreting the needs of homeless men: interviewing in context   251
Karin Schlücker

Part Five: Biographical resources in education and training   **263**

eighteen   In quest of teachers' professional identity: the life story as   265
a methodological tool
Marie-Françoise Chanfrault-Duchet

nineteen   Narratives, community organisations and pedagogy   285
Rosemary Du Plessis, Jane Higgins and Belinda Mortlock

twenty   Doctors on an edge: a cultural psychology of learning and   299
health
Linden West

twenty-one   Intercultural perspectives and professional practice in the   313
university: what's new in Germany
Lena Inowlocki, Maria Teresa Herrera Vivar and Felicia Herrschaft

Index   331

BIOGRAPHICAL METHODS AND PROFESSIONAL PRACTICE

An international perspective

Edited by Prue Chamberlayne, Joanna Bornat and
Ursula Apitzsch

The POLICY
P~P
PRESS

First published in Great Britain in March 2004 by

The Policy Press
University of Bristol
Fourth Floor
Beacon House
Queen's Road
Bristol BS8 1QU
UK

Tel +44 (0)117 331 4054
Fax +44 (0)117 331 4093
e-mail tpp-info@bristol.ac.uk
www.policypress.org.uk

British Library Cataloguing in Publication Data
A catalogue record for this book is available from the British Library

Library of Congress Cataloging-in-Publication Data
A catalog record for this book has been requested

ISBN 1 86134 492 9 paperback

A hardcover version of this book is also available

Prue Chamberlayne is a Senior Research Fellow and **Joanna Bornat** is Professor of Oral History, both in the School of Health and Social Welfare, The Open University. **Ursula Apitzsch** is Professor in Sociology and Political Science, J.W. Goethe University, Germany.

Cover design by Qube Design Associates, Bristol.
Printed and bound in Great Britain by Bell & Bain Ltd, Glasgow.

Notes on contributors

Ursula Apitzsch is full Professor of Political Science and Sociology at the J.W. Goethe University, Frankfurt-am-Main, Germany and member of the board of directors of the Frankfurt Centre for Women's and Gender Studies. She was coordinator of the Targeted Socio-Economic Research project 'Self-employment activities of women and minorities: their success or failure in relation to social citizenship policies' (SEM), and now leads the European Commission Research and Technological Development project 'The chances of the second generation in families of ethnic entrepreneurs: intergenerational and gender aspects of quality of life processes (ethnogeneration)'. Her publications include *Migration und Traditionsbildung* (Opladen, 1999), 'Biographical analysis: a "German" school?', with Lena Inowlocki, in Chamberlayne et al (eds) *The turn to biographical methods in social science* (Routledge, 2000), and a monograph for the *International Review of Sociology*, entitled 'Self employment – gender – migration' (2003).

Daniel Bar-On is Professor of Psychology at Ben-Gurion University of the Negev, Beer Sheva, Israel. Born in 1938 in Haifa to parents of German descent, he worked for 25 years as farmer, educator and then secretary of the Kibbutz Revivim. He pioneered field research in Germany on the psychological and moral after-effects of the Holocaust on the children of the perpetrators. His book, *Legacy of silence: Encounters with children of the Third Reich* (Harvard University Press, 1989), has been translated into French, German, Japanese and Hebrew. He has brought together descendants of survivors and perpetrators for five intensive encounters (the To Reflect and Trust group, shown by the BBC on 'TimeWatch', October 1993), as well as students from the third generation of both sides. Another of his books, *Fear and hope: Three generations of Holocaust survivors' families* (Harvard University Press, 1995), was published in Hebrew, English, German and Chinese, and he has since published *The indescribable and the undiscussable* (Central European University Press, 1999). He has been appointed to numerous professorial chairs and received top-ranking awards in the US, Germany and Italy. Together with Professor Sami Adwan, he directs the Peace Research Institute in the Middle East (PRIME).

Joanna Bornat is Professor of Oral History in the School of Health and Social Welfare at the Open University, where she writes courses on social care and ageing. She has a long-standing interest in oral history, reminiscence and remembering in late life and has researched and published articles, book chapters and edited collections in these areas. She has been joint editor of *Oral History* for over 20 years and is a founder member of the Centre for Ageing and Biographical Studies at the Open University.

Prue Chamberlayne taught for many years at the University of East London, where she was director of the Centre for Biography in Social Policy, and coordinator of the seven-country EU-funded SOSTRIS project ('Social Strategies in Risk Society, 1996-99'). She has since been a Senior Research Fellow in the School of Health and Social Welfare at the Open University, where she has explored the use of biographical approaches in professional training (in the field of homelessness) and evaluation (in arts-based community development health work). Her publications include the jointly authored *Cultures of care: Biographies of carers in Britain and the two Germanies* (The Policy Press, 2000), and three jointly edited collections, *Welfare and culture: Towards a new paradigm in social policy* (Jessica Kingsley, 1999), *The turn to biographical methods in social science: Comparative issues and examples* (Routledge, 2000), and *Biography and social exclusion in Europe: Experiences and life journeys* (The Policy Press, 2000).

Marie-Françoise Chanfrault-Duchet is a Senior Lecturer in Language Sciences at the IUFM (School of Education) and at the University of Limoges (France). Her research fields concern biography from the viewpoint of linguistics, literature, education and feminist theory. She has published a book in German on 'autofiction', entitled *Adolf Wölfli, autobiography and autofiction* (Rombach Verlag, 1998) and numerous articles about life story as a genre. She is currently working on the linguistic construction of the self.

Andrew Cooper is Professor of Social Work at the Tavistock Clinic and at the University of East London. In the 1990s, he worked on a series of comparative studies of European child protection systems and practices. With Rachel Hetherington and others, he is author of *Positive child protection: A view from abroad* (1995) and *Protecting children: Messages from Europe* (1997), each published by Russell House Publishing, Lyme Regis. He is currently writing a book with Julian Lousada, entitled *Borderline welfare* (with Karnac Books, London).

Rosemary Du Plessis is a Senior Lecturer in the School of Sociology and Anthropology at the University of Canterbury (New Zealand). She has supervised a large amount of undergraduate and postgraduate work that utilises biographical research strategies, including personal accounts of professional practice. Her current research includes analysis of public debates about fathering and the evaluation of strategies to facilitate public participation in decision making about the application of new biotechnologies.

David Gadd is a Lecturer in Criminology at Keele University, Staffordshire. His research interests include masculinities and crime, domestic and racist violence, psychosocial and psychoanalytic perspectives.

Yasmin Gunaratnam is a freelance researcher and writer who works on issues of race and gender equality in health and social care. She also has an interest in research methods and is author of *Researching 'race' and ethnicity: Methods, knowledge and power* (Sage Publications, 2003).

Maria Teresa Herrera Vivar studied sociology, politics and pedagogy at the J.W. Goethe University in Frankfurt-am-Main, Germany. Her study focus concerns feminist theory, gender relations, migration and racism. She is currently writing her MA thesis on 'Political organizing of immigrant women: between identity politics and multidimensional subjectivity'. She is a counsellor for foreign students at the students' union (AStA)/J.W. Goethe University, and also works at the Women's Association for Self-Defence in Frankfurt-am-Main.

Felicia Herrschaft studied philosophy, cultural anthropology, psychoanalysis and sociology at J.W. Goethe University in Frankfurt-am-Main, Germany. She wrote her MA thesis on philosophy on Karl Mannheim's sociology of knowledge: 'Strange knowledge'. She is currently developing a PhD thesis on experimental spheres and conceptual art, based on her radio programmes with female artists in her public radio show in Frankfurt-am-Maim, *redaktion universal* at Radio X.

Jane Higgins is a Senior Lecturer in the School of Sociology and Anthropology at the University of Canterbury (New Zealand). Her recent research has focused on a narrative approach to teaching sociology in a prison education programme, welfare reform in New Zealand during the 1990s and youth transitions from education to employment.

Lena Inowlocki is Acting Professor in the Department of Social Sciences at J.W. Goethe University in Frankfurt-am-Main, Germany. Her work is mostly in the area of qualitative–interpretive social research, on families and adolescence and on issues of biography, right extremism, migration, culture and knowledge. Recent publications in English are: 'Biographical analysis: a "German" school?' (with Ursula Apitzsch) in Chamberlayne et al (eds) *The turn to biographical methods in social science* (Routledge, 2000) and 'Doing "being Jewish": constitution of "normality" in families of Jewish displaced persons in Germany', in Breckner et al (eds) *Biographies and the division of Europe: Experience, action and change on the 'Eastern side'* (Ashgate, 2003).

Kaja Kaźmierska is an Assistant Professor of Sociology at the Institute of Sociology (Chair in Sociology of Culture) at the University of Lodz (Poland). Her research is based on biographical narrative interview analysis and she works on problems such as collective identity, collective memory, and biographical experiences of the war. She has published *Polish war experiences and ethnic identity: Analysis of eastern borderland narratives* (IfiS PAN, 1999) in Polish as well as numerous papers in Polish and some in English.

Maria Kontos has initiated and conducted several research projects on migration, migration policies, gender, biography and self-employment. She has worked on the EU project 'Self-employment activities of women and minorities' and has been a lecturer in the Sociology Department at the J.W. Goethe University in Frankfurt-am-Main, Germany. More recently, she has been a researcher at the Institute of Social Research at the J.W. Goethe University, charged with the coordination of the EU project 'The chances of the second generation in families of ethnic entrepreneurs'. She has published on migration, self-employment, self-employment policies, social work, gender and biographical methods.

Feiwel Kupferberg is Professor of Educational Sociology at the Danish University of Education in Copenhagen. He has been a visiting professor at the University of California at Berkeley, the Max Planck Institute of Human Development in Berlin, the Berlin-Brandenburg Institute of Social Research, Moscow University and the University of Wisconsin, Green Bay. He teaches in the fields of sociological theory and biographical methods. His most recent books have focused on creativity in an educational context, the professional socialisation of nurses in Denmark, the interplay of individual biographies and societal transformations in Eastern Europe, and the management of the past in postwar East Germany. He is currently working on several book projects within the emerging field of the sociology of creativity.

Riitta Kyllönen is a Researcher at the University of Tampere, Finland. She has done research in Italy for several years, in particular on the interrelationships between family, labour market and the welfare state. She has worked as a (visiting) researcher in the Universities of Modena, Padua, Turin and Urbino. Her doctoral research is a biographical study of how Italian parents reconcile work and family over their life course.

Belinda Mortlock has been awarded a MA in sociology, and has experience of teaching and administering courses in the School of Sociology and Anthropology, University of Canterbury, New Zealand. Currently she coordinates that university's Social Science Research Centre, a multidisciplinary centre set up to facilitate a more collaborative approach to social science research within the university and the broader community. Her research interests include health, gender and the social analysis of life stories.

Ulrike Nagel is Associate Professor in Microsociology at Otto-von-Guericke University, Magdeburg. Her research interests and publications cover the interface between biography and the institutional life course, and her recent studies focus on pathways to modernisation in post-socialist countries undergoing transformation and in the world of work and professions. She has also published in the fields of qualitative research methods with special regard to the non-standardised expert interview and its foundation in the sociology of knowledge.

Wendy Rickard is a Senior Lecturer in Public Health and Health Promotion at London South Bank University, and specialises in teaching qualitative research methods to postgraduate students in the Faculty of Health. She works collaboratively with the National Sound Archive at the British Library, where she has led projects titled 'HIV/AIDS testimonies', 'The oral history of prostitution' and 'Life history for health promotion' (which includes life histories with homeless people, refugees and asylum seekers, and looked-after young people). She is currently working on an associated collection of oral histories with haemophiliacs living with HIV or AIDS.

Karin Schlücker studied psychology, sociology, political sciences and psychoanalysis in Bochum and Frankfurt-am-Main, Germany. Since 1995 she has worked as a Research Assistant at J.W. Goethe University in Frankfurt-am-Main. She is researching for her doctoral thesis on epistemology and methods of qualitative text analysis in social sciences and is participating in a research project on curative interaction in psychoanalytic therapy.

Victoria Semenova is a Professor at the State Humanitarian University (Faculty of Sociology) and Principal Researcher at the Institute of Sociology, Russian Academy of Sciences. She is also a national expert for USAID and the UN Human Development Programme.

Bogusia Temple is a Reader at the Salford Housing and Urban Studies Unit at Salford University. She has an interest in methodological issues in research, particularly in relation to minority ethnic communities. She is currently working, with researchers at London South Bank University, on a Joseph Rowntree Foundation-funded research project looking at service users' views of interpreters. She is also working on research with refugees and asylum seekers. She has published extensively on both general methodological issues and on issues in relation to minority ethnic communities.

Jan Walmsley is a Senior Lecturer in the School of Health and Social Welfare at the Open University. Her research interests are in the history of learning disability and participatory research methods. She is author of *Inclusive research in learning disability: Past, present and futures* (Jessica Kingsley, 2002) with Kelley Johnson.

Linden West is Reader in Education in the Centre for Educational Research at Canterbury Christ Church University College, Kent, UK. He uses biographical methods in his research and teaching including, most recently, in a new MA programme for guidance professionals. He is Convenor of the Life History and Biography Network of the European Society for Research on the

Education of Adults (ESREA) and has worked for a number of universities, adult education organisations and as a broadcaster. He is a qualified psychoanalytic psychotherapist. He is the author of a number of books including *Beyond fragments, adults, motivation and higher education: A biographical analysis* (Taylor and Francis, 1996) and *Doctors on the edge: General practitioners, health and learning in the inner-city* (Free Association Books, 2001).

ONE

Introduction

Ursula Apitzsch, Joanna Bornat and Prue Chamberlayne

This volume is concerned with the relevance of biographical methods and the contextualised understanding of human agency, as keys in professional interventions. Its interest lies in the usefulness of biographical methods in investigating and generating new forms of social practice and in gaining fresh insights into institutional processes. The contributions to this volume portray ways in which biographical methods have been (or are starting to be) applied in various aspects of professional training as well as in partnership with users of services. The volume evaluates biographical practice against a mapping of practitioner and user positioning and experience. It also does so in different contexts, reviewing developments in policy and practice in a comparative European perspective.

The book profits from lively dialogues in international networks of biographical researchers, and draws on research from a wide range of countries. With such an international perspective, there is inevitably a strong emphasis on issues of migration and cultural diversity, gender, and situations of social transformation.

In this introduction, we clarify for readers our particular understandings of the term 'professional practice', and reflect on the differing contexts in which biographically focused professional practice has emerged.

Concepts of professional practice

Our understanding of professionalism concerns relationships of practice where interactions develop and are sustained within contexts that are rarely predetermined or formally defined, and in which the rules of engagement may be shaped under conditions of uncertainty and challenges to established boundaries. This contrasts with a more traditional approach to professional practice, in which social influence and power are what fundamentally differentiates professionalism from other forms of work (Evetts, 2003). It also goes beyond the emphasis on specified codes of conduct, learned and assessed procedures, and membership, which are typically used to define the work and action of occupations such as medicine, accountancy and law. This is not to say that questions of power differentials, knowledge, training and codes of behaviour are not relevant; rather that these more conventional and traditional defining characteristics come to be problematised by a more inclusive and extensive definition. This understanding draws on a wide set of social relationships that are better understood in terms of context and interaction, and consequently biography.

In exploring definitions of professional practice and how these have changed historically, we find ourselves invoking a diversity of theoretical frameworks: symbolic interactionism, the Chicago school of sociology, structural hermeneutics and psychodynamic approaches, together with theories of empowerment and user participation. The individual chapters of this volume reflect a similar range of epistemologies within sociology. Most are tussling with the theorisation of meaning and motivation, and some are working across the apparent incompatibilities of discourse and emotionality.

Irrespective of such differences, we as editors and contributors, and as researchers as well as practitioners, share a concept of professionalism. This assumes that promoting a sense of individual autonomy in a context that encourages social solidarity necessarily involves a process of dialogue and interaction. Interactive contexts include the agency and perspectives of users of services, students and professionals, and the interplay of policy frameworks with broader structural changes, such as labour markets, migration, class, ethnicity, age and gender. The chapters of this volume cluster around three main arenas of social change:

- transformation from eastern to western types of society in Europe;
- major shifts in social and welfare principles;
- experiences of immigration and of new cultural diversities.

The impact of these fundamental transitions on political and organisational contexts, on professional practice, on employment and occupational structures (including the emergence of new professions), and on human relations and experience, is immense, as this volume vividly portrays. The contributors' own wealth of cross-cultural experience also gives testimony to the conditions and structures in which biographical explorations of professional practice have emerged and are developing.

Readers will notice a diversity of methods among the chapters. Several writers have used the biographical interpretive method, many others depend on narrative analysis, while others again make use of the life history and oral history tradition (see Chamberlayne et al, 2000). One strength of each of these methods lies in their capacity to shift between levels of analysis. This capacity is only one example of the potential closeness between biographical research methods, new policy thinking, and effective and sensitive practice. For taking account of interrelationships between micro and macro levels is clearly essential to the contextualising of professional and user experience, to any critical approach to professional practice, and perhaps to professional 'survival' in conditions of uncertainty and instability (Chamberlayne et al, 2002). Understanding and drawing on inner resources and states of consciousness enriches many areas of policy and practice, and comes to the fore in addressing uncertainty and trauma. Awareness of intersubjectivity emerges from many of the chapters as central to both research and practice. Common also is a commitment to citizenship based on a politics of recognition. The dialogic and interactive nature of biographical methods in research and practice inherently implies a relational notion of citizenship (Lister, 1998), just as global conditions require a concept of citizenship that recognises difference. Linking these aspects of policy and practice, Froggett (2002, p 4) writes of

> responsible self-actualising subjects in the context of irrevocable attachments to others …. Sustained recognition demands a continual open-ended dialogue that can only be fully realised if its participants perceive each other as of equal moral worth and reciprocal significance.

We therefore define professional practice as dialogic and relational, and contextualised within processes of political, social and institutional change. The contributions in this volume concern a wide range of person-centred work, including employment, benefits, social work, health promotion, education and training.

Next we focus a little more on certain debates about professionalism in Germany and Britain, our 'home ground' as editors. The German discussion we address concerns in particular the process of interaction between users and professionals in social work and educational situations (Combe and Helsper, 1996; Kraul et al, 2002). By contrast, the British discussions that we focus on concern the effects of regulation on professional functioning, and on issues of partnership and empowerment among users.

In Germany, a more general concept of professional practice and its meaning for the field of social work (as a 'modest' profession) have been widely influenced by Fritz Schütze (1996, 2002) and Gerhard Riemann (2002). Ulrich Oevermann (1996, 2001) and Dieter Nittel (2000) have developed theories of professions and their consequences for the 'under-professionalised' field of education and training.

Following the tradition of Everett C. Hughes (1984), Riemann (2002, p 167f) underlines the importance of finding communalities between types of work that are often considered poles apart.

> Both the physician and the plumber practise esoteric techniques for the benefit of people in distress. The psychiatrist and the prostitute must both take care not to become too personally involved with clients who come to them with rather intimate problems. (Hughes, 1984, p 316)

Hughes wrote these typically provocative remarks in order to emphasise that sociologists should examine a wide range of human practices "regardless of their places in prestige or ethical ratings" (Hughes, 1984, p 316). Schütze underlines the special challenges of professional practice with clients who are marginalised, as is often the case in social work. Such professionals have to deal with the paradoxes of a hierarchical situation in which nevertheless the free consent and collaboration of the client is regarded as necessary (Schütze, 1996, p 193).

For Ulrich Oevermann (2001, p 1), 'practice', or more precisely the German term *praxis*, which derives directly from the Greek term, involves:

> the totality of life expressions of a particular human life [which is] centered around an individuated subjectivity. So it embraces intentionality, but it includes more than that: the term constitutes theoretically the objective and non-reducible reality of a concrete individuated and unique life form, which becomes autonomous by solving its own unique crises.

The autonomous self-regulation of professions is a "structural condition for competent and effective performance of client-oriented services" (Oevermann, 2001, p 2). In contrast to mechanical modes of practice, the intervention of a professional practitioner "is in itself an autonomous practice and as such consists in a service, which is principally, by its very nature, not able to be standardized" (2001, p 2). Oevermann defines the difference between professional and everyday life practice by analysing "microscopically the inner structural logic and dynamics of professional practice" (2001, p 2). Sociological analysis according to objective hermeneutics makes a fundamental distinction between the rules for the generation of objective meanings and an individual's principles in selecting from these possibilities. This differentiates it from individualised action theories on the one hand, and from social technologies or other 'mechanical practices' on the other. Client-oriented professional service consists in 'vicarious crisis management' (Oevermann, 2001). The professional practitioner according to this concept is able to (re)construct social newness in the form of crisis solution just because he/she is released from the time pressure of social action, but nevertheless is able methodologically to reconstruct the sequences of social action in a given situation.

This concept of professional practice is clearly concerned with biographical perspectives, since such practice is founded in professionals and their clients forming a reciprocally binding working alliance in order to solve a specific personal crisis. Through the hermeneutic reconstruction of professional interventions, we gain an insight into how user (and professional) biographies are shaped through interactive efforts to achieve or maintain social integration against the threat of exclusion processes (Apitzsch and Kontos, 2003). All too often, institutional structures and institutionalised life experiences themselves preclude rather than promote the necessary quality of beneficial intersubjective processes, both between professionals and users, and within the lives of users.

Two contrasting influences have been shaping debates about professional practice in Britain: the shift towards managerialist, neoliberal, policies on the one hand, and pressure from user and disability movement activists on the other. Each has had its impact on approaches to professional practice by practitioners, service users and policy makers.

While there are many perspectives that grapple with the drastic extent of change in British social policy, two are particularly germane to biographical approaches. The first is a *psychodynamic perspective*, which seeks to understand distress in terms of unconscious processes, not just in the individual, but also in interaction with group dynamics in families, institutions policy and government. This is sometimes at considerable odds with the second, an *active, service user-focused and empowerment politics* informed by oral and life history methods. We will try to give a flavour of each of these very different stances, following a brief characterisation of recent changes in the domains of regulation and empowerment and their consequences for professionalism.

Innovations introduced during the period of Conservative government (1979-97) have continued apace under two subsequent Labour administrations, and the introduction into health and social care of management strategies more typical of the private sector has served to weaken and undermine professional powers. From a consumer perspective, many might have welcomed restraint on professional domination rooted in a hierarchy of class and education, which seemed to offer little that was negotiable to those who were the recipients of professional decision taking. However, coupled with huge cuts in funding and with the imposition of a managerialist audit culture (expressed in such terms as 'quality' and 'best value'), these changes have led to much disenchantment and demoralisation among professionals in health and social care (Kelly, 1998; Foster and Wilding, 2000). As far as Froggett (2002) is concerned, under commissioned care management, "the distinctive contribution of the front-line practitioner has been all but removed" (2002, p 130). And, in the new evidence-based systems of monitoring and accountability, "knowledge which is diffuse, interpretive, emotionally embedded, and makes connections [is repudiated] ... in favour of that which is discrete, quantifiable, positivistic" (1996, p 125).

Writing from a psychodynamic perspective, Andrew Cooper sees a crisis in authority in which professionalism has been replaced by surveillance, with much naming and shaming. The social work profession in the 1980s and the medical profession in the 1990s have been brought under an external "inspectorial yoke" (Cooper, 2001, p 353). By marketised subcontracting, government has vacated its own role in favour of agencies that have none of the strong intermediate relations between state and civil society that formerly existed in trades unions, local government, and community and professional organisations. And the exercise of autonomous professional judgement, which is so crucial to the managing of risk and vulnerability, has been undermined by a sequence of public humiliations highlighting tragedies and 'failures'.

At the heart of the governance of health and welfare, Cooper finds a cynical corrosion of governance and professionalism, since enforced audit linked to performance outcomes inevitably brings fraudulent misrepresentation. Within this system, Cooper (2002, p 6) claims:

the lived qualitative, subjective and emotional experience of what it is really like at the heart of our educational system and welfare state is presently a form of inadmissible evidence.

Cooper argues that we need a realist epistemology, a "politics of experiential truth" (Cooper, 2002, p 10). In a comparable argument, Gunaratnam and Lewis (2001) discuss how 'political correctness' suppresses the exploration of underlying emotions, such as rage, shame and hate, without which anti-discrimination policies remain distinctly superficial.

The colonisation of social and psychic space by externally imposed criteria, together with severe cutbacks on professional supervision, removes the scope for 'thinking' in professional practice. French and Simpson (2000, p 54) write of the need to "work at the edges between knowing and not-knowing", and the anxiety that this entails. Yet Dartington (2000) detects in contemporary professionals, alongside an impossible overload, an incapacity to work on attachment and dependency. Such work, which was formerly key to case methods in social work as a means of moving clients on, emotionally presupposes space and support for reflexive thinking, as well as good supervision (Schon, 1983).

While the psychodynamic approach argues for the upholding and enhancing of relatively 'traditional' professional practice and expertise, approaches drawing on oral and life history theory and methods have struck a rather different note. These emphasise the perspective of the service user and biography as empowering practice.

The legitimising of the service user voice is rooted in a multidisciplinarity that links the work of psychologists, sociologists and historians, among others. Psychologists of old age, following from the work of Butler (1963) and Erikson (1950), have emphasised the narrative continuity of reflection and agency into late old age (McAdams, 1993; Coleman et al, 1998). Picking up on these ideas, gerontologists (Johnson, 1976; Bornat, 1989) and those working with other marginalised groups, such as people with learning difficulties (Walmsley and Atkinson, 2000), identified the dual reward of biographical approaches for professional practice. On the one hand, they offer opportunities for more individualised and therefore more sensitive and appropriate outcomes with knowledge gained from fully expressed user identities and, on the other, the possibility of more empathic and enabling practice once professionals and practitioners accept that they can learn from the stories they hear.

Research by sociologists working within a humanistic tradition of theorising, such as Plummer (2001) and Gubrium (1993), has provided more user-focused approaches to biographical work with a rich and extensive literature, going back to the Chicago school and more recently drawing on debates in autobiography and narrativity (Stanley, 1992; Josselson and Lieblich, 1993). Central to these debates are questions of truth and composure where the significance of accounts for what they can tell about the present as well as the past in people's lives has come to be seen as significant.

This intertwining of past and present has become a defining characteristic of the role of oral and life history work in professional practice. Eliciting past experience as a basis for understanding present identity and preferences is perceived as a desirable, if not always operationally possible, component of care practice (Clarke et al, 2003; Gunaratnam, 2003, pp 128-9; Walmsley and Johnson, 2003, pp 134-6). Knowledge of how things were, as a measure of how far or how near current practice is from earlier policy and practice, provides professionals with a measure for reflecting on their own and others' practice. In this way, oral history accounts of the history of health and social care provision, of the past of health and social care from the recipient's perspective, of policy developments and of changing approaches to practice now inform the education and training of professionals and are also beginning to fill historical archives in the UK. Rickard's contribution to this volume (Chapter Eleven) provides an overview of these sources and what they are beginning to contribute both to what is known of past contexts in which professional practice operated and to present-day practice in the light of such knowledge.

However, despite the many ways in which a biographical perspective has been recognised as contributing positively to professional practice, the reality of health and social care provision in Britain today is one of political complexity and managerialist dominance. The implications for both biographical approaches and for professional practice are consequently not encouraging. Of key significance in all this are changes in the standing of professionals.

The championing of service users, during the Thatcher era, as a means to softening attitudes towards a market in health and social care has led to their repositioning as 'consumers'. The issue remains, however, to what extent this is a product of "liberal conservatism" (Crinson, 1998, p 227) or a response to user-movement pressure for change (Beresford, 2001). The reconfiguration of professional and service-user relationships around notions of empowerment and choice could be seen as a net loss in terms of professional powers. However, this same shift, if viewed as a result of user-movement pressure, clearly had the potential to encourage professionals to take up new and more sensitive and responsive forms of practice. From the service user's perspective, the gains may seem clear enough, and the contribution of biographical approaches to a more user-sensitive and participative shift in practice has been well documented. Awareness of individual lives in assessment and care planning, for example, has opened up new opportunities for more individualistic and holistic approaches to care practice. Nevertheless, pincered between users and managers, the authority and scope of professional practice has come under pressure in the UK. Emphasis on consumerism and the influence of the user movement has led to a relative neglect both of professional subjectivity and of the relational interface between professionals and users. To summarise, the arguments from Germany and Britain, while by no means comprehensive, suggest the richness and complexity of emergent discussions concerning professional practice, and their interrelatedness with concerns of biographical methods. Their first emphasis lies in pointing to the need for biographically informed practice.

Some German discussions even define professional practice in *the particular character and quality of interactions with clients,* such as forming reciprocally binding working alliances to solve crises, supporting autonomy within hierarchical situations, understanding objective situations and personal meanings. This view insists that such practice cannot be standardised and requires professional autonomy. It points to key tensions in practice, especially concerning contextual issues, such as *the clash between professionalism and neoliberalism,* but also in relationships between professionals and users. The second argued that in order to be able to 'think' and to cope with uncertainty, professionals need space, support and supervision, validation of 'diffuse, interpretive and emotionally embedded' knowledge, and a politics of 'experiential truth', much of which is eclipsed in a regulatory audit culture in Britain.

We have also pointed to the tendency for *uneasy relationships between user empowerment and professionalism,* both by the user movement becoming colonised by neoliberal consumerism and by challenges to professional power, as in the disclosing of lifelong damaging experiences of services. The fuller expression of user identities has exerted important pressure for more individualistic and holistic approaches to care, but often polarised relations between professionals and users.

The chapters take up these arguments, relating them to issues for biographical research in a range of social and welfare practice contexts. They thread through the book's five sections, each of which is organised around key debates in biographical research. In the final part of this introduction we outline the contents of each section with introductions to each chapter.

The structure of the book

In assembling the contributions for a readership that is likely to come from different directions, both professionally and in terms of practice, we have adopted five section headings, each of which engages with the application of biographical approaches. The chapters are organised into sections that match familiar areas of debate:

- putting the subject into policy and practice;
- subjectivity in context;
- self-awareness in research and practice;
- recognising trajectories of disempowerment;
- biographical resources in education and training.

Putting the subject into policy and practice

This section tackles the conceptual and policy dimensions of using biographical analysis comparatively in order to understand the special dynamics of distinctive social processes. Exemplifying cross-level analysis, it starts with an overarching policy piece, followed by a 'case study' of three contributions from a comparative project on migrant women. These show how biographical analysis can lead to major redirections in theory and policy, shifting and broadening the focus of European welfare systems.

Chamberlayne (Chapter Two) discusses ways in which resource structures in different institutional, organisational and national settings either constrain or facilitate the use of action-oriented, biographically informed work, and the challenge posed by case study methods both to the traditional paradigm of social policy and its liberal form. The following three chapters originating from the European project 'Self-employment activities concerning women and minorities' (SEM) by Apitzsch, Kontos and Kupferberg (Chapters Three to Five of this volume) focus on innovation and professionalisation as emerging biographical strategies among marginalised subjects in self-employment. In a resounding critique of existing (masculinist) theories of ethnic entrepreneurship and of 'deficit' assumptions in social policy, their interpretations point to migrants' active ways of surviving as trendsetting coping strategies under precarious life conditions. They also define a 'new professionalism', not based on fixed social models, but resulting from more fluid biographical processes.

Apitzsch (Chapter Three) argues for the efficacy of biographical forms of policy evaluation in showing the need to understand the conditions of agency, creativity and networking, and of gendered socio-cultural dynamics. Referring to new forms of freelance professional practice and entrepreneurship, she asserts that well-targeted facilitative and monitoring policies need to understand personalised biographical case structures in order to give proper advice in situations of crisis. Arguing the biographical as well as social embeddedness of entrepreneurial activity, Kontos (Chapter Four) explores motivation and 'biographical resources' among successful self-employed minority women. Her contribution denotes how trauma and a lack of education have led to a search for alternative forms of social recognition and learning, and to the realisation of an intuited 'unlived life'. Starting with a critique of 'opportunity structures' within classical American sociology, and showing Iranian entrepreneurs developing identities as businessmen in Denmark, Kupferberg (Chapter Five) emphasises the pressures on immigrant communities to be creative and to innovate.

Subjectivity in context

This section brings inner worlds to the fore, suggesting the hidden depths of unconscious resources. It considers ways in which individuals and collectives internalise the impact of past and present socio-historical conditions, incorporating specific aspects of their experience into emerging identities and values, and how biographies may be devalued and revalued within and between changes in historical and political contexts.

Referring to work in Kosovo, Cooper (Chapter Six) appeals for recognition of emotionality as the foundation of all mental activity and creativity, and therefore for a conceptualisation of deep subjectivity within biographical methods. Bar-on (Chapter Seven) draws on his experience of intersubjective group work in the deeply divided social contexts of Israel and Germany to argue the need for interdisciplinary work to grasp the complicated cross-generational psychic effects of the Holocaust, and to understand the impact of changing political contexts on the way basic biographical questions are posed. Semenova and Nagel (Chapters Eight and Nine, respectively) focus on experiences among professionals of social transformation. In a contribution that has great salience in the context of the liberal threat to European welfare, Semenova uses the case of Sergei to show the huge difference in moral worlds between public and private sectors in Russia, and the difficulties of a researcher achieving emotional empathy across such cultural divides. Posing a similar question, Nagel advocates self-questioning and the 'suspension of belief' as key to research in unfamiliar contexts. Her research concerns East German managers' responses to life decisions under German unification, and how these are influenced by the particular forms of 'mental reservation' they had developed within the old regime.

Self-awareness in research and practice

This third section follows the reflections of professionals and researchers as they encounter and learn from engagement with biographical processes in their daily practice. Researchers and practitioners have long been aware of social relationships and psychological meanings in the interview, and this section particularly concerns the confrontation between the biography as it emerges through the interview process and the interviewer or researcher's own understandings and self-awareness. How these relationships and meanings are interpreted, and how the interview brings changes in the interviewer (and hence the practitioner), is a key focus.

Gadd (Chapter Ten) looks at the way political posturing about male violence, prevalent in domestic violence work, can be subverted through biographical approaches that enable a more dynamic and analytical approach to notions of masculinity, and therewith more searching and effective practice. He also shows how, in the process of giving such help, workers' own biographies are inevitably brought into play.

The interview, as an experience and as a process of self-development, is explored in a general overview by Rickard (Chapter Eleven), who discusses the contribution of biographical methods to more egalitarian relationships and interventions in health studies and health systems. Describing her method of open narrative interviewing and in-depth interpretation in some detail, Kazmierska (Chapter Twelve) reflects on her experience as a researcher, as she explores some ethical issues, heightened in the face of unanticipated political responses, such as nationalism in Poland. Also challenging conventional assumptions relating to the ethics of research and its communication, Temple (Chapter Thirteen) discusses problems relating to the translation of interview data in research, pointing out that the positioning of the translator in the discourse should be made explicit.

Recognising trajectories of disempowerment

The emancipatory power of biographical approaches to research and practice has become part of the rhetoric of methodological debate and a major contribution to the motivation of researchers and practitioners. This section takes a critical look at biographical work as a source of empowerment by raising questions about professional practice where biography has been used as a resource. It thus takes a more questioning view of the claims and limits of biographical practice as a means of challenging or altering power relations in health and social care.

Gunaratnam's study of race and gender in a hospice (Chapter Fourteen) explores the ways in which racialised identities can be reproduced and challenged within healthcare services. Bornat and Walmsley (Chapter Fifteen) question claims of empowerment by positioning research in relation to the different stakeholders who gain from biographical work. Their critical review of 'top-down' and 'bottom-up' research designs thus opens up the question of empowerment for wider debate. Kyllönen's study of social workers and lone mothers in Venice (Chapter Sixteen) draws attention to the processes of emergent biographical co-construction and the way in which biographical categorisation can both enable and constrain supportive work with a socially marginalised group. The perversion of a biographical approach in her study of Venetian social workers' construction of lone mothers' personal histories is both a product of their own prejudices and a response to welfarist policies that seek to confirm a marginalised and dependent status in a context of rationed social support.

Schlücker (Chapter Seventeen), making a further interpretation of student research on the needs of homeless people, shows how taking the wider agency setting into account, together with the interpersonal dynamics of the interview, evokes a lifelong experience of hierarchical services, and a very different understanding of 'needs' from those posited by traditional agencies.

Biographical resources in education and training

This final section explores biography as a quality resource in the education and professional practice of teachers, social researchers and doctors. Dealing with very different community and professional settings, and in contrasting countries, they all see readiness to reflect on personal vulnerabilities, and to feel and be disturbed by exposure to otherness, as essential to good practice.

Combining literary with life history analysis of teachers' narratives, Chanfrault–Duchet (Chapter Eighteen) is concerned with how personal lives interact with changes in professional practice in the teaching of French in schools in France. She is seeking to articulate this research in new programmes of teacher training, as a means of helping to solve the long-standing crisis in French education.

This crisis is in part one of professionalism, in which teachers, casting off the role of a secular priesthood transmitting set knowledge, are expected to engage in a new didactics involving 'the self'.

In teaching sociology by 'doing' in New Zealand, Rosemary Du Plessis, Jane Higgins and Belinda Mortlock work with three interrelated sets of narratives: their own as university teachers; their students'; and their students' interviewees, who are community activists. Their contribution to this volume (Chapter Nineteen) shows how, by such community-based teaching, they generate a sociological understanding of community organisations as 'relational settings', in which personal lives intersect with gender constructs, and with shifts in welfare funding and policy discourse, and how this impacts on all concerned. West (Chapter Twenty), working in the East End of London, gives two moving examples of doctors learning to defend their emotional health in the context of stressful inner-city work, and the challenge this sensitive work poses to conventional medical culture and 'what they need to learn'. His concern is with how doctors manage and cope with the distress of others, the interface between personal and public realms in doctors' own lives, and the stories they tell of their biographical work in becoming effective practitioners. Inowlocki, Herrera Vivar and Herrschaft (Chapter Twenty-One), drawing on several years of intercultural university work, first trace (retarded) shifts in policy concerning 'foreign' students in German schools and universities. Using a number of cameo situations, they trace the growing use by minority ethnic students of their own experience, as well as the impact of their presence and views on other students, and how staff can encourage such reflective processes. In particular, they highlight how the participation of minority ethnic students highlights and challenges the homologising and pathologising of mainstream theoretical models concerning ethnicity and migration, while making such challenges can be a lonely and uncertain process.

Concluding remarks

With the perspectives of professional practice and biographical reflexivity as the foundations for this collection, we are delighted to be able to present research that, drawing so directly and profitably on an exploratory and critical approach to the concept of biography in daily life, also makes such a central contribution to policy developments and debates.

Producing the volume has been a long and painstaking process, involving a great deal of language editing (with special thanks to Jude Bloomfield and Katie Costello), and we thank everyone involved for their patience, including the anonymous reviewers whose comments we valued.

References

Abbott, A. (1988) *The system of professions: An essay on the division of expert labor*, Chicago, IL/London: University of Chicago Press.

Apitzsch, U. and Kontos, M. (eds) (2003) 'Self-employment, gender and migration', *International Review of Sociology/Revue Internationale de Sociologie*, vol 13, no 1, pp 67-234, Monographic Section.

Beresford, P. (2001) 'Service users, social policy and the future of welfare', *Critical Social Policy*, vol 21, no 4, pp 494-512.

Bornat, J. (1989) 'Oral history as a social movement: reminiscence and older people', *Oral History*, vol 17, no 2, pp 16-23.

Butler, R. (1963) 'The life review: an interpretation of reminiscence in the aged', *Psychiatry*, vol 26, pp 65-76.

Chamberlayne, P., Bornat, J. and Wengraf, T. (eds) (2000) *The turn to biographical methods in social science: Comparative issues and examples*, London: Routledge.

Chamberlayne, P., Rustin, M. and Wengraf, T. (eds) (2002) *Biography and social exclusion: Experiences and life journeys*, Bristol: The Policy Press.

Clarke, A., Hanson, E.J. and Ross, H. (2003) 'Seeing the person behind the patient: enhancing the care of older people using a biographical approach', *Journal of Clinical Nursing*, vol 12, pp 697-706.

Coleman, P.G., Ivani-Chalian, C. and Robinson, M. (1998) 'The story continues: persistence of life themes in old age', *Ageing and Society*, vol 18, pp 389-419.

Combe, A. and Helsper, W. (eds) (1996) *Pädagogische Professionalität: Untersuchungen zum Typus pädagogischen Handelns*, Frankfurt-am-Main: Suhrkamp.

Cooper, A. (2001) 'The state of mind we're in: social anxiety, governance and the audit society', *Psychoanalytic Studies*, vol 3, no 3/4, pp 349-62.

Cooper, A. (2002) 'The state of mind we're in (2) – "There is only good news"', Unpublished paper given at Keele University, May.

Crinson, I. (1998) 'Putting patients first: the continuity of the consumerist discourse in health policy, from the radical right to New Labour', *Critical Social Policy*, vol 18, no 2, pp 227-39.

Dartington, T. (2000) 'The preoccupations of the citizen – reflections from the OPUS listening posts', *Organisational and Social Dynamics*, vol 1, no 1, pp 94-112.

Erikson, E. (1950) *Childhood and society*, New York, NY: Norton.

Evetts, J. (2003) 'The sociological analysis of professionalism: occupational change in the modern world', *International Sociology*, vol 18, no 2, pp 395-415.

Foster, P. and Wilding, P. (2000) 'Whither welfare professionalism', *Social Policy and Administration*, vol 34, no 2, pp 143-59.

French, R. and Simpson, P. (2000) 'Learning at the edges between knowing and not-knowing: "translating" Bion', *Organisational and Social Dynamics*, vol 1, no 1, pp 54-77.

Froggett, L. (1996) 'Instrumentalism, knowledge and gender in social work', *Journal of Social Work Practice*, vol 10, no 2, pp 119-27.

Froggett, L. (2002) *Love, hate and welfare: Psychosocial approaches to policy and practice*, Bristol: The Policy Press.

Gubrium, J. (1993) *Speaking of life: Horizons of meaning for nursing home residents*, New York, NY: Aldine de Gruyter.

Gunaratnam, Y. (2003) *Researching 'race' and ethnicity: Methods, knowledge and power*, London: Sage Publications.

Gunaratnam, Y. and Lewis, G. (2001) 'Racialising emotional labour and emotionalising racialised labour: anger, fear and shame in social welfare', *Journal of Social Work Practice*, vol 15, no 2, pp 131-48.

Hughes, E.C. (1984) *The sociological eye*, New Brunswick, NJ: Transaction Books.

Johnson, M. (1976) '"That was your life": a biographical approach to later life', in J.M.A. Munnichs and W.J.A. van den Heuval (eds) *Dependency and interdependency in old age*, The Hague: Nijhoff.

Josselson, R. and Lieblich, A. (eds) (1993) *The narrative study of lives* (series), London: Sage Publications.

Kelly, A. (1998) 'Professionals and the changed environment', in A. Symonds and A. Kelly (eds) *The social construction of community care*, Basingstoke: Macmillan, pp 94-112.

Kraul, M., Marotzki, W. and Schweppe, C. (eds) (2002) *Biographie und Profession*, Bad Heilbrunn: Klinkhardt.

Lister, R. (1998) 'In from the margins: citizenship, inclusion and exclusion', in M. Barry and C. Hallett (eds) *Social exclusion and social work: Issues of theory, policy and practice*, Lyme Regis: Russell House Publishing.

McAdams, D.P. (1993) *The stories we live by: Personal myths and the making of the self*, New York, NY: William Morrow and Co.

Nittel, D. (2000) *Von der Mission zur Profession? Stand und Perspektiven der Verberuflichung in der Erwachsenenbildung*, Bielefeld: Bertelsmann.

Oevermann, U. (1996) 'Theoretische Skizze einer revidierten Theorie professionalisierten Handelns', in A. Combe and W. Helsper (eds) *Pädagogische Professionalität: Untersuchungen zum Typus pädagogischen Handelns*, Frankfurt-am-Main: Suhrkamp, pp 70-182.

Oevermann, U. (2001) 'A revised theoretical model of professionalisation', Unpublished paper, Frankfurt-am-Main, pp 1-27.

Plummer, K. (2001) *Documents of life 2: An invitation to a critical humanism*, London: Sage Publications.

Riemann, G. (2002) 'Biographien verstehen und missverstehen – Die Komponente der Kritik in sozialwissenschaftlichen Fallanalysen des professionellen Handelns', in M. Kraul, W. Marotzki and C. Schweppe (eds) *Biographie und Profession*, Bad Heilbrunn, Klinkhardt, pp 165-96.

Schon, D. (1983) *The reflective practitioner: How professionals think in action*, New York, NY: Basic Books.

Schütze, F. (1996) 'Organisationszwänge und hoheitsstaatliche Rahmenbedingungen im Sozialwesen: Ihre Auswirkung auf die Paradoxien des professionellen Handelns', in A. Combe and W. Helsper (eds) *Pädagogische Professionalität: Untersuchungen zum Typus pädagogischen Handelns*, Frankfurt-am-Main: Suhrkamp, pp 183-275.

Schütze, F. (2002) 'Supervision als ethischer Diskurs', in M. Kraul, W. Marotzki and C. Schweppe (eds) *Biografie und Profesion*, Bad Heilbrunn: Klinkhardt, pp 135-64.

Stanley, L. (1992) *The auto/biographical I: Theory and practice of feminist auto/biography*, Manchester: Manchester University Press.

Walmsley, J. and Atkinson, D. (2000) 'Oral history and the history of learning disability', in J. Bornat, R. Perks, P. Thompson and J. Walmsley (eds) *Oral history, health and welfare*, London: Routledge.

Walmsley, J. and Johnson, K. (2003) *Inclusive research with people with learning disabilities: Past, present and futures*, London: Jessica Kingsley.

Part One:
Putting the subject into policy and practice

TWO

Biographical methods and social policy in European perspective

Prue Chamberlayne

The rapid expansion of biographical methods comes at a time of frustration with a number of aspects of social policy, such as positivistic, top-down approaches, the failure to solve issues of expense, efficiency and dependency, and the cultural lag between welfare systems and social change[1]. European welfare systems, already under pressure from neoliberal forces, must reorient to new social realities in the labour market, in relations between public and private spheres, in gender relations, and in notions of citizenship and democratic agency. Biographical methods provide a tool for reconnecting welfare systems with lived experience and processes of social change, and for elaborating and operationalising new social policy concepts such as social capital, active social welfare and social quality. New and still pliable policy terms are in the process of formation, including at the European level.

The focus on the structure of biographies turns the generalising assumptions and procedures of social science on their head, levering social policy away from its alignment with economics and politics, creating new affinities with psychoanalysis, anthropology and literary criticism. This realigning of disciplines is just one aspect of a paradigmatic shift (Kuhn, 1970) towards a new definition of politics and welfare democracy, a more differentiated and cultural approach to welfare resources, and a new set of relationships between public and private spheres.

In his book *Liquid modernity* (2000), Zygmunt Baumann argues that the public agora of debate and negotiation between the individual and common, private and public good, has become empty and urgently needs rebuilding. There is also a discrepancy between the de jure and de facto status of individual lives, the supposed scope for autonomy and self-determination as against the constrained and 'un-free' nature of actual lives. He says that the key to human emancipation lies in relearning forgotten citizenship skills and reappropriating lost citizenship tools, although this must also be done in new and more generous ways than before (Baumann, 2000, p 41). This is surely similar to the Arendtian idea of a new kind of politics, in which people would be recognised for *who* – rather than *what* – they are, and appear to each other not as objects, but as subjects *acting* with words and deeds (Cavarero, 2000, p 21). Hannah Arendt, in *The human condition* (1958), emphasised individuated and individualising 'action', rather than role-based 'behaviour'. Action 'reveals the self rather than concealing him or her behind the social mask', and reinstates distinction and difference in the public sphere, rather than leaving these as "private matters of the individual" (Benhabib, 1996, pp 25-6; see also Cavarero, 2000).

Rethinking relationships between individual lives and social contexts may be easier in some sociological and social policy traditions than in others. In some welfare settings, professional training involving biographical approaches may be borne along by existing currents of intellectual and cultural capital. A particular strength of French social thought (since Comte and Durkheim), for example, still lies in the formal and informal social sphere, which liberalism finds so hard to grasp. Organisational and professional forms support concepts of social solidarity, proximity, animation or habitus. Some while ago, an article in *Le Monde* defined 'proximity' as the everyday work of society on itself and of social subjects among themselves, and promoting such 'work' as the task of relational social services. The article argued that state innovation presupposed rooting its political dynamics in a socially creative civil society, and this transformation was the *sine qua non* of improving service delivery. It is quite hard even to make the English translation 'sound right'!

German concepts of *hermeneutics* (the science of understanding) make a valuable contribution to conceptualising more cultural and active approaches to welfare, and in generating new understandings within *social pedagogy*. German social thinking specialises in the understanding of personal experience and meaning as interactive and social processes, and social pedagogy's long-standing combining of interpersonal and cultural community development work, which revived in the 1970s, spans disciplines and professions that are deeply divided in Britain. As Walter Lorenz (2000) points out, present-day champions of qualitative methods could gain much from the hermeneutic tradition, which developed in opposition to positivist 'objectivity'. Alice Salamon, for example, a founder of social work in Germany in the early 20th century, argued for objectivity to allow for subjectivity by consciously debating and critiquing it. She espoused the evaluation, comparison and interpretation of detail, rather than its amassing, and attention to affect and intentions in the client and in the social worker.

In Britain, where there is often a notable lack of contextual or conceptual fit between biographical methods and policy thinking, there seems nevertheless to be an openness to biographical methods because they offer innovative solutions or points of departure in a situation of perplexity or crisis. Moreover, the espousal of more active approaches to welfare, as expressed in such terms as 'supporting people', competence building and lifelong learning, requires a more personalised approach.

Biographical methods, however, are differently embedded across Europe in different disciplines, in the fields of education, health, or community and social services, and in different religious and political currents.

Europeanisation provides researchers with opportunities to engage in reciprocal learning and understanding of welfare concepts and institutional contexts. Researchers are in a prime mediating position to broaden and enrich political and policy repertoires. However, in creating a common European terminology in social policy, it is important that newly shared concepts are not glossed, but used with a full understanding of their original depth. To safeguard and develop the cultural capital of European social thinking, and to defend the European social model against the regulating and standardising effects of neoliberalism, social policy experts need to recognise and appreciate the differentiated and constantly shifting nature of European cultures and traditions.

This chapter explores some of the ways in which biographical methods challenge established approaches to social policy, and how this challenge varies and is developing in different European welfare systems. It begins by drawing on research I have been involved in concerning 'cultures of care' and 'social strategies in risk society', to demonstrate how comparative work can generate new understandings of welfare contexts and welfare processes, social relations and resources, and processes of social change. In the second section of this chapter, I examine some examples of discussions in different European contexts on the implications of biographical research for social policy. This will centre particularly on what new understandings of subjectivity and social change imply for institutional settings and the training in the social professions. My argument is that biographical methods need hospitable policy concepts in order to animate relationships between research, policy and practice, and that conceptual exchange at the European level is a vital resource in the reinvigoration of social policy.

Life worlds and social policy

My first example of biographical research into life worlds comes from the 'Cultures of Care' project (funded by the Economic and Social Research Council 1992-96). This project set out to extend comparative social policy to the informal sphere by comparing informal home caring in the three welfare societies of East and West Germany and Britain. Apart from making system comparisons, it highlighted the crucial importance of vibrant informal cultures in mediating creative relations between the public and private spheres (Chamberlayne and King, 2000).

The study contrasted two strategies of caring. The home-centred mode drew on outside resources to fortify a private system of caring, while the more outward-oriented mode used caring as a springboard to wider social engagement. The two strategies were by no means physically determined, since it was possible to be more or less housebound and yet maintain dynamic and expanding relationships with the outside world.

Through caring, outwardly connected carers extended their skills, knowledge and confidence. They became flexible, independent and energetic agents, able to make long-term plans and manage crises, and a source of social capital to others. They often formed partnership relations with services – modelling active welfare. By contrast, home-based caring deepened the divide between public and private worlds, reduced knowledge of options, and weakened confidence and negotiating competencies – within the family as well as without. However, an outward orientation was not a matter of willpower or conscious reflexivity, but required both structural and personal support by services, networks, and partners and/or professionals.

From the complex matrix of structures affecting caring strategies, we identified three key ingredients favouring outward connectedness:

- activity routes;
- shared cultures;
- personal support.

Activity routes were all (highly gendered) ways of moving between public and private worlds, and included employment, informal networks and engagement in welfare or community services. Sharing in a *common culture*, most effectively a counterculture, brought personal relationships, trust, and a sense of being fortified and energised to challenge oppressive structures and mechanisms. Feeling *personally supported*, whether through a marriage-type partnership or by a well-liked professional, likewise generated energy and the confidence to take the initiative and to challenge authority.

We were shocked to see carers in Britain who had been outwardly oriented becoming worn down by the precariousness of services and retreating back into the private sphere in ways that restored the gender divide. We anticipated that the same pattern might develop in East Germany following unification, although there were no signs of it during our study period (1992-96). West German carers tended to have particular difficulty in stepping over the domestic threshold, unless they were associated with alternative milieus, where the key ingredients of activity routes, a common culture and partner support were more readily in place.

Our detailed analysis of individual cases suggested why it was that so much more biographical work[2] by carers was needed in some contexts than in others, and why some cultural and structural situations obstructed an outward orientation. The value for social policy of building on life worlds and encouraging moral agency emerged strikingly, as did the rich possibilities from combining what are often discrete areas of gender, life transition and third-sector perspectives. The research indicated that professionals likewise needed to combine biographical sensitivity (for example, to anger, trauma, depression) in caring situations with contextual awareness, particularly of the 'social' sphere of informal networks and associations. This under-recognised and often uncharted arena became both riveting and alive through biographical research.

My second example comes from the seven-country SOSTRIS ('Social strategies in risk society') project, which was funded from 1996-99 under the EC Targeted Socio-Economic Research Framework 4 programme on social integration and exclusion. This research likewise pointed to hidden social and cultural resources, and to the need for social policy to treat service users as resourceful actors rather than victims, and to bolster existing initiatives and experiences (SOSTRIS, 1997-99; Chamberlayne et al, 2002). The project was concerned with how individuals from a range of social groups (unqualified youth, unemployed graduates, lone parents, minority ethnic groups, early retired people, ex-traditional workers) address the uncertainties of modern 'risk' society, and the very different biographical resources, some more facilitative than others, that individuals bring to this task. Overall, we were struck by the way in which our interviewees experienced what were objectively collective situations as lone individuals – the political masking of what C. Wright Mills termed in 1959 the 'public' nature of private troubles. We felt that our research subjects might have been much helped by popular political discussion, for example, of the new gender and intergenerational relationships entailed in early retirement or graduate unemployment, or the new gender and marital projects in single parenting. These topics barely figure in social policy debates and initiatives, yet they were spoken of in eloquent and troubled ways by our interviewees.

The research suggested that policy makers and professionals might learn much from looking at how individuals, acting as social pioneers, handle the challenges of social change. Individuals are at the frontline of social transformation, and their strategies and actions chart the dynamic, multidimensional processes of modernisation. Biographical methods thus seemed to hold the potential of reconnecting social policy with life worlds in politically invigorating ways (Chamberlayne and Rustin, 1999; Chamberlayne et al, 2002).

The SOSTRIS project also experimented with using biographical methods to study agencies that we considered innovative in tackling social exclusion. In all seven countries, the agencies recognised the value of biographical methods in revealing personal clues to strengthen engagement and a sense of usefulness among the participants, in deepening diagnoses of individual problems, in highlighting and profiling the biographical resources of staff and users, and in developing a form of evaluation that would promote rather than detract from person-centred and community development work (SOSTRIS, 1999; Wengraf, 2002). In each of the seven countries studied, this work led to proposals for further collaboration and evoked the potential for new and creative relationships between research, policy and practice.

Let us now move on to explore some aspects of the possible role of biographical methods in creating such dynamism between research, policy and practice, under three headings: subjectivity and culture; institutional contexts; and professional practice and training.

Subjectivity and culture

The idea of 'acting with words' is central to the biographical method. Biographical researchers are constantly astonished by the coherence and eloquence of their subjects' accounts, and the skills involved in crafting a life story. Interviews with homeless people with multiple problems radically challenge the official policy that they are 'incapable' of benefiting from counselling or therapy (Curran, 2000). Interviewees almost invariably point themselves to the meaningfulness of the narrative experience.

The oral history movement in Britain has a tradition of giving voice to the hidden histories and identities of oppressed groups for whom stigma, segregation and disempowerment have been a common experience. Over a 20-year period, it has challenged and greatly influenced policy at the level of practice, leading to the adoption of 'empowerment' as a policy concept, and to the recognition of narration as a means of maintaining identity in institutional contexts and against negative stereotypes. Narrative work in Britain, well established in gerontology, is gaining ground in medicine, occupational therapy, and in work with vulnerable adults and children (Perks and Thomson, 1998; Bornat et al, 2000; Thompson, 2000; Bornat, 2002; see also Chapter Eleven of this volume).

As compared with oral history, biographical methods offer a more interpreted form of subject-centred research, invoking latent levels of meaning both at individual and system levels[3]. The 'Cultures of Care' and SOSTRIS projects illuminated the way welfare regimes interact with informal cultures and structures and are played out through the lives and strategies of individuals. Material policies and practices are filtered through networks of relationships and shared assumptions and meanings, which vary greatly within and between societies[4]. As we said in *The turn to biographical methods in social science* (Chamberlayne et al, 2000, p 9), the social order is not just transmitted, in the way a deterministic cultural studies might emphasise, but experienced and reacted to, which sometimes helps to change it.

In Britain, relationships between structural constraints and individual autonomy tend to be discussed in terms of structure and agency (Giddens, 1984). As Hanses (2003: forthcoming, p 12 of draft version) points out, 'biography' transcends this dualism. Borrowing from biology, 'autopoiesis' describes the dialectic between subject and structure, in which the subject or organism is not just externally determined but has creative scope, even though it cannot escape the structuring of social practice. While in biology and in systems theory, autopoiesis is used to emphasise (creative) adaptation to surrounding structures, Alheit and Dausien (1999, p 7) have stressed that, inasmuch as such creativity affects the external world, it has 'sociopoietic' potential as a centre of change within a social framework[5].

Self-creativity, or 'biographicity', is the capacity to transform practical knowledge into biographical reflexivity, and also to find potential for action and orientation within the 'unlived life' – often in ways that surprise us, or that we only understand subsequently. In learning, "we not only appropriate single experiential elements as components of the social world, but we develop the 'appropriation system' itself", which is open, but also biographically layered (Alheit and Dausien, 1999, pp 12, 13). The 'appropriation system' that is being developed might well be collective as well as individual, since 'sociopoiesis' can contribute to regime changes as well as personal learning:

> If we conceive of biographical learning as a self-willed, 'autopoietic' accomplishment on the part of active subjects, in which they reflexively 'organise' their experience in such a way that they can generate personal coherence, identity, a meaning to their life history and a communicable, socially viable life-world perspective for guiding their actions, it becomes possible to comprehend education and learning both as individual identity work and as the 'formation' of collective processes and social relations. (Alheit and Dausien, 2002, p 17)

Just as Giddens argues that reflexivity and autonomy are essential capacities for the (post)modern world, so for Alheit biographicity is a key qualification for the current epoch. Working with this understanding of subjectivity has major consequences for professional training, as we shall see.

A biographical focus on the unique experience of the individual seeks to capture 'who' the person is (Caverero, 2000), while also gaining insights into social processes. However, this fundamentally challenges the generalising, categorising methodologies in which social policy planning and monitoring are rooted, and the regulatory, evidence-based culture that dominates current health, education and welfare policies. Rustin (2000, p 35) explores the paradox that "while a variety of forms of Western cultural representation have been ... working in various imaginative biographical registers for centuries, social science has ... mostly filtered biography out of its fields of interest". The alignment between social and natural sciences maintains a deep resistance to single or small-scale case approaches, even while they are basic to law, medicine and psychoanalysis. Novels, drama and poetry – further crucial filters for transmitting, creating and understanding culture – also work through the fulcrum of unique experience.

Challenging current notions of 'evidence-based practice', and taking an explicitly pychodynamic approach, Wendy Hollway (2001) calls for attention to the unconscious intersubjective dynamics within which evidence is produced, and use of a psychosocial theory of the subject who is 'defended' against anxiety. She argues that this evaluation method would validate and enhance professional experience, and use the kinds of understanding and evidence that are inherent to professional practices and ways of knowing.

In their study of a working-class estate, Hollway and Jefferson (2000) explore the 'psychological locatedness' of extraordinary differences in fear of crime in what is, sociologically speaking, a common situation. Such use of case studies exemplifies what Hanses (2003: forthcoming, p 8 of draft version) calls the power of biographical narratives to reveal 'self-constitution' or the 'subjective construction of one's own reality'. Narratives offer access to 'something' about actions, their social origins, and how they are embedded in social contexts.

The tentativeness of Hanses' 'something' is echoed in Murard's (2002) exploration of latent levels of wider cultural formation in his interpretation of case studies from the SOSTRIS project. His starting point was the frequent expression in the narratives of extreme vulnerability and fragility, and feelings of being both a victim and an offender, although the crime was utterly vague and indefinite – recalling Kafka's desperate search for an object of his feeling of guilt (Murard, 2002, p 44). Searching for outside sources of such divided subjectivity, Murard discerns a general shift from a 'culture of shame' to a 'culture of guilt', accompanying the replacement of group control by the requirement for self-control. Although people are clearly victims of structural changes, "guilt is a feeling that structures their narration and their life-strategy". It is essential that welfare agencies understand "the emotional and experiential sources of social exclusion or vulnerability" (2002, p 53).

Institutional contexts

Despite their capacity to bridge personal and social levels of analysis, biographical methods do not always do so. The interpretive tradition in North America moved from the Chicago school's interest in urban structures and processes to a focus on more personalised experiences of illness and health[6]. Sensitive ethnomethodological and social interactionist research in Britain in the early 1970s became sidelined by more structural approaches. And biographical methods in the arena of social work in Germany, in the guise of 'reconstructive social pedagogy' have long been focused on treating the case as a 'social text' and on issues of presentation. Reconstructive social pedagogy has thus remained separate from debates concerning 'person–centred social work'. But even this latter emphasises organisation, quality and management, regards case work as long dead, and approaches social work "without a subject" (Hanses, 2001, p 1).

There are now many signs of biographical research paying more attention to social context, including in relation to professional work, as part of understanding obstacles to personal development, and as part of facilitation[7]. The currently somewhat hidden psychodynamic tradition in Britain holds a rich vein of conceptualisation of the mirroring of external worlds in inner psychic states and vice versa[8]. Menzies Lyth (1960) undertook one of the most famous studies of unconscious dynamics within organisations. She was concerned with the way, in hospitals, defences against the fear of dying produce distancing mechanisms, which obstruct nurses' emotional engagement with patients. In our research on homelessness, Chris Curran (2002) and I found ourselves using this kind of thinking to make links between wider social pressures, institutional structures and individual encounters. In professionals' narrations about their handling of difficult boundary and relationship issues with clients, we were struck by a pattern of professionals withdrawing emotionally at key moments of interaction, with the result that social exclusion was reinforced at the very point at which it might have been tackled (Chamberlayne et al, 2002). While the biographies of the particular professionals suggested why they would tend to avoid such engagement, institutional norms and structures actively helped to preclude such interpersonal work – through norms concerning safety and confidentiality, through tight time schedules, and through lack of appropriate training and supervision. At another level, the failure to address the needs of homeless people for emotional and relational work seemed to result from wider social pressures to keep the 'precipice' of existential insecurity off limits. The main concern of homelessness policy under New Labour has been to clear the streets of rough sleepers. To tackle the deeper-lying causes would bring society face to face with its own malaises in the fabric of everyday life and in its institutional services.

The study of person-centred agencies in the SOSTRIS project invariably showed the importance of time and space for experimentation, reflection and supervision in holistic work, and for agencies to pay great attention from their internal as well as their external relationships. Engagement with the inner world, with intense feelings of anxiety and uncertainty, "will not occur by default but only by deliberate purpose, principle, modelling and design" (Wengraf, 2002, p 262).

The fact that European welfare systems and professional training are more rooted in relational concepts of social solidarity than their Anglo-Saxon counterparts does not mean that they adequately nurture human and social capital in their staff or in their clients. Perhaps no society has discovered how to integrate such personal attentiveness into large-scale bureaucracies. Now the regulatory audit culture that already pervades British systems of administration is assailing Europe. This seems a necessary concomitant of the neoliberal project agenda of restoring state services to the market; although, at a more latent level, the mania for control may be a desperate defensive attempt to 'hold the centre' against the speed of change and diversification. As was stated earlier, such regulation is not the only impulse, even in Britain. New Labour concepts cry out for and often support experimentation with more personalised approaches[9]. And indeed, despite British social policy's difficulties with relational concepts, its pluralist structures do produce some remarkable experimentation, as in the US. There is currently a profusion of arts-based health and education work in Britain, which aims to generate social inclusion, and the rights-based empowerment movement in Britain, with its emphasis on cultural difference, has a strong contribution to make to European policy debates.

As has been said, in all seven countries, the agencies represented in the SOSTRIS project wanted to collaborate further in using biographical methods as a means to furthering their own humanistic and democratic goals. All were committed to redistributive values, yet they were exploring alternatives to the conditionality of existing systems, and promoting ways of enhancing biographical resources and social capital. The quality of personal relationships, knowing and valuing 'who' people were, was key in every case: in unconditional 'honour' loans for self-employment projects in southern Italy, fostering neighbourhood support systems in Catalonia, sustained personal mentoring in a youth employment project in East Germany, the use of arts-based methods and the principle that 'everyone has something to contribute' in a community project in London working across deep divisions of race and mental illness, in which staff were given space to work creatively around commonly agreed principles. In the French project concerning family benefits (*Caisse Nationale d'Allocations Familiales)*, the focus was using a biographical approach to transform local welfare cultures – by mutual recognition of expertise between managers, agents and clients, valuing and codifying face-to-face relationships, and fostering empathy as opposed to fear or pity in staff–client relationships.

As Georg Vobruba (2000, p 605) puts it, decisive situations in welfare tend to consist of interactions between two persons. One has an interest in access to inclusion in some dimension, while the other's role is to observe fulfilment of the preconditions linked with this access. The way the two biographies meet in such a situation shapes the nature of the interaction and its outcome, and personal reasons may influence the extent to which the professional can hear and appreciate the particular client.

The debate in Germany on biographical methods in social work now emphasises that such methods cannot simply be voluntaristically 'added in', but imply regime changes. For one thing, a lack of competences in biographicity is all too often institutionally derived. For another, the active ownership of such competences presupposes that users' biographical knowledge resources and horizons of meaning connect up with institutional provisions (Hanses, 2001, p 3). Biographicity depends on inner development in the client, who may for personal reasons be on a downward trajectory or feel overwhelmed. But a client may also be too institutionalised to access his/her own sense of agency, or too moulded by a *habitus* of 'need'. De-autonomisation can also result from norms of professional practice, and from a more personal mismatch between the professional and the user (Hanses, 2001, p 4).

Both Hanses (2001) and Roer and Maurer-Hein (forthcoming) argue that the shift in interaction patterns involved in introducing biographical diagnosis entails a paradigm shift. Different professional skills, identities and organisational structures are required. Placing narrative centre-stage removes the safe question/ answer situation, puts existing professional skills in the background, and loosens boundaries between professions. Existing skills and organisational arrangements appear rather blunt instruments of support, and new repertoires of action and interpretation are needed. Institutions need to be self-reflexive, and ask how certain institutional and professional regimes came into being, which links interactional relationships with organisational development. Personal biographies of managers, professionals and clients within a given organisation are all 'institutionalised interaction histories'. Accordingly, biographising lies at the heart of institutional and organisational transformations.

As Spanò (2002) puts it, it is not enough to demand that individuals become reflexive and adaptable in the new social conditions; the same is required of institutions (see also Wengraf, 2002).

Alheit and Dausien (1999) similarly argue that education systems should not instrumentalise people's biographies, but support biographicity through a new 'interaction order', creating new learning environments. 'Biographising' institutions implies equality (through mutual recognition), openness and social cooperation (1999, p 9).

Professional skills and training

New Labour's 'overthrow' of the 'old' welfare system recognises such problems to a degree, as in its critique of 'dependency', and its attempts to raise standards, as through the National Service Framework for Older People (DoH, 2001)[10]. Its solution in many fields is to import new young idealists untainted by bureaucratic cultures. The new regulatory culture is highly bureaucratised, however, and pay levels are low. Moreover, the difficulties of interpersonal work with people with emotionally damaged lives produces the kind of retreat we have found in the interviews with homelessness workers, and the failure to tackle deeper lying problems is highly dissatisfying. Turnover of staff in all the personal professions in Britain is now unprecedented – in nursing, teaching and social work. New fields of work such as the homelessness sector have been established without substantive qualifications, and a whole generation of social workers has been trained in managerial and legalistic skills at the expense of casework (Froggett, 2002).

Legal history and administrative categories are also central planks of much social policy and social work teaching in Europe, despite a stronger philosophical base. Roer and Maurer-Hein (forthcoming) say that, in Germany, social work's borrowing of concepts from clinical psychology has failed to grasp the social situatedness of the individual, and the use of business methods loses sight of the creativity and resistance of the biographical actor. The non-recognition of the social catches social workers in a conflict, since it is clearly 'there' – it contributes to their burnout and feeling of being like social plumbers. They appeal to Italian psychiatry's giving back of individual problems to society, and argue that biographical methods offer a resource-centred approach. Individuals vary in the extent to which they can own their own life histories, and some may feel like victims or rebels, but the task is to work with their owned aspirations, goals and resources, and to seek biographically suited outcomes. Working with clients' biographies is also highly motivating.

The use of biographical concepts and methods in professional training, in diagnostic and casework, and in the 'biographising' of institutions requires a sharing and exchange of professional and research skills, together with a certain amount of reciprocal 'translating'. Qualitative researchers are particularly well placed to explore and highlight the rich diversity of cultural, intellectual and practitioner traditions in Europe, and to act as discourse mediators, including with policy makers. Skills in narrative interviewing, active listening, and the interpretation of lives and texts are readily acquired by professionals, especially those with psychosocial or casework training. In Germany (Riemann and Schütze), there are long-standing models of biographical workshop training with social work students; in Britain and France, of intergenerational sociological studies of life histories (Thompson, Bornat, Bertaux, Delcroix); and in Britain of extensive infant observation in a range of professional training (Tavistock Centre).

Researchers need the support and advice of professionals around the particular issues of confidentiality and feedback that emerge in biographical interpretive methods. While the anonymised outputs of such biographical research can clearly be used for empowerment purposes, it is tricky to use the processes of interpretation, which are also highly empowering, among groups of users or professionals who know each other. This is because the analysis tackles deeper and more latent levels of meaning and functioning than, say, an oral history approach (compare, for example, Chapters Six and Twenty with Chapter Fifteen of this volume, and see issues raised by Kazmierska in Chapter Twelve). Biographical researchers who want to apply biographical methods in community settings may well need training in group dynamics.

Since training involves learning, there is much scope for exchange between education and other fields. Courses in 'fictional-critical writing' can be used to great effect as a tool of professional development. As Bolton (1994) explains, fictional stories bypass problems of confidentiality and fears of exposure, allowing vital personal and professional issues to be tackled head on. Fictions have exceptional summarising capacities; they provide access to ambiguity and complexity, are a vehicle for self-examination and discovery, and a means of sharing anxieties, fears and frustrations. In courses in which writing is created for the specific group, "the full interplay of story, teller and audience, or text, interpretation and intentionality is retained" (Bolton, 1994, p 60). Stories can help us "outwit our own inner police systems" (1994, p 64, quoting Hughes, 1982), and grasp things in the depths of our minds. They can help us become aware of taken-for-granted glass walls, and extend our responsibility and understanding.

Winter (1986), who initiated this approach, gives a more theorised account of it, drawing on literary and educational theory, and arguing that the role of social science is ethical and emancipatory, rather than about "accurate descriptions" (1986, p 179). Fictional texts raise questions about reality, through an unresolved plurality of meanings and voices, using irony and the Brechtian 'joke of contradiction'. A case study provides not just a rich and plausible description, but also a theory of the structure behind those details. Writing raises the question of who the 'I' is that writes: how do my words relate to my experience or anyone else's? Writing demands a critical response from the reader:

> there are 'gaps' and 'blockages' in the flow of the text which *force* readers to collaborate in maintaining its meaning, by attempting to remedy the gaps and apparent inconsistencies from their own experience. (Winter, 1986, p 178, quoting Iser, 1974, pp 132-3)

This describes processes that are strikingly similar to those involved in the biographical interpretive method in characterising and interpreting the personal and social meanings of narrators' choices in their lives and in their accounts. Winter says the reader has to formulate the unformulated, to spot what 'I' concealed, and ask what the concealments conceal. To do this they have to distance themselves from momentary emotions, to appreciate the ironies in which the characters are enmeshed – this "alienation effect is necessary to all understanding" (Winter, 1986, p 178, quoting Belsey, 1980, p 71).

The intensity of the workshop experience in the SOSTRIS project led us to consider the nature of the sociological and imaginative engagement in the interpretive process. People invariably feel exhausted and exhilarated after workshops. Certainly a high level of emotional energy is involved in mobilising one's own emotional and cognitive experience in order to understand another, and in the constant cross-referencing between the tiniest detail and the wider context. Detailed case presentations, which need about 15 minutes each, also give rise to animated involvement, including teaching material, with participants who otherwise have no involvement with the cases. Cavarero (2000) evokes the complexity of interrelationships involved in telling and listening to stories, when she posits our fascination with other people's stories as our own desire to have our own told by another. Carolyn Steedman (1996) has explored the social uses of other people's stories of the self. As researchers and professionals we need to consider what social uses we are making of biographical work[11].

Winter (1986), speaking of making the aesthetic form available as a method, invokes educational and literary theory of the 1960s, and imaginative engagement as the quest of all teachers (Walsh, 1959). This seems to capture the quality of the workshop experience. For Coleridge, for example, precision denotes a clearly directed energy, springing from and supported by feelings that cannot be entirely brought to light. Is it not such "strong working of the mind" (Knights, 1981, p 142) that is mobilised in the interactive and creative process of analysing and discussing case studies, and in 'emotional thinking' (Waddell, 1989)?

Conclusion

While the social policy relevance of biographical methods is increasingly coming into view, the broader realisation of its potential remains somewhat elusive. This should not take us by surprise if what is involved is a wider paradigm change in social policy involving issues of philosophy of science, social theory, professional training and norms, and methodology. Moreover, new questions are constantly being thrown up, as I have tried to suggest. One of these is how to have an impact on the policy world. Since we are speaking of experience as well as knowledge as a key to understanding, we need to draw senior policy makers and politicians into a process of imaginative engagement. Such people lack the front-line experience that makes practitioners so open to biographical methods. How to gain support at that level is a tough question[12]. Biographical researchers and practitioners also need funding bodies who are willing to give space for collaborative experimentation, and take on trust the value of the laborious processes of biographical case study analysis, and the high level of researcher skills required. They need creative advice in translating innovative research and practice into effective policy proposals, and creating channels of communication with politicians[13]. There is a need for experimentation in transferring the social relations and practices of biographically sensitive, small-scale projects, to mainstream services and large-scale systems of administration. Such experimentation should be comparative, since all countries could gain from a fuller appreciation of each other's social policy concepts, and particularly those that relate to practical interventions 'below' the focus of institutional analysis that predominates in comparative social policy.

We are at the beginning of a potentially much bigger development. Expanding the uses of biographical methods is challenging for social policy and its related disciplines and professions. It presents us with responsibilities, but also the need for intensive forms of collaboration, across disciplines and across cultures and intellectual traditions in Europe. This may sound daunting, but it will surely be a very enjoyable and creative process.

Notes

[1] The term 'biographical methods' in this chapter usually refers to the biographical interpretive method, which commences with open narrative interviewing, and proceeds to detailed case study analysis deriving from a comparison of the lived story and the told story (see Wengraf, 2001). At times, I may use the term more generically, to embrace the whole gamut of life history, oral history and narrative methods.

[2] 'Biographical work' refers to the process involved in developing more self-understanding, as a basis for more reflexive and purposeful strategies. Seeing oneself and one's history differently is not easy to achieve on one's own – it tends to require relational support and interrogation. See Fischer-Rosenthal (2000) and Alheit and Dausien's (2002) concept of biographical learning, each discussed in this chapter.

[3] While oral history is often concerned to 'give voice' and to examine forms of collective representation that give shape to narratives, biographical interpretations are more concerned with exploring the roots of human action, through subjects' own conscious accounts, but also in cultural assumptions and patterns of personal meaning of which they are typically unaware.

[4] The detail of individual case studies often highlighted particularities of societies, for example the way a political schism in a family (such as that of the Spanish Civil War), could 'block' lives several generations later in a family (Hungerbühler et al, 2002). On the other hand, one might generalise about the possible intergenerational transmission of such divisions, as in 'third-generation' effects of the Holocaust. In general, we found much more commonality between societies than we expected, such as that lone parents were more concerned with problems of partnership than with issues of parenting. We also found lone mothering associated with an intergenerational pattern of absent males, however much reasons for that absence might arise from quite different patterns of gender relations, as in Northern or Southern Europe.

[5] It is important to stress that systems theory is typically antithetical to biographical methods. Systems theory is not at all interested in biographical content, but only in adaptability to institutions as a prerequisite of social inclusion (personal communication with Ursula Apitzsch).

[6] For an account of theoretical and methodological developments once biographical methods 'returned' to Germany in the 1970s, see Apitzsch and Inowlocki (2000).

[7] Social interactionist work, such as Goffman's *Asylums* (1961), and oral history's pioneering work in presenting testimonies of experience, particularly of excluded groups, have played a critical role in the shift to user, consumer and empowerment perspectives in social and care work, a shift that also adds impetus to professional reflection. Groups that have been at the forefront of such emancipatory research include older people, people with disabilities or learning disabilities, mental health service survivors, and welfare recipients.

[8] The psychodynamic tradition survives in some journals (such as the *Journal of Social Work Practice* and *Free Associations*), and some professional groups and conferences such as OPUS (An Organisation for Promoting Understanding of Society), and the UK conference series 'Pyschoanalysis and the Public Sphere', which ran for 12 years during the 1980s and 1990s, jointly organised by the University of East London and *Free Associations*.

[9] This produces curious paradoxes, such as the clash between the relational approach of the family-oriented Sure Start programme (targeted at young children) and the statistical basis of educational testing, the Standard Attainments Targets (SATS), in Britain. For a fuller discussion of contradictions surrounding the audit culture, see Cooper (2000).

[10] There are national service frameworks for renal services, long-term conditions, mental health, coronary heart disease and so on.

[11] For a more applied exploration of the complexities of listening and telling, see Shakespeare et al (1993), which discusses the development of such skills in courses and research of the Open University's School of Health and Social Welfare, as in mental health and learning disabilities, and in reminiscence work.

[12] Robert Walker (1985) describes such an experiment. During three two-day workshops on housing benefit in Britain, housing officers were asked to discuss reasons for difficulties in the service, and then how to convince government ministers (with whom they have frequent dealings) that this was true. A number of projective techniques were used, and the climax came in an after-dinner plenary, when a typical client drama was acted out. I do not know whether the drama was ever used to create dialogue with ministers, but such techniques should be tried!

[13] Since the SOSTRIS project ended in 1999, Directorate-General Research in Brussels has initiated a system of clustering to create synergy between projects, although it has no specialist unit mediating between research and policy.

References

Alheit, P. and Dausien, B. (1999) '"Biographicity"' as a basic resource of life-long learning', European Conference, University of Bremen, (www.erill.uni-bremen.de/lios/sections/s4_alheit.html), pp 1-12.

Alheit, P. and Dausien, B. (2002) 'The "double face" of life-long learning: two analytical perspectives on a "silent revolution"', *Studies in the Education of Adults*, vol 34, no 1, pp 3-22.

Apitzsch, U. and Inowlocki, L. (2000) 'Biographical analysis: a "German" school?', in P. Chamberlayne, J. Bornat and T. Wengraf (eds) *The turn to biographical methods in social science*, London: Routledge, pp 53-70.

Arendt, H. (1958) *The human condition*, Chicago, IL: Chicago University Press.

Baumann, Z. (2000) *Liquid modernity*, Cambridge: Polity Press.

Benhabib, S. (1996) *The reluctant modernism of Hannah Arendt*, Thousand Oaks, CA: Sage Publications.

Bolton, G. (1994) 'Stories at work. Fictional-critical writing as a means of professional development', *British Educational Research Journal*, vol 20, no 1, pp 55-68.

Bornat, J., Perks, R., Thompson, P. and Walmsley, J. (eds) (2000) *Oral history, health and welfare*, London: Routledge.

Bornat, J. (2002) 'Doing life history research', in A. Jamieson and C. Victor (eds) *Researching ageing and later life: The practice of social gerontology*, Buckingham: Open University Press, pp 117-34.

Cavarero, A. (2000) *Relating narratives: Storytelling and selfhood*, London: Routledge.

Chamberlayne, P. and Curran, C. (2004) 'Emotional retreat and social exclusion: biographical methods in professional training', Special issue on professional practice, online journal *FQS – Forum Qualitative Sozialforschung* (www.qualitative-research.net.fqs/fqs.htm>www.qualitative-research.net.fqs/fqs.htm).

Chamberlayne, P. and King, A. (2000) *Cultures of care: Biographies of carers in Britain and the two Germanies*, Bristol: The Policy Press.

Chamberlayne, P. and Rustin, M. (1999) *From biography to social policy, final report of the Sostris project*, SOSTRIS Working Paper 9, London: Centre for Biography in Social Policy, University of East London.

Chamberlayne, P., Bornat, J. and Wengraf, T. (eds) (2000) *The turn to biographical methods in social science*, London: Routledge.

Chamberlayne, P., Rustin, M. and Wengraf, T. (eds) (2002) *Biography and social exclusion: Experiences and life journeys*, Bristol: The Policy Press.

Cooper, A. (2000) 'The state of mind we're in', *Soundings*, Issue 15, pp 118-38.

Curran, C. (2000) 'View from the street', Unpublished report of research conducted for Thames Reach/Crisis, London.

Curran, C. with Chamberlayne, P. (2002) *View from the street: Biographical case studies of homelessness*, School of Health and Social Welfare Research Report, Milton Keynes: Open University.

DoH (Department of Health) (2001) *National service framework for older people*, London: DoH.

Fischer-Rosenthal, W. (2000) 'Biographical work and biographical structuring in present-day societies', in P. Chamberlayne, J. Bornat and T. Wengraf (eds) *The turn to biographical methods in social science*, London: Routledge, pp 109-25.

Froggett, L. (2002) *Love, hate and welfare: Psychosocial approaches to policy and practice*, Bristol: The Policy Press.

Giddens, A. (1984) *The constitution of society: Outline of a theory of structuration*, Cambridge: Polity Press.

Goffman, E. (1961) *Asylums*, New York, NY: Doubleday.

Hanses, A. (2001) 'Soziale Arbeit: Dienstleistung oder Fallbezug?', Lecture to the 'Theorie AG' Soziale Arbeit, Bielefeld, Haus Neuland, 30 November-1 December, pp 1-11.

Hanses, A. (2003: forthcoming) 'Biographie und sozialpädagogische Forschung', in A. Hanses (ed) *Biographie und soziale Arbeit*, Baltmannsweiler: Schneider Verlag Hohengehren.

Hollway, W. (2001) 'The psycho-social subject in "evidence-based practice"', *Journal of Social Work Practice*, vol 15, no 1, pp 9-22.

Hollway, W. and Jefferson, T. (2000) *Doing qualitative research differently: Free association, narrative and the narrative method*, London: Sage Publications.

Hungerbühler, W., Tejero, E. and Torrabadella, L. (2002) 'Suffering the fall of the Berlin wall: blocked journeys in Spain and Germany', in P. Chamberlayne, M. Rustin and T. Wengraf (eds) *Biography and social exclusion: Experiences and life journeys*, Bristol: The Policy Press, pp 23-40.

Knights, L.C. (1981) *Selected essays in criticism*, Cambridge: Cambridge University Press.

Kuhn, T. (1970) *The structure of scientific revolutions* (2nd edn), Chicago, IL: University of Chicago Press.

Lorenz, W. (2000) 'Contentious identities – social work research and the search for professional and personal identities', Paper given at the ESRC-funded seminar series 'Researching Social Work as a Means of Inclusion', University of Edinburgh, (www.nisw.org.uk/tswr/lorenz.html), pp 1-13.

Menzies Lyth, I. (1960) *Containing anxiety in institutions: Selected essays*, vol 1, London: Free Association Books.

Murard, N. (2002) 'Guilty victims; social exclusion in contemporary France', in P. Chamberlayne, M. Rustin and T. Wengraf (eds) *Biography and social exclusion: experiences and life journeys*, Bristol: The Policy Press, pp 41-60.

Perks, R. and Thomson, A. (1998) *The oral history reader*, London: Routledge.

Roer, D. and Maurer-Hein, R. (forthcoming) 'Biographie und soziale Arbeit – vom theoretischen Konstrukt zur Grundlage praktischen Handelns', in A. Hanses (ed) *Biographie und soziale Arbeit*, Baltmannsweiler: Schneider Verlag Hohengehren.

Rustin, M. (2000) 'Reflections on the biographical turn in social science', in P. Chamberlayne, J. Bornat and T. Wengraf (eds) *The turn to biographical methods in social science*, London: Routledge, pp 32-52.

Shakespeare, P., Atkinson, D. and French, S. (1993) *Reflecting on research practice*, Buckingham: Open University Press.

SOSTRIS (1997-99) Working Papers 1-9, Centre for Biography and Social Policy, University of East London.

SOSTRIS (1999) Working Paper 8, Centre for Biography and Social Policy, University of East London.

Spanò, A. (2002) 'Premodernity and postmodernity in Southern Italy', in P. Chamberlayne, M. Rustin and T. Wengraf (eds) *Biography and social exclusion: Experiences and life journeys*, Bristol: The Policy Press, pp 61-75.

Steedman, C. (1996) 'Other people's stories: modernity's suffering self', Paper at the Conference 'Autobiographies: Strategies for Survival', University of Warwick, 12 October.

Thompson, P. (2000) *The voice of the past*, (3rd edn), Oxford: Oxford University Press.

Vobruba, G. (2000) 'Actors on processes of inclusion and exclusion: towards a dynamic approach', *Social Policy and Administration*, vol 34, no 5, pp 601-13.

Waddell, M. (1989) 'Living in two worlds: pyschodynamic theory and social work practice', *Free Associations*, no 15, pp 11-35.

Walker, R. (1985) *Housing benefit: The experience of implementation*, London Housing Centre Trust.

Walsh, W. (1959) *The use of imagination: Educational thought and the literary mind*, London: Chatto and Windus.

Wengraf, T. (2001) *Qualitative research interviewing: Biographic narrative and semi-structured methods*, London: Sage Publications.

Wengraf, T. (2002) 'Biographical work and agency innovation: relationships, reflexivity and theory-in-use', in P. Chamberlayne, M. Rustin and T. Wengraf (eds) *Biography and social exclusion: Experiences and life journeys*, Bristol: The Policy Press, pp 247-68.

Winter, R. (1986) 'Fictional-critical writing: an approach to case study research by practitioners', *Cambridge Journal of Education*, vol 16, no 3, pp 175-82.

Wright Mills, C. (1959) *The sociological imagination*, Oxford: Oxford University Press.

THREE

Balancing precarious work, entrepreneurship and a new gendered professionalism in migrant self-employment

Ursula Apitzsch

The structural crisis experienced generally in post-industrial society since the last third of the 20th century has been characterised by the continuous dismantling of jobs and workplaces, with no compensation in sight. This has prompted some intellectuals and policy makers to speak in terms of the 'economically redundant', in much the same way that industrialisation discourse of the 19th century spoke of a 'surplus population'[1].

Also, however, in the eyes of neoliberal economists, a sector of the migrant population in industrial societies seems to have shown itself to be crisis-resistant: entrepreneurial migrants who subsist in an 'ethnic' economy. On the basis of their niche economies, these ethnic groups seem able to develop economic resources out of ethnic networks, ethnic skills and ethnic financing models (Gold and Light, 2000). These resources provide for co-ethnics and pave the way to economic sectors that have been abandoned by members of the dominant society. The possible demand for social assistance seems to be replaced by the hope for 'ethnic succession'; in other words, hope for advancement for and with the ethnic group as well as within the ethnic group itself.

How influential should this model be in rethinking the European social system? Is it capable of providing answers to crisis-ridden developments in post-industrial societies? What sorts of relationships exist between the specific founding conditions of so-called 'ethnic economies' and current European welfare state models?

In the 1990s, the EC initiated a series of programmes intended to secure economic survival for individuals and social groups that had been forced to the outer fringes of the employment market. These policies offered opportunities for access to specific educational and promotional measures developed to realise self-employment and small business projects. In fact, since the mid-1990s, the number of independent businesses founded by migrants has dramatically increased all over in Europe. According to the results of the German micro-census conducted in 1998, the number of self-employment businesses in Germany owned by German men increased by 16% between 1985 and 1998, while those owned by German women increased by 44%; the number of independent businesses owned by non-German men increased by 86%, while those owned by non-German women increased by 119% (Apitzsch, 2000a, p 4). Should these figures be read as an indication of the success of so-called new entrepreneurship in Europe? They could also indicate that those groups subjected to the highest degree of exclusion in the employment market are obliged more actively to explore the option of self-employment as a last resort (Bögenhold, 1990). One must also address the question of the capital (financial, cultural and social) needed to formulate such a strategy in reaction to this process of labour market exclusion, as well as the question of the risks (individual, family and social) that accompany such a course of action. A further research question would address the relationship between individual coping strategies and national and state policies on various levels – supra-national, national and regional – on the one hand, and group processes on the other.

This chapter pursues these questions in three steps: first, it discusses the wider relevance of issues involved in the concept of 'ethnic business' to European self-employment policies as a whole. Here, I refer particularly to the concept of the 'mixed embeddedness of migrant self-employment' in the context of the European welfare model. The chapter considers in particular gender issues that are associated with different forms of biographic processes of self-employment. Second, this chapter presents the empirical results of a study focused on biographical aspects of this topic. It considers the gender-specific implications of new forms of entrepreneurship and professional practice for policy evaluation. In conclusion, this chapter comments on the concept of 'active citizenship policies' in support of self-employment projects.

Ethnic economy in Europe? The concept of the mixed embeddedness of migrant self-employment

The model of the social embeddedness of economic processes

Granovetter addressed the much-discussed topic of the particular resources of ethnic groups in the late 1980s in his model of the social embeddedness of economic processes (Granovetter, 1995). Here he borrowed terminology from Karl Polanyi's *The great transformation*, a critique of capitalism published in 1944 during his exile in England. Polanyi was convinced that a limitation of market logic was indispensable for correcting the ruinous cultural disembeddedment of self-regulated economic systems (Polanyi, 1997, p 112). In American economic sociology, the term 'embeddedness' has been detached from Polanyi's specific meaning, and now refers to all forms of cultural framing of economic processes. Granovetter argues that the economy is embedded within social relationships and that one can no longer rely on the assumption that individuals act merely as atomised players in the neoclassical utilitarianism tradition. Granovetter (1995, pp 128-65) sees successful development as depending on the mediating function of ethnic networks in the dominant societies. The relative success of ethnic business is interpreted by Waldinger (1990) as a specific opportunity structure, which is grounded in various resources (individual or collective) within the society, which in turn facilitates corresponding successful or defective economic development. In general, the success of ethnic economies is very closely tied not only to the specific cultural resources of ethnic groups, but also to the interaction between the structures of the ethnic colony and those of the majority society.

In reviewing the question of the optimistic versus pessimistic evaluation of ethnic economies with respect to social integration, however, Bonacich (1988) and Sassen (1998) have pointed to a more negative view, underlining relevant social costs such as the overlap among ethnic economies, informal economies and black economies.

The mixed embeddedness of self-employment projects in European migration societies

The issue currently pursued by theorists on the topic of migrant business in Europe is that of the function of the social welfare state in causing the success or failure of self-employment. Using Esping-Andersen's definitions (1990), an examination was made of the effects of various European welfare-state systems on the self-employment projects of migrants (Kloosterman, 2000, p 92; Kloosterman and Rath, 2000). Simplifying Esping-Andersen's model, Kloosterman (2000, pp 98f, 101f) referred to two differentiated types, the so-called 'neo-American model' and the so-called 'Rhineland model', with a particular focus on the second model. Highly salaried workers, high levels of unemployment and harsh exclusion criteria regarding migrants' participation in the labour market characterise the highly regulated 'Rhineland' or 'continental European' models. Thus, migrants are forced into self-employment more than other sections of the population, a process that in turn leads to ruinous competition among members of the same small commercial niches. In contrast, the 'neo-American model', according to the above-mentioned authors, provides a relatively hazard-free context for the establishment of new businesses, whereby the financial gains normally exceed the low levels of payments for dependent jobs, which are accessible and plentiful. They expect that the high level of regulation in social welfare economies would have a negative effect not only on the quality but also on the success of self-employment projects. Lastly, the embeddedness of self-employment in ethnic communities on the one hand and in state policies on the other hand is perceived as contradictory.

Rath and Kloosterman (2000, p 14) refer to the precariousness of alleged 'vacancy-chain-businesses', and argue the negative impact of self-employment on social policy in the continental European welfare model:

> Cut-throat competition quickly comes to bear on areas over-saturated by similar business operations.

When one vegetable store opens up, it will soon be followed by a second in close vicinity. According to Rath and Kloosterman, many businesses are only able to survive these circumstances because of informal work and the simultaneous welfare support most of the self-employed are entitled to. The 'entrepreneurs' in a hypothetical case would then, for example, be those migrants who have legal residence permits in Germany or even German citizenship and who thereby receive social benefits, while at the same time making a profit by engaging poorly paid or unpaid family members who are brought into the country for just such purposes, sometimes illegally, sometimes through marriage and thus also entitled to social benefits. References to individual business ideas and professional resources do not show up in this model of self-employment. One store imitates the other. The network of the ethnic colony keeps the incomes of dependent employees systematically low, and any sorts of social contribution made by the state usually serve as subsidies for the ethnic gatekeepers.

The arguments of Kloosterman and Rath suggest, however, that the cause of the supposedly ruinous effect of 'mixed embeddedness' should not be sought in the functional mechanisms of the continental European welfare state as such, but rather in the fact that a very restrictive form of self-employment is pursued, in actuality serving as a revolving door to the informal work sector. This accords with the classical definition of the 'ethnic economy' offered by the *Handbook of economic sociology*:

> An ethnic economy consists of the self-employed, employers, their co-ethnic employees, and their unpaid family workers. (Smelser and Swedberg, 1994, p 650)

Based on the findings of various empirical studies as well as the results of our own investigations, we have good reason to assume that this model of self-employment deals with a male-dominated form of informal work, which is in stark contrast to the model of self-employment characteristic of female migrant workers, as derived from our research.

The feminist critique of the concept of 'ethnic business'

Discussions on ethnic business and ethnic communities began as soon as the first guest workers and their families started arriving in Western Europe, and after the majority of them settled down permanently in their host countries. In the academic field, those discussions for the large part were initiated and impelled by women. Their contributions questioned the assumption of homogeneous ethnic groups and the criteria of membership of such groups (Schmidt, 2000, p 335).

One of the first studies on ethnic business in Europe was by Floya Anthias (1982), concerning the ethnic economy of Cypriots living in London. In her investigation, Anthias described the gender role that is classically attributed to women, namely that of acting as a resource available to serve and assist in male-run business undertakings. The question concerning the role that female business leaders play in ethnic economies was explicitly pursued by Mirjana Morokvasic (1991) in her study of self-employment and minorities in five European countries (France, Germany, Great Britain, Italy and Portugal), conducted between 1987 and 1988. Here the central issue is whether or not female migrants could possibly be capable of developing the potential to act as effective businesswomen themselves. Morokvasic underlined the remarkable independence of that discussion of self-employment in the majority society – including the self-employment of women – from discussion on immigrant business. She suspected that this could be traced back to the totalising and undifferentiated view of immigrant groups, and especially those ethnic groups that are commonly described by family solidarity and the subjection of women to plans made by male relatives. Morokvasic discovered interesting differences in her interviews, regarding the composition of female-run self-employment projects. Female migrants often pursue unusual courses of action which are highly distinct from the forms of entrepreneurship advocated by their male counterparts. By and large, they promote the dismantling of hierarchies, pay their family members a salary (in contrast to male-run businesses), and make an effort to be innovative in both organisational and social terms (Morokvasic, 1991, p 413). They are, to a good degree, obliged to conduct their businesses in this manner because they cannot count on being supported by the solidarity of their community. It is actually often the case that they do not want such support, whereas male-dominated ethnic businesses generally want and get it.

The findings uncovered by Morokvasic's study have been confirmed by new studies, in particular in Germany. After the fall of the Berlin Wall, and this became highly evident between 1994 and 1996, businesses were founded by Turkish women who desired to fulfil occupational wishes that could not be attained in the core employment areas. Family members were rarely engaged, and if they were, were fully paid as employees, a practice that at the time was quite unusual in Turkish family businesses. In their self-perceptions, these women separated themselves internally from their ethnic community, in order to secure their economic path (Hillmann, 2000, p 430).

The social and biographical embeddedness of female self-employment in and outside migration: results of a transnational European study

I shall now explore the question of the 'mixed embeddedness' of self-employment projects within the framework of a European research project, which I coordinated from 1998 through 2001, entitled 'Self-employment activities concerning women and minorities'. The project took place in six European countries: Germany, Denmark, Greece, Great Britain, Italy and Sweden. What made this project special was above all its methodological orientation. In each of the participating countries, 44 biographical case studies were conducted with male and female migrants as well as with native-born women who, due to unemployment or the threat of impending unemployment, chose to pursue self-employment projects. Half of the interviews were conducted with subjects who had been self-employed for a period of one year or more, and half with persons whose self-employment projects had failed within the past year.

The sampling strategy and methods of analysis of the project (see Apitzsch and Kontos, 1997, 2003) will now be briefly outlined. Even though we processed a total of 264 biographical case studies throughout Europe, this does not imply that we were seeking to build a representative sample of all self-employed European migrants. On the contrary, the sampling criteria of existing or impending unemployment as well as our policy orientation – in other words, the selection of one half of our subjects based on promotional measures designed to encourage self-employment – established a bias we were well aware of. For example, it systematically excluded illegal migrant workers. Also, in the control group, which consisted of those who did not take advantage of self-employment policies, illegal migrants were by and large the exception[2]. (Illegal immigrants were found for the most part in the samples taken in Italy and Greece, Southern European countries that have themselves, until recently, been the homeland of emigrants, and have not yet developed a sophisticated system of legal immigration regulations [Reyneri, 2003].)

Sampling was theoretically oriented along the lines of grounded theory (Glaser and Strauss, 1967), whereby the central cases consisted of male and female migrants and native-born females who, due to dismissal, rationalisation and/or a longer period of family care work, no longer had reasonable chances of a profitable future in similar employment. Further study participants were native women and offspring of first and second migrant generations who, despite completed educational and training programmes, were not able to attain traditional waged positions. They had opened small businesses that typically offered personalised services, either with or without the support of policy programmes, or had founded a so-called solo self-employment business that relied solely on the diligence of the owner him or herself. Incomes in the first years seldom reached levels considerably higher than that of unemployment and social assistance, and were in some cases even lower. Extensive expansion in the future was not expected. We asked ourselves which conditions must be present in order to explain such coping strategies. Is it a question of fear, a lack of willingness to take risks, as presumed by some leading professional consulting institutions?

In order to formulate answers to our questions with the empirical material available to us, we constructed transnational clusters of case studies – for example, a cluster of successful businesses founded by migrants not drawing on public funding. These clusters were analysed by transnational research teams employing a classic procedure of sequential analysis, with the aims first of identifying the case structures and forms of coping strategy, and then of evaluating them in a communicative manner within the research group. Sequential analysis follows the idea that any manifest social act expressed in a text is understandable by the presumption that a latent objective meaning – a case structure – is underlying the individual authentic performance that represents a special selection of the objective possibilities (Oevermann, 2001)[3] (for details on the discussion about hermeneutic biographical methods, refer to Apitzsch and Inowlocki, 2000). A further intent was to reconstruct in an abductive way the basic social problems subjects encountered, as a necessary preliminary to making a feasible interpretation of the concrete strategies they adopted in response to challenges and crises[4].

The production of transnational biographical analyses is an arduous and unconventional procedure (in our project rather insufficiently supported by the software QSR NUD*IST). Why did we choose to follow this course of research rather than adapting the traditional methods employed in national comparative studies or in the comparison of ethnic groups? Our procedure seemed to offer us the opportunity of circumventing the danger of reproducing prior information, particularly that characteristic of national typologies. Furthermore, in investigating ethnic groups across national boundaries, we were acutely aware of the possibility of scientific work either reproducing or even producing ethnic categories (Dittrich and Radtke, 1990). We wanted to ensure that the opportunity to recognise more universal development structures would remain open above and beyond national borders and the assignment to ethnic diversities. Therefore, the arrangement in which transnational research teams all analysed the data material collected seemed to be particularly advantageous (in this case, the transcripts of narrative biographical interviews translated into English).

Self-employment as a gendered biographical process between precariousness, entrepreneurship and professional practice

Remarkably clear biographical types could be found, which stood, in fact, in stark contradiction to currently widely accepted assumptions on migrant self-employment. One of these unconfirmed assumptions was that small-scale projects – in particular those run by women – are businesses founded in response to emergency situations in contrast to creative, expansive undertakings, which are classically dominated by men. Our empirical findings reveal a somewhat different structural format.

What proved to be a typical path to self-employment was a desire to attain personal autonomy. Gaining autonomy, however, was closely tied to two very different coping strategies towards self-employment. On the one hand, we found (among both women and men) the action scheme of a radically self-made entrepreneur. On the other hand, we encountered the more or less conscious self-image of a professional practitioner, often connected to the spheres of education, care and health work – typically women's occupations.

The first strategy is estimated to be difficult; the second, however, seems at a first glance to be a contradiction in itself. How can a person in a marginalised position, threatened by unemployment, see herself as a member of a profession or at least as a person acting professionally? Here one has to recall briefly the sociological discussion on what 'profession' actually means. In his classic book *The system of professions* (1988), Andrew Abbott wrote:

> Diagnosis, treatment, interference, and academic work provide the cultural machinery of jurisdiction.... In claiming jurisdiction, a profession asks society to recognise its cognitive structure through exclusive rights.... These claimed rights may include absolute monopoly of practice and public payment, rights of self-discipline and of unconstrained employment, control of professional training, of recruitment, and of licensing, to mention only a few. (Abbott, 1988, p 20)

Abbott sees the mighty 'old established professions' of medicine, jurisprudence and priesthood as the models for professional practitioners who "heal our bodies, measure our profits, save our souls" (1988, p 1). In contrast, the Chicago school of sociology developed a different view of professional practice, seeing it as a specific practice in a continuum of what people actually do in their daily life and at their workplaces (Nittel, 2000, pp 27ff).

Here professional practice develops historically and can take different forms. Of course, there is a difference drawn between professional practice and other forms of everyday practice and work, including within the traditions of the Chicago school and symbolic interactionism. This difference mainly concerns not only the social status of professional knowledge, but also the forms in which it is produced and performed. It is not a personal service to a customer, but rather claims a special license and a special mandate. Hughes (1984, p 288) argues:

> Most occupations – especially those considered professions and those of the underworld – include as part of their being a license to deviate in some measure from some common modes of behaviour. Professions, perhaps more than other kinds of occupations, also claim a broad legal, moral, and intellectual mandate.

This claim concerns the difference between satisfying a customer and advising a client. Professional knowledge is not just expert knowledge applied while performing a role: it is knowledge orientated to a special case. It does not deliver a fixed product, but rather reconstructs the client's practice in order to allow new solutions in situations of crisis (Oevermann, 1996). The client, however, has to approve the solution. Professionalism in the form of 'interventionist practice' (as the German sociologist Oevermann calls it) transcends all mechanical forms of applied knowledge "in the direction of case-specific individuated dialogical practice with a client in his/her autonomous life practice" (Oevermann, 2001, p 9).

Professional practice, however, is fundamentally different, not only when compared with mechanical modes of applying knowledge, but also when compared with entrepreneurial action. Entrepreneurs are forced to position themselves in the market with new ideas and products. The product chosen comes from an array of several possible products. What is crucial to the success of an entrepreneur is not a specific knowledge base but an ability to convince the public. By contrast, members of a profession are viewed as experts in a repertoire of practices. The individual practitioner does not count on his personal charisma but on the charisma of an established profession (Oevermann, 2001, p 8).

Drawing on these distinctions, the following sections discuss two types of coping strategies among self-employed people: as 'new entrepreneurs' and 'new professionals'. We will see that the members of both groups work hard and are deeply motivated, but that their professionalism as entrepreneurs or as practitioners has a very different logic, a fact that has strong implications for policy evaluation.

The new entrepreneurs

The analysis of the interviews has shown that migrant men and women, especially refugees in Northern Europe (Denmark, Sweden, Germany) and migrants in Southern Europe (for example, Pontian Greek minorities in Greece), are very frequently people with good formal qualifications that cannot be used in the labour market of the host society. In our research, a biographical experience they shared with native women was that education was no protection against becoming economically 'redundant'. The members of both groups were active in occupational fields that seemed to be widely removed from their original human resources. Not one of our interviewees wanted to be voluntarily dependent on social support for a longer period of time without offering something in return; furthermore, none wanted to be categorised as 'superfluous'. This rationale was typical of those migrants who identified themselves as 'denizens'. As bearers of valid residence status, they did not feel threatened by expulsion, but rather rebuffed by a felt moral accusation of illegitimate presence in their country of residence. At the same time, they refused humiliating dependent working conditions. A Turkish-Iranian biologist became the owner of a successful second-hand boutique in a large German city instead of assenting to a deskilled opportunity of working as a laboratory assistant. A chemist from Eritrea, who had completed her university degree in Great Britain, opened a firm specialising in ethnic products in Germany. In each case, the new role as entrepreneur offered the opportunity to transfer creativity developed in the obstructed careers to a new arena.

What was decisive to success in each case was a highly personalised form of business diligence and networking. The new entrepreneurs emphasised the need to develop one's own abilities for creativity and innovation without reference to any approved canon of practices. Abilities such as the reorganisation of occupational processes, the development of new supply structures, or the discovery of new consumer niches were seen as creative. Migrants as well as native-born females who acted as 'entrepreneurs' created a market advantage through an inexorable degree of self-challenge and a disproportionate utilisation of the resources of motivation and networking (see Chapters Four and Five of this volume).

What now is the difference between these new entrepreneurs and freelance professionals? Many of the new entrepreneurs had once acquired an academic 'licence', something that in mainstream discourse is regarded as one of the preconditions for acting as a professional. However, it was exactly the use of this educational capital that had been blocked by particular conditions within a certain phase of their lives: migration processes, the increase of dependant work within the field of their expertise, or the glass ceiling effect for women in the sphere of waged labour (Vianello and Moore, 2000). For their start-up as entrepreneurs, they cannot count on their qualifications, but they have to innovate in order to gain customers for their products. Within this strategy, unless they are successful they will not gain the social recognition they are striving for. They can neither rely on their academic credentials for success nor claim a public 'mandate', in contrast with established professions. It is obvious that most of the interview partners are very much aware of this difference and that they are successful in their business because of this awareness. In this chapter, these structural conditions are called the 'case structure' of 'new entrepreneurship', which have been identified in the interviews (also by revisiting sociological theories of professional practice such as those of Hughes and Oevermann). These case structures have been identified through the study of individual biographical processes among our interviewees.

We can now reconstruct the different coping strategies that individual entrepreneurs developed in order to overcome the threat of failure. One possible cause of entrepreneurial failure lies in misunderstanding entrepreneurial acting. I will illustrate this briefly with the case of a Turkish woman, a daughter of 'guest workers', who studied philology and gained a degree in German. Her aim was the social recognition that this qualification would bring, since she knew it would probably not lead to a job. Her coping strategy involved a 'sub-career'. She became a member and later a teacher in a training centre for martial arts; when the club fell into crisis she became the manager and in the end the owner. Despite investing a lot of money borrowed from friends and family members, she could not make a living for herself out of this enterprise. In the interview, she underlined her expertise in teaching martial arts, but laid no importance on activities like book keeping and advertising. The problem was that while she felt entitled to a mandate for professional practice and for (state) financial support, she had not ascertained what the requisite public recognition for this could be based on, other than her (not particularly relevant) degree. Yet in this particular historical situation it is unlikely that society will regard martial arts as a social function of sufficient worth to earn such public support and endorsement.

The case shows how important the biographical reconstruction of a case structure and a coping strategy can be in policy evaluation. New entrepreneurs starting from a marginalised position seek to earn money in order to gain social recognition. They are proud of becoming taxpayers, but at the same time they live with the threat of failure. Most beginners are not specialists in their new entrepreneurial field, and they mostly lack financial capital. Therefore, state-funded start-up bridging allowances can be not only very productive but indeed necessary. At the same time, extended reliance on social benefits would be counter-productive, given the aim of autonomy. Our example shows that access to the resources of an ethnic network is not always helpful. The most helpful policy would be a very precisely targeted facilitative service. Consultancy services should be skilled in shaping diffuse ideas of self-employment into business concepts and detecting hidden resources that match consumer demand. In providing transitional support, such agencies need the competence and skills to support the 'biographical work' of a client in establishing a self-employment business. This suggests that consultancy services themselves be organised not along entrepreneurial lines but in accordance with new forms of client-oriented professional practice.

The new professionals

The discovery of the biographical structure of our interviewees' occupational trajectories, which included the shifting subjective and objective significance of various types of employment in different life phases, was decisive in identifying what biographical processes had led 'new professionals' to self-employment.

A distinctive factor that the interviewees had often discovered in the midst of life crises (such as illness, unemployment, or anxiety in the face of exams), was that their own psychic and health conditions, as well as their (often discontinuous) educational careers, were economic resources that needed to be diligently nurtured and conscientiously adapted to the prevailing socioeconomic environment (Kontos, 2000). Self-employment appeared to be the safest way of autonomously 'tapping into' and 'replenishing' this resource. As researchers, we saw this as an application of 'biographical knowledge' (Alheit and Hoerning, 1989).

The case structure that emerges thereby is one of a freelance businesswoman, with a deep respect for reliable, personally delivered services, who would be expected to function in a capacity of crisis manager for clients, regardless of whether the professional practice in question has to do with self-employment consultancy, childcare certification, or diet counselling. This definition explains why these personally demanding activities are, as a rule, associated with immense vocational satisfaction and inner fulfilment. Furthermore, by and large the biographies reveal that these women did their job in an effective and responsible manner, that they did not want to delegate this work further, and therefore often did not want to expand. As in the classic example of the medical profession, these freelance advisers eschewed advertising, attempting rather to adhere to and emphasise the professional standards of their fields. Admittedly, recourse to professional standardisation – for example, entry certification for private childcare – is only a recently emerging development in self-employment projects.

Like the new entrepreneurs, freelance consultants face deep crises that can now be understood in the light of the case structure of professional practice. In contrast to the entrepreneurs, consultants rely on qualifications and need a mandate. Furthermore, they have to prove their professional autonomy without being members of mighty professional organisations. This becomes even more complicated when the consultant's university degree is in an academic field that is still not fully recognised professionally, like educational studies or care studies (Combe and Helsper, 1996; Schütze, 1996), or when the consultant's professional knowledge comes from previous experience rather than a university degree. Appropriate policy here might offer certification for knowledge from various forms of adult and higher education (Nittel, 2000) and create new autonomous professional umbrella organisations.

Concerning professional mandates, there is a special problem in the field of pre-school childcare and care work with elderly and chronically ill people. The definition of such work as typical women's family work within paternalistic bourgeois societies precluded its recognition as professional practice (Rabe-Kleberg, 1996; Apitzsch, 2000b). The end of this traditional gender contract means that all such work has to be organised in a new and autonomous way, and a new mandate has to be claimed for the relevant professional organisations as well as for the performance of the work itself. The failure to solve these questions is highlighted by the fact that today most of this work is still organised in informal and illegal ways, and mostly performed by migrants. Sociologists refer to 'new maids' in Western European countries. Our research did not include this particular informal practice since our sampling strategy started from official policy initiatives. It was obvious, nevertheless, that official programmes were not trying to include migrants in their attempts to professionalise care work. The biographical records of agencies aiming at collective self-employment for migrant women represented the participants' resources as confined to personal services such as cooking, cleaning and sewing. In fact, these participants were frequently very well qualified, having formal qualifications (such as degrees) from their country of origin that they could have used and developed professionally.

The consequences for many native and migrant women have been a propensity to develop distinctive personal strategies, professional plans favouring new working patterns, and solo entrepreneurship. The clear disadvantage of solo self-employment is the serious lack of social security. In the light of our results, social policies such as the bridging allowance, in combination with support measures for 'new professionalism' and its endeavours towards autonomy, gain a completely new and positive meaning. Here we find support for an expanding model of individual independence, which is transferable to new fields of activity.

Conclusions

Self-employment offers the advantage of being one's own boss, allows time schedules to be tailored to family needs, and creates a situation in which one feels constrained by external factors to be turned to one's own advantage. The downside of solo self-employment is the serious lack of social security despite long working hours. The strategy often documented by Morokvasic in the late 1980s, in which self-employment was accompanied by another (at least part-time) dependent form of employment, has become more or less obsolete given the lack of such opportunities in the current employment market.

The welfare state embeddedness of self-employment varies in Europe from one state to another and is the focus of many a heated and controversial debate[5]. On the basis of the results of our empirical investigations, bridging allowances paid by the state provide support for a meaningful model of independence and allow the transfer of professional knowledge to new fields of activity. We can interpret this initial securing of self-employment as a specifically European variant of the socio-cultural embeddedness of economic processes. Furthermore, considerable differences between female and male self-employment come to light that reveal that women typically attempt to avoid the informal and frequently highly ethnicised work sector, whereas men have often been able to locate and secure the appropriate resources for self-employment projects in ethnic niches. Thus, our results have confirmed the outcomes of a study conducted by Hillmann (2000, p 430) in Berlin:

> The gender-specific consideration of ethnic Turkish trade and industry shows that the current definition of ethnic trade and industry is only relevant for the subgroup of male entrepreneurs of a specific generation of immigrants. (Translated from the German original)

However, support mechanisms for self-employment provided by welfare states are mostly still closely tied to preconditions that are particularly difficult for women, migrants and especially second-generation young adults to fulfil, namely a long-term period of full employment recognised by the national social insurance programme. Furthermore, when citizenship is not the issue, the drawing of a bridging allowance is conditional upon fixed residence status ('denizenship'), which in turn can itself be endangered by the acceptance of such transfers. According to the conditions set forth by the European 'migration model', it is not only refugees and illegal immigrants who are potentially subject to precarious living situations, but rather all migrants for whom residence status is not defined by existing employment or by long periods of prior, socially secured employment. Additionally, those persons who as long-term residents are accorded access to social rights (the right to public education as well as social assistance) and thereby considered to be 'social citizens', in other words not full 'citizens', but rather 'denizens' (Faist, 1995, 2000) could paradoxically endanger their integration by taking advantage of their rights to these social institutions. In Europe, it is clear that residence status in migration processes that extend across several generations, as long as that status is not secured by national citizenship within an EC member state, is becoming more and more precarious. The status of social citizenship (Apitzsch, 2002) may be lost much faster than that of 'classic' citizenship.

A wide range of policies has supported collective self-employment for migrant and native women in Europe. However, one can say that these efforts have failed – and structurally had to fail – when they aim to imitate the 'success' of ethnic business. The critique of ethnic business has shown how counterproductive it is for women's autonomy to rely on male-dominated structures of self-employment.

We discovered that most of the policy programmes targeting special social (or ethnically defined) groups are trapped by the paradox that they work with the hypothesis that these groups embody special cultural and biographical resources. However, the programmes and the access criteria are still deficit-oriented and the results are patronising types of so-called 'active social citizenship policies' that are unable to sustain agency, creativity, and networking.

This paradox can be overcome or mediated only if the recruitment of participants takes their resources and biographical plans into account, in accordance with the structural challenges of entrepreneurship and professional practice. What is needed is reflection on, and empirical investigation into, new types of bottom-up networking that could provide the new entrepreneurs and freelancers with supports for professional self-employment and with structures for more sustainable social security.

Notes

[1] I refer to a discussion in Germany in 1998. Heinz Bude (1998), who gave prominence to the category of the 'superfluous population', was criticised by Heinz Steinert and others (Steinert, 2000).

[2] We are not here concerned with the 'illegal entrepreneurs' that Georg Elwert had in mind when he argued against categorising all illegal migrants as marginalised. According to Elwert (2002), illegal migrants are more often members of the middle or upper classes of peripheral countries, who work in relatively highly paid positions in the highly developed Western countries, in particular in the service sector in order to save money for investments in their home countries.

[3] Oevermann (2001, p 4): "In sequential analysis one first has to make explicit at each sequential local point in a protocol and thereby in the protocolled course of practice itself the objective possibilities which are opened up by the rules for the generation of objective meaning. Then the actual and real selection found in this protocol can be contrastively revealed in the light of this 'foil' of possibilities. As such it has to be explained by the principles or maxims of selection, which were followed by the particular life practice. The sequence of choices composes what I call the case structure

of the particular life practice, which consists in its dispositional features. These are traditionally expressed in well known variables of social science and psychology such as motivational structures, value orientations, life style, milieu specific norms, etc. If you reconstruct a long enough uninterrupted sequence you will identify the case specific regularity of the recognisable selection within this concrete life practice, and thereby arrive at its inner law".

[4] Abduction is a specific form of syllogism for stating an argument, different from deductive and inductive reasoning. Charles Saunders Peirce introduced it in 1866 as reasoning from the result to the rule. Abductive reasoning means making a (methodologically controlled) hypothesis. Different from deductive reasoning, it belongs to 'the logic of discovery'. According to Peirce (1867), the necessary logical circle within abductive reasoning is not a *circulus vitiosus*, but a *circulus fructuosus*. Thus, Peirce methodologically rectifies what in hermeneutics is called a circle or a 'synthesis' of understanding. Abduction is a form of syllogism that is implicitly well known not only to any scientist, but also to any criminal author: starting from the empirical traces of a very specific situation, you have to 'build the case'.

[5] Germany has recently introduced a more extended bridging allowance for solo self-employment, called 'Ich-AG'.

References

Abbott, A. (1988) *The system of professions: An essay on the division of expert labour*, Chicago, IL/London: University of Chicago Press.

Alheit, P. and Hoerning, E.M. (eds) (1989) *Biographisches Wissen: Beiträge zu einer Theorie lebensgeschichtlicher Erfahrung*, Frankfurt-am-Main: Suhrkamp.

Anthias, F. (1982) 'Ethnicity and class among Greek Cypriot migrants: a study in the conceptualisation of ethnicity', PhD thesis, University of London.

Apitzsch, U. (2000a) 'Beratungs- und Bildungsangebote für Selbständigkeitsprojekte in Europa', *Hessische Blätter für Volksbildung*, vol 1, pp 1-13.

Apitzsch, U. (2000b) 'Biographische "Unordnung" und "caring work"', *Feministische Studien extra: Fürsorge – Anerkennung – Arbeit*, pp 102-16.

Apitzsch, U. (2002) 'Biographien in Europa: Neue Dimensionen des Sozialen', in F. Hamburger et al (eds) *Gestaltung des Sozialen – eine Herausforderung für Europa*, Opladen: Leske+Budrich, pp 199-225.

Apitzsch, U. and Inowlocki, L. (2000) 'Biographical analysis: a 'German' school?', in P. Chamberlayne, J. Bornat and T. Wengraf (eds) *The turn to biographical methods in social science*, London/New York, NY: Routledge, pp 53-70.

Apitzsch, U. and Kontos, M. (1997) *Self-employment activities concerning women and minorities: Their success or failure in relation to social citizenship policies*, EC proposal within the 5th framework of Targeted Socio-Economic Research (TSER).

Apitzsch, U. and Kontos, M. (2003) 'Self-employment, gender and migration', *International Review of Sociology/Revue Internationale de Sociologie*, Monographic Part 1, vol 13, no 1, Taylor & Francis, pp 67-234.

Bögenhold, D. (1990) 'Selbständigkeit als Reflex auf Arbeitslosigkeit? Makrosoziologische Befunde einer international-komparativen Studie', *Kölner Zeitschrift für Soziologie und Sozialpsychologie*, vol 42, pp 265-79.

Bonacich, E. (1988) 'The social costs of immigrant entrepreneurship', *Ambrasia*, vol 14, pp 119-28.

Bude, H. (1998) 'Die Überflüssigen als transversale Kategorie', in P.A. Berger and M.Vester (eds) *Alte Ungleichheiten, neue Spaltungen*, Opladen: Leske+Budrich, pp 363-82.

Combe, A. and Helsper, W. (eds) (1996) *Pädagogische Professionalität: Untersuchungen zum Typus pädagogischen Handelns*, Frankfurt-am-Main: Suhrkamp.

Dittrich, E.J. and Radtke, F.-O. (1990) *Ethnizität: Wissenschaft und Minderheiten*, Opladen: Westdeutscher Verlag.

Elwert, G. (2002) 'Unternehmerische Illegale. Ziele und Organisationen eines unterschätzten Typs illegaler Einwanderer', *IMIS-Beiträge*, vol 19, pp 7-20.

Esping-Andersen, G. (1990) *The three worlds of welfare capitalism*, Cambridge: Polity Press.

Faist, T. (1995) *Social citizenship for whom? Young Turks in Germany and Mexican Americans in the United States*, Aldershot: Ashgate.

Faist, T. (2000) 'Social citizenship in the European Union. Residual, post-national and nested membership?', *IIS-Arbeitspapier*, vol 17, Universität Bremen.

Glaser, B.G. and Strauss, A.L. (1967) *The discovery of grounded theory: Strategies for qualitative research*, New York, NY/Chicago, IL: Aldine de Gruyter.

Gold, S. and Light, I. (2000) *Ethnic economies*, San Diego, CA/New York, NY: Academic Press.

Granovetter, M. (1995) 'The economic sociology of firms and entrepreneurs', in A. Portes (ed) *The economic sociology of immigration: Essays on network, ethnicity and entrepreneurship*, New York, NY: Russell Sage Foundation, pp 128-65.

Hillmann, F. (2000) 'Ethnisierung oder Internationalisierung? Ethnische Ökonomien als Schnittpunkte von Migrationssystemen und Arbeitsmarkt in Berlin', *PROKLA*, vol 120, pp 415-32.

Hughes, E.C. (1984) *The sociological eye: Selected papers*, New Brunswick, NJ: Transaction Books.

Kloosterman, R. (2000) 'Immigrant entrepreneurship and the institutional context: a theoretical exploration', in J. Rath (ed) *Immigrant business: The economic, political and social environment*, London: Macmillan, pp 90-106.

Kloosterman, R. und Rath, J. (2000) 'Mixed embeddedness: markets and immigrant entrepreneurs', Paper presented at the EURESCO Conference on 'Self-employment, Gender, Migration', San Feliu (Spain), 27 November 2000.

Kontos, M. (2000) 'Bildungsprozesse, Abbrüche und die Motivation zur Selbständigkeit – Überlegungen zum Konzept biographischer Ressourcen', in U. Apitzsch (ed) *Selbständigkeitsprojekte: Hessische Blätter für Volksbildung*, Frankfurt-am-Main, pp 44-57.

Morokvasic, M. (1991) 'Roads to independence: self-employed immigrants and minority women in five European states', *International Migration*, vol 3, pp 407-20.

Nittel, D. (2000) *Von der Mission zur Profession? Stand und Perspektiven der Verberuflichung in der Erwachsenenbildung*, Bielefeld: Bertelsmann.

Oevermann, U. (1996) 'Theoretische Skizze einer revidierten Theorie professionalisierten Handelns', in A. Combe and W. Helsper (eds) *Pädagogische Professionalität: Untersuchungen zum Typus pädagogischen Handelns*, Frankfurt-am-Main: Suhrkamp, pp 70-182.

Oevermann, U. (2001) *A revised theoretical model of professionalisation*, Frankfurt-am-Main (unpublished manuscript, 27pp).

Peirce, C.S. (1960) 'On the natural classification of arguments (1867)', *Collected papers*, vol 2 (2nd edn), Cambridge, MA: Cambridge University Press.

Polanyi, K. (1997) *The great transformation: Politische und ökonomische Ursprünge von Gesellschaften und Wirtschaftssystemen* (1944, German edn), Frankfurt-am-Main.

Rabe-Kleberg, U. (1996) 'Professionalität und Geschlechterverhältnis. Oder: Was ist "semi" an traditionellen Frauenberufen?', in A. Combe and W. Helsper (eds) *Pädagogische Professionalität: Untersuchungen zum Typus pädagogischen Handelns*, Frankfurt-am-Main: Suhrkamp, pp 276-302.

Rath, J. (ed) (2000) *Immigrant business: The economic, political and social environment*, London: Palgrave Macmillan.

Reyneri, E. (2003) 'Immigration and the underground economy in new receiving South European countries: manifold negative effects, manifold deep-rooted causes', in U. Apitzsch and M. Kontos (eds) 'Self-employment, gender and migration', *International Review of Sociology/Revue Internationale de Sociologie*, Monographic Part 1, vol 13, no 1, pp 117-43.

Riemann, G. (1997) *Beziehungsgeschichte, Kernprobleme und Arbeitsprozesse in der sozialpädagogischen Familienberatung*, Kassel.

Sassen, S. (1998) 'Überlegungen zu einer feministischen Analyse der globalen Wirtschaft', *PROKLA*, vol 111, pp 199-216.

Schmidt, D. (2000) 'Unternehmertum und Ethnizität – ein seltsames Paar', *PROKLA*, vol 120, pp 335-62.

Schütze, F. (1996) 'Organisationszwänge und hoheitsstaatliche Rahmenbedingungen im Sozialwesen: Ihre Auswirkung auf die Paradoxien des professionellen Handelns', in A. Combe and W. Helsper (eds) *Pädagogische Professionalität: Untersuchungen zum Typus pädagogischen Handelns*, Frankfurt-am-Main: Suhrkamp, pp 183-275.

Smelser, N. and Swedberg, R. (eds) (1994) *The handbook of economic sociology*, Princeton, NY: Princeton University Press.

Steinert, H. (2000) 'Die Diagnostik der Überflüssigen', *Mittelweg*, vol 36, no 5, pp 9-17.

Vianello, M. and Moore, G. (eds) (2000) *Gendering elites. A study of political and business leaders in 27 industrialised countries*, St Martin's: Macmillan.

Waldinger, R., Aldridge, H. and Ward, R. (eds) (1990) *Ethnic entrepreneurs: Immigrant business in industrial societies*, Newbury Park, CA: Sage Publications.

Werbner, P. (1999) 'What colour "success"? Distorting value in studies of ethnic entrepreneurship', *The Sociological Review*, vol 47, pp 548-77.

FOUR

Considerations on the biographical embeddedness of ethnic entrepreneurship

Maria Kontos

Over recent decades in most European countries, the long-term decline in self-employment rates has significantly reversed (Apitzsch, 2000; Bögenhold, 2000). These 'new self-employed' differ from the classical type of self-employed in their motives for entrepreneurship. Whether it is the desire for self-realisation, to achieve an autonomous life plan (Hakim, 1999) or, in the case of collective entrepreneurship, a wish for solidarity in the workplace through self-employment (Vonderach, 1980; Heider, 1996), or the goal of gaining access to income (Bögenhold, 1987), the 'new self-employment' seems to have little to do with the classical entrepreneur. Self-employment seems to have become an individual proactive strategy for avoiding unemployment and social exclusion. Meanwhile, labour market policies in Europe have created schemes to support the efforts of the unemployed to start their own businesses. Native men are the greatest beneficiaries of these self-employment schemes, as they are the most privileged group among the unemployed (Meager, 1993, 1996). Although migrants are over-represented among the unemployed, and show the highest rate of increase in self-employment (Apitzsch and Kontos, 2003: forthcoming), they are strongly under-represented among those benefiting from self-employment schemes (Kontos, 1997).

In the concept of self-employment policy, as well as in its implementation and practice, the notion of 'resources' occupies a central position. Policies addressing business start-ups aim to support those who have the most promising business plans. Business success is thought to derive not only from the quality of the core concept, but also from the 'entrepreneurial capacity' of the future entrepreneur; that is, from his or her capacity to realise the business idea fully. This means that the viability of the start-up project cannot be considered separately from the entrepreneur and his or her capabilities. Under circumstances in which migrants obtain disproportionately little support, the concept of 'resources' takes on a socio-political meaning and requires clarifying.

This paper summarises some results of the TSER project (1997-2000) entitled 'Self-employment activities of women and minorities: their success or failure in relation to social citizenship policies'. The aim of the project was to make a 'biographical' evaluation of policies that aim to support self-employment for the socially disadvantaged. Identifying the resources utilised by the actors in the process of becoming self-employed is crucial, since the project seeks to formulate policy recommendations that meet migrants' realities. From the perspective of biographical policy evaluation, a more appropriate policy would not ignore individuals' actual resources and potential, but take them into account and give them support. A biographical analysis reconstructs the process of accumulating resources within the framework of the life process, and in particular the self-employment process (see Chapters Three and Five of this volume).

In its first part, this chapter argues that the concept of resources underlying self-employment policies targeted at the unemployed should be extended to take motivation into account. In its second part, the chapter presents the analysis of three contrasting biographical case studies, to show the biographical processes by which motivation may be mobilised as a resource. The emergent structure of motivation is that of realising 'unlived-life' possibilities, allied to a struggle for recognition. In these case studies, both the stage of immigration – whether first or second generation – and gender are key dimensions.

The concept of resources in the economic sociology of ethnic business

Light (1999, p 1) has recently discussed the concept of entrepreneurial capacity within economic sociology:

> Entrepreneurial capacity means having whatever it takes to succeed in business, but what exactly does it take? In addition to being in the right place at the right time, partially a matter of luck, it takes resources. Entrepreneurs need resources ... the real task of explaining ethnic ownership economies requires one to identify and classify the needed resources.

Resources are reserves of values that can be utilised to accomplish a social or economic task. They refer to economic levels and to education, culture and social relations. Following Bourdieu, Light discusses class resources as 'forms of capital'. He makes a distinction between class and ethnic entrepreneurial resources. Members of socially privileged groups possess class resources. They are "the vocationally relevant cultural and material endowment of the bourgeoisie" (Light, 1999, p 2), and are independent of membership of the dominant ethnic group. Class resources include economic and financial capital; that is, private property and wealth. Human capital – education and skills – is also considered a material resource, since it requires prior financial investment. Moreover, class resources include competencies in high culture that are occupationally relevant. Values, attitudes, knowledge and skills are transmitted in a process of socialisation from one generation to the other, in the family and through attendance at privileged educational institutions. Finally, social capital is control of social relationships that facilitate entrepreneurship, for example, access to social networks. It is obvious that the analytical distinction between these four types of class resources – economic, human, cultural and social capital – does not mean that there is no interplay between them or that they are mutually independent. Ownership of the one sort of resource or capital can strongly influence ownership of or access to another.

Light specifies ethnic resources as resources involved in entrepreneurial activities in the absence of class resources. In this view, ethnic resources are supportive, and entrepreneurship becomes "a classic route out of poverty" (Light, 1999, p 29). He defines ethnic resources as "socio-cultural and demographic features of the whole group which co-ethnic entrepreneurs actively utilise in business or from which their business passively benefits" (1999, p 30). Ethnic resources subscribe to a whole ethnic group, not individual members or classes. Solidarity is a typical ethnic resource. It can be horizontal, referring to the relationship between entrepreneurs or money providers, or vertical, referring to the relationship of an entrepreneur to his/her ethnic employees. Typical forms of ethnic resource, says Light (1999, p 31), are:

> kinship and marriage systems, relationships of trust, ethnic-derived social capital, cultural assumptions, religion, native language fluency, a middleman heritage, entrepreneurial values and attitudes, rotating credit associations, reactive solidarity, multiplex social networks, employer paternalism, an ideology of ethnic solidarity, and a generous pool of underemployed and disadvantaged co-ethnic workers.

The two distinct kinds of entrepreneurial resources discussed by Light (1999) have a great influence on self-employment policy in Germany, albeit at different levels. The concept of 'class' resources – that is, access to economic, educational and social resources – explicitly dominates the discourse of entrepreneurship, establishing a notion of 'standard entrepreneurship' against which business start-ups are measured. On the other hand, the assumption that migrants possess 'ethnic' resources is the secret script that administrators hide behind. They argue that migrants are already well provided for through ethnic networks and channels, and that they therefore do not need the additional support of public policy (Apitzsch and Kontos, 2003: forthcoming).

Statistical analysis has shown that individuals endowed with class resources show a higher propensity for entrepreneurial activity than those without class resources. But the question of why some individuals with access to resources choose to be self-employed and others choose to be employed cannot be answered by this theory. For example, it has long been acknowledged that education is a central resource not only for entrepreneurial activity, but also for integration in the sphere of privileged employed work in the private labour market and in the public sphere (Bourdieu, 1978, 1990). Therefore, the issue that needs to be addressed is whether or not something more than class or ethnic resources is required for successful entrepreneurial activity. What are the underlying mechanisms that determine the choice of self-employment?

A biographical life-process perspective on the concept of resources

The discovery of the importance of social capital for entrepreneurial activity is in a sense the most important discovery of economic sociology in recent decades (Light, 1999, p 18). The concept of the social embeddedness of entrepreneurship, highlighting the role of social relationships in entrepreneurial activities, has also become one of the most prominent concepts in the field (Granovetter, 1985). However, the perspective in which social networks have been studied is either relational (directed towards the analysis of relationships), or structural (aimed at analysing network structures) (Emirbayer and Goodwin, 1994). Although the perspective of entrepreneurial activity as a process with a focus on the acting individual has only recently entered the debate (Cassarino, 1997), its more dynamic perspective of biographical embeddedness should supplement the perspective of social embeddedness of ethnic entrepreneurship.

We adopt a biographical perspective on entrepreneurship, considering that biography is a crucial determinant in the choice of entrepreneurship as a vocation. Among other reasons, this is due to the crucial difference between the pattern of self-employment and that of dependent employment, and the fact that the latter is still central in institutionally determining life paths, plans and expectations in modern societies. The concept of resources underlying self-employment will be discussed from a biographical perspective that is grounded in the assumption that resources emerge during the course of life.

The concept of resources that is central to the economic sociology of ethnic entrepreneurship is also highly relevant to biographical research. However, the concept of resources is more implicit in biographical research, where resource is used as a hyphenated concept in combination with others. Resources are referred to as experiential resources, meaning and action resources and, as an all-embracing term, biographical resources. Erika Hoerning (1989) discusses biographical experience, and the biographical knowledge deriving from it, as action resources. She identifies structural positions of class, gender and generation that generate orientations and patterns of meaning as biographical resources, and stresses the dual character of experience as a resource. On the one hand, experience acts as a resource in constructing "future biographical projects" (Hoerning, 1989, p 154), and on the other it confers potential social prestige and recognition, which facilitate action in society. However, experience and biographical knowledge are not always resources in the sense of a pool of helpful impulses for action and life management. Hoerning stresses far more the ambivalence of biographical experience, which can encourage or discourage, support or hinder. Moreover, she focuses on the self-reflexive character of experience. Experience socialises individuals, so they refer to their experience retrospectively. In this sense, biography appears as a socialising agency.

The concept of biographical resources found further elaboration in the work of Peter Alheit (1995), who developed the concept of 'biographicity' as a key qualification. Biographicity refers to the capacity to integrate new knowledge into biographical resources of meaning, in order to develop a new relationship to this knowledge. He defines biographical resources as the "biographical background knowledge" that enables us to inhabit and utilise the social space in which we live (Alheit, 1995, p 298). The specific character of this knowledge is that it contains more possibilities than can be realised. Following Victor von Weizsäcker (1947, 1956; Zacher, 1988), Alheit calls these possibilities, the potential of 'unlived life'. People have an intuitive knowledge of this potential. Being 'autopoietical systems' (as Luhman developed the term), people can become aware of this surfeit of life experience and utilise it to bring about a conscious change within themselves and in their position in the society. In this sense, Alheit widens the understanding of biographical resources from acquired, to not-yet-acquired experience; that is, to potential experience, which can be accessed through intuitive knowledge of the 'unlived life.'

The theory of biographical trajectory developed by Fritz Schütze (1995) also entails the concept of biographical resources. Trajectories, as sequentially structured biographical phases in which individuals lose their ability to act intentionally, are:

> social processes structured by causal chains of events that one cannot avoid without high costs, constant breakdowns in expectations, and a growing and irritating sense of loss of control over one's life circumstances. (Riemann Schütze, 1991, p 337)

The initial phase of a trajectory, the accumulation of trajectory potential, is a process in which important biographical resources are destroyed. Nevertheless, such phases generally lead, through individual effort, to control of the trajectory or to an escape from it by reorganising the biographical action scheme. Ursula Apitzsch (1996) has stressed that the process of gaining control over the trajectory has not been studied sufficiently in biographical research. The research should bring into focus the latent, hidden potential and resources upon which people fall back to manage crises. For instance, latent intellectual potential, such as the family orientation of young migrant women, can function as a resource for meaning, which supplies the basis for career planning.

Education in the biographies of self-employed migrants: motivation as a resource

By taking seriously a biographical approach to the sequential character of biography and the interrelatedness of biographical phases, we did not limit our analysis to the moment of formal entry into professional life, but tried to reconstruct the biography from the beginning, tracing the search for vocation back to earlier biographical experiences and conditions. Thus, we tried to reconstruct the emergence of the idea of self-employment in the context of biographical experience, and the emergence of biographical plans in terms of the individual drawing on this experience. The analysis of our biographical interviews allowed us to confirm the assumption that finding a vocation, and in this instance becoming self-employed, "is a very long and extremely complicated process, starting in early childhood and sometimes going on until retirement finally releases the person from the burden of choice" (Kupferberg, 1998, p 172; see also Lange and Büschges, 1975; Brown and Brooks, 1984).

Following the principles of theoretical sampling developed within the framework of grounded theory (Glaser and Strauss, 1967; Apitzsch and Inowlocki, 2000; Kontos, 2001), we selected cases fitting the variables of the research question: self-employed migrant men and women and non-migrant women, who had participated in schemes aimed at supporting self-employment projects. The sample included those who failed to establish the anticipated project and those who had succeeded in establishing self-employment projects without the support of policy measures. Each one had to meet the criterion of social disadvantage.

Our analysis confirmed the assumption that the relationship between educational resources and self-employment does not develop in a linear way. In this chapter, we discuss the finding that the idea of self-employment emerges as an alternative biographical plan to institutionalised life-course plans and expectations, as well as to institutionalised barriers and exclusion mechanisms, and as a coping strategy aimed at social integration and recognition. The experience of barriers and obstacles to social integration through education, and thus to the accumulation of convertible human capital, seems to be a key basis for the emergence of the self-employment plan. The strong positive motivation that underlies efforts to realise an alternative biographical plan derives from intuitive knowledge of 'unlived life' and should be considered as a further compensating resource for action. In the following three migrant biographies, this pattern is discussed as a typical underlying path to self-employment, which exists alongside other typical paths, and as a basis for a middle-range theory that will be developed from the empirical material. The three cases represent three different types of migrant biography, across the boundaries of generation and gender:

- a first-generation male migrant;
- a second-generation male migrant;
- a second-generation female migrant.

Our interviews in the Rhine/Main region have shown that many of the interviewed self-employed migrants and self-employed German women had a break in their educational career, or other breaks in their childhood or youth. Few reached degree level. The effects on self-employment seem twofold. On the one hand, entrepreneurial beginners have to develop strategies to compensate for their educational deficiencies. On the other hand, the individual motivation emerging from coping with such failures becomes a visible resource for entrepreneurial activity. Strong motivation is a necessary precondition for overcoming the crisis brought about by stepping outside the institutionally defined 'normal biographical path' of dependent employment. Strong motivation is also essential for acquiring and sustaining commitment to the self-employment project. Formal education appears not to be an unconditional prerequisite for entrepreneurial activity. Furthermore, the break in education can be seen as trauma that leads to motivation and commitment to the self-employment project.

The notion of 'unlived life', producing the motivation on which the self-employment is grounded, is coupled in these biographies with a 'struggle for social recognition'. Axel Honneth (1994) developed the theory of struggle for recognition as the basis for social change from Hegel's *Jenaer Realphilosophie* of 1805/06 (Hegel, 1969). In this theory, social change arises through collective action. Honneth fleshes out Hegel's philosophical theses with insights from Freud's psychoanalysis and the social psychology of G.H. Mead. He argues that a precondition for developing personal identity is recognition from a partner in an interaction. The denial of social recognition is traumatic since it causes damage to personal identity. The reaction to this is the struggle for recognition. There are three levels of social recognition:

- the level of primary relationships, like family and friendship; this recognises the individual as a person with needs;
- recognition of the moral capacity to participate in the community sharing legal rights, thus the level of social solidarity;
- recognition as a person with a social status.

These levels represent a successively widening space of autonomy, as individuals are inclined to broaden their boundaries by trying to achieve recognition at levels to which they have not so far had access. With this theory, Honneth aimed at reconstructing the grammar of social conflict as a collective one. Nevertheless, his analysis of the basis of the structure of social recognition is biographically conceived. Trauma is thought of as a sequence in a biographic chain of experiences and struggle for recognition, as a biographical plan following the experience of trauma. He remarks that the missing link between trauma and struggle is *motivation*. He suggests that motivation be thought of as cognition, entailing a definition of the situation and the construction of a causal relation between the problem situation and its solution. The terms 'unlived life' and 'struggle for recognition' are in this argument interconnected, revealing a 'generative structure' underlying self-employment projects in migration. This idea will be discussed in its specific manifestation in the three case studies[1].

Antonis: self-employment as a struggle for recognition in the society of origin

Antonis is a 54-year-old Greek taxi driver in Frankfurt-am-Main. He was born in a little village in central Greece. After completing six years of primary school he had to move to the nearby town to attend high school. His father's plan was that he would acquire his school-leaving diploma and go to university. Given the strong orientation of Greek families towards education, such a plan was not unusual at that time, even for poor families in rural regions (Tsoukalas, 1987). Nevertheless, Antonis suffered greatly from the experience of separation from his family and village life. It seems that he was not emotionally mature enough for this separation, nor was the financial support from his parents sufficient. The psychic and material deprivation led to Antonis' inner withdrawal from school life. He established a fragile equilibrium of everyday life by integrating into the group of neighbourhood boys who spent most of their free time playing football. As time passed, he became convinced that he would not be able to complete high school with the required grades, and one year before the final examination he announced to his father that he would leave school. This ended with his father throwing him out of the house in a rage. Antonis stayed after that with a cousin and found a vocational training place as a car mechanic. Having finished that, he tried to find employment as a lorry driver before attempting to become self-employed in different sectors, such as lorry driving and hairdressing, but with little success. He then migrated to Germany where his sister was already living. In Germany, he worked first in engineering, without giving up his plan to become self-employed. A well-developed business plan for a trucking transport firm failed due to his educational deficiencies – he could not pass the compulsory exam required to get the permit. So he reduced the plan from a transport firm with several employees to self-employment as a taxi-driver, with himself as the sole employee.

Two points from Antonis' narration are of particular interest: his long-lasting suffering from failing to meet educational expectations, and his tenacious focus on the plan for self-employment. The positive view that Antonis holds of his self-employment project has a double meaning. On the one hand, it has been a means to achieve social and economic integration in society, and with that, social recognition – not only in the host society, but even more importantly, in the society of origin. On the other hand, it has demonstrated to his father the superiority of his own way of achieving social integration, one that circumvented formal education and proved a more reliable path to upward social mobility. Antonis' biographical path is a struggle for social recognition from society and from his father, who denied him recognition of his needs when he was young, including an autonomous decision about his own education.

His success was not feasible without the strong motivation that he developed to cope with the trauma of educational failure and the break with his father. The strength of motivation towards entrepreneurship seems to develop in inverse proportion to the lack of educational capital. On the one hand, the trauma hindered integration in the educational process and was reinforced at the same time by educational failure. On the other hand, the process of reflecting on the trauma and finding some balance led to the development of a strong motivation for entrepreneurship. Antonis refused to follow the biographical plan that his father had developed for him. Rather, he developed his own plan, and risked living a life that was not anticipated in his father's expectations, but an unforeseen 'unlived life'. The awareness of an alternative life plan to that of his father, the awareness of 'unlived life' that had to be lived, became the basis for a strong motivation for his own biographical plan of self-employment. This linked to his aim of gaining social integration and social recognition in his society of origin and, most of all, recognition from his father.

In the biographies of several other migrant men and women, we have come across this interplay between motivation as a resource and negative educational experiences. However, while as a first-generation migrant, Antonis' self-employment project is coupled with the aim of gaining social recognition in the society of origin and from his father, the self-employment plan of second-generation migrants, socialised in the German educational system, emerges from the aim of gaining social integration and social recognition in the host society, as a world that deprives migrants of recognition through juridical and moral exclusion. Under these circumstances, self-employment as a means of social integration and recognition is a functional alternative to higher education that cannot be attempted, because of the discriminatory mechanisms dominating the German education system.

Ömer: self-employment as a struggle for recognition from the receiving society

Gaining social recognition from German society is a key component in the biographical plans of the young self-employed male who has been socialised in the German education system. This is the case with Ömer, who, despite achieving well at school, refrained from going on to higher education for fear that he would fail. His 'struggle for recognition' in the German urban environment was acted out in the surroundings of his Turkish peer group and local gangs who sought to achieve 'respect' from Germans through activities involving violence. Ömer reflected over time with the help of significant others (such as social workers and teachers) on the deeper meaning of violence as a means of social recognition under conditions in which verbal means of communication are lacking. After finishing an apprenticeship as an electrician, he developed a biographical plan to become self-employed in order to acquire 'respect', distancing himself explicitly from the typical migrant sectors of self-employment, such as catering and grocery retail. Recognising resources and limitations, he developed the idea of a security service, directly capitalising on his experience of violence in his self-employment project.

Hülia: self-employment as a struggle for recognition from family and the receiving society

The aim of living the missed 'unlived life' to gain social recognition from the host society through self-employment is found in the biographical narratives of second-generation migrant men and women. However, the biographical accounts of male and female self-employed differ, in that female migrant interviewees of the second generation are concerned not only with gaining recognition from the host society, but also from their own families and ethnic networks. This gender difference can be explored in the conflict that underlies the 'struggle for recognition' of Hülia, a female Turkish entrepreneur.

Hülia is a 28-year-old Turkish woman who owns an advertising firm. She came to Germany at the age of nine. She did well at school and, although her teachers recommended that she continue her education in high school, her parents were reluctant to allow her to do so. Instead she took up vocational training. In the analysis of her narration, we can reconstruct her position in a field of multiple discrimination, devaluation and subjection. In school, she was confronted with racial hatred, which at the beginning of the 1980s was spreading in German schools. Nevertheless, she gained recognition from teachers for her achievements, but her parents remained committed to the traditional woman's role. The migrant situation allowed her to enter paid work and contribute to the family budget. She registered at the labour office to get advice about possible apprenticeships. There, despite having expressed other aspirations, she was directed towards the marginal, economically declining professions of hairdressing or dressmaking. Her very good grades, which would have opened other doors, were disregarded, and she decided to become a hairdresser. Here she was confronted with the gulf in prevailing norms about appearance in the workplace and in her family. In the workplace, she was expected to dress in a modern style and to use make-up; in her family, on the other hand, fundamentalist Muslim principles about women's appearance prevailed. This conflict in cultural values became more dramatic when she married a Turkish man who demanded that she stop working at the hairdresser's and start working in a factory, although she had finished her apprenticeship with excellent grades and been advised to continue. Through the Master course, she would become branch manager, and attain self-employed status. She again tried to adapt, by working extremely long hours full-time in the factory and part-time at the hairdressing salon. She continued to try to convince her husband to allow her to attend the Master course and become self-employed. Obviously, 'adapting' was a pattern that she developed very early on to cope with the different (and frequently discriminatory) expectations of her. In fact, not only did she adapt, but exposed herself to open conflict when she saw that her adaptation strategies were unsuccessful. Finally, she decided to divorce. Following this, she tried to fulfil the goal of self-employment in insurance sales, which she had come across by chance. Later, she worked as a model and developed the idea of building up her own advertising firm. Breaking more conclusively from traditional values, she moved out of the family home while the rest of the family was on holiday in Turkey. Her main goal of gaining a high income through self-employment entailed an exhausting work schedule. It was impossible to include her son, who was living with his father, in this helter-skelter. She developed her own original concept of mothering, based more on a traditional fathering role, in which she assumed that her son would be happier as soon as she earned more money and could satisfy his wishes.

While the conflict on which Ömer developed his self-employment plans concerned lack of social recognition by the host society, the conflict on which Hülia developed hers, including her goal of attaining a high income, derived from the conflict arising out of the divergence of gendered cultural patterns prevailing in her family and in the host society. Her goals related to the desire for recognition, not only from the host society, but also from her family, which continued to treat her as a child. Self-employment was thus a strategy of obtaining both social integration in the society and recognition from her family as an adult person endowed with moral capacity.

Education played a crucial role in this conflict. Hindered in her educational plans, Hülia's wish for further education had to be satisfied through a vocational apprenticeship. Through the apprenticeship, she came across the idea of self-employment. The system of vocational training in the handicraft sector is the only educational field in which self-employment is explicitly talked about as a professional goal. Thus, Hülia was socialised into thinking about self-employment through her apprenticeship; that is, the institutionalised education system. Before building up her advertising firm, she received further training in the process of becoming self-employed. She was also trying to teach herself the methods needed for this work so that self-employment became a learning process for her.

Self-motivated learning as part of the process of self-employment necessary to maintain a business (Kupferberg, 1995) is more evident in the female biography than in the male biography. However, it is not experienced instrumentally solely as a means to be successful in business, but rather for its intrinsic value. This pattern of learning has been observed in the narratives of other migrant women, where they refer enthusiastically to the learning experience of starting up and maintaining a business. Entrepreneurial activity is experienced as a creative learning process, in which women can affirm their abilities and broaden their skills. This seems to blur the boundary between education and self-employment, as self-employment becomes a terrain of lifelong learning, and of self-development through learning.

Consequences for policy

This chapter has shown that motivation is a resource for entrepreneurship deriving from biographical experience, life crises and traumas that can lie far back in a biography. Self-employment is, in this sense, repair work. The motivation for entering self-employment derives from the process of reflection and awareness of 'unlived life' that has to be realised, in relation to a struggle for recognition from the social environment that denied that recognition. The case of Antonis, the first-generation Greek self-employed taxi driver, showed the crystallisation of the 'unlived life' in the wish for economic and social integration in the society of origin and recognition from his father. The case of Ömer, the Turkish second-generation migrant and owner of a security service, showed the crystallisation of the 'unlived life' in the desire for social recognition in the receiving society. And lastly, the case of Hülia, the Turkish owner of an advertising agency, showed the crystallisation of the 'unlived life' in the desire for recognition not only from the host society but also her family. This desire developed against a background of conflict between the differing dominant cultural values in the family and in the host society.

Thus, in each case, the motivation underlying entrepreneurial activity was directed at repairing damage to self-esteem that had occurred in the course of traumatic life experiences. Within the framework of the family, recognition of childhood needs was denied to Antonis. Recognition of Ömer's cultural and moral equality was denied by his social environment, while in Hülia's case both factors applied: cultural and moral recognition from the social environment and recognition of her right to self-determination and moral equality in the family were denied.

This chapter has also shown that this high-level motivation for entrepreneurship is accompanied by low educational attainment deriving from parents' inappropriate educational strategies, or from discriminatory mechanisms in educational institutions. Exclusion from education in these cases is a further negative experience that adds to other traumas. Thus, these people have a low supply of educational capital, but high motivational resources. Motivation is extremely important for coping with the difficulties entailed in the entrepreneurial task: entrepreneurship has to be self-organised, organisational routines have to be invented, and risks taken. The unpredictability of motivation for self-employment in a context of coping with trauma suggests the impossibility of planning for the accumulation of motivation as a resource. Therefore, we cannot refer to motivation as capital, which implies the possibility of its accumulation, but only as resource, which implies its emergent nature.

The interviews with experts conducted within the framework of the project have shown that the institutions concerned with policy making for the promotion of self-employment are rarely willing to open up their instruments to migrant self-starters and self-employed (Kontos, 2000; Apitzsch and Kontos, 2003: forthcoming). A lack of educational capital among migrant self-starters is one of the reasons for refusing support. However, if business start-up support excludes highly motivated candidates who lack formal qualifications, then a great deal of motivation – a scarce social resource (Parsons, 1961) – is being wasted. Good policy practice should not only give access to the resources needed – in the cases discussed this would support compensation for educational deficiencies – but also take the motivational resources of individuals into account.

Note

[1] The interviews were conducted by participants in the 'Biography' course 1998/99 at the University of Frankfurt-am-Main. The Antonis interview was conducted by Irini Siouti and Dora Kotsari, Ömer's interview by Abdul Hamit Cakir, Hülia's interview by Sandra Bauer.

References

Alheit, P. (1995) '"Biographizität" als Lernpotential: konzeptionelle Überlegungen zum biographischen Ansatz in der Erwachsenenbildung', in H.-H. Krüger and W. Marotzki (eds) *Erziehungswissenschaftliche Biographieforschung*, Opladen: Leske+Budrich, pp 276-307.

Apitzsch, U. (1996) 'Biographien und berufliche Orientierung von Migrantinnen', in R. Kersten, D. Kiesel and S. Sargut (eds) *Ausbilden statt ausgrenzen: Jugendliche ausländischer Herkunft in Schule, Ausbildung und Beruf*, Frankfurt-am-Main: Haag und Herchen, pp 133-47.

Apitzsch, U. (2000) 'Beratungs- und Bildungsangebote für Selbständigkeits-projekte in Europa', *Selbständigkeitsprojekte* (Special Issue), *Hessische Blätter für Volksbildung*, vol 50, no1, pp 1-13.

Apitzsch, U. and Inowlocki, L. (2000) 'Biographical analysis – a "German" school?', in P. Chamberlayne, J. Bornat and T. Wengraf (eds) *The turn to biographical methods in social science: Comparative issues and examples*, London/New York, NY: Routledge, pp 53-70.

Apitzsch, U. and Kontos, M. (2003: forthcoming) *Self-employment activities of women and minorities: Their success or failure in relation to social citizenship policies*, Opladen Verlag: Leske+Budrich.

Bögenhold, D. (1987) *Der Gründerboom: Realität und Mythos der neuen Selbständigkeit*, Frankfurt-am-Main: Campus Verlag.

Bögenhold, D. (2000) 'Entrepreneurship, markets, self-employment', *International Review of Sociology*, vol 10, no 1, pp 25-40.

Bourdieu, P. (1978) 'Klassenschicksal, individuelles Handeln und das Gesetz der Wahrscheinlichkeit', in P. Bourdieu, L. Boltanski, M. de Saint Martin and P. Maldidier (eds) *Titel und Stelle: Über die Reproduktion sozialer Macht*, Frankfurt-am-Main: Europäische Verlagsanstalt, pp 169-226.

Bourdieu, P. (1990) *In other words: Essays towards a reflexive sociology*, Cambridge: Polity Press.

Brown, D. and Brooks, L. (eds) (1984) *Career, choice and development*, London, Jossey-Bass.

Cassarino, J.-P. (1997) *The theories of ethnic entrepreneurship and the alternative arguments of social action and network analysis*, European University Institute Working Papers, SPS no 97/1.

Emirbayer, M. and Goodwin, J. (1994) 'Network analysis, culture, and the problem of agency', *American Journal of Sociology*, vol 99, no 6, pp 1411-54.

Glazer, B. and Strauss, A. (1967) *The discovery of grounded theory*, Chicago, IL: Aldine.

Granovetter, M. (1985) 'Economic action and social structure: the problem of embeddedness', *American Journal of Sociology*, vol 91, no 3, pp 481-510.

Hakim, C. (1999) 'The rise of self-employment: the social consequences of new demands for autonomy', Paper presented to the workshop 'Self-employment in advanced economies', Mannheim Centre for European Social Research, University of Mannheim, July.

Hegel, G.W.F. (1969) *Jenaer Realphilosophie*, Hamburg.

Heider, F., Hock, B. and Seitz, H.-W. (1996) *Kontinuität oder Transformation? Zur Entwicklung selbstverwalteter Betriebe. Eine empirische Studie*, Giessen: Focus Verlag.

Hoerning, E.M. (1989) 'Erfahrungen als biographische Ressourcen', in P.Alheit and E. Hoerning (eds) *Biographisches Wissen: Beiträge zu einer Theorie lebensgeschichtlicher Erfahrung*, Frankfurt-am-Main/New York, NY: Campus, pp 148-63.

Honneth, A. (1994) *Kampf um Anerkennung: Zur moralischen Grammatik sozialer Konflikte*, Frankfurt-am-Main: Suhrkamp Verlag.

Kontos, M. (1997) 'Von der Gastarbeiterin zur Unternehmerin. Biographieanalytische Überlegungen zu einem sozialen Transformationsprozeß', *Deutsch Lernen*, vol 22, no 4, pp 275-90.

Kontos, M. (2000) 'Bildungsprozesse, Abbrüche und die Motivation zur Selbständigkeit. Überlegungen zum Konzept biographischer Ressourcen', *'Selbständigkeitsprojekte' Hessische Blätter für Volksbildung*, vol 50, no 1, pp 44-57.

Kontos, M. (2001) 'Sammenlignede overvejelser over kodifikationsmetoden i Grounded Theory og i den biografiske metode', *Dansk Sociologi*, vol 12, no 3, pp 31-52.

Kupferberg, F. (1995) 'Humanistic startups: film establishment as risk management and life planning', Paper to Rent IX Research in Entrepreneurship 9th Workshop in Piacenza, Italy, 23-24 November.

Kupferberg, F. (1998) 'Humanistic entrepreneurship and entrepreneurial career commitment', *Entrepreneurship and Regional Development*, vol 10, pp 171-87.

Lange, E. and Büschges, G. (eds) (1975) *Aspekte der Berufswahl in der modernen Gesellschaft*, Frankfurt-am-Main: Aspekte Verlag.

Light, I. (1999) 'What are the class resources of entrepreneurship?', Paper presented to the conference 'Working on the Fringes: Immigrant Businesses, Economic Integration and Informal Practices', Amsterdam, 7-9 October.

Meager, N. (1993) 'Self-employment and labor market policy in the European Community', Discussion Paper FS I 93-201, Wissenschaftszentrum Berlin für Sozialforschung.

Meager, N. (1996) 'From unemployment to self-employment: labour market policies for business start-up', in G. Schmid, J. O'Reilly and K. Schömann (eds) *International handbook of labour market policy and evaluation*, Cheltenham/ Brookfield: Edward Elgar, pp 469-519.

Parsons, T. (1961) 'An outline of the social system', in T. Parsons, E. Shills, K. Naegele and J.R. Pitts (eds) *Theories of society: Foundations of modern sociological theory*, New York, NY/London: Free Press of Glencoe, pp 30-79.

Riemann, G. and Schütze, F. (1991) '"Trajectory" as a basic theoretical concept for analysing suffering and disorderly social processes', in D.R. Maines (ed) *Essays in honor of Anselm Strauss*, New York, NY: Aldine de Gruyter, pp 333-57.

Schütze, F. (1995) 'Verlaufskurven des Erleidens als Forschungsgegenstand der interpretativen Soziologie', in H.-H. Krüger and W. Marotzki (eds) *Erziehungswissenschaftliche Biographieforschung*, Opladen: Leske+Budrich, pp 116-57.

Tsoukalas, K. (1987) *State and society in Greece*, Athens: Themelio (Greek original).

Vonderach, G. (1980) 'Die "neuen Selbständigen". 10 Thesen zur Soziologie eines unvermuteten Phänomens', *Mitteilungen aus der Arbeitsmarkt- und Berufsforschung*, 2/1980, pp 153-69.

Von Weizsäcker, V. (1988) *Fälle und Probleme: Klinische Vorstellungen*, Frankfurt-am-Main: Suhrkamp.

Von Weizsäcker, V. (1956) *Pathosophie*, Göttingen: Vandenhoek + Ruprecht.

Zacher, A. (1988) *Kategorien der Lebensgeschichte. Ihre Bedeutung für Psychiatrie und Psychotherapie*, Berlin: Heidelberg Springer.

FIVE

Ethnic entrepreneurship as innovation[1]

Feiwel Kupferberg

This chapter is a result of long-standing interest in three different research areas that rarely intersect or are even seen as of mutual interest: biography, entrepreneurship and innovation. The reasons why biographical research and entrepreneurial research have rarely engaged in an effort of interdisciplinary communication are easy to identify. Entrepreneurial research is a branch of business economics that specialises in the founding of new ventures, mainly small businesses (Gartner, 1985), and in particular the problems of legitimisation that such new ventures encounter as they seek to gain trust among potential stakeholders and business partners (Gartner, 1990; Gartner et al, 1992; Aldrich, 1999). These difficulties, which can be summarised as the 'liability of the new' (Stinchcombe, 1965) put organisational issues related to strategies for overcoming the assumed liability of the new at the centre of business-oriented research. This explains why interest in the role of the person in the founding of new ventures is fading (Aldrich, 1989).

Putting biography into analyses of migrant entrepreneurship

William Garnter (1989, p 47), writing from a business economics point of view, has criticised current entrepreneurial research, laconically stating that, "Who is an entrepreneur is the wrong question". Such a position certainly does not reach out to what is the main assumption of biographical research, namely that a detailed knowledge of a person's life history matters and gives researchers a privileged access to the type of life worlds in which reflexive social agents attempt to construct meaning, negotiate identity and choose appropriate strategies of adaptation (Alheit, 1994; Kupferberg, 1995; Horsdal, 1999). Knowing who the entrepreneur is, is far from irrelevant from the point of view of a biographical approach; indeed, it must be the starting point for any meaningful analysis of entrepreneurial phenomena (Kupferberg, 1998, 2002).

Interestingly, biographical research is not the only sub-discipline that entrepreneurial research has declared to be *non grata*. The same enmity or conspicuous indifference can be found, although for somewhat different reasons, among entrepreneurial researchers towards innovation research (Tidd et al,

1997). This is strange, given that we dealing here with two different branches within business economics. There might be several possible reasons why this is the case, for example, academic specialisation aggravated by internal competition for limited resources (financial and social capital) or attempts to achieve a more favourable balance in terms of educational programmes and academic prestige (cultural and symbolic capital). Nevertheless, the main reason why entrepreneurial research has tended to marginalise the phenomenon of innovation – in spite of the fact that the most cited theorist on entrepreneurship, Joseph Schumpeter (1945), emphasised the dynamic aspects of entrepreneurship as an agent of change in the capitalist economy – seems to be the more or less unstated assumption that innovation and entrepreneurship are two different things and that they rarely, if ever, coexist. Indeed, Aldrich and Martinez (2002, p 41) argue that:

> Overestimating the innovating capacity and personal traits of entrepreneurs has hidden the major role of imitation in entrepreneurial processes. Evolutionary theory calls our attention to the numerically dominant role of reproducers, rather then innovators.

Strangely the same lack of interest in the personal motivations and innovative capacities of entrepreneurs has characterised the sub-field of entrepreneurial research that focuses on immigrant or ethnic entrepreneurship. Although this type of entrepreneurship has attracted sociologists for the most part, the traditional knowledge interests of sociologists into what motivates actors and the creative potentials of social agency have been virtually absent. The potentially innovative aspects of a structurally marginal position did indeed figure prominently among the pioneers of entrepreneurial research as well as immigrant entrepreneurship (Light and Karageoris, 1994; Martinelli, 1994; Portes and Rumbaut, 1996). However, this interest has gradually faded away. Current research on immigrant or ethnic entrepreneurship has more or less forgotten its intellectual roots and has abandoned what we have come to associate with sociological curiosity or imagination. Instead, it tends to take its point of departure in the same assumptions that enlighten the business economics point of view in entrepreneurial research that, as indicated earlier, emphasises imitation rather then innovation and reduces entrepreneurship to a question of the legitimisation of a new organisation.

It is precisely these two hidden assumptions that inform current thinking on ethnic entrepreneurship, where the main problem faced is often described in terms of the 'structural opportunity model' (Waldinger et al, 2000). Here, the main suggestion is that immigrant entrepreneurs tend to imitate rather than innovate. The argument runs along the lines that the chances of an imitative business surviving are determined by the competitive situation in a particular area and restricted by the effect of overcrowding. For this reason, the personal motives of the immigrant entrepreneur are irrelevant and can be excluded in any analysis. In this respect at least, the difference between immigrant and non-immigrant entrepreneurs disappears or becomes irrelevant as "the continuum from reproducer to innovator is defined by outcomes, not intentions" (Aldrich and Martinez, 2001, p 44).

This clearly behaviouristic view of entrepreneurs was introduced by William B. Glade in his seminal article 'Approaches to a theory of entrepreneurial formation' (Glade, 1967). Glade's main hypothesis is that "structural or environmental features enter into the building of entrepreneurial theory on the demand side no less than on the supply side of the situational analysis, chiefly as conditions defining the potential opportunity structure" (1967, p 250). The behaviouristic type of explanation offered by the opportunity structure model, which today dominates sociological thinking on entrepreneurship (Thornton, 1992), can be illustrated by a review article by Aldrich and Waldinger (1990) on ethnicity and entrepreneurship. Of the article's 22 pages (exclusive of references), 16 explore those factors that determine the structure of demand and supply of ethnic entrepreneurs; only two are dedicated to a discussion of the appropriate strategies for business success employing a behaviouristic view of agency that excludes motivation as a factor or sees personal motives as irrelevant. In this analysis, strategies are exclusively defined by what is objectively possible, seen from the point of view of demand versus supply.

Aldrich and Waldinger (1990, p 131) characterise the ethnic business sector as one where there is 'intense competition', leaving ethnic entrepreneurs four strategies:

> (1) self-exploitation (2) expanding the business by moving forward or backward in the chain of production or by opening other shops (3) founding and supporting ethnic trade associations (4) cementing alliances to other families through marriages.

Assuming that the demand side is numerically smaller than the supply side, Aldrich and Waldinger (1990, p 112) argue that imitation rather than innovation is to be expected:

> Rather than breaking new ground in products, process, or administrative form, most businesses simply replicate and reproduce old forms. Simple reproduction is especially likely in the retail and service sector, where most ethnic enterprises are founded. Risks, however are high.

The main problem with this model is that it cannot account for the dynamic aspects of immigrant entrepreneurship (or entrepreneurship in general). Should immigrant entrepreneurship be seen as a kind of behaviour that is determined by structural factors such as supply and demand, how do we account for the fact that new actors enter the field at all? What could possibly motivate an immigrant to become an entrepreneur, given that the structure of opportunity gives him or her little chance to use entrepreneurship as a way to gain control over his or her own future? In order to account for this anomaly, some ethnic entrepreneurship researchers have introduced the theory of 'ethnic succession' (Mars and Ward, 1984; Basu and Goswami, 1999). Basically, this theory argues that ethnic entrepreneurship allows for some degree of social mobility in the sense that successive waves of newcomers move into niches abandoned by more established minorities.

Other theories emphasise the importance of ethnic networks as a compensating factor that might possibly increase the competitiveness of ethnic business in the sense that such networks function as social capital (Coleman, 1988). Ethnic networks give immigrant entrepreneurs access to cheap and loyal labour, a *Gemeinschaft* type of financial assistance, as well as tacit business knowledge from co-ethnics (Portes and Rumbaut, 1996). On the other hand, the same ethnic networks also create new constraints on ethnic businesses that further reduces the chances of immigrant entrepreneurs to change their lives (Rezaei, 2002).

What these and similar theories abstract from is the possibility that personal motivations are often the main capital of immigrants (see Chapter Four of this volume). Thus, Sowell, in his comparative investigation of immigrant groups (1996), found that such motivational factors as thrift, the willingness to work long hours and to accept hard work, and the general ability to postpone present consumption in favour of expected future rewards (including the social mobility of the next generation) have been widely underestimated as a crucial dimension in recent immigrant research. Regarding motivation as a particular kind of capital can thus help us better to account for the interesting social fact that immigrant groups have often been able to mobilise social and economic resources that remained hidden before migration.

A case in point would be immigrants from poor areas of the world such as Ireland, Italy, India and Poland who, according to Sowell, prospered in the countries they chose as new home lands.

Sowell found that motivational factors also explain why, for different reasons, some immigrant groups have done significantly better then other immigrant groups (the 'overachievers'). Here the cases of Chinese and Jewish migrants are particularly interesting. In the case of Chinese entrepreneurs, a socially disembedding or 'decoupling' effect releasing normative duties to co-ethnics (Granovetter, 1995), combined with the experience of harsh discrimination, seems to have intensified a tendency to take entrepreneurial risks and to find innovative ways of doing business. For the Jews, the awareness of permanent vulnerability as a historically diaspora nation without a state of their own seems to have led to a heightened sensitivity and greater ability to adapt to shifting demands in unpredictable mass markets as well as a willingness to take extraordinary risks in order to achieve social recognition and prove one's worth as a person (French, 1971; May and May, 1982).

Only the Germans, one of the six immigrant groups Sowell investigates, seem to fit the structural opportunity model. Here the motivational factors, such as thrift and a strong ethic of labour, seem to be constant deriving from particular socialisation patterns in German culture. These same motivational factors also explain why Germany as a nation has done fairly well in the world and why the only reason for migrating would be to use possible differences in structural opportunities to one's personal advantage. Thus, skilled and disciplined German workers found that they were welcome everywhere where their particular skills and work ethics were in higher demand than at home. For all the other immigrant groups, motivation changed with migration; that is, the immigrants became different persons abroad to what they had been at home. It is this personal change that is interesting from a biographical point of view and what ultimately makes the biographical approach highly relevant in order to understand what is at stake when we talk of ethnic entrepreneurship.

The idea that it is possible to study entrepreneurship from a purely behaviouristic point of view is inaccurate or mistaken as it leaves out the important considerations individuals always make when they deliberate whether they should abandon the relatively well-known and secure life as employees for the relatively unknown and insecure life as self-employed (Kupferberg, 2002). Using the behaviouristic approach in the study of immigrant entrepreneurs (men or women) is not only mistaken, it is absurd. It neglects those existential considerations of immigrant entrepreneurs that focus on denial of social worth, or lack of social recognition, which together with feelings of lack of self-esteem and the need to prove one's value by working harder, lead to greater risk taking and innovation in the sociological sense.

In order for sociologists to understand what immigrant entrepreneurship is about, we need to replace the behaviouristic, objectivist business economics definition of innovation predominant in entrepreneurship research with a definition that takes its point of departure in the reflexive agent, seeking to define subjectively constructed meaning in the world, negotiating identity and choosing appropriate strategies of adaptation for this particular purpose. The fundamental question one has to ask is: what kind of meaning and identity is at stake here? Only when we have investigated these subjective aspects can we begin to understand what kind of business strategies the agent has chosen and why. Whether a particular business strategy leads to 'success' in a business sense cannot be abstracted from where the person comes from, what his or her ambitions in life are, how the choice of entrepreneurship as a life form has been influenced by the ability to realise those ambitions and considerations or how the commitment to entrepreneurship influences that person's social status.

'I am proud of myself': innovation as redefinition of legitimate means and cultural values

In order to illustrate the importance of these subjective considerations that the biographical approach seeks to investigate, analyse and reveal, this chapter presents a very striking case of ethnic entrepreneurship that appears in a recent Danish study of ethnic entrepreneurs (Thomsen and Kupferberg, 2001). The interview took place in Aalborg, a city in the northern part of Denmark. The city has about 150,000 inhabitants and is in the middle of a difficult transition from a traditional industrial region, where the majority of the labour force is unskilled, into a post-industrial city, where higher education and information technology is seen as the key to economic growth and employment.

The respondent, whom we can call Rashid, is an immigrant from Iran. At the time of the interview, he was 48 years old, married to an Iranian women with three children (aged eight, 13 and 18). In Iran, he held a job as a rationalisation expert in a large German-owned firm, measuring the movements of workers and calculating how these could be made more effective. The company must have regarded him as a valuable resource. During the 18 years he worked in this factory, he completed a two-year educational programme entitling him to an engineering diploma. At the time of the interview he was the owner of a local grocery. The interview took place in a back room of the store and was interrupted several times when customers entered.

In the interview, Rashid emphasises his first working experiences in Denmark as a period where he was constantly humiliated. He was offered minimum wages in spite of the fact that he had proven himself to be a highly responsible and effective worker. On the first day of a new job, the owner of the factor approached Rashid with a screwdriver', asking, 'Do you know what this is?'. Having received the correct answer from Rashid, the boss turned to the others present, with the comment: 'He also knows the tools'. In spite of this unpleasant start, Rashid soon ran the factory, because the owner for some reason preferred to stay at home. This working period came to an end, however, for economic reasons. The factory was in bad shape, and the equipment was too old for the firm to stay competitive. From the interview, it is not clear whether the factory closed down or whether Rashid lost his job or both.

Rashid emphasises that this period in his life convinced him that he should start a firm of his own. Although the family income was very small (his wife could not get a job in Denmark despite her having a diploma in hotel management from England and Rashid received unemployment benefits that were reduced because he had to pay his monthly trade union membership fee), they nevertheless managed to set aside a small amount of money each month, and after two to three years they had saved enough capital to realise the dream of becoming self-employed. This is the way Rashid describes the difference between his feelings today and before he became the owner of the grocery store:

> I saved money. And then – I could, I could start my own business. And it is this business. And it works ... it's been five years now. And I am very satisfied, very satisfied, not because I earn more. We don't earn much more than we received through public assistance or from the trade union [in Denmark unemployment benefits are administered by the trade unions]. The important thing, and the important thing and the important thing to me, is that my children are proud of me, because I work. And I am proud of myself, the first day I got the store. I paid the VAT and taxes and until this day I don't owe anyone a kroner. And all the goods that are in my store are

my own, I don't have a bank credit. Alright? Because when I feel that our economy is bad, we stop those kind of expenses that we use for entertainment. And in this way there is always a balance … sometimes, I earn less in this store than public assistance, even if I work 14 hours every day. [At this point the interview was interrupted by the arrival of a customer.]

What struck me when I first read this interview (I had not been present at the interview itself, which had been carried out by a research assistant) was the contrast between the expression of very strong subjective motives to start a business and the objectively poor results of that particular business. The business is far from an economic success, it is barely surviving and in order to keep it going the owner has to work long hours – and sometimes even that is not enough. To avoid running into the red, the family is called upon to make sacrifices as well. On the other hand, if the business is good, the family is rewarded by receiving luxuries as gifts for their patience. Later in the interview, Rashid reveals that, at one time, when the business was good, he bought a big and expensive car for his wife to drive in. Being tied to the business, he has no time to drive it himself. At the time business was less good, Rashid could hardly afford to pay dental bills for his children and what is even worse, he is in need of an operation. His foot hurts, but he cannot afford to stay away from the business so he suffers the pain and takes pride in the sacrifices he makes for his children's future. He wants them to get an education and deliver him from his self-chosen predicament.

These elements of patience and sacrifice were clearly present in the period before he went into business. During those lean years, the rewards had to be postponed several years into the future as everything that could be saved went into the savings account. There is thus continuity between past and present, between patience and sacrifice. So what is the difference? The only difference seems to be the element of pride. The very fact that the family was indeed able to save the money necessary to start their own business and the fact that they are able to keep the business afloat both in bad and good times is the source of the pride the father feels and the pride he assumes that his children also feel.

What are the sources of this pride? It cannot be the mere fact that he works rather than being dependent on the social welfare system, although this certainly figures in the complex feelings attached to his own business. Earning his own money is merely a symbol of the personal transformation he has gone through in the process of becoming self-employed. This transformation has to be seen in the context of his personal ambitions in life, given his previous social status in his home country as a person of some importance and the contrasting experiences as immigrant in Denmark, where efforts to confirm his self-identity as an important person are constantly frustrated. He was deliberately humiliated in front of others. There was no relation at all between Rashid's actual social worth as a highly responsible, disciplined and effective worker and his social identity, the recognition he expected in terms of wages as well as deference from the social environment. On the contrary, the latter was systematically and, as he interpreted it, intentionally denied him, as if the environment wanted to send him the following message: 'Stop believing that you are somebody, because you were someone in your home country. Here, we decide who is somebody and who is not'.

So much for the importance of motives, which in this case undoubtedly were the most important source of capital for starting a firm. Forget about financial capital: this was negative from the start and is still a problem that has not been solved but requires patience and sacrifice, both of which require a high degree of motivation. Forget about cultural capital as well. Had he wanted to exploit his educational or cultural capital, which was his original strategy, he would have continued to look for an employer willing to recognise his social worth. It was precisely because Rashid found that his expertise as a highly qualified worker with relevant experience somehow did not matter or was ignored that he decided that the strategy of converting his cultural capital from Iran would not work. What about social capital? The lack of it certainly contributed to his failure to continue his career in Denmark. One gets the impression that he has few if any Danish friends. Social capital figures in some of his fantasies about the future (he dreams of opening a cinema in Copenhagen for his co-ethnics), but does not seem to have played any role in his present business. The family saved the money he needed and he does not employ any co-ethnics, nor his wife and children, in particular the children whom he takes great pride in keeping out of the store so that they can remain proud of their father.

But what about the type of business he entered? How do we categorise his business strategy? Is it a successful strategy or not? Is he an innovative or imitative businessman? It is when we ask these types of questions that the radical difference between the business economics point of view of entrepreneurship and the biographical approach towards the same phenomenon becomes visible. As biographical researchers, we cannot use concepts such as success or innovation as 'objective' or behaviouristic concepts that are independent on the meaning-construction and negotiation of self-identity in which the person is engaged. In other words, 'who the person is' does indeed matter. A business that barely survives, and has little or no future prospects of ever expanding itself out of this predicament would probably fall under the category of 'self-exploitation' that was mentioned earlier. Yet this is certainly not the way Rashid feels about his business. On the contrary, he takes particular pride in precisely those aspects that would make the business economist groan. What is seen as meaningless from the point of view of a behaviouristic science can be very meaningful from the point of view of a sociology emphasising reflexive agency as the core element of the sociological method (Giddens, 1976).

Let us assume that Rashid's business is a success in the sense that it is a meaningful act, given the life experiences of Rashid as an immigrant in a welfare state society like Denmark. What, then, of innovation? Surely there is nothing in Rashid's case that makes him an innovator – or is there? Whereas a business point of view would argue that the structure of the opportunity model would most likely make Rashid an imitator rather then an innovator, a biographical point of view would not necessarily reach the same conclusion. The question is: what do we actually mean when we talk of an innovation? My suggestion is that, when seen from a reflexive agency point of view, what is crucial when we talk about innovation in the sociological sense is that individuals act differently from what is to be expected. In other words, they break or transcend certain norms that are seen as self-evident. What is self-evident or not of course depends on the social context (Ziehe, 1999).

Robert Merton originally suggested this broader sociological understanding of innovation in his groundbreaking article 'Structure and anomy' (1968). Merton's problem in the article is how to explain how a society like the US deals with the social fact of a gap between cultural goals and legitimate means to achieve these goals. Although phrased in a structural functionalist context, Merton's particular approach in reality relies upon the tacit assumption of reflexive agency. Rather than looking for how the 'system' solves the problem at hand, the focus is on how individuals or different kinds of individuals react to the gap between goals and means. Among the different types of reaction (which include conformism, ritualism and rebellion) he mentions innovation. In the way Merton uses this term, innovation is a particular way of coping with the gap between cultural goals and legitimate means, where the individual affirms the former but denies the latter. Individuals of this type indeed want to have access to the same cultural values as the rest (that is, to become rich or successful), but, since they are denied legitimate means, they are put under pressure to innovate. That is, they use whatever means can be found to reach a culturally defined goal even by using means that are defined as illegitimate or illegal by society. In other words, they break certain types of norm in order to gain the feeling of normality in other areas.

How does this theoretical model of pressure to innovate help us to understand Rashid's road to entrepreneurship? Merton's model cannot be applied mechanically since we are dealing with a welfare state society. No one in Denmark is under pressure to steal in order to be able to afford a place to live and to acquire other everyday necessities such as food, clothing or transport. In his interview, Rashid, similarly to other immigrants, praises the Danish welfare system in this respect and makes clear that he takes pride in following the rules in this sense (he pays his VAT, taxes, and so on). From a legal point of view, he resembles the conformist with a ritualistic type of reaction. However, his innovativeness is projected into a different arena: namely the pride he takes in having a business of his own.

We have already mentioned the sources of this pride: economic independence and the moral virtues of patience and sacrifice necessary to uphold this independent state. What is interesting is that neither of these two values ranks highly in Danish culture. As a consumer society, Danes have learned to take pride in immediate satisfaction and self-realisation. As a career society, Danes tend to look upon the small business sector as an area where efforts do not pay.

It has low social status compared with employment in large private or public organisations. A career as self-employed is, for most Danes with career ambitions, the opposite of having a career. In other words, there is no future in it (Kupferberg, 1997).

Nevertheless, career-oriented Danes do start their own businesses, but mostly reluctantly. They certainly do not feel any pride at the time, although this might change if and when the business turns out to be successful (Kupferberg, 2001). What is interesting in Rashid's case is the elevation of status that he associates with becoming an entrepreneur. This feeling is difficult to understand from the point of view of the majority, for it is the opposite of the self-evident legitimate norms of using cultural and, to a certain degree, social capital in order to have a successful career as an employed person. In fact, Rashid entered Denmark sharing precisely this norm. It was only when he experienced the structural exclusion of immigrants who were denied the possibility of taking pride in their achievement through the ordinary means of employment that he was put under pressure to find another source of pride, namely being self-employed. It is in this sense that self-employment does indeed represent a case of innovation. Indeed, it is not everyone that can take pride in working 14 hours a day to keep a business afloat. This requires a break with the self-evident, a creative act. From this point of view, Rashid's act has more creative elements in it than Merton's innovation category. It resembles what Merton calls a 'rebellion', since not only the legitimate means but also the cultural values are redefined.

'They will find some weak point in me': innovation as a means to circumvent discrimination

What about female immigrants who start their own businesses? Are the motives different for this group? If so, in what ways and how can their decisions be explained? My point of departure is the case of Zahrah, an Iranian woman in her early 40s, who owns a small hairdressing business, which she started with financial and other types of assistance and encouragement from her brothers and other Iranians. The business seems to run very well; it gives her a secure income to support herself and her two children. She is divorced from her husband whom she brought to Denmark in order to get married. When the couple became estranged she decided that it was better to live alone with her children.

What is immediately striking about Zahrah is her risk aversion. She had eight years' experience of working as a hairdresser when she came to Denmark, a career she entered after finishing school in Iran and that led to her eventually opening her own hairdressing salon before she emigrated for political reasons. She was born into a family of self-employed. She says:

> My parents were self-employed. My … father, he had a knitting factory and
> it was the work of all the family, my uncles … and everything. And my
> mother … she had something that they sewed … fabric for the shops.

She had a strong network in Denmark that assisted her in building up the
business. Zahrah's brothers, both of whom are self-employed, gave her lots of
advice and massive amounts of support. She could easily borrow the 120,000
kroner necessary to start up the business from her brothers. A further advantage
was that she did not have to hire an accountant to help her with the paper
work: "It is my brother's wife, she comes and helps me to clear up the things".
Her brothers were also instrumental in setting up the business:

> My brothers told me that they can all help me. Give me advice how to
> open a … business …. I started looking a little … if there was anything. So
> I was lucky, I found the first place in the newspaper, it was actually my
> brother who said there was a hairdressing salon [to rent].

In spite of all these advantages, she was not too eager to become the owner of
a hairdressing business. She feared that if she failed, it would "hurt my family
… be a catastrophe". And although the business has been steadily expanding
and seems to run very well, the idea of employing someone else so that she
could spend more time with her children is something that she does not dare
to consider seriously:

> If I would like to employ one, it costs such an awful lot of money, and I am
> a little afraid of that. Maybe it would be a good idea, if I can employ
> someone and see if it works out well, it would be better for me. But I work
> so hard as I do right now, but perhaps … it is something that scares me.

She is also afraid to employ someone because of the extra costs of hiring an
accountant:

> If I get employees, I need a real accountant and all those things – and then,
> then that will bring big expenses. So therefore I am afraid. Maybe it will
> turn out good if I do. But, but … there are some things that … there are
> always limits for the risk [I can take] …. I cannot take that risk now. Maybe
> in a couple of years.

Given the notion of entrepreneurship as risk taking, her strong risk aversion is
interesting. We do not find the particular pride in working long hours in order
to support one's family that we found in Rashid's case. Many of her thoughts
actually go towards reducing her immense workload in order to live up to her
role as mother. Somehow, one gets the impression that she feels a little guilty
about it. However, because of her strong risk aversion she is unable to solve
that dilemma. However, if neither pride nor willingness to take risks can

explain her motive to become self-employed, how do we account for her taking this important step in her life at all? One gets the feeling that she was more or less persuaded by her social environment to change her social status. Her own role seems to have been more or less passive.

Her feelings once she started her business reveal that she was still not convinced that she had done the right thing. She had looked at the premises, rented them and started:

> So it worked! But I was very, very worried because of my language and … now I speak better than at that time. Two years ago. And then … new hair colour … and perhaps they don't like coming here … the customers. But, just after a couple of months I could see "Wow, someone is coming" … as customers, they are all so nice and courteous… I don't have to worry, if there is something…. If I lack some words or something like that, then they can help me.

There are two alternative narratives that might possibly explain her decision to become self-employed. One has nothing at all to do with discrimination: it simply derives from her personal situation as a divorced immigrant women in modern society. As such she was hanging between two cultures. Divorces are unthinkable in traditional societies. They rarely occur because strong pressure is put on both parties to find another solution. However, there is also a strongly gendered culture for both men and women where problems of marriages can be ventilated in a social forum. In modern societies, where divorce is a common phenomenon, it does not represent a break against any strong norms. Precisely for these reasons there are no gendered social fora where the individual can seek emotional support and advice about how to cope with the psychological aftermaths of a divorce.

This leaves women like Zahrah in a situation where they have to find other ways of getting out of their home to engage in talk and socialise with other women. This social need is indeed mentioned as one reason why she decided to become self-employed after her divorce:

> It was so sad, and I didn't want to stay at home, so I didn't want to be a patient [her own word] receiving public assistance or such things…. And so … I had to find a solution. Like getting out of the house and that, shift to some quite different thoughts … be busy with something else like…. Not feel so sad…. It was like a psychological … treatment I gave myself at that time.

Although Zahrah tends to psychologise her situation, her emphasis upon wanting to get out of her home has to be seen in the Danish cultural context where problems related to divorce and how to cope with it have been privatised. It is for this reason that work becomes a kind of refuge from marital problems. Here it is possible to forget one's privatised problems, simply because work keeps oneself busy. In other words, Zahrah diagnosed her situation correctly; unless she wanted to enter a therapeutic treatment, a job would be the best alternative.

However, if all Zahrah needed to do was work, why didn't she simply work as an employed hairdresser? It is when we introduce this problem that we discover a different narrative underlying the former one, one that seems to have been the fundamental motive for Zahrah's self-transformation. Although she had been educated as a hairdresser and worked in the business for eight years, her qualifications were not recognised by Danish hairdressers. When she presented her predicament to the authorities and asked what she was expected to do, she was told that she had to start all over again and re-enter hairdressing training. This would take her four years:

> And so they told me, I can be employed some places, if they want me, or I can become self-employed. But I cannot have, how do they call it, the only difference between a hairdressing salon that has been educated in Denmark and one they has not been educated in Denmark, is that you cannot have a student. That's what they told me.... Then I thought that this is because I don't have a Danish education, it will always give problems in some workplaces ... they will always find a weak point in me ... not like the other common employees.

This is a very powerful statement and it goes to the root of the problem. What Zahrah experienced was simply the naked discrimination of the labour market that all immigrants in Denmark experience in one way or other. Since she was not a man, the way she coped with this discrimination or structural exclusion did not involve a large amount of personal pride, nor was she willing to take great risks in overcoming discrimination. Precisely for these reasons, her motivation to become self-employed is 'purer' than in the case of Rashid. Paraphrasing Durkheim (1965), we could say that we are here observing the elementary forms of immigrant entrepreneurship. Immigrants become entrepreneurs, because the normal roads for a normal occupational work life remain closed to them. As Zahrah puts it, the employers will always "find some weak points in me".

Why is this an innovation? Why is it not simply a case of discrimination that should be deplored? Innovation normally has a positive connotation. How can a situation that derives from something as morally repugnant as naked discrimination be positive? Those who make the latter kind of argument tend to forget that what makes innovation positive is not those negative or deplorable contexts that precede it but the creative ways in which reflexive agents (sometimes) cope with social injustice. Although the situation of an immigrant has little to do with social justice, this does not mean that we should not celebrate and admire the ways individuals like Zahrah somehow manage to find a way out of the bitterness that being a victim of social injustice always brings with it. Surely Zahrah's decision to become self-employed made her a happier person? This is actually how she describes it: "It was happiness to start as [self-employed]". Without this feeling of exhilaration or happiness she would surely never have overcome her own fears and hesitations. Her happiness was pure, because the discrimination she encountered was so naked and because she found a way to escape confronting it for the rest of her working life.

Policy implications

The overall model of ethnic entrepreneurship that this chapter has arrived at suggests that the structural opportunity approach is inadequate, mainly because it ignores reflexive agency and in particular the motivational capital that immigrants draw on when entering business. This motivational capital can take many different forms, however, depending on the life history of the immigrant. From a policy point of view, what should be emphasised is the crucial difference in coping strategies among male and female immigrants. Here the overall pattern seems to be that, whereas the pressure to innovate among male immigrants takes the form of personal pride and high risks, for female immigrants escaping discrimination in itself is the fundamental motive. The motives of the female immigrants in other words are less over-determined or, shall we say, less 'clouded' by other issues.

This general pattern appears not only in the Danish material assembled for the TSER project entitled 'Self-employment activities concerning women and minorities: their successes and failures in relation to citizenship policies', but seems to be general for all countries with strong welfare states such as Sweden, Denmark and Germany. Immigrant men generally seemed to be much more risk-oriented and oriented towards issues of self-pride than immigrant women. What convinced the immigrant men to start their own business were humiliating experiences of discriminatory low wages often compounded by racial slurs from work colleagues, failed attempts to get a job within the profession to which they were formally qualified in terms of years of education and experience, or merely the firm decision not to live off public welfare and the desire to support their own family financially. To let the welfare state replace the immigrant man as the 'breadwinner' in the family was seen as the utmost humiliation and for this reason avoided at all costs.

In contrast to the immigrant men, who are under strong pressure to take more or less uncalculated risks in order to prove their self-worth, among immigrant women these compensatory, self-assertive motives to start one's own business are mostly absent in the three welfare states investigated (Germany, Sweden and Denmark). For immigrant women, the predominant motive for becoming self-employed is experience of naked discrimination, the feeling that 'they will always find some weak point in me'. Problems of self-esteem rarely enter their consideration. From this, it follows that women immigrants as a rule are very reluctant to start their own businesses. The experience of naked discrimination might push them in the direction of self-employment, but they will at the same time be pulled back by the anxieties of the risks ahead or the hard work necessary.

What our biographical interviews with male and female immigrants in welfare states suggest is that training programmes for immigrants have to take into account the different kinds of motivational capital they bring with them. For women immigrants, the main problem is how to encourage them to take risks by reducing some of the risk factors, for example, by access to cheap financial credits, finding the right premises and providing free accounting assistance during the first years. For men immigrants, the problem is the opposite: how to discourage them from engaging with risk and encourage them to be more cautious and rational in developing a realistic business plan.

Whereas in welfare states starting a business of one's own among immigrants is mainly motivated by ethnic discrimination giving rise to male search for pride and risk taking and female risk aversion, the biographical material in the UK – part of the TSER project – seems to suggest that ethnic discrimination as a motive to become self-employed might also take a more discrete form. Here, ethnic discrimination functions less as an entrance barrier to the labour market, and more as a career barrier in the sense that top positions are tacitly reserved for members of the majority (the idea of the 'glass ceiling'). In Italy and Greece, ethnic discrimination functions on a legal level. Immigrants are often unregistered or they lack the legal status of citizen necessary to start their own business. This adds particular aspects to the pressure to innovate.

Thus, one immigrant from North Africa who had entered Greece illegally had to take the high risk of registering his firm in the name of another immigrant who had achieved citizenship status. Whether that immigrant who nominally was in charge of the firm would be willing to give the firm back to its rightful owner when the time came was simply a risk he had to live with. Another highly educated immigrant from North Africa was shocked when he found that most of his countrymen were street hawkers. Slowly he adjusted himself to the reality and became a street hawker himself. In this case, the innovation consisted in reversing his own view of what was morally acceptable according to the culture he came from. He had to redefine his cultural pride as the price for adjusting to the host culture. Facing the reality of massive ethnic discrimination, he had to redefine what was morally proper under the given circumstances.

This moral rethinking is very close to what Merton was thinking of when he introduced the concept of innovation. What he was hinting at might have been the predominant role played by certain immigrant groups in North America, such as the Italian and Irish Catholics as well as the Jews from Eastern Europe and Russia, in industries that at the time were seen as immoral by the Protestant majority: gambling and boot-legging (and possibly the film industry as well), for example, where 'moral' entrepreneurs were strongly engaged to outlaw such outrageous practices. Although only a small minority within the above-mentioned immigrant groups did partake in making a business in these areas, these minorities were clearly over-represented, which is why the literature sometimes talks of an 'ethnic vice industry' (Light, 1977). However, what is a vice in the eyes of the majority can be redefined as a virtue by the minority. There is no such thing as an 'objective' structure of opportunity; rather, it is how individuals subjectively find meaning in a particular opportunity and whether it supports that individual's negotiation of identity that alone makes it possible to evaluate the moral value of the strategies of adaptation chosen.

Note

[1] This chapter draws on the Danish results of the TSER project 'Self-employment activities concerning women and minorities: their success or failure in relation to citizenship policies'.

References

Aldrich, H.E. (1989) 'From traits to rates: an ecological perspective on organizational foundings', Paper presented at the Gateway Conference 'Entrepreneurship', St Louis, MO.

Aldrich, H.E. (1999) *Organizations evolving*, London: Sage Publications.

Aldrich, H.E. and Waldinger, R. (1990) 'Ethnicity and entrepreneurship', *Annual Review of Sociology*, issue 16, pp 111-35.

Aldrich, H.E. and Martinez, M.A. (2002) 'Many are called, but few are chosen: an evolutionary perspective on the study of entrepreneurship', *Entrepreneurship Theory and Practice*, Summer, pp 41-9.

Alheit, P. (1994) *Taking the knocks: Youth unemployment and biography – A qualitative analysis*, London: Cassell.

Basu, A. and Goswani, A. (1999) 'South Asian entrepreneurship in Great Britain: factors influencing growth', *International Journal of Entrepreneurial Behaviour & Research*, vol 5, no 5, (www.emerald-library.com/brev/16005eb1.htm).

Coleman, J.S. (1988) 'Social capital in the creation of human capital', *American Journal of Sociology*, vol 94, supplement, pp 94-120.

Durkheim, E. (1965) *The elementary forms of religious life*, New York, NY: Free Press.

French, P. (1971) *The movie moguls: An informal history of the Hollywood tycoons*, Harmondsworth: Penguin Books.

Gartner, W.B. (1989) 'A conceptual framework for describing the phenomenon of new venture creation', *Academy of Management Review*, vol 10, no 4, pp 696-706.

Gartner, W.B. (1989) '"Who is an entrepreneur?" is the wrong question', *Entreneurship Theory and Practice*, vol 12, no 4, pp 44-67.

Gartner, W.B. (1990) 'What are we talking about when we talk about entrepreneurship?', *Journal of Business Venturing*, issue 5, pp 15-28.

Gartner, W.B., Barbara, J.B. and Starr, J. (1992) 'Acting as if: differentiating entrepreneurial from organizational behaviour', *Entrepreneurship Theory and Practice*, vol 16, no 3, pp 13-32.

Giddens, A. (1976) *New rules of sociological method*, London: Hutchinson.

Glade, W.P. (1967) 'Approaches to a theory of entrepreneurial formation', *Explorations in Entrepreneurial History*, issue 4, pp 245-59.

Granovetter, M. (1995) 'The economic sociology of firms and entrepreneurs', in A. Portes (ed) *The economic sociology of immigration: Essays in networks, ethnicity and entrepreneurship*, New York, NY: Russell Sage Foundation, pp 128-65.

Horsdal, M. (1999) *Livets fortællinger*, Copenhagen: Borgen.

Kupferberg, F. (1995) 'Biografisk Självgestaltning', *Sociologisk Forskning*, vol 32, no 4, pp 32-57.

Kupferberg, F. (1997) 'Soziologie des beruflichen Neuanfangs: von akademischer Lehrtätigkeit zu beruflicher Selbständigkeit', in M. Thomas (ed) *Selbständige, Gründer, Unternehmer. Passagen und Passformen im Umbruch*, Berlin: Berliner Debatte Wissenschaft Verlag, pp 188-207.

Kupferberg, F. (1998) 'Humanistic entrepreneurship and entrepreneurial career commitment', *Entrepreneurship and Regional Development*, vol 10, pp 171-87.

Kupferberg, F. (2001) 'Passagen in die Selbständigkeit – Typische Verlaufsmuster von Hochschulabsolventen', in D. Bögenhold, B. Hodenius, F. Kupferberg and R. Woderich (eds) *Gründerfernstudium: Passagen in die Selbständigkeit*, Fernuniversität-Gesamthochschule in Hagen, Fachbereich Wirtschaftswissenschaft, pp 83-124.

Kupferberg, F. (2002) 'Entreprenörskap som existentiell handling', *Sociologisk Forskning,* vol 39, no 2, pp 68-103.

Light, I. (1977) 'The ethnic vice industry, 1880-1944', *American Sociological Review*, vol 42, pp 464-79.

Light, I. and Karageorgis, S. (1994) 'The ethnic economy,' in N.J. Smelser and R. Swedberg (eds) *The handbook of economic sociology*, Princeton, NJ: Princeton University Press/New York, NY: Russell Sage Foundation, pp 647-71.

Mars, G. and Ward, R. (1984) 'Ethnic business development in Britain: opportunities and resources', in R. Ward and R. Jenkins (eds) *Ethnic communities in Britain: Strategies for economic survival*, Cambridge: Cambridge University Press.

Martinelli, A. (1994) 'Entrepreneurship and management', in N.J. Smelser and R. Swedberg (eds) *The handbook of economic sociology*, Princeton, NJ: Princeton University Press/New York, NY: Russell Sage Foundation, pp 477-503.

May, L.L. (1980) *Screening out the past: The birth of mass culture and the motion picture industry*, New York, NY: Oxford University Press.

May, L.L. and May, E.T. (1982) 'Why Jewish movie moguls?: an exploration in American culture', *American Jewish History*, vol 72, no 1, pp 6-25.

Merton, R.K. (1968) 'Social structure and anomy', in R.K. Merton (ed) *Social theory and social structure*, New York, NY: The Free Press/London: Collier Macmillan, pp 184-214.

Portes, A. and Rumbaut, R.C. (1996) *Immigrant America*, Berkeley, CA: University of California Press.

Rezaei, S. (2002) 'Erhvervsdynamik blandt indvandrere: Selverhverv og netvúrksrela tioner – blokering eller afsæt for socio-økonomisk mobilitet?', PhD thesis, Syddansk Universitet, Det Samfundsvidenskabelige Fakultet, Institut for Organisation og Ledelse.

Schumpeter, J.A. (1945) *Capitalism, socialism and democracy*, London: George Allen & Unwin.

Sowell, T. (1996) *Migrations and cultures*, New York, NY: Basic Books.

Stinchcombe, A.L. (1965) 'Social structure and organizations', in J.G. March (ed) *Handbook of organizations*, Chicago, IL: Rand McNally, pp 142-93.

Thomsen, M.N. and Kupferberg, F. (2001) TSER Project 'Self-employment activities concerning women and minorities: their success or failure in relation to citizenship policies', *Final scientific report: The Danish Case*, Alborg University, Centre for International Studies.

Thornton, P.H. (1992) 'The sociology of entrepreneurship', *Annual Review of Sociology*, vol 25, pp 19-46.

Tidd, J., Bessant, J. and Pavitt, K. (1997) *Managing innovation*, Chichester: John Wiley & Sons.

Waldinger, R., Aldrich, H. and Ward, R. (2000) 'Ethnic entrepreneurs', in R. Swedberg (ed) *Entrepreneurship: The social science view*, New York, NY: Oxford University Press, pp 356-88.

Ziehe, T. (1999) 'Adieu til halvfjerdserne', in J. Berg (ed) *Pædagogik – en grundbog til et fag*, Copenhagen: Hans Reitzel, pp 74-88.

Part Two:
Subjectivity in context

The social subject in biographical interpretive methods: emotional, mute, creative, divided

Andrew Cooper

This chapter asks questions about the conceptualisation of the ontology of the social subject that informs biographical methods of research. Arguing from a psychoanalytically informed view of the subject, I suggest that emotionality and creativity as it derives from our capacity to dream (or what Freud referred to as primary process thinking), and our hesitant and uncertain development as subjects out of infantile states of near complete inarticulacy, are all necessary dimensions of a fully developed concept of what it is to be a subject.

The chapter was first conceived immediately following an experience of listening to the accounts of war trauma counsellors in Kosovo, and this reminded me that the origins of psychoanalysis remain absolutely relevant today for our project of understanding the social subject as always and everywhere simultaneously a psychological subject. In this view, emotionality is the essential foundation of all true mental activity, dreaming the foundation of all creativity. Equally, however, both these functions may be attacked and damaged by the trauma of social and political terror, displacement, upheaval and dislocation. The Europe in which we work today is not so far removed from the Europe of 1900, 1914 or 1945. Biographical research has the potential to grasp the complicated relationship between the psychological and the social subject more fully than any other research method but only, in my view, if it embraces an ontology of deep subjectivity such as psychoanalysis proposes.

Why do Frenchmen wave their arms about?

Here are some extracts from one of Gregory Bateson's 'metalogues' between himself and his young daughter:

Daughter (D): Daddy, Why do Frenchmen wave their arms about?

Father (F): What do you mean?

D: I mean when they talk. Why do they wave their arms and all that?

F: Well – why do you smile? Or why do you stamp your foot sometimes?

D: But that's not the same thing, Daddy. I don't wave my arms about like a Frenchman does. I don't believe they can stop doing it, Daddy. Can they?

F: I don't know – they might find it hard to stop…. Can you stop smiling?

D: But Daddy, I don't smile all the time. It's hard to stop when I feel like smiling. But I don't feel like it *all* the time. And then I stop.

Later:

D: Daddy, when they teach us French at school, why don't they teach us to wave our hands?

F: I don't know. I'm sure I don't know. That is probably one of the reasons people find learning languages so difficult.

★★★

F: Anyhow, it is all nonsense. I mean the notion that language is made of words is all nonsense – and when I said that gestures could not be translated into 'mere words', I was talking nonsense, because there is no such thing as 'mere words'. And all the syntax and all the grammar and all that stuff is nonsense. It's all based on the idea that 'mere' words exist – and there are none.

D: But Daddy….

F: I tell you – we have to start all over again from the beginning and assume that language is first and foremost a system of gestures. Animals after all have *only* gestures and tones of voice – and words were invented later. Much later. And after that they invented school-masters. (Bateson, 1972, pp 9-13)

This exchange serves as well as any to remind us of the obvious: that human subjects are more than language, language is more than 'mere words', and there is much beneath the surface of our communications about ourselves, and beyond our immediately accessible experience of ourselves or others. Researching any subject's biography poses us with the question – how deep do we want to go? And what validates any attempt to go 'deeper' than the subject proffers as data? These are rather deep questions in themselves, and I do not aim to answer them in any systematic way. Rather, I assume in what follows that all biographies are both social and psychological, that both these dimensions have surface and depth, and I explore some facets of their interweaving.

Emotionality, dreaming and trauma

In October 2000, I spent three rather intense days working in Pristina, the capital of Kosovo, where I had been asked to teach and participate in the final assessment of a group of 35 Albanian Kosovar students who had undertaken a year's training in psychosocial responses to war trauma. I found myself travelling to and returning from Kosovo via Vienna, which was the birthplace of psychoanalysis. On my first day in Pristina, I listened, alongside a panel of other tutors, to 20 half-hour presentations by students of their work with Kosovar families who had experienced persecution and terror of one kind or another in the course of the recent war with Serbia. Students had worked in groups locating families in need, engaging with them, and in most instances video recording at least some of their counselling sessions. An extract of video recording accompanied by a process recording of the interaction (an account of the exchange accompanied by a report on the feelings and thoughts and other subjective reactions of the counsellor) formed a central part of the presentation made by each student. But of course, it was the stories they told of the dreadful events in the lives of these families and communities, the stories of the survivors of mass executions, the burning of houses and villages, everything that happened under the rubric of 'ethnic cleansing', that formed the centre of the narratives of their work as it was told to me. These stories, as well as the account of the work undertaken by the counsellors themselves, were related with a dignity and professionalism that impressed itself upon me as time went by – a curious combination of matter-of-factness, intensity, pride, humour and analytical distance. What in the end struck me so forcibly was the absence of any suggestion of hatred or desire for revenge in any of these accounts. I do not think that this had in any sense been suppressed or censored, although how the state of mind that pervaded these presentations came to be achieved is something I confess I do not understand. It is important, however, because the absence of a retaliatory or hating dimension to these workers' emotional stance released them into an ability to concentrate on the emotional task at hand: the mental pain of these families, their suffering, the losses they had incurred, their sense of hopelessness and helplessness, everything that constitutes what we call trauma.

Genuine trauma makes us mute, sometimes literally but more often metaphorically, as our bodies or minds struggle to represent the state of internal devastation through some displaced or distorted means – what we know clinically as the symptom, and what psychoanalysis took as its original object, namely the 'hysterical symptom'. Now, I am not proposing that biographical research, whatever the circumstances under which it is conducted, should attempt directly to incorporate the techniques of clinical psychotherapy or psychoanalysis. I would not even really propose that Kosovar trauma counsellors attempt to do this, and certainly the students of whom I am speaking were not trained to attempt such forms of intervention, never mind the fact that their work is normally undertaken in people's homes, in parks and gardens, sometimes in cafes or orchards. Notwithstanding this, it was clear to me that they were able to facilitate change and development in the lives of their compatriots, often in the space of just two or three meetings. How is this possible?

The answer lies, I think, in understanding the place of emotionality, of emotional experience, in what it is to be a human subject. In their presentations, none of these students displayed overt strong feeling, but it was absolutely clear to me that their capacity to feel, to identify and empathise with the suffering of the families with whom they worked lay at the heart of the success and impact of their work. I think I know this, not just because they often described the grief they felt themselves even if they did not show it, but because I continually found myself overtaken inside by eruptions of grief in response to what I heard. I came to think that part of what I and the other colleague on the panel of assessors who sat through all 35 of these presentations were being asked to do was to endure at an emotional level something of what these counsellors had themselves endured at the level of feeling in their relations with these traumatised families.

To the psychoanalytic practitioner this is a familiar set-up. The therapist listens to the story told by the patient at the level of the articulate, but also and more importantly the inarticulate, at the level of the transmission of unprocessed raw emotional experience. The capacity emotionally to ingest such experience, then think about it and give words to the experience so that it can in some way be offered back to the patient in a form that allows them to integrate this raw and uncivilised dimension of feeling into their minds with the aid of the symbolic capacity that language constitutes – this is what we regard today as being central to the psychoanalytic project. In turn, the therapist receives something of this same processing function from the clinical supervisor.

Mind and emotional experience

The process just described it is not primarily an intellectual, cognitive or interpretive activity. It is primarily a transformative function with emotional experience as its object. It was the psychoanalyst Wilfred Bion (1967, 1970) who elaborated this understanding into a complete theory of mind and of the development of mind. In doing this, he became one of the few psychoanalytic theoreticians to make a genuinely original contribution to the theorising of the ontology of the human subject. The essence of this theory is more or less captured in what I have already said – in the development of mind emotional experience precedes thought, and true thinking only comes into being as a result of the capacity to bring the function of mental attention into sustained relationship with emotion. The accurate or, as I think Bion would have said, 'truthful' apprehension of our emotional states of mind constitutes the foundation of the possibility of having a mind at all. This theory has many consequences that I cannot pursue in this chapter, but among them is that much that passes in our world for thinking, particularly perhaps in the realm of formalised research into human processes, would not in Bion's view really count as thinking at all.

My question with respect to biographical research methodology is now fairly obvious and straightforward. Does the method take proper account, in a *living* sense, of the emotionality of the subject? If so, how is this dimension processed by researchers and incorporated into the analysis and findings of their work?

Should trauma in some sense return us to a state of desperate inarticulacy about our experience, then it is not stretching a point too far to say that Bion, in common with most other psychoanalytic theoreticians, would take the view that we all begin life in a state roughly akin to trauma. Quite irrespective of actual trauma, how far any of us succeed in fully leaving behind the primitive inarticulacy that attends our infancy is a central preoccupation of the psychoanalytic project. In common with Freud, it was Bion's view that dreaming is itself a form of thinking in some sense intermediate between complete emotional inarticulacy, and the full possession of the faculty of mind, for which it is also a necessary constituent. To become articulate about our dreams and to regard dreams as a form of articulation is more or less a sine qua non of the psychoanalytic enterprise. Now, it is well known that one common symptom of trauma is the repetitive nightmare, in which some version of the traumatic event is revisited compulsively and painfully in dreams, sometimes for years on end. The Kosovar students had been trained to try and understand the importance of dreaming, or the absence of it, in the experiences of the people with whom they worked. In their presentations, they frequently described changes in the quality and content of people's dreams, and also, just as important, the *resumption* of dreaming among subjects where this seemed to have ceased in the wake of traumatic experiences; or in some cases if dreaming had not ceased, dreaming about the dead or missing relatives had ceased but was now revived.

Social strategy, creativity and dreaming

Just over 100 years ago, in *The interpretation of dreams*, Freud (1976) described the laws governing the operation of the dream work, or the 'primary process', which was the other name he gave to this kind of thinking. One does not need to delve far into this book to understand that the principles governing the construction of dreams are the same principles that underlie all forms of what we colloquially refer to as creativity. Poetry, drama and the visual and plastic arts all rely upon the operation of the primary process to generate the symbolic coherence that is at the organising principle of a work of art. In fact, it is my contention, not original, that all creativity in whatever walk of life depends upon the operation of the kind of thinking from which dreams derive.

Now, it is a central point of interest of biographical research methods that they emphasise the creativity of human subjects in relation to the social context of opportunities and constraints surrounding the subject as his or her life 'unfolds'. I think the very idea of social subjects who are capable of 'strategic' functioning with respect to their possibilities and predicaments itself implies creative capacity, because strategy entails the imaginative elaboration of a possible future or futures attained through activity in relation to circumstances that are only partly known or predictable. This brings us again to what conception biographical researchers have of the creativity of the sociological subject. The idea that each of us actively produces and reproduces on a day-by-day basis the social structures and systems that are themselves the condition of the possibility of social action and constraint is a great advance upon the terms in which the old agency–structure debate used to be posed in sociological theory. Anthony Giddens' theory of structuration (1984) has always struck me, in this sense, as a profound contribution, and some recent biographical research programmes have deployed his thinking at the level of meta-theory. Equally, I think that, in common with many theorists in the hermeneutic tradition, Giddens remains implicitly wedded to an over-rationalistic view of human nature and of social strategy as a core aspect of human activity. Should socially strategic creativity be ultimately continuous with other kinds of human creativity, and should these necessarily involve the operation of unconscious processes organised around emotional experience, how can we justifiably divorce our research methods from an ontology of the human subject that embraces these dimensions? So, I am asking whether the explicit or implicit ontology of the human subject represented in biographical method is actually adequate to the epistemological project these methods have realised with such notable success.

Much of Freud's early work has its origins in a period of terrible instability and conflict in Western Europe and the world, when mass destruction, warfare and the mass displacement of whole populations made it urgent that we understand better how to respond better to the impact of trauma on individuals and societies. In today's Europe, I suppose that by some measures we have achieved some degree of social progress, but if so, recent events in the Balkans remind us how tenuous and provisional such progress really is. In the new Europe, it may be that economic migration is as prevalent a cause of displacement, dislocation, exclusion and marginalisation as flight from persecution and war. But whatever the focus of our preoccupations and activities as professionals, we each respond to personal, biographical and social experience on the basis of our own history of suffering, conflict and transformation. If we do not, I believe we should. The social subject is, I contend, always and everywhere also a psychological subject. The great strength and power of biographical method applied to the understanding of social life is that it is capable of grasping this complex dialectic more fully and meaningfully than any other method of research. My question is really only this – how deep a concept of the psychological subject are we capable of embracing in such sociological work? Can we do justice to this issue without a living engagement with the emotionality of the subject, the deep sources of their creativity, and the recognition that as subjects we are all ultimately divided from ourselves? Gregory Bateson's daughter, or perhaps it was the lively child in Bateson himself, seemed to see this matter quite clearly, with the freshness of a mind not yet too cluttered with theory. We could try to emulate her.

References

Bateson, G. (1972) *Steps to an ecology of mind*, New York, NY: Ballantine Books.

Bion, W. (1967) *Second thoughts: Selected papers on psychoanalysis*, London: Karnac Books.

Bion, W. (1970) *Attention and interpretation*, London: Tavistock.

Freud, S. (1976) *The interpretation of dreams*, Harmondsworth: Pelican.

Giddens, A. (1984) *The constitution of society: Outline of the theory of structuration*, Cambridge: Polity Press.

SEVEN

A socially and historically contextualised psychoanalytic perspective: Holocaust survival and suffering[1]

Daniel Bar-On

The Holocaust did not only divide humanity into survivors, bystanders, perpetrators and rescuers and define generations as first, second and third generations of each category. The Holocaust also reinforced perspectives that became associated with the construction of collective memory, especially in countries where society identified itself, or was identified by, these categories, specifically Israel and Germany. 'Who was a Holocaust survivor?' was determined first legally and then historically (Gutman, 1990). In Israel, this identity became an important issue in terms of social labelling in the 1950s, and later became salient in terms of self-chosen categorisation in the 1980s and 1990s (Bar-On, 1995a). In Germany, social oblivion makes the social categorisation of victim and bystander during the Nazi era and the Holocaust an 'untold story' (Bar-On, 1989), outside collective discourse and memory (Hardtmann, 1992). Consequently, historical facts become different from their social construction and they may take different forms in the collective memory and discourse of these countries.

I start this discussion with the question: 'Who is a Holocaust survivor?' I look mainly at Jewish society over three generations. My discussion then continues with the question: 'Who suffered more?', which is relevant also for German collective memory.

'The more we learn about the Holocaust, the less we understand': scholars have expressed this view many times during recent years. It clearly reflects the immensity of the Holocaust, the fact that new questions and data are coming up every year, showing us how little we actually know and how much there still is to try to figure out. This statement also suggests, however, that the more knowledgeable we become, the less we can make sense of some simple questions. How, for example, could people do such things to their fellow human beings?

One option that will be stressed here is that such questions can be answered differently within the context of different disciplines and social contexts. Therefore, it may well be that only through an interdisciplinary effort can one try to make sense of very complicated human phenomena such as the construction of collective memory after the Holocaust.

This chapter is based on a critical view of the role of individual psychoanalysis in interpreting the social impact of the Holocaust (Spence, 1980; Bergmann and Jucuvy, 1982). My critical view on the role of psychoanalysis in interpreting the after-effects of genocide and holocaust is based on three points.

First, *the fragility of the language of Holocaust survivors*; that is, their inability to find words to express what they went through, which I wrote about in *Fear and hope* (1995a) and in *The indescribable and undiscussable* (1999b). This issue was overlooked and suppressed by those who used powerful psychoanalytic interpretations and concepts to describe the after-effects of the trauma (Bergmann and Jucuvy, 1982). Perhaps it was a necessary first step to focus the attention of the helping professions, but it also created secondary stigmatisation and ambiguity around the difference between normality, abnormality and normalisation (Bar-On, 1999b).

Second, *a lack of distinction between the indescribable and the undiscussable*, two impediments to human discourse (Bar-On, 1999b) related to trauma. The first represents the intersubjective inability to make sense of the construction of facts within separate individual frames of reference. Levinas (1990) describes it through his concepts of the totality of the self and its limited ability to contain the infinity of the 'otherness of the other'. The second impediment, undiscussability, represents the disappearance of certain facts, silenced by society, including the helping professions.

Third, *the illusion of the monolithic representation of the ego*: the latest literature about victims, perpetrators and bystanders of massive violence suggests that the monolithic representation of the ego or the self is an illusive construction (Spence, 1980; Rosenthal, 1998; Bar-On, 1999c; Bar-Tov, 1999). According to this perspective, the disintegration of the ego into bits and pieces that do not fit each other is the norm, rather than belonging to the outcast or the abnormal. The quality of the dialogue between these bits and pieces (or the lack of such a dialogue), instead of their integration into one monolithic entity, can tell us something about normalcy under extreme stress (Bar-On, 1999c)[2].

These issues suggest that psychoanalytic concepts are important but have to be historically and socially contextualised in order to further the understanding of social and individual construction, relating to extreme, human-made collective acts of violence. I would like to introduce such a historically and socially psychodynamically oriented perspective regarding the two questions identified above that are still on the scientific agenda:

- Who is a Holocaust survivor?
- Who suffered more during and after the Holocaust?

The present discussion of these questions exemplifies the importance of integrating historical and social with psychoanalytical perspectives into studies that have previously been dominated by historians and jurists, or discussed separately within disciplines like philosophy, poetry or psychoanalysis. If we can look at the collective, intersubjective and intrasubjective processes within a common frame of reference, we may be able to grasp better the complexity of the phenomena we are trying to understand.

Who is a Holocaust survivor? A historically and socially contextualised psychodynamic perspective

Mainstream historical literature was based on legal aspects, limiting the boundary around definitions of Holocaust survivors (as well as impairment as a result of the Holocaust) to those people who suffered directly from Nazi persecution and the extermination processes (Bauer, 1982; Gutman, 1990). This definition includes a few hundred thousand Jews who survived the death and concentration camps, or who survived by hiding in the woods, in Catholic monasteries or among gentile families while under Nazi occupation, as well as others who fought among the partisans. Today, the interesting question is: 'Why did this legal definition become so important for postwar Jewish society, overshadowing other possible definitions?'

The restitution agreement between Israel and Germany, for example, and later between Jewish organisations and Germany after the Second World War, included individual European refugees who lost their career and capital as they fled from Nazi persecution. There were some differences in recognising their claims depending on whether they had fled from Germany, Holland, France, Norway or other countries. However, this definition – 'Who is eligible for restitution claims?' – was a legal definition backed by and large by legal, fiscal and medical evidence. Why were these so widely accepted by postwar society?

Perhaps in light of the immense magnitude and severity of the unfolding of the Holocaust after 1945 more 'objective' definitions were, to some extent, comforting. It released the signifier (the bystanding and perpetrating societies) and the signified (the so-called survivors) from further inquiry (How did it happen? How could people do such things to their fellow people? Why did the world stand aside?). The issue of 'Who is a survivor?' was settled for the time being and did not need further elaboration. Since then, however, times have changed. Today, we are more aware that there may be no such objective definition of types and categories, as these are socially constructed in Jewish and Israeli collective memory, as well as in the non-Jewish societies. While some people may feel negatively labelled as Holocaust survivors, others may feel excluded by that definition, suggesting a gap between their life history and the construction of their identity and biographical life story (Bar-On, 1995a; Rosenthal, 1998).

In a newspaper article on Yom Hashoah (Holocaust day in Israel), Tamar Katko, a daughter of Holocaust survivors, told her story (*Haaretz*, 13 April 1999). According to her, Holocaust survivors should be defined as *those who did not go on reliving the Holocaust daily* after the war. By this she meant those who succeeded in emotionally surviving its after-effects. In her parents' home, the Holocaust was preached daily, emotionally, cognitively and behaviourally. Her parents, therefore, could not be defined as survivors of the Holocaust because, from her perspective, they did not survive it.

In contrast to her story, at a seminar at Ben Gurion University on the psychosocial effects of the Holocaust[3], one student declared: "I am a second generation of Holocaust survivors. I do not believe there is such a thing. I came here to see what you were talking about". Other students were ready to attack her but I tried to support her subjective perspective by asking: "Who are we to tell her what to feel in this respect?". It turned out that she was one of the most brilliant students and did an excellent final paper on how the Holocaust was represented in schoolbooks in Israel and how this representation has changed over the years.

Today, unlike the 1950s or the 1960s, we cannot tell or decide for others anymore who Holocaust survivors are. Once the mental after-effects of the Holocaust on the second and third generations had been acknowledged and become widespread, the legal definitions had to be re-examined. For example, the literature suggests that the silencing or obsessive talk and the so-called 'normalisation' of survivors' experiences during the first years after the Shoah had a traumatising effect on some of their children (Danieli, 1980, 1998). Was this true *only* for legally defined survivors? What about those Polish Jews who fled to Russia at the beginning of the German invasion into Poland and left all or most of their family members behind, never to see them again? These people did not fit into the 'objective' legal definition of survivors. Although they did not enjoy a good life, thanks to their flight, their lives were less endangered (Bar-On, 1995a). But did they not suffer from guilt feelings for leaving behind their relatives who perished? Did they not silently mourn the loss of their family members? In an interview, Anya, a Polish Jew, argued with herself, as if she were still trying to explain to us, to herself, why she left her family behind to fall into the hands of Nazi murderers. We see how even her two granddaughters are still caught up in Anya's traumatised discourse (Bar-On, 1995a, pp 201-26).

What about those Jews who left Europe during the 1930s, emigrating to Palestine or to the US, leaving most of their family members behind and later watching in panic and helplessness as these relatives were caught by the Nazi death machine? Again, these refugees may have enjoyed relative physical safety during the years of the war, but did they not also feel guilty? Did they not mourn their lost relatives? Most of them did not even dare to express these feelings openly. They felt lucky, comparing their fate with that of the *real* survivors who experienced the Shoah. When interviewed in the early 1990s, however, we heard that they silenced and normalised the past just as the survivors did and that their descendants suffered from similar unspoken guilt and mourning behind the 'double wall' of their parents' (Bar-On, 1995a).

From a more historically-socially contextualised psychodynamic perspective, the question of the validity of control group studies on the after-effects of the Holocaust on the following generations of Holocaust survivors has to be re-examined, given that such after-effects are also likely to be found among groups such as the Second World War refugees. Based on the legal definition, control groups for the survivors are usually Jews who come from the same European countries but who had emigrated early enough not to be caught under Nazi occupation. For example, results were recently published of a control group study that claimed that there were no special psychological after-effects among descendants of Holocaust survivors (Bar-On, 1995a). However, when one examines the control group, it seems that these were mostly refugees. Can one really claim that they did not go through the same processes of loss, guilt, anguish and mourning, combined with a feeling of illegitimacy of having such feelings at all? Could they really serve as a control group for Holocaust survivors?

One could ask: 'Does this mean that every Jew who lived during the period of the Second World War was a Holocaust survivor?' Or perhaps were survivors only those people who defined themselves as such? To some extent, the latter became a more common perspective with intergenerational change, perhaps as a late collective identification with those who were excluded from the legal definition. In Israel, non-European third-generation Jewry, mainly Sephardic families who immigrated to Israel from Afro-Asian countries, also 'adopted' the Holocaust as their 'identification card' as Israelis (Bar-On, 1995a). We can observe these intergenerational changes in Laura's family (Bar-On, 1995a, pp 265-91). She grew up in Libya and knew about the Holocaust through her relatives who were detained in Bergen-Belsen and felt guilty for her inability to do anything to help them. Her son, Vitorio, grew up in an Israeli immigrant camp during the 1950s, together with Holocaust survivors. He hated them because they managed to leave the camp and receive state support, while he and his family, together with other North African immigrants, were left behind. He felt "they deserved what had happened to them because they did not listen to Jabotinsky [a right-wing Zionist leader] who warned them about the Nazi". In contrast, Liat, Laura's granddaughter, who grew up in Israel in the late 1970s, felt that the Holocaust had become part of her personal heritage, although she knew relatively little about what had happened during that time.

These examples show how complicated the issues of defining a Holocaust survivor are from a socially contextualised psychodynamic perspective. Still, one can try to set some boundaries in order to distinguish survivors from non-survivors at least when referring to immediate survivors before we consider their descendants. Let us go back to Laura's story. She lived in Libya under Italian Fascist and German Nazi occupation, where the total annihilation of the Jews was not implemented during that time, although she experienced trauma and loss in her personal and family life. Still, her family story had continuity because her social environment was not destroyed. The life stories of Holocaust survivors of that era have been broken by the massive victimisation of the Nazis (Bar-On, 1995a)[4]. Those survivors had survived the camps, the ghettoes and life with the partisans in Nazi Europe, but the Nazis murdered most of their family members and disrupted their social context, and their broken family stories represented that sudden disruption.

These examples offer three criteria that may be part of an intuitive distinction between survivors and non-survivors, apart from the subjective perspective of how one feels about such a definition. Immediate survivors can be characterised by the following:

- most of their family members perished in the Holocaust;
- their children grew up without grandparents;
- while telling their life stories, the external traumatic events overpowered the family history and broke up its continuity.

Some of the after-effects of the Holocaust may overlap with the after-effects of emigration or with persecution in the countries of origin. These may also overlap with specific family dynamics and individual coping patterns. Yet there is a consensus among researchers that the impact of fear, hunger and helplessness, of surviving a death camp all alone, of being in hiding for long periods as a young child, of suffering extreme loss and humiliation, resulted in the most severe symptoms of post-traumatic stress disorder (Danieli, 1998). This is an a priori assertion, even if survivors exhibited a high level of resilience and strong ambition to continue with life after the Holocaust.

While these criteria may be applicable for defining first generation survivors, when we move from the immediate survivors to the second generation, we see already that we are dealing with 'fuzzy categories' or boundaries (Wittgenstein, 1953). The issue of fuzzy boundaries between survivors and non-survivors becomes even more apparent when we approach the third generation. The latter tends to generalise the impact of the Holocaust beyond direct family ties and mix them up with the impact of other traumatic or formative collective events (Bar-On and Selah, 1991) into a more general collective memory of being victimised. Selah and Bar-On, for example, found that Israeli students of African-Asian origin had similar knowledge and understanding of the Shoah, expressed similar strong emotions and held similar attitudes toward the Shoah as did students of European origin. The latter group included respondents who came from families of Holocaust survivors as defined by conventional standards.

In the Bar-On and Selah study (1991), we concluded that the traumatic experience of the Holocaust became the focus of a more generalised feeling of being victimised expressed by younger Israelis of the 1980s and 1990s (Segev, 1992; Bar-Tov, 1999). The Holocaust became a common legend for secular Jews in the Diaspora as well as a collective construction of the Israeli 'siege mentality' that took over in the mid-1970s as part of a deeper social and political power shift (Bar-Tal, 1997). First, there was an estrangement of survivors in the 1950s and early 1960s, through the moralistic judgment of Israelis towards those who 'went like sheep to slaughter'. This was replaced in the 1980s by transforming the Holocaust into a political tool to address current problems with the Arabs. For Begin, in the 1982 Lebanon war, Arafat became a continuation of Hitler while the Israeli Jews were again all alone just as the world stood aside during the Holocaust.

To summarise the answer to the first question, 'Who counts as a Holocaust survivor?', it seems from a historical and social psychodynamic perspective that the original 'objective' historical and legal definitions and their identity as survivors were necessary for a postwar society that was trying to normalise life as quickly as possible. These 'objective' definitions came under attack from different perspectives, including the individual psychodynamic perspective, especially when considering the after-effects of the Holocaust on the interpsychic and intrapsychic processes of second and third generations. Viewed from the context of our current perspective, the further one was removed from the events, generation-wise, the fuzzier the perspective became on what had happened during the Holocaust – to whom and how? This lack of clarity, on the other hand, led to the development of different collective and culturally subjective reconstructions of what the impact of those catastrophic events had on us, as the second and third generations after the Holocaust. This development was also part of a wider contemporary development, putting more emphasis on the subjective definitions than on legal objective ones; that is, how people construct their identities as well as the social and cultural reconstruction of historical realities (Bar-Tov, 1999). These observations bring us directly to the second question of this paper: 'Who suffered more?'

'Who suffered more?' and 'We suffered too'

Why is the issue of rating suffering during and after the Holocaust important for Jews and Germans? Suffering means pain, and pain is usually individually and collectively memorialised or repressed. It varies considerably in terms of subjective perception, but is difficult to rate or compare intersubjectively (Wittgenstein, 1953). Why has comparison and rating become such an important issue in the construction of collective memory after the Holocaust among both Jews and Germans? This is the issue that will now be discussed in this chapter. First, I discuss the Jewish and Israeli construction of this issue. I then go on to and discuss the German aspect of 'we suffered too' as one way of marginalising collective German responsibility for the Holocaust (Bar-On and Gaon, 1991).

When confronted with stories of the immediate survivors of the Shoah, we feel completely overwhelmed. Would we have been able to endure such extreme situations of hunger, physical and mental distress and humiliation? Zipke, trying to identify with her mother's experiences in Mydaneck and Auschwitz, used to imagine herself feeling hungry for hours, or having cancer, just to come up with the conclusion "that it is nothing compared to what my mother had to go through there" (Bar-On, 1995a, pp 62–81). This feeling of helplessness and loss of control when encountering extreme suffering was usually overcome in early confrontations (in the public domain) with survivors by two opposite psychological mechanisms. First, by playing down survivors' suffering, using the accusations that 'they went like sheep to the slaughter', Israelis tried to distance themselves from what actually happened during the Holocaust. This was a typical accusation in 1950s Israel, based on the Israeli construction of heroism and the struggle of Israeli society for its survival before, during and after the 1948 war with the Arabs (Segev, 1992). It was, however, also a defence mechanism against one's own feeling of being overwhelmed by helplessness, lack of control and guilt towards the survivors, at a time when Israelis could not deal with these complex feelings openly. This can be seen as part of the 'just world' hypothesis (Lerner, 1975). According to this, the suffering of the victims is attributed to their own (lack of) deeds or their 'nature', thereby making it easier for the bystander to create a distinction between themselves and the victims. Such an intrapsychic repair strategy (Rosenthal, 1998) may help control the uncontrollable, or may help overcome the shattered assumptions concerning the benevolence of the world (Janoff-Bulman, 1992).

The second strategy was to develop *a scale of suffering* of who suffered less and who suffered more. Once one can scale suffering, it becomes more controllable in the eyes of the beholder. This universal tendency was unwittingly supported by some of the survivors themselves. We hear from Tamar (Bar-On, 1995a, pp 227-45) how her family would gather during Passover; those who were in Auschwitz sat at the head of the table with their descendants. They used to lead the ceremony. Those who were in hiding sat next to them. Near them sat those who ran away to Russia (like her mother) and at the end of the table those who immigrated to Israel before the Second World War. This last group had no 'right' to speak about suffering at all. This hierarchy of suffering may make no sense to those of us who have not been there, but it had a subjective 'logic' for those survivors. This was especially true for those who wanted to control the current family situation and to set up an order indirectly created through their interpretation of what they went through during the Holocaust.

We know of other families in which this 'scale of suffering' was set up in the opposite direction, according to the Israeli value judgment of 'like sheep to slaughter'. In these families, the 1948 heroes would typically sit at the head of the table, while the survivors would sit at the lower edge and keep quiet. Some survivors, in presenting themselves as Sabras (metaphorically, a fruit that has thorns outside but is soft and sweet inside), tried to hide the fact that they were actually Holocaust child survivors (Bar-On and Mor, 1996). Others silenced their experiences of the Holocaust for many years (Keren and Almaliach, 1994). In the past few years, there have been examples of a couple of famous Israeli army generals who, before their release from military service, confessed that they were actually child survivors who initially hid their Holocaust background and acted like Sabras, as they were afraid that disclosing their original background might stigmatise them and harm their military career.

These two hierarchies – one elevating the Auschwitz survivor and the other, contrastingly, the Sabra hero – represent two of the basic value hierarchies of Israeli society: Shoah (Holocaust) and Tkuma (Redemption) (Bar-On, 1995a, pp 168-88). The first represents the heroism of the victimised, those who survived the Holocaust. The second represents the heroism of fighting for the independence of the State of Israel. Many saw a contradiction between these two hierarchies. I want to suggest that they actually complement each other within the Israeli society of the 1980s and 1990s in which victimisation and heroism were closely interwoven, indeed reinforced each other. Both relate to the outcomes of wars and do not tell us anything of how people cope with the stress of daily life (Bar-On, 1999c). This kind of symbiosis, therefore, can be seen as a shield against an unknown future of life in the Middle East in which one has to develop new roles beyond being victims or heroes, associated mostly with wars and military experiences (Kimmerling, 1993)[5].

Keren and Almaliach (1994) tell us the story of a kibbutz, in which the young survivors were never accepted as full members because they were 'not good enough'. They were good enough to fight (and some also to die) together with the Sabras during the 1948 war and to go together into Jordanian captivity, but not to become full members of the same kibbutz. Even after they were later accepted as full members, this feeling hindered them from telling their Holocaust life stories right up to the late 1990s. It could well be that Tamar's initial description of her family's scale of suffering was in a way an 'inverse scale of suffering' in comparison with the more dominant type of Israeli 'redemptive heroism' that prevailed after the 1948 war (Keren and Almaliach, 1994).

However, it would be a mistake to believe that this was only an Israeli problem. Holocaust survivors were not encouraged to tell their stories in other social contexts as well. One survivor, who listened to one of my lectures on my book (Bar-On, 1995a), told me of her first encounter with her cousin in London after the Second World War. He was the only living relative she could find after she had survived the Warsaw ghetto as a teenager. His first remark when they met was "Do not tell us, we don't understand". Asking her what he meant by that sentence, she replied that the message being communicated by her new social environment was: "Try to become part of us, but don't try to make us part of what you went through there". Anya tells us about an almost identical reaction when she arrived in Israel and met her relatives here after 1945 (Bar-On, 1995a, pp 201-26).

The question 'Who suffered more?' became even more obscure when descendants of survivors and descendants of Nazi perpetrators began meeting each other (Bar-On, 1995b). In these encounters, it became obvious that the descendants of Nazi perpetrators also suffered from silence at home, although the content of that silence was very different from the silencing of the survivors. When the Germans found out about the atrocities their fathers had committed during the Shoah, it created a total breakdown in family communication. In the BBC documentary of the To Reflect and Trust group (*Time Watch*, 1993), one of the Jewish members suggested that the German members of the group suffered even more than himself, "When I finally learned what my parents went through during the Holocaust, I get to a pair of good people. When they find out what is behind the silence in their family they get to a terribly evil person, sometimes two, and there is no solace for them. They have to live with this pain and evil forever".

At the same time, we learned that many German people talk about the war years using the rationalisation 'we suffered too' (Bar-On and Charny, 1992). This may of course be true, as many of them went through the war and experienced hunger and bombardment. However, it becomes a moral rationalisation when they use their own suffering to undermine the responsibility of Germany for the suffering of other victims, specifically those of the Holocaust. Analysing interviews with the descendants of Nazis in Germany, the acknowledgement of the suffering of Jews was measured in comparison with their own suffering during and after the war (Bar-On and Gaon, 1991). We found that the descendants of the perpetrators related more to the suffering of the Jews than the interviewees whose parents have not been perpetrators during the Holocaust. I suggested that for the descendants of the German Nazi perpetrators, this kind of defence was not sufficient. It still exposed them to their father's atrocities and they had to use stronger moral arguments to come to grips with that past (Bar-On and Charny, 1992).

It is important for mental health professionals to try to clarify that suffering can be *different* in just the same way as other emotions and life experiences, but it cannot be scaled as we have no reference point against which to verify this scaling. Even if we have a natural tendency to scale suffering, we have to learn to hold it as being *different but not more or less*. For example, while working in a seminar with students at my university, interviewing survivors and descendants of survivors, this kind of 'holding the differences concerning suffering, without scaling them' became a major task of the facilitators. This was even more important when they encountered German students who studied in a similar seminar in Germany (Bar-On et al, 1997). As one of them phrased it, "Only then did we learn that we both are sick people with opposite illnesses, like two sides of the same coin".

Conclusion

In this chapter, I have presented a historically and socially contextualised psychodynamic perspective as a way to engage with two difficult questions: 'Who is a Holocaust survivor?', and 'Who suffered more?'. It seems essential that, in an era that is changing faster than ever before, people will need confidence to be open to and cope with the changes they are living through. The problem is that we are the first generation who knows that the reason why many of us are not coping with current changes is because so much of our energy is still preoccupied with past traumatic events. However, we are also paralysed by this awareness, as we still know so little about what can be done to reduce these after-effects and prevent new after-effects from happening.

Notes

[1] This chapter was prepared during my stay at Yad Vashem International Institute of Holocaust studies. I thank Professor Yehuda Bauer, the Director of the Institute, Professor Dr Inge Marszolek from Bremen University (Germany) and Dr Ifat Maoz from the Hebrew University of Jerusalem for their helpful comments on earlier versions of this chapter. Part of this chapter was presented at the Psychoanalytic Society conference in Jerusalem in December 1999 (Bar-On, 1999a).

For correspondence, please write to Professor Daniel Bar-On, Department of Behavioral Sciences, Ben Gurion University of the Negev, POBox 653, Beer Sheva 84105, Israel. Tel: 972 7 6472035; fax 972 7 6472932; e-mail danbaron@bgumail.bgu.ac.il.

[2] As an example of such a limit to the individual psychodynamic perspective, I want to cite Gilbert (1950), who tried to diagnose the Nazi perpetrators with regular psychiatric diagnostic tools. Had one taken them seriously, these perpetrators would have ended in the psychiatric hospital instead of being hanged. Kolchar, for example, did not understand that diagnosing Eichmann as a mentally unstable personality had nothing to do with his atrocious acts. These were socially and historically contextualised in the Nazi regime. In these cases, the psychiatric diagnosis could have served the German postwar society that tried to dissociate itself from the perpetrators and from where they originated (Bar-On, 2000).

[3] Every year at Ben Gurion University, we conduct a seminar on the psychosocial after-effects of the Holocaust on second and third generations. In this seminar, students interview and analyse biographical life stories of survivors and their descendants.

[4] As a point of interest, I do not count myself as a descendant of Holocaust survivors. My parents left Germany in 1933 after Hitler came to power. My mother went back and rescued her parents in 1935. Other family members managed to leave. The fact that I grew up with grandparents, and that many of the family left in time, changed the context in which I grew up. Many of my friends were less lucky in these respects.

[5] In our To Reflect and Trust group, which is composed of descendants of Holocaust survivors and descendants of Nazi perpetrators, the issue of victimhood was raised in the following way: both groups can easily identify and talk with the role of the victim in themselves. It is much more difficult to identify and talk with the victimiser within oneself. But once one can identify that part of oneself and let the two parts talk with each other, who are we if we let them both go? Did the over-identification with the victim (and victimiser) not hinder us from developing additional roles in ourselves (Bar-On, 1995b)?

References

Bar-On, D. (1989) *Legacy of silence: Encounters with children of the Third Reich*, Cambridge: Harvard University Press.

Bar-On, D. (1995a) *Fear and hope: Three generations of the Holocaust*, Cambridge: Harvard University Press.

Bar-On, D. (1995b) 'Encounters between descendants of Nazi perpetrators and descendants of Holocaust survivors', *Psychiatry*, vol 58, no 3, pp 225-45.

Bar-On, D. (1999a) 'A critical view on the role of psychoanalysis in interpreting the social impact of the Holocaust', The Psychoanalytical Society's conference, Jerusalem, December.

Bar-On, D. (1999b) *The indescribable and the undiscussable: Reconstructing human discourse after trauma*, Budapest: Central European University Press.

Bar-On, D. (1999c) *The other within us: Changes in Israeli identity from a socio-psychological perspective*, Jerusalem: Mosad Bialik and Ben Gurion University Press (in Hebrew).

Bar-On, D. (ed) (2000) *Bridging the gap*, Hamburg: Koerber.

Bar-On, D. and Charny, I.W. (1992) 'The logic of moral argumentation of children of the Nazi era', *International Journal of Group Tensions*, vol 22, no 1, pp 3-20.

Bar-On, D. and Gaon, A. (1991) '"We suffered too": Nazi children's inability to relate to the suffering of the victims of the Holocaust,' *Journal of Humanistic Psychology*, vol 31, no 4, pp 77-95.

Bar-On, D. and Mor, Y. (1996) 'The "as-if" "Sabraness" of second generation Holocaust survivors: a biographical and narrative analysis of one interview', *Sichot*, vol 11, no 1, pp 36-48 (in Hebrew).

Bar-On, D. and Selah O. (1991) 'The "vicious cycle" between current social and political attitudes and attitudes towards the Holocaust among Israeli youngsters', *Psychologia*, vol 2, no 2, pp 126-38 (in Hebrew).

Bar-On, D., Ostrovsky, T. and Fromer, D. (1997) '"Who am I in relation to the other?" German and Israeli students confront the Holocaust and each other', in Y. Danieli (ed) *International handbook of multigenerational legacies of trauma*, New York, NY: Plenum.

Bar-Tal, D. (1997) 'Formation and change of ethnic and national stereotypes: an intergrative model', *International Journal of Intercultural Relations*, vol 21, no 4, pp 491-523.

Bar-Tov, O. (1999) 'Kitsch and sadism in Kazetnik's planet: the Israeli youth visualizes the Holocaust', *Alpaim*, no 17, pp 148-75 (in Hebrew).

Bauer, Y. (1982) *The history of the Holocaust*, Danbury, CT: Franklin Watts.

Bergmann, M.S. and Jacuvy, M.E. (1982) *Generations of the Holocaust*, New York, NY: Basic Books.

Danieli, Y. (1980) 'Countertransference in the treatment and study of Nazi Holocaust survivors and their children', *Victimology*, vol 5, pp 3-4.

Danieli, Y. (1998), *International handbook of multigenerational legacies of trauma*, New York, NY: Plenum.

Gilbert, G.M. (1950) *The psychology of dictatorship: Based on the examination of the leaders of Nazi Germany*, New York, NY: Ronald Press.

Gutman, I. (1990) *The encyclopedia of the Holocaust*, Tel Aviv: Yediot Aharonot (in Hebrew).

Hardtmann, G. (1992) *Spuren der Verfolgung*, Gerlingen: Bleicher.

Janoff-Bulman, R. (1992) *Shattered assumptions*, New York, NY: Free Press.

Keren, N. and Almaliach, D. (1994) 'Community under siege', in D. Bar-On and D. Fromer (eds) *The second reader – After-effects of the Holocaust on second and third generations*, Beer Sheva: Ben Gurion University, Mifal Leshichpul (in Hebrew).

Kimmerling, B. (1993) 'Militarism in Israel: society', *Theory and Critics*, vol 4, pp 123-40 (in Hebrew).

Lerner, M. (1975) 'The justice motive in social behavior', *Journal of Social Issues*, vol 31, no 3, pp 1-19.

Levinas, E. (1990) *Totality and infinity: An essay on extiority*, Pittsburgh, PA: Duquesne University Press.

Rosenthal. G. (1998) *Three generations of the Holocaust*, Germany: Kassel.

Segev, T. (1992) *The seventh million*, Jerusalem: Keter Publication (in Hebrew).

Spence, D.P. (1980) *Historical truth and narrative truth*, New York, NY: Basic Books.

Time-Watch (1993) *The children of the Third Reich*, London: BBC.

Wittgenstein, L. (1953) *Philosophical investigations*, New York, NY: Macmillan.

EIGHT

Professional choices between private and state positions in Russia's transformation

Victoria Semenova

The impact of organisational structures is a much-discussed issue in Russia and elsewhere today; for example, state-run organisations, international companies, or small private firms on professional hierarchies[1]. Positions are often ranked in relation to salary levels, social functions (such as service orientation and responsibility), issues of autonomy and control, type of management (such as degrees of hierarchy), and systems of social security (such as sickness and pension benefits) (Parsons, 1964; Balzer, 1996).

The subjective meaning of a professional career choice between 'private' and 'state' employment is usually considered in terms of a dilemma between more social security (in a state enterprise) and more career opportunities (in a private enterprise). Kivinen (1993) argues that, in the British context, more and more professionals prefer the private sector for its speedy response to new ideas and its promise of better financial rewards. Some scholars emphasise the political aspects of the dilemma. For example, researchers emphasise that state-sector employment in France enhances professional 'autonomy', 'power' and 'success' (Geison, 1984).

The cultural or, more precisely, moral differences between organisational structures in the context of Western Europe are often portrayed as opportunities in the state sector to exert more influence on societal transformation and the production process, as against more egotistical money and career opportunities in the private sector. The state can protect income and status. However, in some contexts, the professional can also deteriorate into 'organisation man' (Rosenberg, 1966)[2]. Yet, as Balzer (1996, p 6) suggests, in the 19th century Russian context:

> The model of the civil servant as bureaucratic modernizer was a powerful alternative to the model of the free professional.

Presented in this way, the state–private dilemma affects the career, status and even the moral world of professionals, depending of course on the cultural context of a particular society. Nowadays, however, the difference is considered mainly as an organisational difference within one overall economic structure: that of the market economy.

In the case of contemporary Russia, the dilemma between 'private' and 'state' employment is more fundamental for several reasons. First, formerly Soviet professionals (or intelligentsia) knew only one system of employment – that of the state. As most forms of social welfare were provided by the state this entailed dependence on the state. For a professional, the position of 'working for the state' meant 'service for the state', which became the core point of both economic status and professional culture. The historical background of the Russian intelligentsia also enforced 'service for the state' as a value. This specific type of professional ethic dated from the pre-revolutionary era when 'service for the people' meant a strong orientation towards public service as people's enlightenment, a kind of 'missionary' function. Functions of 'service for the state', 'service for the people', and the wider social function of 'bearer of culture', were more familiar to Russian professionals than the function of 'rational actor' with expectations of autonomy and control (as an expert). As a result, in the pre-revolutionary Russian context, professionals were more likely to identify themselves with other 'collective actors' (in the sense of belonging to the group of professionals who were equally dependent on the state) than with 'individual actors' with some kind of autonomy from the state.

Work for private firms in modern Russia is a relatively new phenomenon. Private firms did not make their appearance until the beginning of the 1990s and emerged as a result of Westernisation, meaning intervention from outside along with market reform. It is a newly emerging structure, therefore, with a new system of work relationships and an ethos unknown to the majority of employees. Moreover, this system is in the process of being shaped and adapted to Russia's particular cultural context and its own cultural history.

In the first instance, the new managerial style in private firms is alien to the majority of the Russian workforce, including professionals. People even leave their well-paid private positions out of dissatisfaction with the system of employee–employer relationships in that sector, because the western-oriented managerial style is so alien to the majority of the Russian workforce (Yadov, 1997). Second, the distance between 'private' and 'state' spheres became a key factor in social and economic differentiation during the period of transformation in Russia. Levels of income, social prestige and social security depended to a marked degree on whether one was working for a state or a privately owned enterprise (Zaslavskaya, 1993). Third, changes in the employment system created more varied opportunities in the choice of profession and career development. However, despite an increasingly diverse occupational world (where the state remained attractive to many but was no longer the sole player), many professionals continued to prefer the security of government positions where a fixed salary and pension were guaranteed and they could continue 'to fulfil their mission' to the people.

This leads to the conclusion that professional choices largely hinged on the cultural distance between these two occupational sites.

This chapter, therefore, will concentrate on these questions:

- What is the difference in business culture between these two spheres in the eyes of professionals?
- What are the significant advantages and disadvantages of each situation from the standpoint of career choice?
- Are these different cultural models the leitmotif of professional choice?

In order to investigate organisational structures from the point of view of the individual, and to compare them as cultural systems or different cultural milieus, researchers usually use very general dimensions involving oppositions such as:

- *systems of power* (vertical-horizontal relations, democracy-authoritarianism);
- *the communication system* (managerial styles, such as order-inconsistency);
- *the role of the individual* (collectivist-individualist);
- *job motivation* (achievement goals, quality of 'personal relations within the collective') (Hofstede, 1996).

These general criteria serve well as a primary matrix for analysing unstructured data, such as in-depth interviews with professionals describing the characteristics of their job position in their own words.

Method

My observations and interpretations of the interview data are based mainly on the case of one person who holds two jobs at the same time: an official job (his work for a state enterprise), and an additional one (his work for a private firm). Concentrating on this extreme case as the main object of investigation[3], I would like to stress my research interest in a situation where a choice is made between two positions. This provides an opportunity to pick up most of the "problematic aspects of case structure – the problem, the context, the issues, and the meaning" (Creswell, 1998, p 120). An extreme case is used here as an instrument to illustrate the problem and to observe the opposing, controversial, features of the phenomenon, in order to reconstruct a systematic picture of their differences in terms of culture.

This method of basing the research on one case may be called a 'clinical approach' as the object of our interest is not practice or pattern behaviour, but the 'basic underlying assumptions' of a particular business culture that lie behind them. The experience of someone simultaneously involved in both structures is a useful instrument for such an approach, as it provides an opportunity to understand the combination of individual, organisational and even national characteristics of the phenomena.

The biographical interview with Sergei (not his real name) was conducted in 1996. He was then 39 years of age. He is a Muscovite, a specialist in computing (a computer programme specialist by education). Until 1994, he was a computer programmer working for the Social Science Institute (state-owned Institute for Social Information). His tasks included writing, testing and maintaining computer programmes for users. In 1994, he started his additional job as manager of a private firm that sold computer equipment (head of the department responsible for public relations with governmental structures).

Why did I choose this case for further analysis? What was of special interest there?

First, by his age and speciality, Sergei represented an active age cohort on the modern Russian labour market. In addition, he was a highly educated professional with good positions in both firms. This meant he enjoyed a certain degree of autonomy in each work place and control over the production process. This gave him the opportunity, on the one hand, to be deeply involved in the work situation and, on the other, to analyse his job situation quite critically.

In the Russian context, so-called 'balancing positions' are relatively common nowadays: about 20% of the workforce 'strike a balance' between the private and the state sector. For them, a career strategy of part-time employment in a state-owned enterprise serves to bring a feeling of security in an unpredictable social situation, while an additional job in the private sector is a source of good money in order to survive. However, as I pointed out earlier, our interest lay not in the professional strategy from the economic point of view but in its cultural background. Sergei's case proved most useful in this regard. He maintained a 'balancing position' between the two as he had reasonable motivation for remaining in both. He could not make a definite choice. During the in-depth interview, he tried to describe his job situation at both firms in order to explain why he was still on 'both sides' and what his fears and anxieties were on each side.

Second, his unstable situation of choosing and 'balancing' between two positions brought about a lot of reflection in his personal account. That was important for his further life strategy. By weighing up the advantages and disadvantages of each position, he was touching on the central meaning of his immediate individual life world, and this had practical consequences for his future career. His account took the form of reflexivity and a dialogic form of textuality, which was of specific interest to the researcher[4].

On the basis on this extreme case, I tried to search for the cultural meaning of his hesitation in order to reconstruct the subjective images of both places as differing cultural systems and to define their differences in the eyes of professionals.

Methodologically, this was a semi-structured, in-depth biographical interview, where the job position became the central topic as a result of the interviewee trying to understand himself. He analysed his status in the private firm in great depth according to various dimensions. For him, the interview served both as an attempt to understand the 'self' and to shed light on his experience of the new type of employment, as yet unknown to the majority of outsiders. His narrative about the job at the state-owned enterprise (the institute) was triggered by the interviewer's question *'Why would you not leave your previous place of work, if you are so successful in the firm?'* The answer took the form of a comparison between the two situations and argumentation for his half-decision. I shall analyse these two passages from the interview in two dimensions: first, the subjective attitude towards the opportunities of each position, and second, the subjective meaning of his hesitation at the moment of choice as expressive of cultural distance between two business cultures.

Subjective attitude towards opportunities in the private firm

On the whole, Sergei was satisfied with his current status in the private firm: he did not have any conflicts with his boss, so in general his attitude towards the firm was a positive one. The firm was currently developing and maintaining its place in the computer market. When he started there were only 10 employees, but later there were 30-40.

The description of his 'private' job situation was quite profound. It can be summarised in three main dimensions: his attitude towards power; his attitude towards managerial style; and his own motivation.

Sergei's attitude towards power emerges from his account which he started with a description of the system of hierarchy in his firm and its vertical job relations. This could be interpreted as subjectively the most important and significant aspect of the job situation.

He put himself roughly at the 'middle level and higher' and called his status 'the status of responsibility':

> people who have energy and opportunity ... executives who bear a certain
> amount of responsibility ... [who are] empowered .... It means the ability
> to take decisions, or, rather not the ability, but the power to do so, from a
> certain level.

He understood 'being in power' as the status of responsibility (executives, empowered, the power to do), a space for opportunities (energy and opportunity, ability) and a challenge for making decisions. He talked at length about it, as it seemed to be a new aspect of the job situation that he had never experienced before. He saw it as a *new advantage* of his position in a private firm. Its central meaning was in line with the high esteem in which 'autonomy' and 'control over the process' were held, known to be important features in the Western-type professional model.

He also distinguished two other levels in the power structure: those who are lower ("clerks, secretaries, who do not bear responsibility") and those who are much higher (the owners – "the difference between the owners of the firm and hired employees is simply enormous. It's like the distance between here and Vladivostok").

The discovery that there were restricted opportunities for further upward mobility in his career (that he could never become an owner) came as bad news and a disappointment. At the beginning, he had been very ambitious and thought he could easily overcome that distance and become an owner, but later he became disappointed when he understood that he never could reach that 'top' status.

His reflection about closed social class and restrictions on future achievement was a significant personal discovery concerning the 'private' firm compared with the previous (Soviet-type) job system. In the Soviet-type system, after achieving a middle-level status of responsibility (nomenclature), you could hope to continue moving 'up' without any restrictions. In this new situation, it was economic background (individual financial capital) that prevented the individual from overcoming the strict barrier between 'employee' and 'owner'. Despite this disappointment, Sergei was on the whole satisfied with the status of 'responsibility' or 'power' that he had achieved, as he did not have it previously.

Sergei had developed his own understanding of management style. According to Sergei, in order to succeed in one's firm, one should know:

> the technology of business ... [the] technology of relations with partners ... have practical experience and be quick [to learn by doing; to be quick in picking up knowledge] ... have personal energy and responsibility [for decisions taken] ... loyalty to the firm.

That was 'a norm' he learned during his job there.

At first, he simply listed these characteristics as qualities required for any 'responsible' person at his firm. It appeared that professional success at his firm depended on 'expert skills' and 'individual achievement' and coincided with the western-oriented professional model. But later, while describing the system at his firm in more depth, he dwelt on his own case as an example:

> Sergei (S): It is not obligatory, but it is better if you know somebody in the firm. It rarely happens that somebody is taken on as the result of an advertisement and just an interview and inquiries – that hardly ever happens. On the whole, as far as I can judge by what I see in our firm, if a person doesn't know anybody, his chances of being taken on are very small. Or he should be able to show ...

> Interviewer (I): A trial period?

> S: If during the trial period, he manages to prove that he is a real professional, that he can solve the problems that are entrusted to him. But there are very few who can do that. On the whole, it is, of course, *a question of personal acquaintance. I, for instance, was taken on only because my friends knew my personal qualities. Only because of that, I was given a degree of responsibility and freedom in decision-making* [emphasis added by author] because they knew what I could and what I could not do.

I: So that, in a certain sense, they sacrificed professionalism?

S: Yes, of course. Personal loyalty certainly plays a role. Of course!

From the narration, it was evident that 'expert skills' as a required quality for a newcomer are sacrificed to 'personal loyalty'. It became clear that professional skill meant less here than 'personal connections' with the boss or, in other words, than the personal loyalty of the employee. So managerial style was based not on the rational choice of experts and competition of their skills but on personal relations and loyalty. This gave rise to uncertainty and instability in those who worked there. As a result, despite his good position at the firm, Sergei was anxious about possible instability in the future.

Later he described the system of employee–employer relations in the firm:

> Of course, there were cases when someone was simply told: from tomorrow you're not working here any more.... Without any motivation. I think that was an extreme case of toughness.... I consider that this mechanism is not functioning properly at the present stage of development of our economy and business. Let's put it that way.

> There is complete arbitrariness. Yes, you can say that.... It is, of course, a question of terminology. Is it complete arbitrariness or.... After all, if a person goes to work in a private firm, he should clearly understand that he can be sacked at any moment. If he makes ... certain mistakes. When he starts working for a firm, he should understand where he is going and what the rules of the game are. That there are such things as the personal characteristics of the boss, the rules of the game and all the rest. This means that there are no norms. Let us say, if a firm has a certain turnover or employs a certain number of people, there exist a number of rules for the employees and so on. We don't have that. In our firm, personal relations with the management of the firm play an important role ... of course, there is always a strong personal element in people being accepted for employment.

In describing the type of job relations, Sergei tried to be loyal (he is a part of that system, and he is in a good position in his firm) but he tried to find some justification for such arbitrariness. Nevertheless, his negative attitude towards the managerial style was evident from his use of such terms as 'toughness', 'arbitrariness', 'no norms', 'a question of personal acquaintance'. According to Sergei, the managerial style was based on 'the personal element' and 'power', and decisions in relation to employees that should recognised as irrational or inconsistent (no norms).

Those mainly negative characteristics also have a personal emotional aspect. Sergei is satisfied with his own status, but this system of work relations did not satisfy his moral feelings. He disagreed with power relations based on personal connections and arbitrariness without any sign of rationality or normative order. His pauses and hesitations before any mention of kinds of relations could be seen as evidence of his attempt to justify and to adapt to the new system. He tried to reach a moral compromise but was not convinced of its justice.

It is curious that he should be so angry about a power structure based on 'personal connections'. He was familiar with 'personal connections' as a type of hiring and firing system from the Soviet-type command economic system. He seems to be more shocked by the type of relationship based on toughness and arbitrariness, which were unknown and alien to him.

His motivation towards the part-time job in the private firm is rather complicated. On the one hand, when he started his job he simply had the pragmatic aim of having a well-paid job in order to feed his family in hard times ("most of the time I work for this firm where I'm well-paid"). Later, however, he also felt the need "to be a part of the team", to be loyal to the firm, to work for it:

> Well, in the beginning that plays a role, but later it develops into loyalty towards the firm, ie to what extent a person stands up for the interests of the firm…. But this question is directly connected with the question of money, because, in fact, it means defending the interests of the firm in respect of its profitability, its revenue and all the rest. For instance, reducing the amount of money the firm has to pay [to another firm or state structure]. It is often something intangible. One can't always immediately work out how much to pay in a given situation. If you are able to lower the sum to a certain level, nobody might even know you had done it…. Yes, you do that unconsciously, because you look upon the affairs of the firm as your own. Of course, you may consider it a virtue and display it.

For Sergei, the salary he received from the firm at first only represented a form of financial support for his family and later appeared to be an adequate reward for his loyalty, a measure of his 'power' and his 'worth' and real importance to the firm. The firm does not just give him money to survive, but 'money' as a reward for his professional value, the equivalent price for his individual capital.

The cultural meaning of his private job is to be important, powerful – and adequately paid (unlike in the state enterprise, where he received much less money and irregularly). It is a form of compensation for his moral compromise with its unjust system of relations.

> In this particular case, I am talking about how much I am needed by the management of the firm. I am very much needed and I should never forget that. It doesn't mean that I should play on this, but simply always bear it in mind, so as to correctly evaluate my strengths, my abilities, my prospects and my career. The wish to be very needed by my firm…. The feeling that you are needed, constantly needed is, really, one way of making a career, because

a career is not only your job, but depends on the extent to which you are needed as a specialist, as an employee, by that particular firm.

This passage makes it clear that he is constructing a new identification for the professional as a professional who is 'working for the organisation' instead of the previous identity of 'working for a state service'. Rosenberg called this 'organisation man' (Rosenberg, 1966), which does not coincide with the market model of 'working for profit'.

That means that the 'status of responsibility' and 'being in power' referred to earlier are also a part of his devotion to the firm's interests. Defending the firm's interests, therefore, is more important for him than professional interests and 'service for society', even though he is dissatisfied with the managerial style (hiring and firing system, toughness, personal power of the boss). He does not exclusively adopt that ethos to replace another, but nevertheless he feels that he is part of it.

His image of 'I' within the framework of the private firm is constructed as the image of the individual 'self' in an alien milieu: he is uncertain about his future relations with the boss; he criticises the system of communication and the relations with his peers and those of 'lower' status. On the other hand, he is proud of his autonomous status and 'the firm's need of him'. He has an entirely rational attitude towards the firm that he has to adapt to, but the rules of the game are unknown to him here.

The systematic reconstruction of this image suggests the model of 'working for the organisation' (or 'working for the boss') rather than 'working for the state' or 'working for private profit'.

Out of this subjective picture, it is possible to reconstruct the system of job relations in a private firm in the Russian context as having a strong vertical structure. The professionals are given more autonomy and responsibility (status of responsibility). The need for and significance of expert skill is only given lip service (while in reality it is sacrificed to personal connections). Individual achievement is connected with loyalty to those in power. There is inconsistency in managerial style and norms. The way Sergei presents it, the private firm does not have a well-articulated rational need for expert skills. This is demonstrated by a hiring and firing system based on 'personal connections' inherited from the Soviet system (instead of a western-oriented, skills-based competition type).

Subjective attitudes towards his job position in the state firm

As I mentioned earlier in this chapter, when describing working for the 'state', Sergei dwelt only on those aspects that prevented him from leaving that workplace; that is, the advantages of state employment. The interview passages devoted to the 'state' job will be analysed accordingly as in opposition to the first one; that is, 'What I do not have in my first job where I'm well paid'.

Power and horizontal relations

First, in contrast to his private firm, Sergei did not mention any aspect of hierarchy. This could be explained by his different attitude towards the normative mechanisms in the private and state jobs. The state position is a traditional one; he became used to it during his first socialisation into a familiar organisational system and so its normative mechanism does not bother him now. Compare this with the private job where this was most important to him: "There are no norms here. We used to have set rules – 'You must do this, you mustn't do that' – but now we don't have any". He would have liked such norms in order to feel secure and know the way to the 'top' of the hierarchy, but the private firm does not provide him with that.

On the other hand, in his state-enterprise position, he is not oriented towards 'achievement' and an upward career, which is why the vertical dimension is less important for him there. What does Sergei like best of all at his state job? He says it is "human relations with people" (horizontal connections) and he considers them to be very different from the system of horizontal relations at his new place.

> Sergei (S): In my new work [the private firm] there exists a micro-community that affects human relations. All these completely everyday, simple conversations about the family, about common interests and all the rest exist much less [at the new place of work] and I think of them as an element of the past. Because, formerly, everybody worked in a government institution, and there were these relations outside the actual work, which were very highly developed. Human relations. People talked a lot to each other, spent a lot of their working time talking to each other about human affairs. They were forced to converse with each other and they brought part of their home life with them to their work. One could do that then. Now there is no time for that. If there is, it is not more than 1% of the working time.

> I: So the main reason is lack of time?

> S: There is neither the time nor the possibility, because no owner, having money or making money with the help of other people, of hired labour, will enjoy seeing his employees spending half an hour or an hour discussing how they spent last weekend.... But, before, that was in the order of things in any workplace of whatever kind, except, perhaps, factories, where the production process cannot be interrupted. But everywhere else connected with science, culture and even health, in short, in many branches of public life, that is how things were. In private firms this sort of behaviour is, to put it mildly, not greatly welcomed.... And here [in the institute] I remain in touch with that part of the past, which warms my heart.... It gives me the strength to adapt my behaviour to the private firm.

According to Sergei, the highly developed horizontal relations of the Soviet-type enterprise are the key aspect that is missing in the private firm. He even seemed to be idealising it because of its absence in the new place.

However, what is most significant here is the stress on 'human relations' in the sense of extensive non-instrumental communication with one's peers. Compared with the hierarchical system and competition at his private firm, that is the main thing that warms his heart: "they talk about human affairs" without thinking about money issues.

By contrast, his account of the private firm contained no in-depth analysis of horizontal relations. There were only brief remarks to show that horizontal relations were friendly enough amidst the signs of individualism and competition: "We have friendly relations but do not communicate ideas, know-how"; "No owner making money will contemplate talking [informally among colleagues] for more than 1% of working time". However, one more sentence seemed to be important here, showing that he was not satisfied with the amount of informal communication in the private firm: "It is not enough for me". So, non-instrumental personal communication on equal terms was a significant feature of the previous business culture. It was the basis for emotional comfort in the workplace for the respondent, "people brought part of their home life with them to their work".

Sergei's image of his state position could be constructed as the image of 'we': his own self as a collective actor in communication with equal others. Horizontal community and emotional ties with equals were at the heart of the previous culture as opposed to rational and vertical relations at his new place of work. This opposition enables us to characterise individual attitudes towards these two business cultures as 'collective equality' versus 'individual achievement'.

Motivation: emotional and rational background

Sergei's language when talking about his state employment was much warmer and less critical than in passages about the private firm. First, he described the character of the job and his duties at the state institute:

> I find the work in the institute interesting. It is analytical work combined
> with human relations. Though I must say that the work here is more creative.
> The atmosphere in the institute gives me the strength to realise myself here.

Managerial work and responsibilities made him proud of his position in the private firm, but the creative, interesting, analytical work in his state employment satisfied him emotionally, and served as a kind of moral support that gave him the strength to realise himself in the alien surroundings of the new job.

Emotionally, then, he was more satisfied with this kind of job ("I find it interesting"). The most important word here is 'interesting', which was never mentioned in relation to the private sector job. There, he was satisfied with and proud of his status of responsibility, but here he was motivated by emotional involvement and 'interest'.

He is faced, then, with the emotional choice of an interesting job as opposed to the rational choice of an influential job. Speaking in terms of a former Soviet stereotype, he says that one should "never think about financial reward, it's the job that should be of interest". Sergei considered the Soviet-type job ethos as emotionally meaningful. In his own words, "the work was part of their life and people brought part of their home life with them to their work". It is striking that he never mentioned any outcomes of that job, only the process of communication itself. This is in line not only with business culture but also with Russian national mentality in general, as has been mentioned by many authors; that is, the importance of 'being', 'belonging', 'reflexivity' – as opposed to the 'results', 'achievements' and 'productivity', which are important in western-type cultures (Lickachev, 1990; Lebedeva, 1999).

Lifetime orientation: past and present

The section in Sergei's interview about his state position is also very nostalgic. One of the most important reasons for him to retain his state position is its nostalgic link with the past:

> It may sound paradoxical, but the institute links me, in many ways, to the past. In my new work, I have to start much from the beginning; I have to change myself in many ways and in order to be able to do that I need strength. The changes that are required of me in this work on a psychological and moral plane need to be fed and supported by the past. The relations in a private firm differ greatly from those in a government department.

Psychologically, his state position acted as a stable mechanism and psychological support for him as he adapted to a new kind of life project and a new type of morality (which he was not satisfied with, as we remember). In his vision, the former Soviet kind of morality was clearer and better justified than the one at his new place of work.

Here, then, the comparison of state and private positions takes on the meaning of 'known past' and 'unknown and alien future'. The state-job position in the respondent's vision seemed to be idealised when compared with the private one. He dwelt only on its positive features, and constructed it mainly as a horizontally oriented structure where relations on equal terms were more significant than vertical power relations. The most important aspects were psychological comfort and communication. As a type of 'known past', it seems to be emotionally acknowledged by the majority of former-Soviet people.

Cultural difference between the two models

On the basis of the individual case of Sergei (who is not old enough to be typically 'Soviet') serving as an extreme case standing between 'private' and 'state' business cultures, the cultural distance between these two models could be described in the following way:

PRIVATE	STATE
– toughness, arbitrariness	– warmth, human concern
– power hierarchy	– horizontal relations
– individual achievement	– collective equality
– responsibility for decisions	– no decision making
– inconsistency	– norm-based
– moral compromise	– moral comfort
– rationality	– emotional choice
– money	– psychological comfort
– results-oriented	– process-oriented
– unstable and unknown future	– link to known past

Sergei's attitudes towards these two work situations correspond to two different work cultures (Hofstede, 1980), in particular the dichotomy between market-oriented and command-oriented work cultures.

Cross-cultural studies distinguish between individualistic and collectivist values in the determination of individual choice (Triandis, 1994; Hofstede, 1996). Similarly in this case study, these two types of job position are subjectively presented as two fundamentally different work cultures. In answer to the general question, does Russian national culture correspond to one or other of these character types, empirical studies have shown that it lies *somewhere between* them and that is why it could adapt to the market-oriented style in the same way as Germany, Finland, Austria or Israel (Yadov, 2002).

The choice in this dichotomy also depends on several other dimensions: 'individual achievement – collective equality'; 'result-oriented – process-oriented'; 'unknown future – known past'; 'rational – emotional'. What is important here is that when faced with the choice between these two types, Sergei always made an emotional choice in favour of the Soviet as against the market-oriented type. This was despite having rationally underlined the advantages of the private firm (autonomy, status of responsibility, adequate evaluation of his personal and professional capital).

The private model is painted in negative colours, as unknown and morally and culturally alien to the respondent. He tries to be neutral since he understands the need to adapt to it. Here the respondent feels that he is a responsible person with a certain kind of autonomy and control over the production process but that he serves his organisation's interests more than his professional duty requires. The state-sector image is described in emotionally more pleasant colours as it represents connection with the known past and nostalgia for the 'best days of his youth'. That job situation also coincides with his professional interests and sense of duty towards others – service to the public.

Conclusion

Thinking of Sergei, it is evident that it is mainly biographical factors, such as previous work experience, that prevail in his emotional choice. More generally, this suggests that representatives of older generations who went through their first socialisation process in Soviet times (Soviet-type business culture) could not adapt to a new business culture quickly. They feel closer to the state culture emotionally and personally, since it was a part of their former biographical project, constructed in the time of their youth. This is why they see it as a part of their own life, as the 'known past', and now experience frustration and negative attitudes to any new form alien to their previous job aspirations.

Emotional adherence to Soviet-type business culture means that the genetic code of the previous system is still very strong and is a dominant factor in the professional's choice of career. The psychological continuum in this opposition lies not only in the dimension of 'known past' and 'unknown future' but more deeply as a moral compromise for the Soviet-type professional between 'working for the public' and 'working for the organisation'. More extensive research based on 40 interviews with Russian professionals shows graphically that only a limited section of the former intelligentsia could adapt quickly to the new western-oriented business ethos. Others are still living in the framework of various kinds of earlier traditional Russian cultural models (Semenova, 1997).

There is a very practical aspect to this psychological conflict in the context of Russia: large western corporations based on an ethos of individual achievement could not prosper in Russia if they provoked this conflict between norms and ethos within the majority of the Russian work force. Their cultural orientation towards the 'market managerial order' or 'individualism' is out of step with Russian mass psychology.

This last remark underlines the importance and fruitfulness of the chosen research strategy of concentrating on one case study. As I have demonstrated, the clinical approach to investigating work cultures provides an opportunity to reveal the most hidden basic cultural background, namely collective biographical experience.

Notes

[1] 'Professional' is used here to mean the full gamut of professional, technical and managerial occupations. It is the group referred to in state socialist parlance as 'the intelligentsia'.

[2] Rosenberg (1966, p 89), focusing on specialist employment in large organisations, suggested that the Prussian bureaucrat should be called the original 'organisation man'.

They were regimented with an iron hand, driven to work, constantly supervised and spurred to greater exertions by the hope of material reward and social honours and fear of punishment.

[3] This case is used as a good illustrative example out of a set of 40 interviews with professionals conducted during 1995-96 for the collective project 'On transition to the middle class: professional strategies of young intellectuals' (grant from the Central-European University; the author was team leader). The interviewer was Elena Meshcherinka. The results of the whole research are published in Semenova (1997) and Meshcherinka (1997).

[4] Turning to the example of Dostoevsky's textuality and innovative author's position, Bakhtin, in his metalinguistic analysis, showed that Dostoevsky invented a new type of textuality that openly concentrated on the personal reflexivity of the actor. Textually, his method was represented as a *dialogic form* of textuality or 'microdialogues'. In Dostoevsky's texts, the actor is not 'He' or 'I' but 'You', acting as the reflected 'other'. In order to show these dialogue relations, Dostoevsky withdrew himself from the scene as an interpreter of the action and presented only long dialogues between his heroes as acting and reflecting 'selves'. From this, Bakhtin concluded that the author's main method of interpretation of 'the other' was to concentrate on her/his reflexivity by giving him/her the freedom to speak openly without any overt interpretation by the author. According to Bakhtin, a *dialogic relationship* between the author and 'the other' means, therefore, openness towards the inner world of 'the other' by means of her/his free textuality (cited from Kozlova, 1992). In my own research, my main concern was to concentrate on Sergei's personal form of textuality in order to understand his reflexivity about his work position 'between two worlds of work'.

References

Balzer, H. (ed) (1996) *Russia's missing middle class: The professions in Russian history*, New York, NY: M.E. Sharpe.

Creswell, J. (1998) *Qualitative inquiry and research design: Choosing among five traditions*, London: Sage Publications.

Geison, G. (ed) (1984) *Professions and the French state*, Philadelphia, PA: University of Pennsylvania Press.

Hofstede, G. (1980) *Culture's consequences: international differences in work-related values*, Newbury Park, CA: Sage Publications..

Hofstede, G. (1996) 'Riding the waves of commerce: a test of Trompenaars "model" of national character', *International Journal of Intercultural Relations*, vol 20, no 2, pp 189-98.

Kozlova, N. (1992) 'Sociologiya povsednevnosti: pereostenka cennostej' ('Sociology of everyday life: re-estimating values'), *Obschestvennyi nauki i sovremennost*, no 3, pp 47-56.

Lebedeva, N. (1999) *Vvedenie v etnicheskyuy i cros-kyltyurnyuy psichologiyu* (*Introduction in ethnic and cross-cultural psychology*), Moscow: Klyuch.

Lickachev, D.S. (1990) 'O natzionalnom charactere ruskich' ('About Russian national character'), *Voprosy philosophii*, no 4, pp 3-6.

Meshcherkina, E. (1997) 'Biographical reconstruction: educational and professional strategies of adaptation in the market economy', in V. Voronkov and E. Zdravomyslova (eds) *Biographical perspectives on post-socialist societies*, St Petersburg: Centre for Independent Social Research, pp 158-66.

Parsons, T. (1964) *Essays in sociological theory*, New York, NY: Free Press.

Rosenberg, H. (1966) *Bureaucracy, aristocracy and autocracy*, Boston, MA: Beacon Press.

Semenova, V. (1997) 'On transition to the middle class: professional strategies of young intellectuals in Russia', in M. Kivinen (ed) *The Kalamari union: Middle class in East and West*, Aldershot: Ashgate, pp 151-9.

Triandis, N. (1994) *Culture and social behavior*, New York, NY: McGraw-Hill.

Yadov, V. (1997) 'Social identifications in post-Soviet Russia: empirical evidence and theoretical explanation', *International Review of Sociology/Revue Internationale de Sociologie*, vol 7, no 2, pp 10-16.

Yadov, V. (2002) The research report on the project 'Work relations on Russian enterprises' (unpublished paper).

Zaslavskaya, T. (1993) 'The monitoring: results of the first six months', *Economic and Social Change: The Monitoring of Public Opinion*, no 6, pp 5-8.

NINE

Maintaining a sense of individual autonomy under conditions of constraint: a study of East German managers

Ulrike Nagel

This chapter deals with the biographical situation and coping strategies of highly educated cadres under the authoritarian regime of the former German Democratic Republic (GDR). It draws from a study of work biographies of contemporary East German managers who had previously been economic cadres in the GDR. The second part of the chapter considers methodological difficulties of cross-cultural research, particularly in the arenas of post-socialist transformation research and migration research. The problem of providing an adequate framework of interpretation for the social phenomena of a culture unfamiliar to the researcher will be captured by the notion of lacking the 'common sense knowledge of social structures' (Garfinkel, 1972) of the life world under scrutiny.

The database of this study consists of 17 narrative interviews with East German managers who had been economic cadres under socialism and who succeeded in retaining leading positions after the Berlin Wall came down in 1989[1]. At the time of the GDR, they all belonged to the operative elite of the economic system, but not the political elite. As managers of former GDR companies, it was they who put the economic transformation into practice. They were aged in their early 40s in 1989 and about 50 in 1999, the time of the interview.

A central concept of this chapter is that of 'the institutionalised life-course regime'. While this is applied to the former GDR in the first instance, my argument is that modernisation and globalisation processes are increasingly bringing lives in 'Western' societies under the sway of institutionalised life-course processes, not least in welfare systems. Research on economic managers shows the effectiveness of interpretive methods in revealing the interplay within individual responses between cultural (and family) traditions and institutionalised life-course forms. It also suggests both the rich potential of biographical research for macro-sociological diagnosis and prognosis, and the importance of biographical understandings for working 'with the subject', as is being promised in the 'new' social policy.

Since interpretive data analysis bears much in common with casework strategies underlying social welfare services, its results can be understood as an additional empowerment of personnel in social work and even in social policy, 'additional' in the sense of both further detailing the professional knowledge base and sensitising awareness of latent consequences of action and intervention. This chapter gives an illustrative example of unexpected – and unwanted – outcomes of social policies and leads to some heuristic concepts that might serve as a tool while 'working with the subject'.

The life-course regime of the GDR

The data analysis started from an experience common to almost all the interviews, a phenomenon that repeatedly presented itself at status passages throughout the life course; namely, the experience that the state held a tight rein over life-course decisions. Decisions that in Western political culture would be considered to be within the realm of individual choice and autonomy – such as whether to go to university or not, what profession to choose, where to look for employment, whether to move from one company to another – were heavily influenced by government institutions, including state administration, school boards, and economic organisations and companies.

When first encountering this phenomenon, the research team tended to categorise it as repression of individuality and autonomy and the experience related to it as a feeling of vulnerability and a violation of the individual's claim to autonomy, which no doubt it was. However, this was only half the story. The young people were directly channelled into professions and firms which meant that they were denied freedom of choice, but at the same time they were given the chance of higher education and careers. Although they may have been unable to take up the discipline they would have chosen for themselves, they did have the privilege of studying at university. They had access to rapidly advancing careers and their subsequent applications for changes of position were sometimes accepted. Given these facts and experiences, the notion of pure repression is misleading; it omits the fact that this institutional life-course regime provided, as well as denied, opportunities for higher education and upward mobility.

There are numerous examples that illustrate this paradox. One of the managers wanted to study economics and specialise in foreign trade, but was accepted at university to study chemistry; another hoped to study electronics but was admitted to industrial economics; another manager, having been offered teaching at a university for two years, and who was looking forward to this change in occupation, was refused permission to transfer by the director of his company (who belonged to the next higher status group). Another manager wanted to make a horizontal shift, but was told, 'We need you where you are'. Another still was offered a promotion to a different company, and was punished for his refusal by having to stagnate in his current position for many years. Each one of the interviews contains a remarkable number of comparable experiences. It is important to note that this applies mostly to those who were considered part of or destined for the socialist avant garde, and not so much to those with lower aspirations and no desire for leading positions.

For the functional elite, or so-called intelligentsia, the life-course regime of the GDR typically created a paradox, by simultaneously opening up opportunities for participating in the *nomenclatura* on the one hand, and on the other neglecting individuals' need for autonomous choice, and disregarding individual inclination and preference (be it for profession, occupation or position). The characteristic trait of this regime, and at the same time the reason for calling it a 'regime', was its power to form and determine the processes of individualisation and professionalisation, and its general overruling of personal needs (Fehér and Heller, 1979; Hanke, 1995; Engler, 1996; Frommer, 2000).

This interference by state institutions in the sphere of personal freedom very much resembles what, in the world of Western social welfare, is called the *processing of people*, in which institutions of social control and social care virtually predetermine life decisions. Such processing can also be observed when people's rise in their careers is not through their own choice but is a result of other people's interests, such as employers, who profit from it. The dependency structure that tends to underlie such careers can also be found in migration biographies.

With regard to the manager study, it could be objected that an 'institutionalised life course' as a means of allocating and orienting people's lives is a necessary and common tool of politics, in democracies as much as in authoritarian regimes. It could also be pointed out that many young people lack a clear conception of their future education and profession at the time when they have to make choices, and that channelling and creaming off, as observed in the GDR, are the harmless mechanisms of any life-course regime. I am not convinced by this line of argument, and would rather emphasise the difference between the institutionalised life course in Western industrial countries, where labour markets and social welfare institutions serve as the mechanisms of allocation (Kohli, 1985, 1988), and countries like the GDR, where allocation was centrally planned and organised by state institutions. I consider that the kind of channelling found in the GDR, following the principles of achievement, social background and adherence to the state philosophy, enforces an attitude of submission and a readiness to be controlled (Fehér and Heller, 1979). Any disobedience or opposition to the culture of institutional decision making about individual life courses, even criticism of the institutional channelling and specific decisions, endangered what opportunities were offered. By extrapolating this to the whole of society, one can easily envisage a climate of public conformity and manifest loyalty (Pollack, 1990; Engler, 1996).

The database clearly shows the biographical consequences of the life-course regime for those who had to live under it. The managers' institutionally processed and regimented life courses and careers, on the one hand, were developed by having autonomy and individual choice denied, and on the other by taking advantage of imposed structures of education, career training and upward mobility. In the end, however, they generated in the individual a mental reservation towards the power system and those in charge, towards the political culture and state philosophy (Pollack, 1998).

This mental reservation did not usually develop at an early age, during the passage from school to university, or university to work, or at the beginning of their career. Rather, it took shape later, as they grew older and developed greater confidence in their social standing and responsibilities as company managers or production managers, when they had acquired greater competence and professional skills in their workplaces and developed a deeper insight into the mechanisms and failures of an antiquated economy.

The typical professional experience of this generation was paradoxical: they were introduced to leading positions during the 1970s, but then, at a time and age when their qualification and know-how, initiative and creativity should have been at their best – that is, during the 1980s and at the age of about 40 – they found themselves managing a structurally rigid, stagnating economy that was less and less capable of meeting the demands of consumers and industry. And while they were maturing personally and professionally, they continued to be ruled by the institutional life-course regime; personally initiated biographical changes were repeatedly denied; biographical stagnation was required against individual wishes for change; they risked being demoted if they reacted negatively; they would invest their energy in professional projects and, halfway through, find themselves overruled, for reasons unknown or determined by shifts in state policies.

Conformity with, and mental reservation against, the political system formed the tension around these biographies. At the beginning of their careers, the institutional life course seemed acceptable as a prominent formative power in individuals' biographies, but eventually, the managers found that the impositions of the institutional life course were increasingly at odds with their needs. As individuals, they would secretly start to oppose the rule, first by building up a mental reservation, then with more openly expressed disagreement and even protest against imposed biographical changes.

It should be stated here that this mental reservation, which was built up steadily over the course of a life, can be looked upon as the seed, or one of the seeds, of the Velvet Revolution[2]. Analysis of the manager interviews leads to the conclusion that the GDR lost its grounds of legitimacy not so much because of the economic shortages or the growing amorality of the political class, or disillusionment over the state philosophy of equality and the superiority of collectivism, but as a result of the state or party monopoly over the life course. This monopoly, after being successfully implemented for the first 30 years of the GDR with its enormous career opportunities, started losing support with the reduction of opportunities for the cohorts born in the 1960s onwards and the virtual self-recruitment of the elite, not to mention the increasing insight into and contact with the Western world and other Eastern European countries of so-called Goulash Communism (such as Hungary and Poland).

The life-course regime as experienced by the manager generation under study became arbitrary inasmuch as its claims to legitimacy – social progress, equality and the superiority of socialist governance under the leadership of the party – were seen to be invalid. The earlier balance between conformity and misgivings, typical of the generation under study, broke down when the 1960s cohorts, at the age of about 30, realised that their chances of an acceptable standard of living and membership of the elite were in jeopardy, and altogether worthless in comparison to conditions in Western societies.

Following this line of thought, it seems plausible that it was this generation of 1960s-born cohorts that transformed the mental reservation of their elders into open protest, as in the case of the Leipzig demonstrators and the refugees to the embassies of neighbouring Warsaw Pact countries. The thesis that state monopoly over the individual life course was a principal cause of the decline of the GDR hints at an irony of fate. For the life-course regime that was to be the means of restructuring traditional bourgeois-capitalist society and bringing about equality and justice, turned out to be the very source of reservations against those who supported and enacted it, the political class, and these reservations bore the seed of the Velvet Revolution.

It has to be added that this mental reservation was by no means the preserve of those from the former bourgeois environments that survived under socialist conditions. It was as much to be found among managers who came from formerly lower strata of society; that is, those who profited the most from the upgrading of working and farming classes. In other ways, however, social background and family traditions had a significant effect on the different ways of coping with the tensions arising from the institutional life-course regime. This finding is very much in line with the generally accepted view that traditional class structures turned out to be much more persistent over time than the political elite would have liked them to be.

The following section deals with three class-specific strategies for coping with various features of the institutionalised life-course regime of the GDR, strategies in which a prominent role was played by subcultures and family traditions.

Strategies for coping with the institutionalised life-course regime

There were three widely differing strategies for coping with the institutionalised life-course regime, strategies that left room for a sense of autonomy. These are set out a little later in this chapter and discussed more broadly in relation to the overall process of modernisation. They are then followed by some thoughts on the potential of biographical research for macro-theoretical reasoning. Since the focus of attention is on the processual character of these strategies and on the social background from which they emerge, they are classed as modes of identity work (Schütze, 2001, p 6)[3] and defined as the processes of incorporating common orientations, especially moral orientation schemes, into personal identity in such a way that they serve as guidelines to personal behaviour. Individuals, in their multi-layered biographical projects, draw on such common schemes while simultaneously keeping a distance from them, as a means of meeting contradictory demands and negotiating paradoxical situations.

'Discursive' identity work and 'disenchantment'

Families generating this type of strategy characteristically used a double orientation framework, partly motivated and enforced by the authorities, and partly stemming from bourgeois society's past but still functioning and accepted schemes of orientation, such as Christian religion or an educated bourgeois worldview (*Bildungsbürgertum*). In these cases, the family functioned 'backstage'. Imposed decisions in matters of education and vocational development were made explicit, and openly discussed and worked through (Freud, 1969). The family provided compassion and comfort when individual options were thwarted. It was a place where the potential crisis inherent in the experience of being overruled was talked about, and where criticism of the front stage – the rule of the authorities – was allowed.

Parents who provided this kind of background tended to be found, not only in environments and social positions greatly removed from the power system or among those for whom socialist transformation meant social downgrading, but rather among those who had gained from the socialist transformation and belonged to the cadres themselves. In all these families, the mental reservation seemed to be partly inherited from the parents and went hand in hand with a capacity to cope and to deliver the necessary account of loyalty.

In the course of their upward career, managers from this 'discursive' social background sooner or later reached a point of no return in the face of constraints from authority, and their sphere of individual autonomy was unforgivably compromised. This was a disenchanting experience and led to a crisis of political loyalty and detachment from civil commitment. Yet the inner detachment did not interfere with their show of loyalty or affect their career; quite the opposite, in fact. However, although their careers seemed unaffected, managers who had reached disenchantment underwent a mental transformation long before the Velvet Revolution. As they pursued their careers, their performance as cadres remained plainly undisturbed. It is important to understand that the detachment, as well as the events in which it was rooted, were dealt with backstage, where they were recognised as undue interferences in the sphere of personal freedom, in contrast to public rationale. For these managers, the subsequent breakdown of the political system did not cause a personal crisis; it solved more problems than it created. For them disenchantment in the socialist state's philosophy of collectivism, equalisation and central planning had taken place long ago, and when the Velvet Revolution occurred it could be said that they had already done their identity work.

'Confined' identity work and 'insulation'

In marked contrast to discourse and criticism as a frame of orientation and a way of maintaining a sense of autonomy and dealing with the tensions of the life-course regime, is the tendency to deal with those tensions by 'insulating' their wounding effect. This means looking back on one's life and seeing events and episodes *minus* the suffering derived therein. It is as if the individual has undergone a process of blocking off the wounding effects of experiences of denied autonomy and becoming detached from the events that generated them. In this mechanism, the crisis potential is not eliminated by professional success but is seen to belong to other people's lives and experiences.

The Freudian term of screen memory (*Deckerinnerungen*) comes to mind here, and it is this screening that hides the experiences of wounding and suffering from the narrators, although not from the interpreter. In the interpretation, strong mechanisms can be seen at work, serving the function of keeping the memory free from the wounding impact of the institutionalised life-course regime. It is as if the latent meaning structure of events and the mental reservation that derives from it are forcefully kept under control through the mechanisms of normalising, legitimising and de-dramatising. In these cases, identity work is not focused on the experience of denied autonomy itself but on working off these discomforting recognitions until it becomes second nature to ignore their wounding and critical impact and is insulated from them. The resulting absence of crisis leads to a sense of autonomy, of being in control.

It seems that the experience of having a family member or the family tradition (perhaps as merchant or entrepreneur) socially downgraded by the authorities played a crucial role in this type of identity work, and this coping mechanism probably emerged in the earlier generation. The crisis of political loyalty had to be insulated because life must go on and one's own or the children's future must be taken care of. Whenever disconcerting experiences arose, there was recourse to mechanisms of insulating the wounding impact and of neutralising, normalising and de-dramatising the event. In the long run, it is easy to see how the practice of blocking off the crisis potential of the experience of being overruled became ingrained. This is not to say that the managers had an uncritical attitude to the system, but this criticism never reached the point of an overt crisis of loyalty; the mechanism of normalising was constantly at work to keep dissent under control and bolster the necessary show of loyalty.

It is important to understand that the purpose of insulating any disconcerting feelings was to guarantee the individual's favourable public behaviour, favourable to those who had power over the life course, the authorities. Although this was successfully mastered to the extent that those feelings did not interfere with the outward show of political loyalty, the side effect was a trace of mental reservation, and this played an important role when the Velvet Revolution took place. In this situation, everybody – and especially members of the *nomenclatura*, such as the managers – had to face up to questions of loyalty and responsibility. The functioning of the political class and authorities was exposed and easily seen to be lacking. This put the pattern of insulation – normalising and de-dramatising the contradictions within the socio-political system – under the utmost strain, but it continued to serve its purpose by shielding these managers from the discomforting recognition of their share in the state of affairs.

Reviewing their personal involvement in the socio-political system, these managers argued that, since they had always had their doubts and their mental reservations, there was no reason for them to worry about their participation or even share of guilt. The question of guilt was dealt with by placing the blame for failure on the political class; that is, by assuming that the decisions had been made by others, while they themselves were only agents, and that economic inefficiency could be blamed on an unmotivated labour force. Seen from this angle, their personal achievements appeared considerable; they had managed to keep things going in difficult conditions and could be proud of their feats. And since, once the failures of the system came out, there was not much cause for regret, it made sense to stop worrying over the past. This 'full-stop' solution to questions of loyalty and guilt may be read as a context-specific adaptation through the mechanism of insulation. With its help, there seemed little likelihood of a personal breakdown caused by insights into personal responsibilities for an authoritarian regime.

Still, as can be observed from accounts given to us of the years following the Velvet Revolution, the full-stop solution did not manage to still the conscience on questions of loyalty and guilt. These managers did not succeed in making peace with their past. They continued to argue the pros and cons of the GDR and got caught in a mixture of critical and favourable opinions, each critical remark being balanced by a favourable one and vice versa. It is as if the habit of insulation carried on almost undisturbed by the change of times. In the author's opinion, this was generally the case among those who were formerly placed among the operative elite. In less prominent status groups, the mechanisms guaranteeing loyal behaviour were probably less deeply rooted and thus more easily shaken off during the process of transformation.

'Canonical' identity work and 'masking' (Ausblenden)

The third and last mode of coping with the life-course regime was to be found in families with a strong attachment to the state philosophy and the ruling Socialist Unity Party. For these families, the socialist state and party philosophy was the canonical frame of reference; it was the framework for their definitions of situations and overruled any perceived contradictions. This mode of coping was centred round the mechanism of masking social facts and experiences that contradicted the canonical order of things and the brute facts that might arouse doubt. This mechanism of masking contradictions, and explaining the ones that could not be ignored as the personal failure of those who were responsible, was a particularly effective way of maintaining a sense of autonomy and even of superiority. It nurtured habits of thought that inhibited the notion that the outer world constrained and denied personal autonomy. Where these families suffered the irritation of being confronted with a different and 'deviant' world view, such as the Christian tradition, the parents took action to put things right and redefine wrong thoughts and feelings in the light of the socialist tradition. It would appear that family socialisation kept a tight rein over the development of the children's ways of thinking.

By successfully inhibiting thought, the mechanism of masking was very influential in creating loyalty towards the state philosophy and the party that represented and executed it. It also dealt with the crisis potential of the life-course regime in that it helped to inhibit 'wrong' feelings. The family's attachment to the political system brought additional incentives for loyalty and even gratitude. Children of these families were destined to enjoy all the opportunities the system had to offer: higher education, university study abroad (mostly in the Soviet Union), and a cadre career.

However, the fact was that the life-course regime did interfere with individual options, there really were incompatibilities between institutional and individual life-course choices, and neglected yet latently sensed contradictions and discrepancies between the theory and practice of socialism did exist. Again, the result was mental reservation, and the interview texts reveal traces of suppressed crisis experiences – in episodes and remembrances – that can be reconstructed. The mental reservation was compounded by the recognition of ongoing economic shortages, deficiencies of economic policies and, most of all, incompetent, unsatisfactory personnel both among workers and management. Compared to such personnel, and thanks to their canonical orientation, the managers felt superior and in command, and this mentality was not even shaken by the advent of the Velvet Revolution.

In contrast to both the other modes of coping with the life-course regime, the remembered events and experiences were treated in a matter-of-fact way, leaving no room for deliberating and interpreting their meaning and impact on one's life course. They were definitively fixed and the definitive argument lay in their consistency with the canonical knowledge base. The definitions and loyalties erected during the GDR times even resisted the challenge of the Velvet Revolution. The end of the GDR was seen as a punishment for individual inefficiency and deviation from socialist dogma. The former attitude of having 'vision' and knowing better now turned into a powerful shield against any possible thoughts of personal and ideological involvement in its shortcomings.

Contexts of modernisation and globalisation

The phenomenon of mental reservation deriving from the experience of being processed by the institutional life-course regime is by no means exclusive to the social world under study, but can also be observed in Western European nation states in general. This will now be discussed in relation to the current modernisation and globalisation of these societies, followed by a methodological remark on the comparative value of quantitative and qualitative research. In the final section of this chapter, some of the problems of the manager study will be reconsidered and put in perspective for further transformation research.

European and even worldwide developments of modernisation suggest that more and more people are being processed by the rule of law of the nation state and institutions of the welfare state. This is true not only of the 65 million unemployed people in Europe, many groups in social care, and some groups of migrants, but also increasingly the employed and even those in better positions. In one way or another, the life courses of more and more people tend to be processed, and processed both ways (downward as well as upward), as a result of economic trends and profit imperatives, business cycles and cycles of rationalisation, and shifts in political and social affairs, as well as changes in scientific knowledge.

Generalising from case studies, it can be supposed that the increase in experiences of being processed by political and economic institutions will be paralleled by an increase in the phenomenon of mental reservation towards power systems, and will release and promote mental reservation towards the overall modernisation process and its agents – the political and economic systems. It may further be expected that the familiar decline in numbers of voters in state elections is but a statistical translation and expression of the collective biographical experience of institutional processing and the ensuing mental reservation toward the power systems.

Continuing this line of argument and giving it a methodological turn, I maintain that biographical research holds much more potential for macro-sociological diagnosis and even prognosis than it has produced so far. And certainly a comparative perspective, across cultures and societies, is one way of strengthening this potential for theorising. Biographical researchers still tend to keep a distance from macro-sociological reasoning, in ways that are overly modest. They still tend to consider that macro-analysis and diagnoses of our time are the preserve of grand theory and grand statistics, whereas there are sufficient grounds to believe in the potential of in-depth qualitative methods for generalisation (Strauss and Corbin, 1990).

A methodological retrospective

At the beginning of the research project on East German manager biographies, it became obvious that none of the researchers was prepared to deal with the difficulties of cross-cultural comparative research. As West Germans, they lacked – regarding the GDR – what Garfinkel (1972) has described as common sense knowledge of social structures; that is, tacit knowledge of socialist society and why it is so. The manifold prejudices that ruled and still rule West-East and East-West German mutual perceptions made things worse in terms of methodical understanding and interpretation. In research, such prejudices have to be carefully attended to. In retrospect, it seems that the first real phase of data analysis occurred when the research group worked on its lack of feel for the institutional structure of the GDR.

In the very first sessions of data interpretation, something paradoxical happens. Although the researchers may be aware of the fact that they are moving in unfamiliar social and cultural terrain, and because of this very insecurity, they cannot but rely heavily on their accustomed forms of understanding. If they do not attend to this paradox at the start, by explicating the frames and schemes they are relying on, the following will happen: the first generalisations, the first codes, will tend to take the shape of one-dimensional classifications and abstractions. The social phenomena under consideration will tend to be subsumed into accustomed everyday ways of seeing: they will look either black or white, reasonable or unreasonable, repressive or permissive, this *or* that, obeying the logic of binary schemes.

This is the moment when the interpretive researcher becomes suspicious and realises that the interpretation has taken a wrong turn. Instead of reconstructing the unfamiliar according to its own rationale, the researcher has made it his or her own, and thus missed what he or she was expecting to discover, the paradoxical nature of things, the black *and* the white, the interweaving of contradictory elements, the opaque nature of events and experiences, the complex and often seemingly unreasonable patterns of action and interaction at work, which at the same time make life meaningful, liveable, bearable and rewarding.

Not taking care of the intricacies of reconstructing and framing social issues under conditions of cultural *Fremdheit* (a social world that is strange and unfamiliar) may lead to ethnocentric explanations and the reproduction of stereotypes. If, on the other hand, we methodically and meticulously control the operation of interpretation while studying otherness, we will reach a deeper understanding while also broadening our perspectives of our own society and ourselves.

A closer inspection of this process of methodical reflection reveals that, in order to understand the observed life world, one cannot but rely on one's everyday understanding, on the frames and codes of one's own culture – this is always the basis for interpretation. Since we can only generate our theories on these grounds, we are obliged to permanently double-check the views, cultural codes and language patterns we are dealing with, that is, cultural frames and schemes such as the conception of the 'normal biography', life-course scripts and regimes, patterns of participation, the possibilities and risks of institutionalised opportunities, patterns of biographical development and change, and so on.

As Goffman (1977) puts it, frames organise our experience and thus allow us to feel in control and see the world as calculable. In studying foreign cultures, all this gets lost and the researchers experience a loss of trust in their schemes and codes. When doing research on unfamiliar life worlds *within* their own society, they rarely feel as if they are losing trust in their capacity to understand and validate their findings. Should one of the tentative interpretations of a text fail, they always have others in stock to turn to. However, in transformation (and probably migration) studies, they may not have such alternatives – there is a cultural gap between two cultures. The gap is not altogether different from the challenge of interpreting a different life world within their own society, but it is deeper and thus demands more with regard to methodical strategies of controlling each and every step in the interpretation process (Oevermann, 2001).

In my view, this requirement to double-check the findings, insights, results and generalisations while developing them in the process of interpretation, epitomises the difference between the analysis of unfamiliar societies and analysis of one's own society. Formulated as a rule of interpretation, it might be called the rule of 'heightened suspension of belief' in the sense of heightened doubt in one's formulations[4]. This suspension of belief in the researcher's reasoning compensates for the lack of common-sense knowledge of social structures that would otherwise steer them through situations of interpretive doubt. It takes shape by making explicit the schemes and notions that govern the researcher's understanding. Only when these are made explicit can they themselves become an object of scrutiny and criticism, and be monitored, therefore, for adequacy in the case under study. In this interpretive process, as with every good professional practice, the professional as much as the studied individual is 'the case'. It is this very interrelatedness that epitomises the difference between interpretive and quantitative analysis.

Understanding otherness: heuristic concepts

It is essential in transformation research to set out from the beginning the heuristic concepts that direct the process of theory building. The following dimensions are suggested as heuristic concepts for interpreting data and checking the process of understanding otherness. They could be seen as aspects of the formative power of the given. The list embraces three fundamental conditions of individual life:

- the embeddedness in the social world of a nation state in the sense of a universe of discourse (Strauss, 1978);
- the logic of material production and reproduction in the sense of a sphere of economic and vocational necessities (Kohli, 1994);
- the legacy and latitude of individuation according to generation, environment, race and gender; that is, according to ascribed roles that shape the habits of the heart and scripts of life (Mannheim, 1980).

The universe of discourse

The life-course regime of a society and the structuring of status passages: the ways in which the basic socio-political values of the state (for example, freedom and equality in Western capitalist societies, equality in the former socialist countries) are institutionally shaped, bureaucratically instrumentalised, and biographically processed. In this view, the constitutional values of a power system play a dominant role in structuring social life. Such values are not treated as negligible because of their universal symbolism, but as materialising in institutional practice, above all in relation to status passages. They inhabit and predetermine the individual's identity formation and biographical achievements. This symbolic horizon gives an overall orientation, via the institutionalised life-course regime, to individual actions and endeavours.

The political culture and interrelations between public and private spheres: the image people have of the power system, authorities and administration, which influences coping strategies and ways of handling personal affairs, and hints at commitment and resentment towards civil affairs.

The semantic structure of the culture: historically inherited cultural codes that form the collective identity, such as religious ideas, concepts of a good life and of a humane and civil society, the concept of temporality, that is, the sequence of existence as linear or cyclic. Together, these codes are suggestive of 'awareness' in the society under study of the crisis potential of social change, and they serve as a normative point of reference.

The sphere of economic necessity

Economic reasoning: among the major issues structuring societies as a whole and the individual life course in particular are the acknowledged ways of securing reproduction in the present and in the future. They are usually represented in mighty concepts such as social market economy and achievement society, and embrace not only the outlines of the economic relations between capital and labour but at the same time the socio-political preconditions of the economic sphere, such as opportunity structures, chances of participation, and solutions to the question of distribution.

Work traditions: the division of labour among social groups such as ethnic groups, gender-specific groups and nationalities is a powerful means of balancing individual expectations with the society's distribution of rewards. There are routine ways of recruiting personnel on the basis of ascribed membership roles that delineate in advance individuals' aspirations, their political party and trade-union orientation, their vocational and professional inclinations.

Vocational and professional cultures: Vocational and professional cultures might seem to be loosening their grip on the individual because modern life demands several changes of workplace, work project and professional skills. Yet, the study of modern biographies and identity work shows that vocational and professional training and education are still formative in processes of individuation. Even where the life course seems discontinuous, vocational and professional cultures shape the common-sense knowledge of social structures. They orient the individual's search for identity, and serve as a frame of reference in situations of insecurity. The 'architecture' of vocational and professional career ladders (or their absence) and the typical paradoxes and patterns of failure and achievement continue to have an impact on individual lives.

Life scripts

Social background: it is maintained here that the social background not only implies a position in the social structure but acts as the interpreter or mediator of the institutional life-course regime, thus forming the habits of the heart, the perspective on self and society. In the interpretive line of thought, differences of environment can be described as interpreting the relationship between self and society with regard to the individual's room to manoeuvre their own affairs. Social background is not so centred round status, but seen as an agent of individuation that is connected with a particular social stratum, more loosely though than when seen from a macro-sociological angle.

Generational agendas: the notion of generation may also be reconsidered from a micro-sociological perspective, and not be seen as the binding force of collectively shared, epoch-making events. Rather, it is almost the reverse: it seems preferable to define a generation by the collectively shared everyday experience of institutional practices and public affairs. It is only in relation to these routines of defining situations, of framing experience, of tacitly knowing what is and what is not, that the researcher can reconstruct the formative character of great historical events, such as the Prague Spring (1968), the students' revolts, the Velvet Revolution of 1989, Chernobyl, and the changes of practice they may bring about.

Personal fate: this points to tensions deriving from objective determinants in the sense of ascribed roles such as membership of a gender or race group with associated patterns of behaviour. The concept also evokes circumstances immediately influencing the individual because they are the child of a certain time and space, and have had the respective unavoidable collective experiences of migration, transformation, colonisation, revolution, genocide, and so on.

Conclusion

In interpretive research, these issues need to be double-checked on the basis of theoretical sources. Especially when doing transformation research, all issues need to be followed up both from the point of view of the interview interpretation and from the point of view of the theoretical knowledge base. The latter is needed in order to be able to review empirically observed practices with their difficulties and patterns of orientation, as ways of making sense of and enacting general social structures.

In fact, the lack of a common-sense knowledge of social structures, which at first sight seems to be a disadvantage in transformation research, may finally turn out to be an advantage, because the process of understanding otherness encourages us to become aware of our own frames of reference.

Notes

[1] The project was funded by the German Research Association (1998-2000). The research team consisted of two West German sociologists and one from Hungary who had been living in East Germany since 1988. Data collection and analysis followed the method of open narrative interviewing.

[2] The coming down of the Berlin Wall in November 1989 was called the Velvet Revolution because of the unexpectedly peaceful course of things when the mass of East German people that had gathered in front of the Wall near the famous Checkpoint Charlie suddenly crossed the borderline and set foot on West Berlin ground without being held back by East German military and police forces.

[3] The description of identity work given here leans heavily on Schütze (2001) while adapting the concept to the study of managers.

[4] A 'heightened suspension of belief' implies an attitude of systematic doubt about the validity of one's own ways of looking at the world when dealing with another society. The expression is borrowed from literary studies and derives from the notion of 'the willing suspension of disbelief' in the fictitious world of a novel or a play.

References

Engler, W. (1992) *Die zivilisatorische Lücke; Versuche über den Staatssozialismus*, Frankfurt-am-Main: Suhrkamp.

Engler, W. (1996) '"Kommode Diktatur" oder "Totalitäres System"? Die DDR im Kreuzverhör der Enquete-Kommission', *Soziologische Revue*, vol 19, no 4, pp 443-9.

Fehér, F. and Heller, A. (1979) *Diktatur über die Bedürfnisse: Sozialistische Kritik osteuropäischer Gesellschaftsformationen*, Hamburg: VSA-Verlag.

Freud, S. (1969) 'Erinnern, Wiederholen und Durcharbeiten', *Gesammelte Werke*, vol 10, pp 127-36.

Frommer, J. (2000) 'Psychoanalytische und soziologische Aspekte personalen Identitätswandels im vereinten Deutschland', *Zeitschrift für qualitative Bildungs, Beratungs- und Sozialforschung* (ZBBS), vol 1, no 2, pp 365-83.

Garfinkel, H. (1972) 'Common sense knowledge of social structures: the documentary method of interpretation', in J.G. Manis and B. Meltzer (eds) *Symbolic interaction: A reader in social psychology*, Boston, MA: Allyn and Bacon, pp 356-78.

Goffman, E. (1977) *Rahmen-Analyse: Ein Versuch über die Organisation von Alltagserfahrungen*, Frankfurt-am-Main: Suhrkamp.

Hanke, I. (1995) 'Sozialstruktur und Gesellschaftspolitik im SED-Staat und ihre geistig-seelischen Folgen', in Deutscher Bundestag (12. Wahlperiode) (ed) *Materialien der Enquete-Kommission "Aufarbeitung der Geschichte und Folgen der SED-Diktatur in Deutschland"* (Band III/2), Frankfurt-am-Main: Suhrkamp, pp 1180-213.

Kohli, M. (1985) 'Die Institutionalisierung des Lebenslaufs', *Kölner Zeitschrift fuer Soziologie und Sozialpsychologie*, vol 37, no 1, pp 1-29.

Kohli, M. (1988) 'Normalbiographie und Individualität: Zur institutionellen Dynamik des gegenwärtigen Lebenslaufregimes', in H.-G. Brose and B. Hildenbrand (eds) *Vom Ende des Indididuums zur Individualität ohne Ende*, Opladen: Leske+Budrich, pp 33-53.

Kohli, M. (1994) 'Die DDR als Arbeitsgesellschaft? Arbeit, Lebenslauf und soziale Differenzierung', in H. Kaelble, H.F. Kocka and H. Zwahr, *Sozialgeschichte der DDR*, Stuttgart: Klett-Cotta, pp 31-61.

Mannheim, K. (1980) 'Strukturen des Denkens', in D. Kettler, V. Meja and N. Stehr (eds) *Strukturen des Denkens*, Frankfurt-am-Main: Suhrkamp.

Oevermann, U. (2001) 'Das Verstehen des Fremden als Scheideweg hermeneutischer Methoden in den Erfahrungswissenschaften', *ZBBS*, vol 2, no 1, pp 67-92.

Pollack, D. (1990) 'Das Ende einer Organisationsgesellschaft – systemtheoretische Überlegungen zum gesellschaftlichen Umbruch in der DDR', *Zeitschrift für Soziologie*, vol 19, no 4, pp 292-307.

Pollack, D. (1998) 'Die konstitutive Widersprüchlichkeit der DDR. Oder: War die DDR-Gesellschaft homogen?', *Geschichte und Gesellschaft,* vol 24, no 1, pp 111-31.

Schütze, F. (2001) 'Zur trinationalen Zusammenarbeit zwischen den Universitäten Lodz, Wales/Bangor und Magdeburg im Bereich der Mikrosoziologie und der Kulturstudien', Magdeburg, unpublished manuscript.

Strauss, A. (1978) 'A social world perspective', in N.K. Denzin (ed) *Studies in symbolic interaction: An annual compilation of research* (vol 1), Greenwich, CT: Jai Press, pp 119-28.

Strauss, A. and Corbin, J. (1990) *Basics of qualitative research: Grounded theory procedures and techniques*, Newbury Park, CA: Sage Publications.

Part Three:
Self-awareness in research and practice

TEN

Biographical reflections on the problem of changing violent men

David Gadd

After a lengthy period of neglect within criminology, the study of men's violence towards female partners gained a high profile during the 1980s as a consequence of feminist activism and feminist research with victims and survivors. Attention was drawn to the pervasive and extensive nature of violence against women, the greater danger posed by men that women know (as opposed to male strangers), the continuous relationship between physical and sexual assaults and emotional abuse, and the criminal, sometimes fatal, consequences of this abuse (Dobash and Dobash, 1980; Kelly, 1988; Hester et al, 1995). Yet, it was not until the mid- to late 1990s that the British government undertook to develop a coordinated response to the problem of 'domestic violence' (Home Office, 2000).

The model of intervention that followed was heavily inspired by experimental work undertaken in the US, notably by Ellen Pence and her collaborators in Duluth, Minnesota (Pence and Paymar, 1993). However, the extent to which North American ideas and practices were imported unmodified into the UK is easily overstated (Newburn, 2002). Many British practitioners have been sceptical of the value of 'one-size-fits-all' provision (Bell, 2000). In fact, the National Practitioners' Network (now RESPECT) has, in recent years, looked more explicitly at Scandinavia and Australia for examples of 'good practice' than it has towards the US. Similarly, proposals to introduce pro-arrest styles of policing have been received less favourably in the UK than in the US by women's groups, victim support organisations and the police themselves (Goodall and MacKay, 1998). Indeed, whatever the policy documents say, many British practitioners have been keen to infuse New Labour's preoccupation with evidence-led practice with a fair dose of the social work values they picked up when they entered the field (Vanstone, 2000; Robinson, 2002).

The establishment of the UK's first Women's Unit in 1998 no doubt aided women's activists who had been organising local support for tackling the problem of violence against women – notably from the police, local councils and social services – since the early 1980s (Hague and Malos, 1995). Many towns and cities gained their own 'domestic violence forums', where representatives from Women's Aid worked hard to coordinate the efforts of social workers, lawyers, housing officers, police officers and probation officers in order to enhance the safety of women and children. To this day, services remain desperately under-funded in this field. However, by the end of the 1990s, many domestic violence forums were successfully attracting grants from the National Lottery, industry, private trusts, and the various community safety and crime prevention budgets the Home Office distributes.

The imperatives of the government's evidence-led practice agenda, together with the high profile of agencies whose primary mandate involved working with offenders, increasingly meant that the issue of women's safety became coupled with the question of how to change violent men (Mullender, 1996). Early signs of success in Duluth, and subsequent evidence of change among men who attended two Scottish projects that mimicked the US exemplar (Dobash et al, 1996), helped foster the growth of specifically pro-feminist cognitive-behavioural programmes for perpetrators of domestic violence in both probation services and the voluntary sector (Scourfield, 1998; Scourfield and Dobash, 2000). Confident of the effectiveness of these programmes, in 1999 the Home Office singled out two cognitive-behavioural probation programmes for perpetrators for Pathfinder status (Hamill et al, 1997). These 'accredited programmes' will be used by the Home Office as exemplars to inform best practice within the English and Welsh Probation Services.

Many feminist scholars, women's activists and practitioners alike remain (appropriately) sceptical regarding the feasibility of the task being undertaken here. The research data suggest that these cognitive-behavioural interventions have only proved effective for a small minority of men (Browne and Herbert, 1997; Mullender, 2000). While there are no hard and fast rules that enable practitioners to predict which men will benefit most from particular interventions, there is some evidence to suggest that certain groups of men are more likely to 'change' than others (Dobash et al, 1999; Morran, 1999; Morran and Wilson, 1999). Those whose change can be most readily demonstrated in evaluation studies are those who are typically:

- the most motivated to stop being violent before they receive 'treatment';
- unhindered by serious addiction and mental health problems;
- not from minority groups;
- literate, and more accustomed to doing 'homework assignments'.

Those working with men have used these findings to raise concerns about the cultural specificity of the interventions on offer and the state's (unduly punitive) responses to those currently deemed 'untreatable' (Browne and Herbert, 1997). Conversely, those specifically concerned with supporting women have tended to be more worried about the unintended consequences for women and children of erroneously raising expectations about the possibility of change (Burton et al, 1998; Lee, 1998). Many men, perhaps the majority of those who are clients on these programmes, use their attendance abusively (and before this, the delay imposed by waiting lists), encouraging their partners to endure further violence under the promise that change will eventually come. Some violent men learn to use programme techniques (particularly taking 'time-outs') to control partners without breaking the law. Others avoid prosecution and punishment altogether by convincing their partners that their behaviour is changing very gradually. Unfortunately, the vast majority of men registered for anti-violence programmes – including those exposed to the best examples of practice in this field – fail to complete their courses (Burton et al, 1998; Bell, 2001). Moreover, many of those men who are coerced into attending group work programmes by criminal justice agencies become more resistant to change as the 'help' they are offered is conflated with 'punishment' and/or 'thought manipulation' (Fox, 1999).

Of course, many abused women neither want nor expect their partners to undergo any radical transformation, only for the violence to stop (Hoyle, 1998). Given this, it is tempting to conceptualise most violent men's failure to change as incontrovertible evidence of men's vested interest in women's subordination. In his book, *The violences of men*, Jeff Hearn (1998, p viii) seems to make this assumption:

> Men remain violent to women through social power and control ... combined with physical size and strength, reinforced by social power and control that reduces intervention against them.

Hearn observes that men's talk about violence, whether to friends, researchers or practitioners, is laden with effective repudiations, justifications and excuses. Conversely, others, like James Messerschmidt (1993, 2000), have argued that men are only violent towards women when their access to other legitimate resources for 'accomplishing masculinity' is severely constricted. From Messerschmidt's perspective, white, middle-class, educated men are less likely to be violent to partners than poor, black and working-class men, because they are more able to 'prove' their manliness in non-criminal ways, for example, by engaging in intellectual argument or through the accumulation and display of material goods.

Messerschmidt's work sits at the other end of the interpretive spectrum to Hearn's when it comes to making sense of the link between what people say and how they behave. Whereas Hearn reduces all men's talk to discursive 'techniques of neutralisation' (Groombridge, 1999), Messerschmidt assumes that people say just what they mean, *telling it like it is*. This is a position that I have taken issue with elsewhere (Gadd, 2000a). However, to summarise, my view is that the tensions between Messerschmidt's and Hearn's perspectives beg the question of how to theorise a masculine *subject* that is neither entirely transparent nor the faithful reproducer of social discourses. Furthermore, these tensions also open up the empirical question of how non-violent men accomplish their 'masculinities', a question that is all the more pertinent when asked of those men who claim to be able to help violent men find non-violent alternatives. As Collier (1998, p 173) puts it, are we asking those men who attend criminal justice interventions to become like their *re-educators:* to reproduce 'normal men', exhibiting 'normal masculinities'?

Defended psychosocial subjects

It was with these questions in mind that I became interested in the theoretical and methodological ideas put forward by Jefferson and Hollway (Hollway, 1989, 1996; Jefferson, 1994; Hollway and Jefferson, 1998), ideas that I had developed during my doctoral research project into the life histories of 'men who are violent and want to change' and 'men who work with violent men to help them change' (Gadd, 2000b). Hollway and Jefferson (1998) argue that those aspects of social life that we routinely attribute to 'gender' are better conceptualised as the product of individuals' biographically driven investments in power-conferring positions in a multiplicity of discourses. Drawing on the work of Melanie Klein[1], Hollway and Jefferson argue that anxiety is fundamental to the human condition and has to be constantly defended against. This psychic defending can be done by taking up 'safe' positions in social discourses – laden as they are with ethnic, classed and gendered assumptions – as well as through splitting and projecting vulnerabilities onto others.

Furthermore, Hollway and Jefferson (1998, 1999, 2000) argue that the assumption of a 'defended' subject demands a methodological approach premised on the fact that researchers can never get complete and unfettered access to 'the truth' of interviewees' experiences, an approach sensitive to the slips of the tongue, absences, avoidances and contradictions in interviewees' narratives. Those using the 'Free Association Narrative Interview Method', Hollway and Jefferson advocate, must assume that interviewees cannot explain their actions fully. Hence, the interviewer's job is to probe absences and avoidances in the narrative account, to glean a clearer sense of where the interviewee's defences lie. The interviewer-cum-analyst then seeks to move beyond these defences by working through different interpretations of what was said, not said, gestured and inferred at the analysis stage of the research.

Four years ago, I decided to use this method to interview eight men who had been violent to their female partners and seven men and two women who were working for a voluntary sector project aimed at tackling men's violence to women and children. In the remainder of this chapter, I focus on the story told to me by one of the male practitioners in my sample[2]: a man I have renamed 'Jack'.

Introducing Jack

Jack, white, aged 47, was a man of small build, who was studying for a doctorate in humanities. He was a single parent with two sons, and a theatre worker for a project campaigning to make men take responsibility for their violence. Jack was a man who prided himself on his community activism, both with regard to raising awareness about domestic violence, and in terms of tackling bullying in schools. Methodologically, my interviews with Jack were unusual because Jack appeared more 'defended' in his second interview than his first. At the time of our first interview, Jack was very upset and tired, having stayed up most of the previous night because his wife (who lived overseas) had been arrested for assaulting his eldest son (Ian). During this first interview, Jack seemed very vulnerable and upset, this emotional state perhaps causing him to say things he may have otherwise been more guarded about. By the time of our second interview, Ian was living with Jack, and Jack himself seemed much less anxious, and slightly more guarded.

Jack's background

Given the 'last rites' five times during his first week of life, Jack's Catholic parents figured that he was 'saved to do something' and hence had him 'groomed' as a priest. Jack told me he was never quite sure what exactly this 'something' was, except he knew it involved "a reflex to deny oneself": a feeling that putting oneself first was 'self-indulgent' and a 'terrible thing to do'.

Jack said he "deeply" respected his father for his community activism in the trade union and the church, for his 20-year commitment to an "appallingly inhuman" production-line job that kept the family out of poverty, and because, unlike other men of his time, he did not engage in domestic violence. However, Jack also said he had "very ambiguous feelings" towards his dad and never "felt a terribly deep connection with" him.

> I had friends ... whose fathers drank, and gambled and beat their wives....
> Domestic violence then.... It just happened.... It was part of the culture.
> And my father didn't err do these things except that he, I think, neglected
> my mother really, and therefore, you know, left the burden on her. So there
> is this sense of ... a very distant, erm, kind of authoritarian figure who, who
> was brought in at the last minute, who was the final threat, the final court.
> And [coughs] dad was always very against being frivolous. Or there was
> always this sense that, "Well that's all very well if you want to be a footballer
> or an actor...". [But] You had to get on and earn a living.... The boys ...
> were expected to get on educationally.

When I followed these 'ambiguous feelings' up in my second interview, Jack reported being "totally crushed" when his father had dismissed his footballing aspirations. Jack also recounted his "vivid memories" of the times when his dad "beat the living daylights" out of his older brother for playing Bob Dylan's album 'God On Our Side'. But Jack continued to structure most of his childhood recollections around his father's neglect of his mother. Jack could remember a family holiday during which his father unexpectedly left his pregnant mother to care for their eight children so that he could attend a trades union meeting. Jack's mother "never knew" how much her husband earned: "She would have to manage. And if she didn't manage would be told off". Jack claimed that his father was able to "stay free" of chastising the children because he "left the burden" on his wife. In fact, Jack's sister had observed that their mother singled Jack out for more physical chastisement than the other children, in spite of the fact that Jack was "the one who would try and help mum".

Jack now felt that his "mum was a product of her time", explaining

> it must have been impossible for her to say to anyone, "I'm being neglected or … psychologically abused". Because what she would get back is, "Ah but he's a good man…. You're so lucky".

Until recently, though, Jack had wondered if his mum singled him out for physical chastisement because of the "grief" he, like his father, caused; whether he was, like dad, "this creature who caused them a lot of hassle".

Despite his reservations about the church, Jack had always been "attracted" by the "theatricality" of the pulpit – not least because it offered a "safe space" in which he could say what he "thought before anybody could contradict". It was not until his early teens that Jack

> began to … feel a pull towards … ideas which were at odds with … a very oppressive world…. I started to look at the priests, and looking at my brother's back and the price people were paying at school for saying … 'Who says God exists?'.

Inspired by a teacher who was "fierce" but "cared passionately" about ensuring that children had access to literature and poetry, Jack began investing his energies in the school's drama productions instead. However, disheartened when the teacher suddenly left and teased by his peers, Jack eventually gave up on acting too. He told me:

> I'm frightened of physical confrontation. Always have been…. As a boy I was bullied a lot …. 'Cos I'm little…. And I was a nance … a poof … because I was. I liked acting, I was fair-haired…. I was top of the class all the time in the secondary school…. It's why I'm very protective of my sons. Very protective of anyone who has been hurt really…. My basic fix is that I never fitted with this concept of whatever a man is. I couldn't even hack it because I couldn't even look like it…. And the armoury I developed was verbal…. I used to have to construct this protective barrier through people who were bigger than me, who protected me because they liked me being funny. And actually I survived secondary school by these big lads who thought I was fun … who literally and physically would act as my minders … if I was threatened. So I've always been, erm, unable to relate to this macho, you know, this violence, this fighting and yet [long pause, sigh] was faced with it and forced to collude in it…. When I look back, you know, it was like, unbearable to think of the kind of things one was saying and thinking ….

Aged 15, Jack also became active in a small socialist collective led by a teacher (a man he now thinks of as a "fundamentalist", a "robotic Marxoid") who would read Lenin's *What is to be done?*, and offered Jack the job of "tsar for education". Jack's political interests persisted throughout his university years. Jack's father paid for Jack to study English Literature, hoping Jack would become a teacher; an investment he was not prepared to make in his daughter.

Having completed his university education, Jack took up work with a leftist theatre group, where he learnt how to design his own "theatre of the oppressed", making:

> theatre accessible to working class, and gay or black or whatever community were in struggle and campaigning ... to mobilise people ... to understand the world in order to ... to free ourselves to act, to change it.

It was this work that inspired the projects Jack later developed in relation to bullying and domestic violence.

Jack's intimate relationships with women and children

Although he described himself as a "pathological talker", Jack claimed he always "froze" when trying to chat women up. He depicted himself as lacking in confidence when it came to initiating romantic relationships with women. He met Jane, a feminist activist, through his theatre work after he had left university. Jane subsequently became the mother of his first child. However, Jack and Jane's relationship ran into trouble before the child was conceived. Jack explained:

> When we had this child Jane decided that, and already was, I part knew, but that she was a lesbian and that she was going to become woman-identified. And this house had to be a 'women-only' house. And I had to go. And I said, "Okay. That's the politics at the time. And we can share him. And that's groovy. 'Cos ... these are the moments we're living in".... So I did go. We shared Ian, although I had the main care of him ... I think a great deal of the impulse of what was going on [for me] was a ... sort of historical guilt that one had to redeem this thing.... Everything that happened could be interpreted as fitting the oppressive, oppressor/oppressed jigsaw.... Behind that personal interpretation lay a history that was appalling ... in which women.... Things had to change. There is no doubt about that. And men were and continue to be [sighs], erm.... It was like, on the one hand there was all this politics which was right and one had to struggle and change and men had to change. And on the other hand, there was this specific relationship in which those things ... were damaging decisions that would have been made differently ... if one hadn't been trying to be so fucking 'right on' basically!

Several years later, Jack married another woman (Julie) with whom he had his second son. Jack believed that Jane and Julie were not entirely dissimilar.

> [They] aren't exactly similar. It's very unfair ... pointless saying that. But they have similarities in the sense that they were both very angry and ... needy kinds of people ... with a lot of problems ... because of their childhood and stuff.

Both women were violent to their sons – something that Jack found "unbearable". Both women were (according to Jack) "deeply unhappy people", "intelligent", politically active and thus "interesting", "charming", but "low in self-esteem". Both women had experienced men's sexual violence prior to meeting Jack. In both relationships, Jack felt he carried more than his share of the emotional and material responsibilities associated with childcare.

Jack told me that when Julie and he separated it "affected him deeply", not only because "of the way that Julie was suffering from depression" but also because *he* "didn't want to end up with another child whose parents had split up". Through the therapy Jack pursued at this time, he came to identify that he had a tendency to think

> that one had to do everything ... to look after everyone ... a, 'Men must do this to compensate'.... I think it's the flip side of the, if you like, uncaring male.... I think, erm, my, you know, a basic impulse with me is a fear that things will get out of.... There will be chaos.

Jack regretted that his adoption of this "rescuer position" had made it very difficult for his partners to find out what his "needs" were, but he argued that it had helped him develop a very close relationship with his sons. Thus, Jack had been able to support his youngest son, Terry, when he was bullied at school and when his mother left. Jack told Terry:

> No matter what happens, I'll support you.... My first instinct will be to get behind you. No matter what.... I think Terry knows that and I think I've encouraged him very strongly to express his feelings, his anger and his feelings about what happened with Julie.... I wish it had been said to me more.... If he feels genuinely hurt he keeps with that hurt until he feels that it's been resolved.... I want him to grow and ... be a man who can express his feelings without needing ... to use violence.

This is not to say Jack saw himself as exceptional, although he probably had done in the past, as his closing statement from our first interview suggests.

> Doing all this work around men's violence, it just strikes me, you know, in looking at oneself, is that the temptation is to see oneself as some kind of exception.... And I just ... I suppose I would want to feel I didn't fit

whatever being a man was ... size-wise and a lot of other ways. And I just think that is true of so many men. And the great tragedy is that is true.... The redeemable feature of all this is that we're all victims ... of a social structure and context that needs challenging.

During our second interview, Jack disclosed that Julie had written to him asking if they could give their marriage another try. Jack had turned her down, telling her that he could not "risk it" for his sons "that she might go again".

Analysis

Given the synonymy Hearn (1998) and Messerschmidt (1993) attribute to violence and maleness/masculinity, their theories offer very little that might help us make sense of the lives of men like Jack – men who 'shrink' from violence and have made challenging 'oppression' their life projects. Indeed, if anything, Jack's story should caution us against all theories that assume that 'the social' or 'cultural values' (whether macho, sexist or otherwise) are unproblematically reproduced from one generation to the next. Jack was both like and unlike his well-respected, authoritarian, providing father. He was equally like and unlike his industrious, self-sacrificing, but sometimes volatile mother. If Jack was reproducing a 'discourse of violence', then it was one that assumed "women to be victims of oppression" and that "there are no excuses for violence" towards them. Jack accomplished his masculinity by asserting his difference from the violent and authoritarian men he knew as a child.

In line with Hollway and Jefferson's (2000) thesis, there was evidence that Jack tended to fluctuate between what Kleinians call 'paranoid-schizoid' and 'depressive positions'. Indeed, one might have expected such fluctuation from Jack given that the time of our first interview was one of such high anxiety for him. Although Jack was able to recognise good and bad in his partners and his parents, he was prone to splitting the world up into victims and oppressors. While his abusive mother was a 'product of her time', his father was afforded no such excuses. In Jack's relationships with adult women, he positioned himself as a 'rescuer': a position that required him to put his 'needs to the backburner' in order to 'save' those who were victims of oppression. One of the problems this created was that Jack's partners 'never knew' what his needs were – possibly leading them to feel they were not needed, undesired. As a single parent, Jack endeavoured to 'get right behind' his sons, positioning himself as a positively involved father, unlike his own father, a man who, like many, left 'the burden' on his wife. This investment legitimated Jack's, perhaps defensive, unwillingness to risk getting back with a woman who had once left him for another man, in spite of all the material and emotional support he felt he had offered her.

However, at other points in our interviews, Jack was less willing to resort to these kinds of dichotomies. During our interviews, as in everyday life, Jack was re-'narrativising' his account; reworking it, reinterpreting his explanations when they did not quite capture the complexity of his experiences. Jack's reluctance to complete his sentences about what men and women were 'like' might suggest a move away from paranoid-schizoid thinking. 'Control' was probably the missing word at the end of his sentence, "my basic impulse is a fear that things will get out of …", signalling that Jack had begun to recognise that his "doing everything to look after everyone" was not just about being 'selfless', but also his own fear of chaos and desire for order. Similarly, Jack's 'desire to understand the world' seemed to be related to his capacity to empathise with others; empathy that undermined his tendency to resort to an oppressor/oppressed interpretation of gender relations.

It is this shifting of subjectivity that makes the concepts 'masculinity, masculinities, femininity, femininities' seem all too static to capture the gendered contours of individual men and women's lives. This is why Jack's story fits better with what critical autobiographies and ethnographies – like David Jackson's (1990) *Unmasking masculinity* and Paul Willis' (1977) *Learning to labour* – have told us about men's experiences, than some of the more discursive and narrowly cognitive analyses of men's talk. What these ethnographies and autobiographies reveal is that it is humour and banter that typically enable boys – especially articulate ones – to deny feelings of vulnerability by projecting weakness onto stigmatised others. As a child, Jack's fear of being labelled a 'nance' probably motivated his complicity with the 'hard nuts', while his sense of having failed the church and disappointed his father may well have underscored his admiration for those exhibiting alternatives to traditional masculinity: his rebellious brother, his 'fierce but caring' drama teacher, socialist visionaries, his industrious mother and perceptive sister. Similarly, Jack's 'reflex to deny' himself resonates with Catholic notions about human sinfulness, socialist and pro-feminist commitments to equality, many anti-sexist men's feelings of guilt and contempt for other men, as well as more traditionally masculine notions of the protecting and providing family man (Lupton and Barclay, 1997; Seidler, 1997).

Conclusion

In sum, by theorising a psychosocial biography, it is easy to see how Jack's lifelong feeling that to put oneself first was a "terrible thing to do", his dread of chaos, and his fear of being this hassle-causing "creature" were rendered meaningful and manageable through his investments in totalising world views. These investments were manifested in practice that sought to mobilise the "oppressed" to "understand the world in order to change it", as well as his parenting. The key advantage of the psychosocial approach advocated by Hollway and Jefferson is that it enables one to perceive a motivated subject and hence agency in the context of a shifting subjectivity.

How exactly the social and psychic are sutured within this approach is not entirely clear. For example, why did Jack's identification with "anyone who is hurt" get conflated with an idea of women and children as "victims" and "men" as oppressors? Hollway and Jefferson's approach encounters a 'chicken and egg'-style problem here. Did anxiety, born out of the contradictions Jack experienced between his own sense of justice and his experience of male privilege, first motivate his investment in anti-oppressive styles of masculinity? Or was Jack already an anxious child – someone who always felt slightly unrecognised and misunderstood, who sought to explain his psychic unease in terms of those particular social contradictions with which he was routinely confronted?

My speculation is that Jack's experiences of feeling emotionally "crushed" by his father, of being bullied by his peers, and intimidated by the church, were all implicated in both his capacity to recognise vulnerability in others and his tendency to disown his vulnerabilities, as many men do, by positioning himself as a rescuer/protector. Indeed, I would suggest that this is a more common feature of 'masculinity' among men of Jack's class and educational background than most analyses of men's lives commonly concede. The implication of this at the level of practice is that the question of changing violent men is infinitely more complicated than the 'what works?' agenda allows for. Men are constantly changing, but this change is inextricably rooted in individuals' biographically mediated subjectivities. When academics talk of the performance of 'masculinities', they are actually referring to the manifestation of psychosocial dynamics that are resistant to rational reconstruction (for example, through cognitive-style re-education programmes) precisely because they are so biographically embedded.

This is not to say that individual men cannot change. Only that the majority of men subject to criminal justice interventions will find it nearly impossible to adopt the anti-oppressive masculinities sometimes assumed by men like their social workers, counsellors and group facilitators. Indeed, these may not be the most desirable options for male ex-offenders to pursue anyway. Were they adept sociologists, those disproportionately disadvantaged men who are more routinely the subjects of criminal justice interventions might well ask of Jack to what extent he achieved his intellectual position of *difference* by accumulating the 'cultural capital' offered to him by his family, the church and higher education institutes (Bourdieu, 1984; Hall, 2002) – capital that was less readily passed on to his sister. To what extent was Jack's assumed anti-oppressiveness the product of his authority to depict, as opposed to his capacity to empathise with, the experiences of those (men and women) who were not like him? We ignore this structural argument at our peril. But to my mind, the *detail* of Jack's case suggests that our explanations need to keep in view both the powerful social determinants that mould individual life trajectories *and* the psychic contingencies that render these lives full of choices (see also Bion, 1988). Given these tensions between the social and the psychic, it is relatively futile to pursue analyses that decontextualise 'attitudes' from the web of complex narratives that comprise individual men's understandings of their own lives. As Jefferson (1994, p 29) puts it:

> Without ... sensitivity to the difficulties of uniting social and psychic processes – often pulling in different directions – it is not possible to theorise masculinity in a way that men will recognise.

Nowhere is this clearer than in the field of men's violence, where academic attention to the issue is often evoked superficially to fuel the demonisation of a small group of unknown dangerous men – most glaringly in the light of the recent media coverage of sex crimes against children (Evans, 2003). The critique of masculinity falls on deaf ears when 'ordinary blokes', practitioners and academic commentators alike can safely reassure themselves that they have little or nothing in common with those men who are physically violent to women and children. To be sure, intervention work with offenders constitutes only a small part of the project of reconstructing masculinities. To engender real change, we must ensure that this broader project addresses both the social and the psychic dimensions of men's experiences. Otherwise, those doing intervention work will only collude with those who feel more comfortable with the notion that violence against women is caused by individual pathology, as opposed to anything connected to the socio-cultural and socio-historical construction of masculinities.

Notes

[1] See Klein (2000) for an accessible example of Klein's account of defence mechanisms.

[2] See Gadd (2000b) for an analysis of one of the 'admittedly violent' men's life stories.

References

Bell, C. (2000) 'Men and violence', *Working with men*, vol 1, pp 12-13.

Bell, C. (2001) 'Counselling intervention with men who batter: partner safety and duty to warn', in P. Millner and S. Palmer (eds) *The British Association of Counselling, Reader*, Volume 2, London: Sage Publications, pp 197-207.

Bion, W.R. (1988) 'A theory of thinking', in E.B. Spillius (ed) *Melanie Klein today: Developments in theory and practice, mainly theory*, London: Routledge, pp 178-86.

Bourdieu, P. (1984) *Distinction: A social critique of the judgement of taste*, translated by R. Nice, London: Routledge & Kegan Paul.

Browne, K. and Herbert, M. (1997) *Preventing family violence*, Chichester: John Wiley & Sons.

Burton, S., Regan, L. and Kelly, L. (1998) *Supporting women and challenging men: Lessons from the domestic violence intervention project*, Bristol/York: The Policy Press/Joseph Rowntree Foundation.

Collier, R. (1998) *Masculinities, crime and criminology*, London: Sage Publications.

Dobash, R.E. and Dobash, R.P. (1980) *Violence against wives*, Somerset: Open Books.

Dobash, R.E., Dobash, R.P., Cavanagh, K. and Lewis, R. (1996) *Research evaluation for violent men*, Edinburgh: Scottish Office Central Research Unit.

Dobash, R.E., Dobash, R.P., Cavanagh, K. and Lewis, R. (1999) *Changing violent men*, London: Sage Publications.

Evans, J. (2003) 'Victims and vigilantes: thinking psychoanalytically about anti-paedophile action', *Theoretical Criminology*, vol 7, no 2, pp 163-90.

Fox, K. (1999) 'Changing violent minds', *Social Problems*, vol 46, no 1, pp 88-103.

Gadd, D. (2000a) 'Deconstructing male violence', Unpublished manuscript, Keele University.

Gadd, D. (2000b) 'Masculinities, violence and defended psychosocial subjects', *Theoretical Criminology*, vol 4, no 4, pp 429-49.

Goodall, K. and McKay, H. (1998) *Police classification and responses to domestic violence incidents*, Edinburgh: The Scottish Office.

Groombridge, N. (1999) 'Book review: the violences of men', *British Journal of Criminology*, vol 39, no 3, p 467.

Hague, G. and Malos, G. (1995) 'Inter-agency approaches to domestic violence: issues for probation', *Probation Journal*, vol 42, no 4, pp 220-5.

Hall, S. (2002) 'Daubing the drudges of fury: men, violence and the piety of the "hegemonic masculinity thesis"', *Theoretical Criminology*, vol 6, no 1, pp 35-62.

Hamill, U., Hayward, S., Wynn, P. and Craven, P. (1997) 'Practice note: Merseyside groupwork programme for men who are violent and abusive to their partner's', *Probation Journal*, vol 4, no 1, pp 220-4.

Hearn, J. (1998) *The violences of men*, London: Sage Publications.

Hester, M.A., Kelly, L. and Radford, J. (1995) *Women, violence and male power*, Buckingham: Oxford University Press.

Hollway, W. (1989) *Subjectivity and method in psychology*, London: Sage Publications.

Hollway, W. (1996) 'Recognition and heterosexual desire', in D. Richardson (ed) *Theorising heterosexuality*, Buckingham: Open University, pp 91-108.

Hollway, W. and Jefferson, T. (1998) '"A kiss is just a kiss": date rape, gender and subjectivity', *Sexualities*, vol 1, no 4, pp 405-23.

Hollway, W. and Jefferson, T. (1999) 'Gender, generation, anxiety and the reproduction of culture', in R. Josselson and A. Lieblich (eds) *Making meaning of narratives*, London: Sage Publications, pp 107-40.

Hollway, W. and Jefferson, T. (2000) *Doing qualitative research differently: Free association, narrative and the interview method*, London: Sage Publications.

Home Office (2000) *Multi-agency guidance for addressing domestic violence: The government's campaign to tackle violence against women*, London: The Stationery Office.

Hoyle, C. (1998) *Negotiating domestic violence*, Oxford: Clarendon Press.

Jackson, D. (1990) *Unmasking masculinity*, London: Unwin Hyman.

Jefferson, T. (1994) 'Theorising masculine subjectivity', in T. Newburn and E.A. Stanko (eds) *Just boys doing business*, London: Routledge, pp 10-31.

Kelly, L. (1988) *Surviving sexual violence*, Cambridge: Polity Press.

Klein, M. (2000) 'Notes on some schizoid mechanisms', in R. du Gay, J. Evans and P. Redman (eds) *Identity: A reader*, London: Sage Publications.

Lee, S.-J. (1998) 'Summary of findings from an evaluation of the work of Nottingham agenda', Unpublished manuscript, Nottingham.

Lupton, D. and Barclay, L. (1997) *Constructing fatherhood: Discourses and experiences*, London: Sage Publications.

Messerschmidt, J. (1993) *Masculinities and crime*, Lanham, MD: Rowman & Littlefield.

Messerschmidt, J.W. (2000) *Nine lives: Adolescent masculinities, the body, and violence*, Boulder, CO: Westview Press.

Morran, D. (1999) 'Violent men: terrifying others, scared of themselves?', *Working with men*, vol 2, pp 3-5.

Morran, D. and Wilson, M. (1999) 'Working with men who are violent to partners – striving for good practice', in H. Kemshall, H. Pritchard and J. Pritchard (eds) *Good practice in working with violence*, (Good Practice Series 6), London: Jessica Kingsley, pp 74-90.

Mullender, A. (1996) *Rethinking domestic violence*, London: Routledge.

Mullender, A. (2000) 'Reducing domestic violence... What works? Perpetrator programmes', *Policing & reducing crime briefing note*, Policing and Reducing Crime Unit, London: Home Office.

Newburn, T. (2002) 'Atlantic crossings: "policy transfer" and crime control in the USA and Britain', *Punishment & Society*, vol 4, no 2, pp 165-94.

Pence, E. and Paymar, M. (1993) *Education groups for men who batter: The Duluth model*, New York, NY: Springer.

Robinson, G. (2002) 'Exploring risk management in probation practice: contemporary developments in England and Wales', *Punishment & Society*, vol 4, no 1, pp 5-25.

Scourfield, J.B. (1998) 'Probation officers working with men', *British Journal of Social Work*, vol 28, pp 581-99.

Scourfield, J.B. and Dobash, R.P. (2000) 'Programmes for violent men: recent developments in the UK', *Howard Journal of Criminal Justice*, vol 38, no 2, pp 128-43.

Seidler, V. (1997) *Man enough*, London: Sage Publications.

Willis, P. (1977) *Learning to labour: How working class kids get working class jobs*, Farnborough: Saxon House.

Vanstone, M. (2000) 'Cognitive-behavioural work with offenders in the UK: a history of an influential endeavour', *Howard Journal of Criminal Justice*, vol 39, no 2, pp 171-83.

ELEVEN

The biographical turn in health studies

Wendy Rickard

This chapter offers an overview of existing biographical methods in health studies. The focus comes from my own efforts over the past few years to draw together a picture of some potentialities, possibilities and challenges of using biographical methods in health studies, both in research with marginalised groups and individuals, and in university teaching. I came to the topic initially from British oral history work in the two different – but both highly politicised – areas of HIV and AIDS (for example, Rickard, 1998, 2000) and prostitution (for example, Rickard, 2001; Rickard and Growney, 2001), work that I undertook in the context of being a health promotion practitioner. Hence, in terms of a broad range of biographical methods, the focus here dwells for the most part on oral history, life history and narrative approaches.

The rise of biographical methods in health

In the past two decades, there has been a perceived rise in the use of biographical methods in health studies, and a number of reasons have been cited to explain why this has occurred. First, modern biomedicine has been criticised for neglecting the patient or the lived experience side of health-focused encounters (Cornwell, 1994; Hogarth and Marks, 1998), and since the mid-1980s, biographical methods have gained precedence as a way to humanise medicine and redress this imbalance. They have been used in order to look at the stories of patients or the recipients of health interventions and their interaction with the increasing array of health professionals (for example, Brody, 1988; Kleinman, 1988; Hunter, 1991; Epstein, 1995; Greenhalgh and Hurwitz, 1998). Hogarth and Marks (1998) suggest that this biographical turn in health studies is firmly linked to changing power relations between health professionals and recipients of healthcare. They note that:

> a renewed emphasis on narrative in the late twentieth century can be linked to the declining power of professionals and the re-conceptualisation of patients as complex individuals powerfully conditioned by familial and early childhood experiences on the one hand, and as consumers with demands and rights on the other. (Hogarth and Marks, 1998, p 147)

Second, and perhaps slightly in contrast to this point, biographical methods have also been used to record the history of professions and of witnesses to their medical achievements, potentially reinforcing notions of professional power. For example, the 'Wellcome witnesses to twentieth century medicine' seminars promoted interaction between medical scientists, clinicians and historians in order to record advances that have been made in medicine (Tansey et al, 1999). The National Sound Archive at the British Library contains life-story data from a range of professional groups including the Royal Society of Chemistry, the Royal College of Nursing, founders of the Geriatric Specialty, the Institute of Physiotherapists, the Wellcome Trust Oral History of General Practice (1935-52), Community Pharmacy and Psychiatric Nursing. Other work has included histories of local government welfare workers, health visitors, general practitioners (GPs), geriatric medicine specialists, midwives, district nurses and hospice workers[1]. While the histories of medical science and of medical institutions have become established areas of concern, the history of medical practice remains a developmental area, and multilayered institutional work that looks across professional groupings and across the traditional health/social care divide may prove important for the future.

Third, Michael Bury (1998) and others have detailed and challenged arguments about the extent to which the rise of biographical methods in health is linked to modernity's creation of an intense sense of personal identity and selfhood, followed by the age of the subjective in postmodernity. Bury exposes the way that opposing strains in postmodern health analysis, from emphasis on fragmentation, difference and possibility, to emphasis on increasing organisation and surveillance in daily life, fail to encompass the range of "organisational and experiential elements that go to make up contemporary existence" (Bury, 1998, p 25). Others disagree and continue to support a postmodern thesis. Throughout these debates, a key ongoing challenge remains the need to understand better lay people's complex relations to medical science and medical practice, and biographical methods are likely to remain important tools.

The contribution of biographical methods in health

Biographical methods have been hailed as groundbreaking in promoting participatory and inclusive approaches to health research, in documenting hidden histories and in improving health work through detailed dialogue with communities. For example, in the field of learning disability, Jan Walmsley (1995) and others have used biographical methods to contribute to the development of more sensitive policies for care and support (Phillips, 1990; Atkinson, 1998; Rolph, 1998, 1999; Stuart, 1999). Similarly, in the care of people with dementia, John Killick (1998) and others have used biographical methodologies as a way to help people value their memories and retain coherence as individuals. At the same time, biographical methods offer opportunities of leaving a record for relatives, acting as an educational resource for residential staff in nursing homes and offering a tool for assessing older people's community care needs (Dant and Gearing, 1990). Other studies have used biographical methods to explore explanatory models of illness, importantly highlighting differences between patients and staff models of particular medical conditions. Some conditions explored to date include diabetes, cancer, leprosy, Parkinson's disease, traumatic brain injuries, multiple sclerosis, strokes and typhoid[2].

In extending this kind of work, biographical methods may offer significant opportunities to understand a broader range of health conditions, and particularly to focus on the interception between formal and informal caring practices, traditional and complementary medicine. As Paul Thompson has suggested (in Bornat et al, 2000, p 8), to include:

> a user's perspective of health and welfare, (as is implied by many biographical methods) ... is not simply a question of adding a complementary source....
> [I]t is more likely to challenge and subvert understandings of care and control, the boundaries between health and welfare, the location of centres and margins and notions of status and eligibility in all sectors of society and conditions of life.

Such studies have also highlighted social and cultural issues that are frequently underestimated by clinicians and potentially act as a key catalyst in reshaping future practice and policy. For example, Whiteford and Gonzalez (1995) undertook a study of perceptions of stigma of 25 US women who sought medical treatment for infertility and, through the use of biographical methods, showed how the form and manner of medical interventions transformed their private pain to a public, prolonged crisis. Challenging health service policies in this way has been an important development. Related notions of community involvement, openness and transparency underpin many recent health policy statements emanating from the current UK government (Watson and Platt, 2000), and biographical methods in health research look set to continue to provide important analytical tools within this policy agenda in health.

In growing areas of health research, such as public health and health promotion, biographical methods may have particular importance. Deborah Lupton (1995, p 81) has proposed that: "The risks which are selected by a society as requiring attention may ... have no relation to 'real' danger but are culturally identified as important". This selective perception of risks is derived from clinical medicine and epidemiology, disciplines that have tended to inform health promotion initiatives to date. Biographical methods offer possibilities for reconceptualising the real risks experienced by people and refocusing the policy agenda. My own work on occupational health and safety issues reported in prostitute's life histories aims to encourage refocusing of policy attention. It aims to prompt services to focus away from the primacy of sexual health concerns spurred by the HIV epidemic since the mid-1980s, and towards a more holistic view of the health concerns of the whole person (Rickard and Growney, 2001).

Such studies have a potentially important political role in countering victim blaming, exploring conflicts of interest and expectations between policy makers, service providers and clients of health services, and highlighting some unwillingness of governments and health agencies to respond to 'uncomfortable' political realities. A further example lies in Ruthbeth Finerman's work (1995), which drew on biographical methods to explore parental accountability for child survival, showing that concepts of selective neglect and parental incompetence were being incorrectly used to explain patchy results in reducing infant and child morbidity and mortality rates in Guatemala. As Jenny Popay and colleagues have recently suggested (Popay et al, 1998, p 637), biographical methods potentially offer ways to observe 'mediating influences' between individuals and their capacity to act, such as autonomy, control, identity and the central role of narratives in the 'construction' of self-identity.

Interest in social exclusion and health inequalities has developed in recent years. Some health research has suggested that patterns of adult health and even mortality are clearly linked to events in infancy, suggesting association for some disease conditions to events 50 or 60 years before. The relationships at birth, health in infancy, circumstances in childhood, education and social mobility as the individual grows up are very complex. To disentangle all this, health studies to date have relied largely on longitudinal birth cohort studies, yet biographical methods could clearly play an important future role. For example, there is an increasing range of important biographical work on life-stage issues[3]. Future studies are likely to follow politically determined social objectives such as ideas about social capital, defined as "the features of social organisation such as networks, norms and social trust that facilitate co-ordination and collaboration for mutual benefit" (Putnam, 1995, p 67). In this context, Somers (1994) has argued that the experience of social action is constituted through narratives and suggests a strong case for looking at people's perceptions of 'episodes' in their lives and the ways in which these may orientate or fail to orientate action at the individual and collective level.

In terms of different client groups, Joanna Bornat and Graham Smith (1999) suggest that the most extensive biographical work in the health arena to date has been with older people, particularly that focusing on reminiscence (Cornwell and Gearing, 1989; Smith and Bornat, 1999). However, the age range of people worked with through biographical methods in health is becoming more fluid, as studies with a primarily historical focus are increasingly accompanied by a social-scientific analysis. For example, in response to the AIDS crisis, biographical methods have been central to work with younger people in documenting the social history of the epidemic (Garfield, 1994; Small, 1995; Berridge, 1996; Rickard, 2000), understanding political responses, individual values and wider social issues of citizenship (Carricabburu and Pierret, 1995; Squire, 2000), as well as in addressing training issues for health professionals (Marshall and O'Keefe, 1995).

Inherent tensions

Using biographical methods in health studies also presents researchers and practitioners with a number of inherent tensions. One particular claim for biographical methods in health is related to promoting human agency. For example, it has been suggested that biographical methods drawing on patient narratives can provide meaning, context and perspective for the patient experience and help explore the life-altering capability of illness. In diagnosis, narratives encourage empathy, promote construction of shared meaning, and supply useful analytical clues and categories. For GPs, Smith and Bornat (1999, p 771) characterise this as the assistance of biographical methods in recognising the 'interconnectiveness' of people's lives. Hunter goes as far as suggesting that narrative construction is "the principle way of knowing in medicine" (Hunter, 1991, p 209), building on psychoanalyst Michael Balint's earlier suggestions that listening to patients is as important as pronouncing what is wrong with them (Balint et al, 1996). At the same time, health professionals have increasingly recognised the extension of their skill base outside traditional realms. For example, Tricia Greenhalgh and Brian Hurwitz (1998, p 6) have suggested that:

> When doctors take a medical history, we inevitably act as ethnographers, historians and biographers, requiring to understand aspects of person-hood, personality, social and psychological functioning, as well as biological and physical phenomena.

Through biographical methods, opportunities to speak from experience and to be listened to hence become a basis for effective human agency on both sides (Bornat, 1989). It is perhaps in this area that the potential of biographical methods in health is foremost.

However, those who employ biographical methods face serious challenges in representing and interpreting evidence about agency. Here, debates about mediated and unmediated voices abound. For example, in relation to one of my own specialist areas of study, prostitution or sex work, biographical methods have served as an important means to give prostitutes a voice and to enable a proliferation of stories to emerge from people expert in their own lives. This biographical information has undoubtedly countered misinformation and misrepresentation in the health arena on many levels (for example, Rickard, 2001). Yet, the importance of heeding the voice of experience through the unmediated voice of the prostitute has also disabled a thoroughly feminist critique. Biographical methods have constituted a chronicle of the sex industry that is often contradictory and selective, in terms of who can claim to speak for prostitutes, and has fed into a wider contemporary feminist aversion to speaking for others. Some commentators such as Belinda Carpenter (2000) argue that this latter use of biographical methods effectively silences new ways of thinking about prostitution. Those who use biographical methods in other health arenas may have to find ways to address such dilemmas in claiming agency as a key benefit of the approach and in further exploring notions of collaboration and shared authorship. Some may argue that the problem lies in feminism's difficulty in dealing with contradictory viewpoints rather than biographical methods' problem in revealing them, a key claim for biographical methods being that it highlights choices and helps people make them.

Some authors have started to consider a range of other tensions raised by the context in which biographical methods are employed. For example, with the recent promotion of evidence-based practice as the mantra for health researchers, relying heavily on risk and probability evidence from population samples in randomised control trials and large cohort studies, debate has raged about where subjective narrative accounts can sit in terms of current best evidence (Sackett et al, 1996; Greenhalgh, 1998; Traynor, 2000). Tensions remain about the apparently totalising ambitions of some proponents of systematic research approaches and how they fit with biographical methods. It has been suggested by some that biographical methods inherently make evidence more complicated, nuanced and untidy, and medicine has a traditional objection to this seemingly 'anti-scientific' practice. It will be interesting to see how these debates continue to develop in future and whether the tensions are resolved or heightened.

Interdisciplinary dialogue

It is argued that biographical methods offer ways of engaging in interdisciplinary dialogue between professionals working in different health disciplines and with those working across non-health-related fields. For example, exciting recent interdisciplinary ventures have included historians appointed to work in partnership with health practitioners[4]. However, where such appointments remain rare, certain problems can emerge in the early process of interdisciplinary dialogue across what Bornat (2000) has referred to as 'parallel universes'. One problem relates to differences in the maturity of ideas within different health-related disciplines and differences in willingness to learn from the existing experience of people in disciplines who have been experimenting with the methods for longer time periods but perhaps not in a health context. While historians may not speak explicitly about the social and psychological characteristics of recipients of biographical methods, they are often speaking directly of these issues within a different language base. Working in a faculty of health brings me into contact with psychologists, occupational therapists, physiotherapists, sociologists and those with wider interests in cultural studies, innovation studies and human relations. Learning to reinterpret biographical evidence across professional specialities is a key future challenge to ensure there is limited 'reinvention of the wheel'.

To aid cross-disciplinary communication about biographical methods in the health arena, clarity about different analytic approaches and terminologies employed is particularly needed. For example, biographical methods have gained currency to provide insight into the meanings of clients' experiences and to develop a shared view between client and therapist of the need to engage in a particular treatment, by locating therapist and client within 'a story' (Frank, 1996; Mattingley, 1998). Health research that started to emerge in the mid-1990s drew on a whole range of analytical terms and methods. These included occupational storytelling and story making (Clark, 1993), volitional narratives (Helfrich and Kielhofner, 1994), therapeutic 'emplotment' (Mattingley, 1994), narrative methods (Bruna, 1987; Larson and Fanchiang, 1996; Ryan and McKay, 1999), life-history approaches and narrative configuration (Polkinghorne, 1995; Price-Lackey and Cashman, 1996), literary folklore (Dolby-Stahl, 1985), hermeneutic case reconstruction (Rosenthal, 1993) and discourse analysis (Nessa and Malterud, 1990). While a broadening of methodological and analytical developments presents exciting possibilities and potentialities, some have argued that we risk fragmenting people's lives into specialisms, jargonising their experience and dislocating people from their own biographies.

A lack of a culture of sharing material from biographical studies in health could also, perhaps, be a risk. During the course of my oral history work with people living with an HIV or AIDS diagnosis, we set up a central UK oral history collection at the National Sound Archive of the British Library. As well as contributing new interviews to this collection, the curator was eager to offer others collecting similar kinds of data the opportunity to deposit their recordings in this central and publicly accessible resource, subject of course to any anonymity and confidentiality clauses requested by interviewees. Some highly valuable contributions were made as a result, but some academics did not want to deposit their collections and the reasons remain unclear. Such obstruction to data sharing could potentially be experienced in a range of health arenas, particularly those connected with politically charged issues, lucrative drug contracts or new surgical procedures. A future challenge, therefore, might be to encourage and enable continued altruism in sharing biographical health data.

Biographical approaches as therapeutic intervention

Narratives are in themselves intrinsically therapeutic or palliative, and there is now clear evidence that talking and writing about one's problems can improve health outcomes in a variety of conditions. For example, in reminiscence work with older people, life histories play a developmental role in assisting with transitions such as the loss of a partner and changes in health status. They also help to achieve acceptance of lived life in late old age and understanding of frustrations that link to familial history (Smith and Bornat, 1999). Other recent edited collections, centring on notions of trauma, draw on biographical methods to discuss the complex issues surrounding memory, false memory, remembering, forgetting, silences, identity and life histories (Dwivedi, 1997; Rogers et al, 1999). There has arisen a keen interest in recent years about the extent to which biographical methods offer possibilities for informal therapy as a by-product, an issue that was debated recently in a special issue of the UK journal *Oral History* (1998). Conclusions drawn suggested caution in making assumptions that anyone using biographical methods could claim a therapeutic role and pointed to inherent dangers in the biographical process that were highlighted by interviewees and interviewers. While celebrating the exciting possibilities of biographical methods in health, we must develop more in-depth understanding of the ethical implications of the approach and what Jo Stanley (1996, p 25) has termed "the psychic costs to the interviewee and the interviewer" (see also Rickard, 1998).

On a more formal level, psychotherapists and others have developed approaches to narrative therapy that are used to achieve specific clinical outcomes. For example, referring to the indigenous rights of the Tainui people of the Waikato in New Zealand, John Winslade speaks of narrative therapy as "likened to a process of restoring rightful ownership of what has been stolen away by dominant stories" (Monk et al, 1997, p xi), while Gerald Monk describes the narrative approach as "co-exploration in search of talents and abilities that are hidden or veiled by a life problem" (Monk et al, 1997, p 3). The emphasis of Monk and his colleagues has been on what they term 'optimistic orientation', seeking stories of hope, success and vindication by constructing a history of the preferred story of the client in the therapeutic encounter, through a process of self-redefinition rather than further problematising their lives. Emphasis is also placed on doing therapy respectfully through a process of "promoting the construction of a client's life without enfeebling her in the process" (Drewery and Winslade, in Monk et al, 1997, p 32). The process is envisaged as one of co-authoring, creating shared meanings, and coordinating the counselling relationship as one of mutual meaning making (Epston and White, 1992).

However, my (perhaps naïve) view is that we need to substantiate these claims by developing a better understanding of similarities and differences with other therapeutic approaches. The book that Monk and colleagues (1997) published about their narrative therapy approach describes the benefits emerging from this kind of counselling across a range of client groups and in a range of settings. Such emphasis on the 'how to', on collaborative processes and on the apparent benefits of narrative therapy have had a tendency to be framed within an evangelical tone and many have not to date been accompanied by a reflexive, balanced, critical reflection of challenges and complexities. One task for the future is to temper this enthusiasm with more critical reflections on the strengths and weaknesses of biographical methods used therapeutically. In particular, we perhaps need to document instances where biographical approaches are problematic or unsuccessful in clinical encounters and this will hopefully provide a clearer indication of the boundaries of their usefulness.

Health databases

The millennium project titled 'The Century Speaks' was a collaboration between BBC local radio and the British Library. It yielded a huge amount of material on health that became accessible on the World Wide Web when CADENSA went online in November 2000. This collection, the huge archives of QUALIDATA held at the University of Essex, and the growing collection of audiotapes held at the Wellcome Library for the History and Understanding of Medicine, present three British examples of the possibilities for secondary analysis of existing biographical data relating to health. The Database of Individual Patient Experience (DIPEX), based in the Division of Public Health and Primary Health Care at the Institute of Health Science, University of Oxford, offers a further multimedia resource. Its objectives include conducting illness narratives with an 'appropriate' sample for each condition; identifying issues, questions and problems that matter to people when they are ill, and using these to identify outcome measures that reflect patient's concerns; and sharing experiences and feelings about treatment choices. The challenge for health researchers and practitioners for the future lies in establishing innovative ways of working with such databases and documenting any difficulties with methodological processes encountered in doing so.

Health training in biographical methods

Finally, a key area for development in relation to biographical methods and health appears to lie in the training sphere. A key focus of recent writing about biographical methods in health has been to provide clinicians with the tools required to understand the significance of narratives, and their usefulness in the diagnostic encounter, in the therapeutic process and in training and research (Greenhalgh and Hurwitz, 1998). Existing evidence suggests that first-person narrative approaches to medical training can be an effective method of sensitising students to the experience of living with certain medical conditions and help to develop increased empathy (Marshall and O'Keefe, 1995). In education, narratives are often memorable and enforce reflection. They help to set a patient–centred agenda, challenge received wisdom and generate new hypotheses. Anecdotes or 'illness scripts' are the form in which we accumulate health knowledge and health professionals need to understand their role in authoring "the text-that-is-the-patient" (Greenhalgh and Hurwitz, 1998, p 12). They also need to reflect on the multiplicity of readings that a text engenders, becoming aware of the nuances, and to appreciate fully the moral choices in healthcare.

Through a questionnaire survey to individuals and departments working in higher education, Al Thomson (1998) recently evaluated an increasing wave of undergraduate and postgraduate courses developed in universities across Britain that utilise biographical methods or oral history methods more particularly. He noted that the courses surveyed were "creative, imaginative, stimulating, engaging and 'hands-on' in relation to both skills and ideas" (Thomson, 1998, p 4). Particular exemplars such as the biographically based courses in health and social welfare pioneered at the Open University were given prominence. Courses organised by health and medicine departments and faculties across the UK were fairly well represented (see Thomson, 1998, p 57, table 4), but in terms of undergraduate course content, health sciences constituted the smallest content area compared with other disciplines like history, women and gender studies, and sociology. Clearly, there is room for the further development of educational programmes in health that focus on biographical methods, in adult education, higher education and professional training. Networks and information exchange among those who are starting to develop such training approaches will hopefully offer future students and health practitioners quality training that blends theory and practice.

Conclusion

While biographical methods in health studies offer a huge range of stimulating opportunities, like other qualitative approaches in healthcare, their future contribution in an area that has been traditionally dominated by the quantitative paradigm will remain complementary until we can demonstrate their catalytic potential. My own battles with science-based ethics committees to gain permission for student study in this area are frequently reduced to defending philosophical principles behind the approach. I look forward to a time when we can move beyond such basics to establish a firm footing for biographical methods across a spectrum of health-related arenas. To do so, we will have to reduce the gap between theory and practice, and seek better implementation and dissemination of research, particularly looking to a future where indicators that capture the impact of research on policy and practice are given closer attention. We may also need to think carefully about the traditional written portrayal of this work, which often does not adequately portray the energy and dynamism of its oral roots, and does not reflect the multimedia technology revolution in which research drawing on biographical methods is increasingly positioned (with the availability, for example, of CD-ROMs and DVDs).

Notes

[1] An example of histories of local government welfare workers in working with the homeless can be found in Adams (1989) and that of health visitors in Peretz (1989). For examples of histories of general practitioners, geriatric medicine specialists, midwives, district nurses and hospice workers, see Bornat et al (2000).

[2] Examples of work on these conditions include: diabetes (Ternulf Nyhulin, 1990; Callaghan and Williams, 1994; Cohen et al, 1994); cancer (Tischelman, 1997); leprosy (Kakar, 1995); Parkinson's disease (Pinder, 1998); traumatic brain injuries (Nochi, 1998); multiple sclerosis (Robinson, 1988; Monks and Frankenberg, 1995); strokes (Manzo, et al, 1995); and typhoid (Diack, 2001).

[3] This includes, for example, the biographical work of Young and Cullen (1996) on preparation for death.

⁴ For example, at the Primary Care/General Practitioners Centres at Glasgow University (Scotland), Graham Smith was employed (at the time of writing) as an oral historian. His projects included work on the career histories of both older and younger GPs, exploring ways that they are informed by informal or hidden practices, and an analysis of the impact of surveillance medicine on GPs' constructions of patient and professional identities within the GPs' own life histories.

References

Adams, J. (1989) 'Caring for the casual poor', *Oral History*, vol 17, no 1, pp 29-35.

Atkinson, D. (1998) 'Autobiography and learning disability', *Oral History*, vol 26, no 1, pp 73-80.

Balint, E., Courtenay, M., Elder, A., Hull, S. and Julian, P. (1996) *The doctor, the patient and the group: Balint revisited*, London: Routledge.

Berridge, V. (1996) *AIDS in the UK: The making of policy 1981-1994*, Oxford: Oxford University Press.

Bornat, J. (1989) 'Oral history as a social movement: reminiscence and older people', *Oral History*, vol 17, no 2, 16-20.

Bornat, J. (2000) Conference Address, 'Biographical methods and professional practice', International Sociological Association, London, October.

Bornat, J., Perks, R., Thompson, P. and Walmsley, J. (eds) (2000) *Oral history, health and welfare*, London: Routledge.

Brody, H. (1988) *Stories of sickness*, New Haven, CT: Yale University Press.

Bruna, J. (1987) 'Life as narrative', *Social Research*, vol 54, no 1, pp 13-32.

Bury, M. (1998) 'Postmodernity and health', in G. Scambler and P. Higgs (eds) *Modernity, medicine and health: Medical sociology towards 2000*, London: Routledge, pp 1-28.

Callaghan, D. and Williams, A. (1994) 'Living with diabetes: issues for nursing practice', *Journal of Advanced Nursing*, vol 20, pp 132-9.

Carpenter, B. (2000) *Rethinking prostitution: Feminism, sex and the self*, New York, NY: Peter Lang Publishing.

Carricaburu, D. and Pierret, J. (1995) 'From biographical disruption to biographical reinforcement: the case of HIV-positive men', *Sociology of Health and Illness*, vol 17, no 1, p 85.

Clark, F. (1993) 'Occupation embedded in a real life: interweaving occupational science and occupational therapy', *The American Journal of Occupational Therapy*, vol 47, no 12, pp 1067-78.

Cohen, M.Z., Tripp-Reimer, T., Smith, C., Sorofman, B. and Lively, S. (1994) 'Explanatory models of diabetes: patient practitioner variation', *Social Science and Medicine*, vol 38, no 1, pp 59-66.

Cornwell, J. (1984) *Hard-earned lives*, London: Tavistock.

Cornwell, J. and Gearing, B. (1989) 'Biographical interviews with older people', *Oral History,* vol 17, no 1, pp 36-43.

Dant, T. and Gearing, B. (1990) 'Key-workers for elderly people in the community – case managers and care co-ordinators', *Journal of Social Policy*, vol 19, no 3, pp 331-60.

Diack, L. (2001) 'The myth of a beleaguered city: Aberdeen and the typhoid outbreak of 1964 explored through oral history', *Oral History*, vol 29, no 1, pp 62-72.

Dolby-Stahl, S. (1985) 'A literary folkloristic methodology for the study of meaning in personal narrative', *Journal of Folklore Research*, vol 22, pp 5-70.

Dwivedi, K.N. (ed) (1997) *The therapeutic use of stories*, London/New York, NY: Routledge.

Epstein, J. (1995) *Altered conditions: Disease, medicine and story-telling*, London/New York, NY: Routledge.

Epston, D. and White, M. (eds) (1992) *Experience, contradiction, narrative and imagination: Selected papers*, Adelaide, Australia: Dulwich Centre Publications.

Finerman, R. (1995) '"Parental incompetence" and "selective neglect": blaming the victim in child survival', *Social Science and Medicine*, vol 40, no 1, pp 5-13.

Frank, G. (1996) 'Life histories in occupational therapy clinical practice', *The American Journal of Occupational Therapy*, vol 50, no 4, pp 251-63.

Garfield, S. (1994) *The end of innocence: Britain in the time of Aids*, London: Faber and Faber.

Greenhalgh, T. (1998) 'Narrative based medicine in an evidence based world', in T. Greenhalgh and B. Hurwitz (eds) *Narrative based medicine: Dialogue and discourse in clinical practice*, London: British Medical Journal.

Greenhalgh, T. and Hurwitz, B. (eds) (1998) *Narrative based medicine: Dialogue and discourse in clinical practice*, London: British Medical Journal.

Helfrich, C. and Kielhofner, G. (1994) 'Volitional narratives and the meaning of therapy', *American Journal of Occupational Therapy*, vol 48, no 4, pp 319-26.

Hogarth, S. and Marks, L. (1998) 'The golden narrative in British medicine', in T. Greenhalgh and B. Hurwitz (eds) *Narrative based medicine: Dialogue and discourse in clinical practice*, London: British Medical Journal.

Hunter, K.M. (1991) *Doctor stories: The narrative structure of medical knowledge*, Princeton, NJ: Princeton University Press.

Kakar, S. (1995) 'Leprosy in India: the intervention of oral history', *Oral History*, vol 23, no 2, pp 37-45.

Killick, J. (1998) 'Climb up the family tree and look at the vista from there: writing work with people with dementia', *Oral History*, vol 26, no 1, pp 81-5.

Kleinman, A. (1988) *The illness narratives: Suffering, healing and the human condition*, New York, NY: Basic Books.

Larson, E.A. and Fanchiang, S.C. (1996) 'Life history and narrative research: generating a humanistic knowledge base for occupational therapy', *American Journal of Occupational Therapy*, vol 50, no 4, pp 247-9.

Lupton, D. (1995) *The imperative of health: Public health and the regulated body*, London: Sage Publications.

Manzo, J., Blonder, L. and Burns, A. (1995) 'The social and interactional organisation of narrative and narrating among stroke patients and their spouses', *Sociology of Health and Illness*, vol 17, no 1, pp 307-27.

Marshall, P.A. and O'Keefe, J.P. (1995) 'Medical students' first-person narratives of a patients' story of AIDS', *Social Science and Medicine*, vol 40, no 1, pp 67-76.

Mattingley, C. (1994) 'The concept of therapeutic emplotment', *Social Science and Medicine*, vol 38, no 6, pp 811-22.

Mattingley, C. (1998) *Healing dramas and clinical plots: The narrative structure of experience*, Cambridge: Cambridge University Press.

Monk, G., Winslade, J., Crocket, K. and Epston, D. (eds) (1997) *Narrative therapy in practice: The archaeology of hope*, San Francisco, CA: Jossey-Bass.

Monks, J. and Frankenberg, R. (1995) '"Being ill and being me": self, body and time in MS narratives', in B. Ingstad and R. Whyte (eds) *Disability and culture*, California: University of California Press.

Nessa, J. and Malterud, K. (1990) 'Discourse analysis in general practice: a sociolinguistic approach', *Family Practice*, vol 7, no 2, pp 77-83.

Nochi, M. (1998) '"Loss of self" in the narratives of people with traumatic brain injuries: a qualitative analysis', *Social Science and Medicine*, vol 46, no 7, pp 869-78.

Oral History (1998) 'Memory, trauma and ethics', *Oral History*, vol 26, no 2.

Peretz (1989) 'The professionalisation of childcare', *Oral History*, vol 17, no 1, pp 22-8.

Phillips, M.J. (1990) 'Damaged goods: oral narratives of the experience of disability in American culture', *Social Science and Medicine*, vol 30, no 8, pp 849-57.

Pinder, R. (1998) 'Striking balances: living with Parkinson's disease', in M. Allott and M. Robb (eds) *Understanding health and social care: An introductory reader*, London: Sage Publications.

Polkinghorne, D.E. (1995) 'Narrative configuration in qualitative analysis', *Qualitative Studies in Education*, vol 8, no 1, pp 5-23.

Popay, J., Williams, G., Thomas, C. and Gatrell, T. (1998) 'Theorising inequalities in health: the place of lay knowledge', *Sociology of Health and Illness*, vol 20, pp 619-44.

Price-Lackey, A. and Cashman, J. (1996) 'Jenny's story: reinventing oneself through occupation and narrative configuration', *American Journal of Occupational Therapy*, vol 50, no 4, pp 306-14.

Putnam, R. (1995) 'Bowling alone: America's declining social capital', *Journal of Democracy*, vol 6, pp 65-78.

Rickard, W. (1998) 'Oral history: more dangerous than therapy?', *Oral History*, vol 26, no 2, pp 34-48.

Rickard, W. (2000) 'HIV/Aids testimonies in the 1990s', in J. Bornat, R. Perks, P. Thompson and J. Walmsley (eds) *Oral history, health and welfare*, London: Routledge.

Rickard, W. (2001) '"Been there, seen it, done it, I've got the T-shirt": British sex workers reflect on jobs, hopes, the future and retirement', *Feminist Review*, vol 67, no 1, pp 111-32.

Rickard, W. and Growney, T. (2001) 'Occupational health and safety amongst sex workers: a pilot peer education resource', *Health Education Research*, vol 16, no 3, pp 321-34.

Robinson, I. (1988) 'Personal narratives, social careers and medical courses: analysing life trajectories in autobiographies of people with MS', *Social Science and Medicine*, vol 30, no 11, pp 1173-86.

Rogers, K.L., Leydesdorff, S. and Dawson, G. (eds) (1999) *Trauma and life histories, international perspectives*, London/New York, NY: Routledge.

Rolph, S. (1998) 'Ethical dilemmas: oral history work with people with learning disabilities', *Oral History*, vol 26, no 2, pp 65-72.

Rolph, S. (1999) 'Enforced migrations of people with learning difficulties: a case study', *Oral History*, vol 27, no 1, pp 47-56.

Rosenthal, G. (1993) 'Reconstruction of life stories: principles of selection in generating stories for narrative biographical interviews', in R. Josselson and A. Lieblich (eds) *The narrative study of lives, volume 1*, Newbury Park, CA: Sage Publications.

Ryan, S. and McKay, E.A. (1999) *Thinking and reasoning in therapy: Narratives from practice*, Cheltenham: Stanley Thornes.

Sackett, D., Rosenburg, W., Muir Grey, J., Haynes, R. and Richardson, W. (1996) 'Evidence based medicine: what it is and what it isn't', *British Medical Journal*, vol 312, pp 71-2.

Small, N. (1995) 'Living with HIV and AIDS', in B. Davey, A. Gray and C. Seale (eds) *Health and disease: A reader*, Buckingham: Open University Press.

Smith, G. and Bornat, J. (1999) 'Oral history, biography, life history: broadening the evidence', *The British Journal of General Practice*, September, pp 770-1.

Somers, M. (1994) 'The narrative construction of identity: a relational and network approach', *Theory and Society*, vol 23, pp 605-49.

Squire, C. (2000) 'Situated selves, the coming-out genre and equivalent citizenship in narratives of HIV', in P. Chamberlayne, J. Bornat and T. Wengraf (eds) *The turn to biographical methods in social science*, London/New York, NY: Routledge.

Stanley, J. (1996) Letter to the editors, *Oral History*, vol 24, no 2, p 25.

Stuart, M. (1999) 'Stories of shame and esteem: women with learning difficulties and the right to tell tales', *Oral History*, vol 27, no 2, pp 47-57.

Tansey, E.M., Christie, D.A. and Reynolds, L.A. (eds) (1999) *Wellcome witnesses to twentieth century medicine*, London: The Wellcome Trust.

Thomson, A. (1998) *Undergraduate life history research projects: Questionnaire analysis*, University of Sussex Monograph.

Tischelman, C. (1997) 'Getting sick and getting well: a qualitative study of aeteological explanations of people with cancer', *Journal of Advanced Nursing*, vol 25, pp 60-7.

Traynor, M. (2000) 'Purity, conversion and the evidence based movements', *Health: An Interdisciplinary Journal for the Social Study of Health Illness and Medicine*, vol 4, no 2, pp 139-58.

Turnulf Nyhulin, K. (1990) 'A contribution of qualitative research to a better understanding of diabetic patients', *Journal of Advanced Nursing*, vol 15, pp 796-803.

Walmsley, J. (1995) 'Life history interviews with people with learning disabilities', *Oral History*, vol 23, no 1, pp 71-7.

Watson, J. and Platt, S. (2000) 'Connecting policy and practice: the challenge for health promotion research', in J. Watson and S. Platt (eds) *Researching health promotion*, London: Routledge.

Whiteford, L. and Gonzalez, L. (1995) 'Stigma: the hidden burden of infertility', *Social Science and Medicine*, vol 40, no 1, pp 27-36.

Young, M. and Cullen, L. (1996) *A good death: Conversations with East Londoners*, London/New York, NY: Routledge.

TWELVE

Ethical aspects of biographical interviewing and analysis

Kaja Kaźmierska

It may seem obvious to say that biographical research differs from all other sociological research. The differences apply to research techniques, procedures of analysing biographical material and something that can be called a 'style of work', which covers the very time-consuming research stages of material collection and analysis. These and many other specific features of biographical research are grounded in theoretical and methodological assumptions which vary for particular types of biographical work. However, the outstanding characteristic of this kind of work is that the research material is biography.

Each biographical story is unique. The situation of its creation is not – and cannot be – standardised. This is what makes biographical work different from other, more traditional, techniques and applies especially to unprepared stories that are recounted and recorded in the presence of a researcher. Whereas biographical accounts that are written down can be changed and amended, narrative is the outcome of face-to-face interaction, which involves both a narrator and a researcher. It follows that the process of collecting narrated biographies and their subsequent analysis is related not only to particular methodological procedures, but also to a situational context and to different aspects of interpretation connected with the case of a given person who is not just a respondent in the research, and not just the anonymous author of a life story. Altogether, these circumstances may generate different sorts of questions: how valid are the accounts? How representative are they? Is it possible to make generalisations from the biographical analysis, as well as questions about ethical aspects of biographical interviewing?

This chapter concentrates on the latter issue. My comments will mostly concern the method of narrative biographical interview with which I work. In this type of interview, people are stimulated to tell the stories of experiences they have lived through (Schütze, 1983). A narrator is expected to give an extempore account of their life without being interrupted by the listener (researcher). The interview is recorded and then carefully transcribed. It is very important, therefore, to create an atmosphere that encourages the narrator to talk about their life. The researcher should stimulate the narration in such a way that the narrator can be sure that their personal story is what the researcher is interested in, and that the researcher is ready to listen to their experiences

(Hermanns, 1987). The text of the interview is analysed according to the detailed procedure of narrative analysis. First, the researcher examines the communicative schemes of the text (to see to what extent the text is an autobiographical extempore narrative), and then begins on a structural analysis of the text (that is, looking for the structure of the sequence of narrative units and the placing and build-up of commentaries). Structural text analysis is one of the main stages of the research process. The next step is analytical abstraction (generalities shared by other biographies and distinctive features of the studied text) (Schütze, unpublished).

My discussion on the ethical aspects of biographical interviewing mainly concerns the stages during which the material is collected and subjected to detailed structural analysis. I also consider in this chapter the problem of collective work on narrative interviews. Although texts of interviews are analysed according to analytical procedures, the process of interpretation requires the application of different perspectives and frames of references. This is why a narrative is usually discussed and analysed in a group (Riemann and Schütze, 1987).

What happens when somebody tells their life story?

Telling a life story requires both physical and psychological effort. When an individual decides to share their life experiences honestly and fully they have to devote their time and energy to concentrate on past experiences, put them in some sort of order to present them as a life story, and last but not least tell their biography, which may entail speaking for extended periods of time. It is also assumed that in most cases the biographer tends to create a favourable picture of himself or herself, often unconsciously, and that they have some expectations of their role in the research.

Telling an autobiographical story is a personal matter, to some degree. Although one could do it with a stranger, the biographer and listener need to establish a certain relationship. There has to be a specific 'atmosphere' between the two people, a little sympathy and a little confidence (Hermanns, 1987). The time required by a narrator to tell their life story is greater than in 'classical' interviewing, and this factor helps to strengthen the relationship between researcher and informant. The setting of the interview (often the informant's home) also helps, by making the interaction less formal.

So, let us sum up the narrator's point of view. Narrators devote their time, build a sort of confidence with their listener (the researcher), use different strategies (sometimes unconsciously) to present themselves, and have a certain idea of their role in the research project.

And what of the researcher? In other research methods, the researcher often is not involved in the actual process of collecting the necessary data, whereas, here, he or she usually takes an active part in this stage of the work. Here, researchers know their informants, who are not anonymous individuals. They have met them, know them by name, and most of all, they have shared their life experiences with them. Their presence during the process of life storytelling makes them a 'co-author' of the story, in a way. All these circumstances influence the researcher's attitude not only towards the narrator they listen to, but to the problem under study.

The researcher also has certain expectations. He or she hopes that their informant will tell them a life story that can be useful for their research, that it will be created according to the researcher's methodological procedures (in the case of biographical narrative interview, it should be an extempore narration about life experiences), concentrated on a particular topic (especially when a story is to be structured by topic), and so on. They also expect the narrator to put some effort into creating a substantial story and be quite honest in their presentation.

These expectations on the part of the narrator and the researcher can be treated as a model that, in each case, is fulfilled by concrete circumstances. These may be modified by the specific biographical situations of an informant, such as whether or not they are talking about harmful experiences. It is very difficult to talk about traumatic life experiences and many people find it impossible to share this type of experience. Besides, speaking about trauma may be supported by culturally grounded patterns that make it possible or impossible for individuals to tell their stories. Nonetheless, when a narrator discloses their suffering, this is always difficult both for the informant and for the listener (Inowlocki, 1993; Engelking, 1994). On the other hand, such narratives can function therapeutically. In a recent edited volume, Rosenthal and co-authors emphasise the therapeutic dimension of biographical interviewing (Rosenthal, 1998). The volume's contributors describe cases in which long-suppressed traumatic experiences are narrated, and then the cathartic effect that ensued.

I have quite often been in situations when narrators tell me something and then declare that they had never mentioned it to anyone else before. These statements referred not only to events that were hard to describe because of their traumatic nature, but also to situations that narrators were ashamed of, or to autobiographical commentaries emphasising a change in attitude, and comments on past events and behaviour. Researchers, therefore, should be prepared for this kind of interaction where they play the role of 'good listener'. (I would disagree with those who claim that, since they are not psychologists, they are not interested in the informant's feelings or problems that are not related to the particular topic under study. I have sometimes heard such opinions expressed in discussions at conferences and seminars devoted to biographical methods.)

Another important matter is whether or not a narrator is telling their story for the first time, or whether they are 'trained' (or well versed) in telling stories, as in the case of people whose profession requires such skills. For example, it is much easier for teachers or storytellers to construct a narrative than therapists, let alone therapy patients, since they possess the skills and strategies appropriate to presenting life experiences. In situations where the narrator has difficulties expressing feelings, it would seem so much easier to be the listener, or researcher. Nevertheless, the researcher must be able to distinguish a routine narrative from an extempore account.

I intend to analyse the complications that may arise between narrator and researcher which contribute to the difficulties in interpreting their mutual relationship. I believe these complications are associated with the ethical aspects of biographical interviewing.

What can happen at the stage of collecting life stories?

First, a researcher may treat his informant as one more 'talking machine' that they must listen to. Very often researchers focus on their own idea of a research project and look for material to confirm it. They may lose sight of the fact that each life story is a unique biography. However, should they be unwilling to go beyond the framework of their own expectations and, to some extent, interpretations, they may miss crucial aspects of analysed biographies and, therefore, important features of a case. Viewed from this angle, each life story is important, even when an informant is talking about an aspect of their life that seems uninteresting to the researcher. Thus, a listener (researcher) must learn to be appreciative, even when the story they are listening to is not exactly what they would like to hear in the context of their research project. I have sometimes felt that I was 'wasting my time' while listening to a story I could not use for my research material. I felt a little uncomfortable when thanking the narrator for their story, for I felt quite the opposite. However, it often turned out later that this 'useless' life story could serve as supplementary material to the main data or, indeed, reveal new aspects of a problem.

Second, during the process of storytelling, a narrator may present ideas with which the researcher disagrees. The question arises as to how to react when the disagreement is not about trivia but serious moral choices, for instance. What a researcher could – or rather, *should* – do is discuss this matter after the interview. They can then express their disapproval – of prejudice, for instance. However, the matter is more complicated in practice, of course. For example, once I listened to a woman who expressed very strong nationalism and prejudice against Lithuanians. She was born in Vilnius before the Second World War. The city is now the capital of Lithuania, but before the war it belonged to Poland and was treated as a symbol of Polish hegemony on the Eastern border. As a displaced person, she cannot forgive Lithuanians who, according to her, "occupy Vilnius". During the process of storytelling, this woman was clearly expecting non-verbal signs of communication confirming her position. I found myself playing the role of ally, a trusted person who shared the same point of view. I did not confirm the narrator's statements verbally, but neither did I express any disapproval, because I was anxious to avoid a confrontation. First, I did not want a confrontation in which the woman would be offended. Second, I felt that this was the best way of obtaining this kind of authentic story. I thought that, had I not accepted the role of ally, I would have been treated as a stranger and an enemy. I needed to be identified as being on 'the same side'. Although I did not say a word to confirm the woman's attitudes, the situation was quite clear. Despite my doubts, this life story was perfect for my research, and served as one of the model narratives.

Other examples concern narrators who, while talking about their war experiences, expressed strong prejudice against Jewish people. I listened to their stories, totally disagreeing with their views, but was uncertain whether I should discuss their attitudes after the interview. Was it my role to start a discussion? After all, I was a stranger/visitor who had asked the favour of listening to their life story and I had been welcomed. Presentations like these enabled me to obtain very fruitful material. On the other hand, I always experienced a sort of cognitive dissonance when I was 'co-author' of such accounts by the very fact of listening to them.

Third, in the process of collecting life stories, narrators are informed about the main aims of a research project, but they do not usually know how their biography can be analysed. In the method of biographical narrative interview, the analysis of a life story is more important than the analysis of a life history, where a life story is defined as 'subjective' narrated life experiences, and life history as the 'objective' experiences or events that a person has lived through (Rosenthal, 1993).

Narrators usually imagine that a researcher will refer to their life history, the events described. They have no idea about structural text analysis, the aim of which is to describe and interpret the construction of their story. Narrators do not realise that their every word is carefully transcribed and then analysed, including 'slips of the tongue'. They do not know that the researcher is not only interested in what they say (life history), but also in how they say it (life story) and what the reasons are for constructing a biography in a particular way. Thus, narrators usually have in mind a 'traditional' image of material analysis, in which the story is a 'means' of studying socio-historical reality (Helling, 1990)[1]. They believe that the researcher will choose the best parts of the account, the most interesting matters, and will omit those that are left unelaborated. These expectations, in fact, are entirely false. The researcher's aim is to analyse the narrator's meaning, which has been systematically produced in the individuals' accounts (Apitzsch and Inowlocki, 2000) – that is, to treat the life story as the very 'topic' of research.

Although narrators are usually informed about the aim and expected results of the project and the informants' role in the research, it is my opinion that there is a discrepancy between the narrator's image of their contribution to the research and the researcher's idea of their work. This raises the question: do we, as researchers, explain to a narrator the complicated procedures and consequences of text analysis, or simply let them keep their idea of the research project? This question becomes important in that it may affect the results of text analysis.

What happens during the process of analysis?

Careful work on narratives enable us to discover various features of the biography, such as prejudice, 'dark' aspects of biography, and reasons for erasing some events or experiences from consciousness (Schütze, 1992). There are two ways in which parts of a biography are 'faded out' of awareness. First, it is done from the perspective of the present. A narrator tends to hide past life experiences from their listener in order to present themselves in a better light. This kind of omitting can be very easily identified with the help of structural text analysis. The moment in the story when the narrator tries to omit some experiences may be marked by evidence such as a plot coming to a sudden end or contradictions in the presentation of life experiences (Schütze, 1989).

Second, the process of omitting certain experiences started in the past, and this has affected later experiences. This sort of fading out of awareness is unintentional and much more difficult to identify. Asking additional questions after the main part of the interview may help the researcher identify reasons why certain aspects of a narrator's biography came to be omitted. These omissions are very often connected with traumatic experiences (Schütze, 1989).

Analysis provides the researcher with tools to uncover experiences that have been erased from consciousness, classify them according to types, and interpret the reasons for the way the narrator projects their story. When the text of an interview is analysed as a specific type of data, there is only the *potential* for ethical ambivalence. However, the situation becomes more complicated when the analysis is associated with a particular person that may result with the informant being identified. The narrator has agreed to tell a researcher their life story (probably with quite different expectations of research analysis), whereas the researcher analyses it in depth, including details that the narrator perhaps would prefer to keep hidden. In other words, there is an issue concerning how far a researcher may investigate such personal material as a life story and to what extent the researcher may use the confidence that has been established with the narrator to justify detailed analysis of different aspects of the narrator's experiences. In order not to abuse their privacy, researchers are sometimes obliged to obtain the informant's written consent to use their story. Such documents are not required in Poland, for example, whereas they are in the US. There is also a rule that information such as the narrator's name, details connected with places, and anything else that could help identify the person, must be changed. However, this situation remains controversial for at least two reasons: one I would call the 'narrator–researcher relationship', and the other the 'narrator's appearance in public discourse'.

As regards the narrator–researcher relationship, telling one's biography is a rather personal matter and, in fact, narrators decide what part of their experiences they want to share. Researchers, on the other hand, often concentrate on what has not been told, what has been faded out of awareness, and try to find the reasons for this. Their aim is not simply to study the narrative itself but to reveal general social phenomena and processes. Nevertheless, when researchers analyse the text of a narrative they see and know more than perhaps its author would like to reveal. In many cases such work may perform the therapeutic functions of storytelling; in my opinion, however, this does not absolve the researcher from responsibility for abusing the narrator's image of their role in a project.

The second reason, as I have said, is to do with the presentation of a text in public discourse. Although the narrators are anonymous, there is always a chance that they may be identified, or that they will recognise themselves.

I have had at least two such cases in my research experience. Once, I published a fragment from an interview with a woman talking about her experiences during the Second World War. I quoted a section where there was a very touching story about her grandfather who, at the age of 90, decided to visit his homeland on his own. The fragment was published in a book commemorating the European Year of Older People and it was presented as an example of how contemporary older people talk about older people they knew and keep in their memories. I learned by chance that the author of the interview (whom I did not know because a colleague had conducted the interview) recognised herself and felt offended at being classified as an old person.

Another example concerns the wartime life story of a woman who experienced the Second World War in Vilnius. She describes a scene she had observed at the beginning of the war when the Soviet occupation of the eastern border of Poland began:

> And here there is my experience because, as I said, our soldiers were throwing some of their things into the forecourt. When I was going out, there were perhaps a few sabres – we lived in this house in an outbuilding – so I was going out across the yard by the forecourt and I witnessed this scene in the forecourt. This Jew with a red armband took a sabre out of a sheath and read 'Honor et Patria', and burst out laughing: "Ha, ha, ha they defended the country with *honour*". So it was a *very* strong experience, I rushed back home and along the way started crying. It was probably the beginning of *this* that is called patriotism.

This part of the narrative was once analysed during a seminar in a region and city other than where the woman lives. The analysis tended to show that the narrator was expressing her experiences by using the rhetoric of prejudice. According to one theory of stereotypes and prejudices, they should be analysed as particular communication structures influencing specific forms of argumentation and narration (van Dijk, 1984; Czyżewski, 1997). This scene was discussed, therefore, as an example of the language of prejudice. Although this sort of analysis does not relate the rhetoric of prejudice to an actual person's attitudes, it may appear to do so.

During the seminar somebody identified the narrator because he knew her. Then, in a face-to-face interaction, this person explained that the narrator did not hold such attitudes and that such an interpretation was very unjust in view of the woman's identity, her ideas and opinions.

I discussed this narrative in my book (Kazmierska, 1999), but I concentrated on quite another aspect of the life story. I did not emphasise this particular fragment and problems related to it for two reasons. First, the problem of prejudice was not the main issue in my book. Second, I realised that I might have the chance of giving the book to the narrator (which I did) and she could very easily have identified herself. I would not risk such a confrontation, because I shared the opinion about the narrator expressed at the meeting. On the other hand, the fragment was worth analysing because it represented one of the important problems of Polish-Soviet-Jewish relationships on the eastern border during the Second World War. It is also interesting because of the symbolic universe to which the narrator refers.

This example points to another problem. Is it only the narrator who has the 'right' to expect this sort of privacy? Or do researchers also have the 'right' to withdraw from certain aspects of analysis that seem to them to be controversial? For instance, a researcher may find the situation of personal contact with a narrator too difficult because of her or his own emotional involvement, or because of certain aspects of identity. This may happen when the identity of a listener (researcher) and a narrator are dominated by other forms of identification. For example, again in relation to the Second World War, these roles may be influenced by identification with victim and perpetrator. According to Rosenthal and Bar-On (1992), this may influence the interaction between the interviewer and interviewee and, consequently, the life story. Rosenthal describes an interview with a Jewish narrator in which she acknowledged being the descendant of a perpetrator (Rosenthal and Bar-On, 1992). However, this relationship may also be affected by the ability to confront such situations. I know that for some of my German colleagues, the task of interviewing victims of war would be too difficult, whereas others are prepared to do it, although they are fully aware of the special meaning of the situation (Rosenthal, 1998). This example demonstrates that the relationship between researcher and narrator is truly interactive, something that becomes very clear when a narrative is analysed in a group.

Group discussion

As has been mentioned before, narratives are usually interpreted in groups. Procedures of text analysis tend to provide objective bases for interpretation. In addition, collective discussion of a text narrative provides an opportunity to analyse various frames of interpretation and different aspects of certain phenomena. The value of such analysis is especially obvious when cross-cultural perspectives are represented (for example, when people from different social worlds or cultures discuss a case).

According to my experience, collective discussions show the importance of the relationship between researcher and narrator. This specific intimacy that has been built up during the process of storytelling is 'verified' in public presentation. The researcher presenting their case knows more about the narrator and interprets their story in the context of the whole interaction. Although they always describe this context, others treat the narrative only as a text for analysis, whereas for the researcher it is the story of a particular and individual person.

Thus, the researcher may be confronted with a situation that has already been discussed in this chapter. Collective analysis sometimes reveals aspects of the narrative that are difficult for the researcher to study because of their background knowledge of the narrator. The question of ethical aspects acquires another meaning. To what extent should a researcher remain 'loyal' to a narrator and to what extent should they be 'faithful' to the task of objective description of social phenomena when studying narratives? Group discussions help to clarify this dilemma. A researcher is confronted with frames of reference that they have perhaps not taken into account. Sometimes they have to revise their perspective and face the problem of an interpretation that they would like to omit.

Conclusions

Quantitative methods do not show the contexts of people's opinions and choices; rather, they exemplify certain points, or stages, of life without the personal aspects. Respondents are mere numbers in representative samples. Qualitative research, and the biographical approach in particular, enables us to study social reality and see it continuously reinterpreted by social actors. It enables us to describe how individuals give meaning to their experiences. This is why I strongly believe in the biographical methods with which I work. However, the ethical aspects of biographical interviewing have been a frequent source of problems for me, as I have explained earlier in this chapter. The comments I have presented are the result of my own research experience of situations when I have felt uncomfortable about the discrepancy between my expectations and those of the life stories' narrators.

The closer a researcher is to an individual's experience when revealing the latter's social, cultural as well as emotional and personal context, the more their research can be considered to be humanistic. At the same time, however, more ethical doubts arise: how far should a researcher go with their interpretation, and to what extent can somebody's biography be treated as mere research material?

Note

[1] I refer here to the distinction presented by Helling (1990) when she discusses differences between a 'traditional' way of biographical analysis where the material is 'a means' of studying socio-historical reality, and interpretive analysis where the nature of the narrative account becomes 'a topic' of the research.

References

Apitzsch, U. and Inowlocki, L. (2000) 'Biographical analysis: a "German" school?', in P. Chamberlayne, J. Bornat and T. Wengraf (eds) *The turn to biographical methods in social sciences: Comparative issues and examples*, London: Routledge, pp 53-70.

Czyżewski, M. (1997) 'Repatrianci i wypzdzeni: wzajemne uprzedzenia w relacjach biograficznych', in M. Czyżewski, A. Piotrowski and A. Rokuszewska-Pawlek (eds) *Biografia i tożsamość narodowa*, Lódź: Wyd Katedry Socjologii Kultury, pp 159-72.

Engelking, B. (1994) *Zaglada i pamięć*, Warsaw: IfiS PAN.

Helling, I. (1990) 'Metoda badal biograficznych', in J. Wlodarek and M. Ziólkowski' (eds) *Metoda biograficzna w socjologii*, Warsaw-Poznań: PWN, pp 13-37.

Hermanns, H. (1987) 'Narrative interviews – a new tool for sociological research', *Approaches to the study of face-to-face interaction*, Wyd Uniwersytetu Lódzkiego, *Folia Sociologica 13*: Lódz, pp 43-55.

Inowlocki, L. (1993) 'Grandmothers, mothers and daughters. Intergenerational transmission in displaced families in three Jewish communities', in D. Bertaux and P. Thompson (eds) *International yearbook of oral history and life stories*, vol 2: *Between generations, family models, myths and memories*, Oxford: University Press.

Kaźmierska, K. (1999) *Doświadczenia wojenne Polaków a ksztaltowanie tozsamości etnicznej. Analiza narracji kresowych*, Warsaw: IFiS PAN.

Riemann, G. and Schütze, F. (1987) 'Some notes on a student research workshop on biography analysis, interaction analysis and analysis of social worlds', *Biography and Society Newsletter*, no 8, pp 54-70.

Rosenthal, G. (1993) 'Reconstruction of life stories: principles of selections in generating stories for narrative biographical interviews', in R. Josselson and A. Lieblich (eds) *The narrative study of lives*, vol 1, Newbury Park, CA/London: Sage Publications, pp 59-91.

Rosenthal, G. (ed) (1998) *The Holocaust in three generations of the Nazi Regime*, London/Washington DC: Cassel Wellington House.

Rosenthal, G. and Bar-On, D. (1992) 'A biographical case study of a victimizer's daughter's strategy: pseudo-identification with the victims of holocaust', *Journal of Narrative and Life History*, vol 2, no 2, pp 105-27.

Schütze, F. (1983) 'Biographieforschung und narratives Interview', *Neue Praxis*, no 3, pp 283-93.

Schütze, F. (1989) 'Kollektive Verlaufskurve oder kollektiver Wandlungsprozess. Dimensionen des Vergleichs von Kriegserfahrungen amerikanisher und deutscher Soldaten im Zweiten Weltkreig', *Bios: Zeitschrift fur Biographieforschung und Oral History*, vol 1, pp 31-110.

Schütze, F. (1992) 'Pressure and guilt: war experiences of a young German soldier and their biographical implications', *International Sociology*, vol 7, no 2, pp 181-208 and no 3, pp 347-67.

Schütze, F. (unpublished) *Outline for the method of biography analysis*, Notes for students.

Van Dijk, T.A. (1984) *Prejudice and discourse*, Amsterdam: Benjamins.

THIRTEEN

Ghost writers: using biographical methods across languages

Bogusia Temple

What this volume demonstrates, as did *The turn to biographical methods in social science* (Chamberlayne et al, 2000), is that there are undoubted benefits in research with people who are different to you in terms of widening perspectives and horizons. When language is a barrier to communication, many researchers and service providers employ translators and interpreters to try to harvest these benefits. However, ensuring that perspectives other than that of the researcher can be heard is not a straightforward task. In this chapter, I am interested in the implications, when translating, of Spivak's (1993, p 189) call to "discriminate on the terrain of the original", and the value of using biographical methods to attempt to do this. For researchers, these issues matter because, as I argue later in this chapter, the choice of interpreter or translator influences the research 'findings'. The service provider is also reliant on the person acting as a go-between for the two languages. Ultimately, the kind of service a non-English speaker receives may depend on whether or not service providers have addressed some of the issues raised in this chapter.

Here, I ask: does it matter what languages we are discussing? In other words, is there a politics of translation? I use an example from my work with Polish communities to discuss the value of biographical methods in this area, as well as to point out some of the issues involved in the approach I have chosen.

Much of what is published about using interpreters is a sort of practical 'how to' list, rather than a concern with the methodological implications of employing an interpreter (see, for example, Phelan and Parkman, 1995; Johnson et al, 1999; and for an exception, Edwards, 1998). The insights researchers have gained from looking at cross-language communication in the field of translation as an active process are rarely applied to interpretation across languages, although there are undoubted lessons to be learned from such work. I use the term 'translation' throughout to include both written and oral accounts, since researchers often treat both in the same non-problematic way. The written translation is usually all the researcher has to represent an interview.

Universal and conditional translation

All too often, cross-language research in health and social care assumes, sometimes by default, that there is only one correct perspective on the social world. Researchers using this model believe that they *produce* – and *do not influence* – 'findings'. In other words, when the 'correct' method is used, findings exist independently of the researcher. Translators pose practical difficulties, not methodological ones. For example, methods such as 'back translation' can be used to ensure one agreed end product; the research *process* is ignored. I call this model *universal translation* because it implies that the particular translator is not important, since the end product is always the same[1].

There is an alternative position: that researchers and research participants produce accounts of their research. To extend this model to include cross-language research, then, should translators be involved, they also have an influence on what is produced. I call this *conditional translation*, since the process of translation influences the end product; in fact, the translator is an integral part of that process. This is my preferred approach to translation.

Building on the work of Liz Stanley (1990), I see the mapping of the *intellectual auto/biographies* of both researcher and translator as part of a reflexive methodology that can be used to operationalise this conditional approach to translation. This mapping involves a discussion of the position of all involved in the research with recognition of the social grounding of all knowledge claims. The researcher, research participant and translator each bring their own views to the research. A translation, like all aspects of research, is always open to challenge. Similarly, Barbara Godard describes translation as "a truly associative process, an ongoing appeal to memory and to a private thesaurus, a pingpong of potentially infinite rebounds" (quoted in Simon, 1996, p 23). Godard sees translation as a way of ordering relations between languages and cultures, as an art of approach rather than one concerned with 'target languages' (that is, the languages you are translating between) and conditions of arrival.

However, the argument that all research accounts are auto/biographical in nature itself raises a number of issues with regard to translation.

A politics of translation

Many writers have argued that there is a language hierarchy (Spivak, 1992, 1993; Lauret, 1999). In her overview of English studies, Maria Lauret (1999) argues that the familiar image and discourse of margin and centre is relevant to English as a discipline, with English *literature* at the centre and women's post-colonial 'black' and ethnic *writing* at the periphery. She suggests that, to challenge 'cultural imperialism':

> The English language, likewise, in all its variety of uses both at home and
> abroad, should become more of an object of scrutiny than at present it is –
> English departments and English curricula usually do not include any study

of language *per se*.... As long as the 'universality' of English as a language is taken for granted and remains unexamined and unproblematic, just so long will English as a discipline remain complicit with the legacy of empire. Only when English is no longer 'a study which occludes its own specific national, cultural, and political grounding' can it become a discipline in a very important sense, 'in its own right' rather than one which perpetuates cultural imperialism in the very act – these days – of disavowing it. (Lauret, 1999, pp 134-5)

The same point could be made about much cross-language research in the social sciences. While sociologists, for example, may agree that language constructs as well as describes social reality, the significance of these insights in research with people whose first language is not English is often ignored and "the approval of Headquarters" (Lauret, 1999, p 125) is sought. For Lauret 'Headquarters' (HQ) is an idea of 'England' and 'English' in some pure or unadulterated form and can take hold in many guises, such as the evaluation of 'major writers' or the demand for standards and 'correct' English. This resonates with the idea of a single correct translation. Gayatri Spivak's (1992, 1993) and Homi Bhabha's (1994) challenge to the Western view of HQ as the neutral English language has yet to make the impact in research that it has made in translation studies. The field of translation studies holds many valuable lessons for cross-language researchers.

Spivak (1993) and many others (for example, Bassnet, 1994; Simon, 1996) have demonstrated that translation is more than a word-for-word matching across languages. For example, Spivak urges the translator to think not only in terms of logical connections between words, but also to look at texts as 'rhetorical devices'; that is, in Spivak's view, each account presents a perspective on an issue. There is, then, no simple relationship between what a translator reads, or an interpreter hears, and the written research account that is produced out of it. If all accounts are in fact produced, different translators may produce different translations, and the choice of translator becomes crucial in the same way as the choice of researcher.

Spivak's work on translation presents all researchers with issues in the political naming of 'others'. She asserts that, in translation, "meaning hops into the spacy emptiness between two named historical languages" (Spivak, 1993, p 180). Her 'politics of translation' highlights the hierarchies implicit in translating into the language of a country with a particular history. Spivak recognises the power differentials between languages and countries and, while accepting that transnational hybridity may challenge fixed notions of 'otherness', argues that this is via a process of "linguistic and esthetic [sic] assimilation" (Simon, 1996, p 154) by Anglo-American writers. In other words, which particular countries and languages are involved in translation is important.

These points can be illustrated by Molly Andrews' (2000) work in East Germany. Andrews' work shows how "social and individual identity will be recast as a response to acute political change" (2000, p 184). This is particularly relevant here, since she shows that what is memorable can change rapidly when the political climate changes. The 'narratives of countries' change as well as those of individuals within them.

> When people who are neither heroes nor villains in the current construction of the East German past tell their stories to an outside audience, their words are often interpreted through a meaning-making lens which is not their own. When East Europeans speak the unspeakable – ie the details of their non-heroic lives – their stories are rejected…. In time, it is likely that the stories do change, not because respondents feel that finally they are able to speak of a past which really did happen, but rather because they have found ways of narrating their life stories for popular consumption and approval. (Andrews, 2000, p 189)

Andrews documents the flood of Western sociologists and oral historians into East Germany at a time when their East German colleagues had lost their jobs. Only outsiders, it seemed, could be 'objective' and pick out what is significant. Andrews argues, and my work supports, the view that all researchers, including those from the West, bring their own – and their country's – narratives, to their research[2]. This does not mean that outsiders' views are not valuable; no, it is always useful to have a comparative perspective. However, no perspective is 'objective', since we all come with our own social and cultural baggage.

Spivak argues that the translator, therefore, must be able to "discriminate on the terrain of the original" (1993, p 189), and not assume that the perspective of the researcher or the translator is irrelevant (a point discussed later in this chapter). That is, they must engage with issues concerning the position of the original author and the situation from which they are writing. Others, for example Cooper (2000) and Wengraf (2000), also warn that it is no longer defensible to cross national boundaries without first researching and defining norms and assumptions of culture. This process involves mapping the terrain or narrative of a country.

The messages from the work of researchers such as Andrews, Watson, Wengraf and Cooper are often taken on board in cross-language research by employing translators who speak the language involved. However, this in itself is not enough. Spivak's call to discriminate on the terrain of the original means that the position of the translator must be a concern and choosing someone by language ability alone does not ensure that research participants' views will be heard. As Sherry Simon (1996) asserts, we cannot simply discover 'cultural meanings' as if they existed within separate cultures or indeed separate languages.

Researchers are increasingly aware that any 'matching' of the social characteristics of researcher and research participant is methodologically problematic (for example, Twine and Warren, 2000, discuss 'racial matching'). The same issues also arise when assumptions are made that matching researchers' and participants' languages is sufficient to ensure understanding of perspective. Researchers engaging with translators and using an approach such as that suggested by conditional translation have to tackle the murky waters of their own terrain. I will demonstrate this point in relation to my own research with Polish communities in England.

Insider or outsider? Or, what is the 'terrain of the original'?

My research with Polish communities in England has spanned more than 10 years (for example, Temple, 1992, 1997 and 1999). The topics I covered vary greatly. Increasingly, as people who arrived from Poland immediately after the Second World War have retired, views on ageing and homeland have featured. I have now carried out interviews with over 40 people, some of whom I have interviewed on three separate occasions.

My initial contacts were formed by getting in touch with a Polish Saturday School teacher in a northern town in England. Participant observation at a Polish Club and interviews with 10 households provided a wealth of information about household divisions of labour and life histories. Following on from this research, I have carried out interviews all over the UK, trying to include both first- and second-generation men and women of various ages who described themselves as 'Polish'. I have also interviewed visitors from Poland as well as Polish-Americans. Life histories and issues of ethnicity and diaspora have been central, given the lack of research with long-established white refugee communities in England. The interviews have been structured to varying degrees according to the topic under consideration. For example, while researching the existence (or otherwise) of 'Polish families', my interviews were specifically focused on definitional issues of Polish identity and changes in those definitions over time and across context. The life-history interviews were less structured, since people focused on various parts of their lives for different lengths of time. Interviews were conducted in the preferred language of the person being interviewed. I always translated and transcribed those in Polish into English, so that I could transfer text directly from the interview to my writing. Each interview was taped, and the names of people were changed so that they cannot be identified.

My language skills have always been an asset. Once, however, time constraints induced me to employ a translator to listen to my taped interviews and to interpret from the tape and write up the interview in English. The experience was salutary (Temple, 1999). The translation I received of Mrs Donowicz's [all interviewee's names are pseudonyms] interview, for example, was not 'wrong', in the sense that totally inappropriate words had been chosen. However, the translation seemed to bear little resemblance to the interview I had carried out. Particular problems arose with translating words such as 'have to', 'can' or 'must' when talking about women's lives. Did this mean they were saying that they were constrained by society and, therefore, had – but did not want – to live as they did? Or did they 'have to' because, as my translator was suggesting, women's nature led them to that way of living? These words are not difficult to translate literally but the words chosen are crucial to the sense they give of an account. I learnt that there are many ways to interpret, in the broadest sense of the word, a discourse.

Looking back over the translation with my translator raised my awareness of many issues. Of particular relevance here is the problem of 'where did the translations come from?'. In other words, what is the terrain of the text? Why was my version different from Mrs Larkowska's, my translator? She had lived in England for about 10 years. We discussed many issues in Polish and our views were significantly different. Discussing women's employment in Poland, for example, Mrs Larkowska said:

> You don't understand about Poland. You haven't lived there. Going to work ... queuing ... looking after the children. Women have to go out to work. I wanted to stay at home but we couldn't afford it. They say women are treated the same as men under Communism but the men don't do anything at home. We do everything.

In discussing why this was so, she explained:

> We had equality rammed down our throats. The home was the only place my husband could say no. It was like ... like fighting them ... you can't make me do it. The government didn't care about what went on in the home ... someone did it ... that was enough.

For Mrs Larkowska, the women I interviewed were not fighting for equality, they were making matters worse:

> They [women] do everything. Equality is about sharing the work. If a woman goes out to work, looks after the children and the house ... why is that good? It is better to make men do their share ... they are lazy. If a woman agrees to do everything, they will agree ... but children want their mothers ... that's the way life is.

Talking about recent changes in Poland (second interview, 2000), Mrs Larkowska said:

> At least now we own something. Men can work hard and make money for their families. Women don't have to work until they drop. That's equality.

Beyond differences of country of birth and upbringing, there were generational differences between us. Mrs Larkowska's views corresponded to those of some of the older women I interviewed. They did not agree, however, with those of the younger women, including Mrs Donowicz, the woman whose interview she had translated for me, who was herself a recent arrival from Poland.

How could I choose a translator for Mrs Donowicz's interview? If I chose according to language ability and grammatical correctness, I would chose Mrs

Larkowska. If I chose according to who would be most sympathetic to Mrs Donowicz's perspective, I would do the translations myself. However, as well as looking into Mrs Larkowska's views, I had to examine how I came to my current views and how they would influence how I translated. My views may be similar to those of Mrs Donowicz, but there are also differences between us. I am interested in feminist ideas, which are seen by many in the Polish community I grew up in as decidedly 'not Polish'. I speak fluent Polish. However, my interpretation or translation may not be the same as that of someone from Poland. I was born and brought up in England, although I have been influenced by the teaching of history from a non-British perspective and have appreciated a different cultural heritage.

If my beliefs are a result of a variety of influences, the same can be said of Mrs Larkowska's and of the people I have interviewed:

> I don't think the Poland they [refugees after the Second World War] are longing for and dreaming of exists anymore. We have hamburgers and French fries and wear jeans. Also we went through things they didn't ... a Communist regime ... occupation ... shortages. But some of us long for those days now. We had security. They wouldn't understand that. They think we have been brainwashed or are lazy. (Interview with Mrs Pokasz, a Polish woman visiting England)

The terrain of these translations cannot be travelled using language alone as a guide. This woman's interview came to mind when I read Andrews' (2000) work. There is a presumption by many Westerners that all Polish people welcome capitalism. They certainly welcome freedom, but that does not necessarily mean they welcome capitalism. Mrs Pokasz's views were supported by others in Poland but were not appreciated by the people I interviewed, who viewed Mrs Pokasz and people like her as dupes or as having 'sold out'. This may have been a lack of understanding due to different experiences and life histories since the Second World War. So, as Spivak argues, it is not enough to be able to speak the language. Moreover, identifying the terrain of a translation is no easy matter either, as cultures cannot be split into 'Polish' and 'English' parts.

Discussion

Choosing a translator as a representative of 'the terrain' is problematic since particular beliefs cannot be mapped onto cultures in any straightforward way. Knowing a translator's views on the issues being researched, however, is crucial to an understanding of the product the researcher ends up with. Knowledge of each individual and the social context of their views is part of the process of building mutual understanding.

It is unusual for a researcher to be able to pull translations apart in the way that I have done. However, all researchers can discuss perspectives to open up debates about similarities and differences. In my research with people who speak languages, I do not understand, I make debates about perspectives part of the research itself.

Although I advocate the *conditional translation* model, there are issues of representation when choosing translators. Concerns over representation always arise in research with communities. When there are two languages in play, the difficulties are compounded. This translation model at least builds these issues into discussions about perspective. People do not represent their cultures, and within a culture there may be different views that are all authentic within a particular context. Particular views cannot be attributed to a culture using language as the yardstick. Rather, the context of debate is crucial. This is clear from Mrs Larkowska's views on equality, quoted earlier in this chapter. Many women in England would agree with her 'Polish' perspective on the overloading of women in society. However, she situates her beliefs firmly within a resistance to Communism in a particular period in Poland's history.

Trying to do justice to difference by discriminating on the terrain from which views originate is, therefore, a tricky business. Attributing causes to differences in perspective may be impossible. I will never be able to say for definite whether or not the differences between my translator and myself were due to the fact that we were born and raised in different countries, or were from different generations, or met with different intellectual (including political) traditions over our lives. I feel it is necessary to point out to people who ask me to translate for them that my views have been strongly influenced by feminist writings. Mrs Larkowska acknowledges that her aversion to socialism/Communism may colour her translations. We both agree there is no neutral text that we can produce for readers. However, the discussion of these complex influences has to be engaged in should the strictures of an all-embracing HQ be broken. It follows from this that, in order to avoid cultural tourism, researchers employing translators need to become involved in debates about 'the public–private spaces' we create in all conversation (Griffiths, 1995). A way to engage in such debates is by discussing intellectual auto/biographies. Without attempting to ask 'what does this concept mean to this person within this language/culture?', we are implicitly assuming that there is a correct ahistorical perspective. The art of translation lies in managing the tension that exists between recognising the cultural specificity of meaning while looking for similarities between different language speakers. I believe that this balancing act is unavoidable.

Notes

[1] See Bryman (1988) for a fuller exposition of this view of research and Edwards (1998) for a discussion of the consequences of its application to language interpretation.

[2] See also Watson (1993) for a development of the argument that concepts and events need to be seen within a country's own historical framework.

References

Andrews, M. (2000) 'Texts in a changing context: reconstructing lives in East Germany', in P. Chamberlayne, J. Bornat and T. Wengraf (eds) *The turn to biographical methods in social science: Comparative issues and examples*, London: Routledge, pp 181-95.

Bassnet, S. (1994) *Translation studies*, London: Routledge.

Bhabha, H. (1994) *The location of culture*, London: Routledge.

Bryman, A. (1988) *Quantity and quality in social research*, London: Unwin Hyman.

Chamberlayne, P., Bornat, J. and Wengraf, T. (eds) (2000) *The turn to biographical methods in social science: Comparative issues and examples*, London: Routledge.

Cooper, A. (2000) 'The vanishing point of resemblance: comparative welfare as philosophical anthropology', in P. Chamberlayne, J. Bornat and T. Wengraf (eds) *The turn to biographical methods in social science: Comparative issues and examples*, London: Routledge, pp 90-108.

Edwards, R. (1998) 'A critical examination of the use of interpreters in the qualitative research process', *Journal of Ethnic and Migration Studies*, vol 24, no 1, pp 197-208.

Griffiths, M. (1995) *Feminisms and the self: The web of identity*, London: Routledge.

Johnson, M., Noble, C., Matthews, C. and Aguilar N. (1999) 'Bilingual communications within the health care setting', *Qualitative Health Research*, vol 9, no 3, pp 329-43.

Lauret, M. (1999) '"The approval of headquarters": race and ethnicity in English Studies', in M. Bulmer and J. Solomos (eds) *Ethnic and racial studies today*, London: Routledge, pp 124-35.

Phelan, M. and Parkman, S. (1995) 'Work with an interpreter', *British Medical Journal*, vol 311, pp 555-7.

Simon, S. (1996) *Gender in translation: Cultural identity and the politics of transmission*, London: Routledge.

Spivak, G. (1992) 'The politics of translation', in M. Barrett and A. Phillips (eds) *Destabilizing theory: Contemporary feminist debates*, Cambridge: Polity Press, pp 177-200.

Spivak, G. (1993) *Outside in the teaching machine,* London: Routledge.

Stanley, L. (1990) 'Moments of writing: is there a feminist auto/biography?', *Gender and History*, vol 2, no 1, pp 58-67.

Temple, B. (1992) 'Household strategies and types: the construction of social phenomena', Unpublished PhD thesis, University of Manchester.

Temple, B. (1997) 'Watch your tongue: issues in translation and cross-cultural research', *Sociology*, vol 31, no 3, pp 607-18.

Temple, B. (1999) 'Translating the translators, interpreting the interpreters', in M. Banting, J. Elliott, M. Dongchao, D. Oates and B. Temple (eds) *Inside the translation machine: Pro/feminist writings on translation issues in women's studies*, Manchester: Women's Studies Centre, University of Manchester, pp 48-55.

Twine, F.W. and Warren, J.W. (eds) (2000) *Racing research, researching race: Methodological dilemmas in critical race studies*, New York, NY: New York University Press.

Watson, P. (1993) 'Eastern Europe's silent revolution: gender', *Sociology*, vol 27, no 4, pp 471-87.

Wengraf, T. (2000) 'Uncovering the general from within the particular: from contingencies to typologies in the understanding of cases', in P. Chamberlayne, J. Bornat and T. Wengraf (eds) *The turn to biographical methods in social science: Comparative issues and examples*, London: Routledge, pp 140-64.

Part Four:
Recognising trajectories of
disempowerment

FOURTEEN

'Bucking and kicking': race, gender and embodied resistance in healthcare

Yasmin Gunaratnam

Concerns about how to work with and across differences of ethnicity, culture, language and religion are central to discussions on policy and practice development in the health and social care services in Britain (Alexander, 1999), where references to the need for cultural 'awareness', 'sensitivity' and 'competence' are commonplace. These concerns have taken on further meaning with the renewed attention to 'institutional racism' (Macpherson, 1999) in public sector services, and with the extension of race relations legislation (2000 Race Relations [Amendment] Act) to these services. However, despite the increasing attention being given to the need for culturally sensitive and anti-discriminatory professional practice, what is missing from British policy and professional education initiatives is any meaningful engagement with the complex relationships between lived, biographical experiences of race and ethnicity and needs for care. For example, how might social difference[1] affect the ways in which professionals interpret and respond to the requests, silences, faces and bodies of service users? How might biographical experiences of race and ethnicity affect, and be affected by, the everyday, micro-interactions within services, such as those interactions that take place in relation to eating, toileting, washing and touching? I believe that these 'tiny' details of somatic experiences of race and ethnicity are critical in producing the nature and quality of intercultural care, and they are the focus of this chapter. By 'somatic', I am referring to how race and ethnicity (in interrelation with other differences such as gender, class and disease/disability) are 'felt' and given meaning, emotionally and physically, through the body, affecting the very fabric of care needs, practices and interpersonal relationships between professionals and service users.

Using the case study of Maxine, a black Jamaican service user drawn from my ethnographic research in a London hospice (Gunaratnam, 1999), I will argue that biographical approaches to race and ethnicity can play a significant role in enabling professionals to engage with the nuances of somatic experience. This argument is grounded in my experiences in education and training with health and social care professionals where I have used biographical narratives to make less abstract some of the rich, but often dense, theoretical work on the relationships between lived experiences of race and ethnicity and wider social discourses and contexts (for examples, see Brah, 1996; Hall, 1996). While there can be significant gaps between academic theory (particularly in relation to critical race, feminist and cultural theory) and discussions of intercultural practice, I have found that professionals are open to – and enthusiastic about – using and applying theoretical concepts to their practice. In many cases, theory can be empowering to professionals, naming and legitimising some of the complex dynamics and experiences that they meet in their everyday work (Hollway, 2001), but that are largely unrecognised in professional and service development.

By examining how biographical approaches can be used to enrich intercultural and anti-discriminatory practice, three main areas of discussion structure this chapter. The first outlines some of the limitations in current approaches to professional practice in multicultural contexts and makes explicit how biographical narratives might be used to address and overcome these limitations. I then move on to present an analysis, centred upon biographical accounts of the physical care of Maxine. In this analysis, I will link themes in biographical stories of gendered and racialised violence, reports of Maxine's *anorexia nervosa*, and portrayals of her anxiety about being touched, lifted and washed by hospice nurses towards the end of her life. I argue that the interrelations between the body, the emotional and the social, and how these are narrated, produced and performed in biographical accounts, are vital in understanding the complex power relations between white staff and service users racialised as 'ethnic minorities'. The final part of this chapter discusses how biographical narratives might be used to connect different sites of experience and to gain insights into racialised experiences of care.

Using biographical approaches to race and ethnicity

A principal strand of my argument about the value of biographical approaches in understanding somatic experience of race, ethnicity and social difference lies in the extent to which practitioners and researchers are able to use the approaches to move beyond thinking about race and ethnicity in relation to rigid, one-dimensional categories. For instance, in relation to training and education resources in hospice and palliative care (for examples, see Firth, 2001), which provide care to people with terminal and sometimes chronic diseases and conditions, it is not so much that the racialised body is unrecognised in discussions of professional practice; rather, it is that its recognition is fetishised, mainly in relation to ethnicity, culture and religion. What I mean by 'fetishised' is that assumptions are made about how ethnicity, culture and/or religion can *determine* psycho-physical experiences and care needs, leading to highly prescriptive and restrictive approaches to intercultural care. In what I called 'fact-file' resources (Gunaratnam, 1997) that are aimed at providing discrete, 'factual' information to practitioners about death-related rituals in different ethnic and religious groups, the body and bodily practices are central:

> Of basic and particular consideration ... and questions frequently asked by
> nurses, are whether there are last rites, whether there are rules about who
> can touch the body, questions about confession, about prayers, about leaving
> the dead person alone. (Neuberger, 1987, p 4)

I am not disputing that such questions and information can be valuable to
practitioners. Rather, my argument is that the danger with such categorical
approaches to race, ethnicity and intercultural care is that an individual's body
can *become* their racialised identity. That is, race/ethnicity/religion can eclipse
both individual experience and also other social differences such as gender and
class that can criss-cross and mediate the meanings of race, ethnicity, culture
and religion in people's lives. Care needs are then seen in relation to a narrow
spectrum of racial and ethnic categories, in which assumptions are made, and
clear lines are drawn between those grouped as being 'Muslim', 'Jewish' or
even 'the African-Caribbean community' (Green, 1992) and needs for care.

These categorising approaches not only put people into ideal-type 'boxes' of
ethnicity, culture and religion, but they can also lead to perceptions of
intercultural care in terms of unrealistic dichotomies of either 'getting it right',
or 'getting it wrong' (Gunaratnam, 1997). Through my experiences of research
and training, I have found that such dichotomies can be unhelpful, restrictive
and anxiety-producing for practitioners, while also serving to divert attention
away from complicated emotional and socially structured experiences of
difference for service users. In my experience, a central dilemma in intercultural
care that is rarely addressed in policy and practice development is how
practitioners can grasp something of the *specific ways* in which race and ethnicity
are produced and can have effects in individual lives, while not losing sight of
broader social *patterns,* particularly when these patterns are based upon inequality
and oppression.

In working with these tensions between the unique and the patterned in my
own research, I have found it useful to think of research and professional practice
in terms of a 'doubled practice' that needs to work both *with* and *against* racial
and ethnic categorisations (Gunaratnam, 2003). In relation to approaches to
practice, this entails an engagement with how individual experience might be
affected by race and ethnicity without making assumptions about what these
experiences are. It is here that the value of biographical approaches can really
be seen.

In broad terms, by addressing the detail of biographical accounts, both
researchers and practitioners can move beyond categorical thinking and gain
insights into the nuanced meanings and effects of race and ethnicity in individual
lives. In this respect, I am convinced by Knowles's (1999, p 130) argument
that:

> Consideration of individual lives ... brings endless variation to racial categories
> making it possible to take into account important differences between
> occupants of the same categories.

For me, the value of biographical approaches to 'race' and ethnicity can be summarised in relation to four main points:

- Biographical accounts can be used to engage with embodied subjectivity. With this recognition, the work of practitioners/researchers involves using processes of interpretation to examine how the social, the embodied, the emotional and the interpersonal are produced, felt and have effects in the stories that individuals tell about their lives.
- The approaches are able to engage with the interrelations between the individual and the social context in which race and ethnicity are always at play yet can also be obscured and masked (Higginbotham, 1992).
- The process of engaging with individual biographies allows for – and can be sensitive to – a heterogeneity of experiences. This is important in recognising some of the uniqueness of the ways in which other social differences interact with and inflect biographical experiences of race and ethnicity.
- The process of interpreting biographical narratives (Hollway and Jefferson, 2000; Wengraf, 2001) gives attention to the production of accounts (the interview or service interaction) as a site for the negotiation and reworking of identities, bringing intersubjective relations (including unconscious processes) and the identity of the researcher/practitioner into view[2].

Despite the great potential value of using biographical methods in professional practice, it is important to make clear that attention to individual biographies does not by itself generate sensitive and anti-discriminatory practice. The processes of how we trace, map, connect and juxtapose narrative themes in accounts (Wengraf, 2001) and how we locate present perspectives and actions within a history of personal, interpersonal and social contexts (Scheff, 1997; Wengraf, 2000) are critical.

This chapter makes explicit what such processes of interpretation can look like and how they can lead to more complex approaches to intercultural care and anti-discriminatory practice in the discussion of Maxine's case study that follows.

Maxine's story: narratives of gender, migration and settlement

Maxine was a black Jamaican woman, a 63-year-old mother of 10 children, who lived on her own in a council house and described herself as "a fighter". I had first met Maxine through my participant observation in the hospice day centre, and I subsequently interviewed her in her home. Shortly after our first interview, Maxine's health deteriorated and she was admitted into the hospice for terminal care. She spent just over a month in the hospice before she died, and during this time I visited her several times. With Maxine's permission, I tape-recorded one of our conversations in her hospice ward.

Maxine had migrated to England in the early 1960s. Her story of migration and early settlement in our first interview was characterised by accounts of both domestic and racist violence. Maxine first spoke of her experiences of domestic violence in an account about her migration, when I had asked her about her reasons for migrating:

Yasmin Gunaratnam (YG): So why did you come here?

Maxine: Because of my stupid husband (...)[3] he, he send and said if I don't come, I won't get any maintenance for me and the children .... I tell my parents, I'm not going, for one of my reason, he was very cruel to me. He beat me you know (...) and I was thinking about that (...) so (...) my, my parents they're old-fashioned (...) they said, "Where I bound (...), I have to go. It's my husband, anything he said, I should do". You know they are so old-fashioned, they get on your nerves.

YG: Umm (...) so you felt you had to come?

Maxine: (...) Yeah, they put the pressure on me you know (...), "That is your husband. Where you bound, you must", you know, they just put it (...) back home in the country (...) they lift husband higher than God, you know. I said to me Mum, me Granny everybody (...) I said, "Would you like to be out here and get a telegram that he beat me to death?". They said they're praying (...). So I said, "It doesn't matter to you if he beat me seven days a week". So I just (...) come (...). Yeah (...). He was terrible you know, uum, it's another doctor I had (...). Doctor H, she was a woman. I went to her one Saturday morning, he started beat me (...) blood coming through me nose and me mouth and [clears throat] .... I tell her I fall down the stairs (...) and it was in those big block of flats (...) so she said, "You could fall down the stairs (...) bang your mouth or your nose (...), that's what giving you this bleeding. But, you didn't fall down (...) the stairs" .... And she give me a letter to Tower Bridge Court and she said to take it there Monday morning (...) and they'll write to me, write to me and they summons him to court 'cause me knee bruise up, me feet up, everywhere (...).

The gendered, ethnic, cultural, and regional identifications that are evoked in this account of Maxine's migration situate Maxine's particular experiences of gendered violence and mark out some of the dynamics between biographies, emotions, bodies and social relations that I want to explore in relation to Maxine's care within the hospice. In this respect, my analysis is concerned with the particular narrative connections between traumatic racialised and gendered experiences and how these connections might be used to understand Maxine's emotional investments in her body. In order to explore these relationships in further detail, I want to examine this account of gendered violence within the context of Maxine's accounts of racist violence. In the extract below (that followed closely in sequence to the preceding extract), Maxine talks about two incidents that took place in her early period of settlement:

> Uuh (...) twice I get lick (...). I thought I'd lose me eye (...) some boy rolling up er (...) snow ... and they said, "Here, here, here one is coming (...)" and they threw the snow straight in my eye. Oh gosh (...) and they run off and (...) "Monkey go back home and go climb (...) em tingy (...) banana tree (...)". So I said "You see how lucky we are? Have you got a banana tree? (...) But you have to bloody go, go and go buy it at green grocer though". [Laughs] "We, we cut our own. So you see, we are blessed people". They just run off and laugh. When I expect Yvonne [daughter] they, they say, "go home". I hear this "Go home. Go home", until it really used to get me sick. "Go home monkey" (...) and this boy (...) I was about (...) gone seven months pregnant with Yvonne (...) and the boy give me one lick in me back .... Big lump of snow, that they roll up ... and all you could hear is 'Boom' and they don't do it to white, just black (...) and ... I was with two of me, my husband cousin and they say [voice getting louder], "Max. Max. What you think you're doing? Let them boy go on". And I run them down with the big belly (...) and they run into a shop [laughs]. Every time I pass that shop (…) and I'm in this country from 1961 (...) every time I pass that shop (...) I stand up and give a little laugh, 'cause I remember that's where they run.

This extract is again marked by identifications of race and gender. Maxine is clear that it is her blackness that signals her out as a target for violence. She leaves no room for doubt about the racist nature of the attacks. The direct reports of the vocabulary of racist abuse in the first incident are all too familiar, in which the representation of African-Caribbean people as 'monkeys' speaks of dehumanisation, racial inferiority and a biological and spatial otherness (see Young, 1990) that can threaten the order of white, urban street life.

Within this narrative context, I am specifically interested in how Maxine's stories of racist violence serve systematically to disrupt the polarised subject positions of 'victim' and 'aggressor' that circulate within dominant discourses and representations of racist violence. In each account, Maxine is simultaneously 'victim' and agent. In the first story, she reappropriates and reworks the very dehumanising material of verbal abuse to challenge and belittle her attackers and to empower, rehumanise and dignify black people as 'blessed'.

In the second story, despite the depiction of her heavily pregnant body (perhaps even because of it) and the inaction of two male relatives, Maxine scripts herself as the heroine of the narrative, who chases the attackers away – an incident that is also cited as an enduring source of future satisfaction. Both stories serve to restore a sense of self, objectified and degraded by racist violation. However, the stories are also ambivalent in the sense observed by Brain (2002, p 164) in auto/biographies of *anorexia nervosa*, where narrative can enact "both a painful recounting of past horrors and enabl[e] a translation of trauma into language" through which emotional trauma can be both 'relived' and 'relieved' in the storytelling process.

The recognition of these complexities, ambivalence and points of resistance are specifically important in relation to a doubled practice that challenges racialised categorisation. As Warner has argued with regard to gender (1996, pp 52-3), "There is a need to privilege those stories which disrupt ... finite categories and which give way to the possibility of different positions which are fluid rather than ossified into gendered bodies".

The attention that I have given here to themes that disrupt 'traditional' relations between 'dominant' and 'subordinated' identities within Maxine's stories are of significance not only in freeing up our thinking about how racialised difference is lived, but are also important in interpreting Maxine's experiences of care within the hospice.

Biographies and caring practices

During my many visits to Maxine in the hospice, she talked about being unhappy with aspects of her nursing care. In one (tape-recorded) conversation, Maxine talked about feeling excluded by particular nurses who gave "special" attention to their "favourite" service users:

> They have their favourite and I'm not saying it for a lie. It's true (...) when they would say "Oh lovie, darling, you want your (...) bed wash now" and tings like that.

Maxine talked about these practices in providing a context to a story of being lifted and moved by nurses in the course of being taken to be washed.

When she described the incident to me, Maxine said that she felt unsafe and 'like a piece of meat', framing the incident as objectifying, but also racialised: "Those girls [nurses] no respect no black people". Maxine talked about feeling particularly unsafe when being lifted, and drew attention to the fact that a nurse had frightened her by shouting: "She ball at me, man, and I don't like people frighten me". At the time when Maxine was describing the incident to me, I found it difficult to fully understand the representation of this incident as racialised. Furthermore, in Maxine's medical case notes, I also found that Maxine's nurses had noted her specific anxieties on being lifted, suggesting that Maxine's anxiety and 'paranoia' needed to be taken account of in her care.

As Maxine's health continued to deteriorate, she became increasingly reluctant to let the nurses attend to her basic hygiene needs. Two weeks after our conversation about this incident, I noted in my fieldwork diary after a visit to Maxine:

> She has been in the hospice a month now and is clearly deteriorating. She is incontinent and when I last saw her, her face was dirty and she was lying

in urine. Apparently she had not let the nurses wash her. But when she talked to me, she expressed the need to be washed.... Towards the end of my visit with her, she said that she felt like she was a donkey. She talked about working hard and feeling tired, and people continually prodding and poking the donkey. I then asked her what she would like the donkey to do. She was quite adamant in her reply and said that she wanted the donkey to buck and kick its heels in the air.

In bringing these different representations of Maxine together and considering them within the context of her biographical accounts of gendered and racist violence, I want to use my analysis to speculate upon the embodiment of Maxine's identifications, in which her body was both an expression and a site for the representation, regulation and resistance of identifications (Foucault, 1973, 1977). Psychoanalytical themes are valuable here in challenging the notion of a pre-given, rational subject and in addressing the erratic, volatile and unconscious dimensions of subjectivity and identification.

The particular value of attention to unconscious dynamics in the analytic process is perhaps best illustrated in interpreting another biographical narrative about Maxine that came from a hospice nurse. After Maxine's death, one of her homecare nurses told me that Maxine's daughter had reported to hospice staff that Maxine had had a history of eating disorders, marked by long periods of *anorexia nervosa*. This disclosure led to further re-readings of my interviews with Maxine, through which I identified narrative traces that provide some insights into the positioning of Maxine as someone with *anorexia nervosa*. For example, Maxine had told me that when she was first diagnosed with cancer, her response was to tell the doctor that:

I'm going to stop eat. I know I'll be hurting myself ... but I'm sick and tired of people, I was getting scared to go out the road and just kind of pad meself, holding out my old coat I feel better, 'cause it make me look big [laughs].

YG: [Laughs] So why were you going to stop eating Maxine?

Maxine: 'Cause of everybody saying I'm not eating (...) and I'm eating, and Doctor R, she asks me every time I go there.

This extract can be read as representing something of the threatening nature of concerns about Maxine's eating, and Maxine's defensive resistance to such threats. However, it also reveals something about the significance of her reported use of not eating in response to threats. Yet, following closely after this extract was Maxine's suggestion that this episode of weight loss was not *anorexia nervosa*, but anorexia related to her cancer.

The point of addressing this question about Maxine's anorexia is to make explicit how processes of interpretation, and attention to the unconscious, can be used to make sense of the contradictions between representations of Maxine's identity from others and her own identifications, and also the contradictions and tensions within narrative accounts themselves. These are important issues for practitioners, because in this instance the different sources of biographical information about Maxine gathered through the research process reflect the different types of biographical information that practitioners routinely have to manage and make sense of. In other words, practitioners do not just have to interpret biographical accounts from service users, but can also gain information from case notes and other practitioners and carers, all of which must be examined, interpreted and used to inform their care.

The important point in terms of my interpretation is that questions about Maxine's *anorexia nervosa* cannot be sidelined through reference to her own biographical accounts. How we interpret accounts and the assumptions that are made about subjectivity are highly significant in this respect. Biographical and narrative methods use psychosocial models of subjectivity that reject a reading of accounts as transparent, self-knowledgeable representations of experience (Hollway and Jefferson, 2000; Wengraf, 2001). Rather, these psychoanalytically inspired approaches assume levels of a psychic defensiveness, in which 'the interviewee is always "motivated not to know certain things about themselves and always produce ... told stories, which avoid such knowledge" (Wengraf, 2000, p 144). These approaches to subjectivity have guided my interpretations, and the relevance that I have given to the questions raised about Maxine's *anorexia nervosa*. Although speculative, I believe that these questions are important in exploring the somatic interfaces and tensions in Maxine's wider accounts of violence and in making sense of her experiences within the hospice. Indeed, the ambiguity of Maxine's *anorexia nervosa* and the connections between it, social difference and her resistance to physical care, captures Prosser's (2001, p 65) conceptual locating of the somatic as:

> Neither body nor psyche proper, the 'somatic' is that interface that cannot be touched directly. This psychic dimension of the body, or corporeal dimension of the psyche ... can be touched and known only by the unconscious sending out of messages onto the skin.

As a black Jamaican woman, Maxine had talked about being systematically denied control of her body through gendered violence, gendered-racist violence, and cultural acceptance of this violence. It is my contention that narrative themes in Maxine's accounts of her family relationships, domestic and racist violence, caring practices, questions about Maxine's *anorexia nervosa*, and wider social relations need to be connected in order to explicate and 'touch' something of the complexity of the somatic that is evoked in representations of Maxine's care. I want to suggest that recognising embodied, racialised and gendered experiences in Maxine's narratives is critical in making sense of her fear and anxiety about physical touch within the hospice and her subsequent refusal to be washed and kept clean.

I also want to address the power relations involved in the connections that I am making. Twigg (1997, 1999), for example, has argued in relation to the 'social bath'[4], that forms of intimate care, particularly those relating to bathing and washing, involve the negotiation of a complex set of boundaries. These boundaries involve touch, space, intimacy, bodily exposure, vulnerability and status differences between service users and professionals that can produce a myriad of power relations. She has suggested that such power relations can create particular vulnerabilities for older people. In relation to nakedness, she writes (Twigg, 1997, pp 224-5):

> To be without your clothes in the context of those who are clothed is to be at a disadvantage…. Bathing in the community inevitably involves such nakedness in front of another who is clothed. For older people it may involve a second form of asymmetry in the sense of bring naked in front of someone who is young. Nearly all representations of nakedness in modern culture are of youthful bodies. There are very few unclothed depictions of ageing.

These power relations become more complex when considering issues of 'race', gender and illness, where representations of black, older and sick bodies are non-existent. Furthermore, in my interviews with Maxine, physical contact was not talked about in ways that were caring or pleasurable, but was spoken about, almost exclusively, in relation to experiences of violence. In drawing upon the range of accounts that I have presented, my argument is that Maxine's biographical accounts of violence need to be seen as a part of the conscious and unconscious frameworks of meaning surrounding Maxine's anxiety in being touched, lifted and washed – like a 'piece of meat' – by hospice nurses. It is also relevant that, although Maxine's nurses appeared to acknowledge her anxious behaviour as an issue that was significant in her care, this behaviour was categorised as pathological and labelled as 'paranoid' in her case notes.

The lines of the argument that I am developing are further complicated in two main ways. First, although my research involved group interviews with hospice nurses, at this early stage of the research I had not grasped the significance of interviewing nurses about the care of specific service users that were a part of the study. (This development in methodology occurred much later in the research[5].) The material that I have drawn upon in this chapter, therefore, has not been able to explore the particular dynamics of the nursing practices involved in Maxine's care, although my research with hospice staff has been drawn upon to examine a range of possible interpretations. At one end of the spectrum of interpretation, it is possible that the objectifying elements of nursing touch described by Maxine were forms of more general and organisationally 'structured defence mechanisms' (Menzies Lyth, 1988 [1959]) developed to help practitioners avoid painful and difficult feelings. The ways in which Maxine experienced being touched could have been part of a 'protective touch' (Estabrooks, 1989) used to distance and 'protect' nurses from Maxine's suffering.

However, it is also possible that the touches Maxine described were racist practices, marked by objectifying or even aggressive 'meat-handling' touches, that resonated with Maxine's experiences of domestic and racist violence.

Second, anxiety, paranoia and hypersensitivity to touch and noise are often a part of the progression of many forms of terminal illness with a range of causes (for example, disease progression, treatment regimens, as well as the psychological trauma of awareness of impending death) needing specific management and care (see Regnard and Tempest, 1997). Thus, the range of these subjective, social and biomedical meanings also needs to be considered as a part of the shifting and complex narrative relations evoked in the reports of Maxine's care.

Caring practices

Despite the complexities of Maxine's story and the acknowledgement of her anxieties by the hospice nurses, my analytic attention to different sites of embodied experience and social relations suggests that Maxine's care within the hospice cannot be seen as holistic. Expressions of Maxine's anxieties about physical care were not explored by staff within the broader context of her biographical history, but were regarded as pathological rather than as connected to – and expressive of – the trauma of bodily violation. The possible multiplicity and interconnectedness of physical, emotional, social and cultural elements converging within the expression of Maxine's anxieties, then, were lost, preventing hospice staff from situating and linking Maxine's care to her ambivalent and evolving experiences within the hospice. My reporting of Maxine's narrative, in which she uses the simile of a donkey, speaks of burden, physical weakness, further violation and the wish to resist. It gives added depth to her story of feeling objectified and unsafe when being touched and lifted by nurses, and it can also be used to make sense, at least in part, of her resistance to being kept clean.

However, we also need to ask further questions in order to avoid reinscribing Maxine into dominant representations (see Bhavnani, 1993) of older, sick, black women as 'victims'; that is, representations that I feel Maxine herself resisted. In my research interactions with Maxine, she had suggested that her physical appearance and personal hygiene were important to her. Maxine had also expressed a desire to me to be washed, at a time when she was refusing physical nursing care. To draw upon Bordo's (1993, p 196) rhetorical question of anorexic women: 'Do we really choose the appearances that we reconstruct for ourselves?', I would ask: 'Can Maxine have really chosen the lack of care that she created for herself?'. What I am suggesting is that Maxine's 'choice' to resist physical forms of care can be read as simultaneously empowering and diminishing, in which representations of subjective and corporeal autonomy were linked paradoxically to bodily and emotional neglect. In my interpretation, these relations were played out in the dynamics between trauma and restoration, control and lack of control, and disease progression, blurring the binary distinctions between 'doing' and being 'done to' that mark dominant representations of care.

What is significant is that expressions of these complex relations appear to have been invalidated, misconstrued and/or avoided by hospice staff, leading to practices that reaffirmed and colluded with the diminishing aspects of Maxine's ambivalent 'choices'. These choices can in turn be seen as being related to racial, ethnic, cultural and gendered identifications that serve to give specific meaning and significance to Maxine's complicated needs and her resistance to care.

Conclusion

Through this discussion of Maxine, I hope to have demonstrated some of the ways in which attention to biographical narratives can be used to gain insights into somatic experiences of difference in the caring services. However, the complexity of the issues raised by Maxine's case also suggests that the links between biographical narratives, experience and emotions are ragged, placing particular responsibilities on the analytic process to go beyond literal interpretations of biographical accounts, or what Hollway and Jefferson (2000, p 10) have critiqued as the "telling it like it is approach". In relation to Maxine, my own approach to analysis has sought to interrogate biographical accounts of Maxine, with regard to care practices, unconscious defences against anxiety, and broader social power relations. Thus, the analysis draws attention to the complicated ways in which biographical experiences are put together, resisted, hidden and worked upon in accounts in ways in which the embodied trauma of racialised and gendered oppression might be both relived and relieved (Brain, 2002).

The challenges for theory, research and professional practice are substantial in this respect. We need approaches that are able to take account of – and connect – social, embodied and emotional contexts to biographical histories and interpersonal power relations, with the ever-ready willingness to question the nature of these connections in response to the unique complexities of individual experience. With this in mind, our approaches to research and professional practice are also obliged to shift. The issues, then, are not so much about the rigidities and prescriptions that are involved in notions of 'getting it right' that circulate in the education and training literature on multicultural care (Gunaratnam, 1997). Rather, what I am suggesting is the need to create possibilities and spaces for 'less deluded knowledge' (Haraway, 1997) about social difference; that is, knowledge that is responsive to the multiplicity of possible meanings and consequences of difference in individual lives, knowledge that recognises somatic experience, and knowledge that can testify to and engage with trauma.

Notes

[1] By social difference, I am referring to how differences such as race, ethnicity, gender, class and disability carry historical and political meanings that structure and organise both individual and social relations. For further analysis, see Avtar Brah (1996), who provides a sophisticated theoretical rethinking of difference.

[2] Due to the constraints of space, reflexive examination of my own positioning within my research interactions with Maxine and in the interpretive process is not included in this account.

[3] The transcription codes that I have used are: ... indicates where the account has been edited; (...) refers to pauses in the interview account.

[4] 'Social bath' is the term used to describe the provision of assistance with bathing in the home for older and disabled people as a part of 'community care' service provision in England.

[5] My exploration of professional care practices in the hospice took place through 14 group interviews with a range of hospice staff (nurses, doctors, social workers and members of the chaplaincy team) and observation of hospice nurses on homecare visits. Physical touch was an under-explored theme both in the group discussions and in the observational research, although emotional distancing through constructions of racialised difference (the divisions between 'us' and 'them') by professionals was evident throughout the research. The racialised emotional dynamics of physical touch have not been explored in the nursing literature, except in relation to differences in cultural norms about touch, and this is clearly an area that needs further investigation.

References

Alexander, Z. (1999) *Study of Black, Asian and ethnic minority issues*, London: Department of Health.

Bhavnani, K.-K. (1993) 'Tracing the contours of feminist research and feminist objectivity', *Women's Studies International Forum*, vol 6, no 2, pp 95-104.

Bordo, S. (1993) *Unbearable weight: Feminism, western culture and the body*, Berkeley, CA: University of California Press.

Brah, A. (1996) *Cartographies of diaspora: Contesting identities*, London: Routledge.

Brain, J. (2002) 'Unsettling "body image": anorexic body narratives and the materialization of the "body imaginary"', *Feminist Theory*, vol 3, no 2, pp 151-68.

Estabrooks, C.A. (1989) 'Touch: a nursing strategy in the intensive care unit', *Heart and Lung*, vol 4, pp 392-401.

Firth, S. (2001) *Wider horizons: Care of the dying in a multicultural society*, London: National Council for Hospice and Specialist Palliative Care Services.

Foucault, M. (1973) *The birth of the clinic: An archaeology of medical perception*, London: Tavistock.

Foucault, M. (1977) *Discipline and punish: The birth of the prison*, Harmondsworth: Allen Lane.

Green, J. (1992) *Death with dignity: Meeting the spiritual needs of patients in a multi-cultural society*, vol 2, London: Macmillan Magazines.

Gunaratnam, Y. (1997) 'Culture is not enough: a critique of multi-culturalism in palliative care', in D. Field, J. Hockey and N. Small (eds) *Death, gender and ethnicity*, London: Routledge, pp 166-86.

Gunaratnam, Y. (1999) 'Researching and representing ethnicity: a qualitative study of hospice staff and service users', Unpublished PhD thesis, University of London.

Gunaratnam, Y. (2003) *Researching 'race' and ethnicity: Methods, knowledge and power*, London: Sage Publications.

Hall, S. (1996) 'Introduction: who needs identity?', in S. Hall and P. du Gay (eds) *Questions of cultural identity*, London: Sage Publications, pp 1-17.

Haraway, D. (1997) 'The virtual speculum in the New World Order', *Feminist Review*, vol 55, pp 22-72.

Higginbotham, E. (1992) 'African-American women's history and the metalanguage of race', *Signs*, vol 17, no 21, pp 251-74.

Hollway, W. (2001) 'The psycho-social subject in "evidence-based" practice', *Journal of Social Work Practice*, vol 15, no 1, pp 9-22.

Hollway, W. and Jefferson, A. (2000) *Doing qualitative research differently: Free association, narrative and the interview method*, London: Sage Publications.

Knowles, C. (1999) 'Race, identities and lives', *Sociological Review*, vol 47, no 1, pp 110-35.

Macpherson, W. (1999) *The Stephen Lawrence inquiry: Report of an inquiry*, London: Home Office.

Menzies Lyth, I. (1988) *Containing anxiety in institutions: Selected essays*, London: Free Association Books.

Neuberger, J. (1987) *Caring for dying people of different faiths*, London: Austen Cornish and Lisa Sainsbury Foundations.

Prosser, J. (2001) 'Skin memories', in S. Ahmed and J. Stacey (eds) *Thinking through the skin*, London: Routledge, pp 52-68.

Regnard, C. and Tempest, S. (1997) *A guide to symptom relief in advanced disease*, Hale: Hochland and Hochland.

Scheff, T. (1997) *Emotions, the social bond, and human reality: Part/whole analysis*, Cambridge: Cambridge University Press.

Twigg, J. (1997) 'Deconstructing the "social bath": help with bathing at home for older and disabled people', *Journal of Social Policy*, vol 26, pp 211-32.

Twigg, J. (1999) 'The spatial ordering of care: public and private in bathing support at home', *Sociology of Health and Illness*, vol 21, no 2, pp 381-400.

Warner, S. (1996) 'Constructing femininity: models of child sexual abuse and the production of women', in E. Burman, P. Alldred, C. Bewley. B. Goldberg, C. Heenan, D. Marks, J. Marshall, K. Taylor, R. Ullah and S. Warner (eds) *Challenging women: Psychology's exclusions, feminist possibilities*, Buckingham: Open University Press, pp 48-61.

Wengraf, T. (2000) 'Uncovering the general from within the particular: from contingencies to typologies in the understanding of cases', in P. Chamberlayne, J. Bornat and T. Wengraf (eds) *The turn to biographical methods in social science: Comparative issues and examples*, London: Routledge, pp 140-64.

Wengraf, T. (2001) *Qualitative research interviewing: Biographic narrative and semi-structured method*, London: Sage Publications.

Young, L. (1990) 'A nasty piece of work: a psychoanalytic study of sexual and racial difference in "Mona Lisa"', in J. Rutherford (ed) *Identity: Community, culture, difference*, London: Lawrence and Wishart.

FIFTEEN

Biography as empowering practice: lessons from research

Joanna Bornat and Jan Walmsley

The use of biography and autobiography today, compared with only 20 years ago in the UK, is now ubiquitous in work with vulnerable people in care settings. Biographical materials exist implicitly and explicitly in a variety of forms, from documents (such as case notes, patient histories, and care plans) to more journalistic public accounts in the media following instances of abuse or fatal accident, as well as in service users' own accounts often presented in the form of life storybooks, or audiovisual recordings. The use of autobiography and biography has also become a common research tool in health and social care settings in the form of life stories and histories, oral history, narrative studies, and biographical interpretive methods. Collectively, these have come to be known as 'biographical methods' (Bornat, 1994; Walmsley, 1995; Chamberlayne et al, 2000, Bornat, 2001; Bornat, 2002; Coleman, 2002; Webster and Haight, 2002).

In tandem with this shift towards a more subjectively understood idea of care has been the claim by some authors, though not all, that such approaches empower participants, enabling them to take control of their own stories, to reverse roles with researchers, to claim ownership, to retain the right to interpret rather than allow the 'academic gaze' to take over, and even to bring about change in the direction of their lives (Bornat, 1989; Frisch, 1990; Booth and Booth, 1998; Hirsch, 1998; Thompson, 2000). Whether or not any of these empowering outcomes is measurable or achievable remains a focus for constant debate.

In this chapter, we make our own contribution, exploring ways of positioning biographical research and practice on a top-down/bottom-up matrix. In so doing, we arrive at a more questioning appraisal of claims for empowerment through biographical work. *Questioning*, but not necessarily being judgemental. It is not our intention to recommend or suggest that any one positioning on the matrix is more or less desirable than any other. In what follows, we offer a matrix as a form of self-evaluation and reflection on research processes. In doing so, we consider such issues as ownership, power in research relationships, presentation, structure and process. We apply the matrix to our own work retrospectively, with revelatory outcomes for us, as this chapter will show. If we had been in a position to apply it as we worked through the projects we describe, then it is possible that our research strategies might have developed rather differently.

What the matrix does not do is offer any straightforward answers; if anything, it reinforces complexity. For this we make no apologies. In our opinion, some of the claims for empowerment through biographical research rest on 'unmeasurables', such as feelings of self-worth and reclaimed identity. Other claims rest on ideals of authenticity and commitment. These, too, have a tendency to be elusively over-simplistic and to evade implications of partisanship and bias by avowing political certainty. For example, outcomes that include to 'give voice' beg questions of 'whose voice and whose gift?'. As Hammersley (2000, p 19) argues, researchers may appropriately show commitment in their selection of research topics and use research to illustrate the implications of particular commitment, but should also remain questioning and sceptical about their own commitment. We suggest that the matrix offers a critique of process to be used as a self-evaluative tool, one that, in this context, offers the possibility of reflection and comparison and ultimately greater awareness of the distinctive contributions of different biographical approaches.

The matrix

The matrix presented in Figure 15.1 is inevitably simplistic. It is a diagrammatic representation of a wide range of practices and definitions of research. However, in its simplicity we present it as a tool whereby biographically oriented researchers – both academic and non-academic, paid and unpaid – might be interested to position their methods and outputs. First, however, some definitions of terms are required. By 'research', we mean any activity in which a person or group of people undertakes to solve a problem, or finds ways to answer a question they or others have posed using stated methods to arrive at an argued conclusion. 'Practice' for us is activity, in this case relating to health and social care, that involves social relationships that are recognisable as having common and observable characteristics, roles and interactions often, but not always, guided by rules and procedures.

Positions along the research–practice matrix describe activity that is more or less practice- or research-oriented with a midpoint represented by action research in which researchers may be practitioners seeking to bring about change in a practice setting[1].

'Top-down' in the matrix includes research that is generated and carried out by those who are personally detached from the subject or research topic. Commitment or partisanship should not be an issue, nor should the kind of soul-searching that claims shared identity in order to avoid accusations of oppression. A top-down researcher may show great commitment and partisanship in relation to a subject or topic with whom they have little in common. What defines top-down, as far as we are concerned, is by whom and how the research idea and process are generated. Defining characteristics are distance, physical, social, professional, and power, whether located in class, ethnicity, disability, sexuality, gender or age. Identifying such differences and distance is one thing; it is quite another to judge them. For, as Daphne Patai (1991, p 150) argues:

> no controversy attends the fact that too much ignorance exists in the world to allow us to await perfect research methods before proceeding. Ultimately we have to make up our minds whether our research is worth doing or not, and then determine how to go about it in ways that let it best serve our stated goals.

With these points in mind, we have positioned examples of research methodologies and methods in the top left-hand quadrant of the matrix. These include quite different approaches: biographical interpretive, ethnographic and life history.

'Bottom-up' research is that which is generated from ground level by those who are, in most cases, the recipients of practice as service users or members of the public. Their roles may be many and varied, as Peace (2002) suggests: they may be initiators of research and they may analyse and plan the process. However, their position within the structures of health and social care provision is non-professional and without bureaucratic or administrative power. We have located life storybooks and reminiscence work in the bottom right-hand quadrant of the matrix as these, to us, are examples of biographical work carried out by service users, though the extent to which they generate or control these activities is of course an issue that use of the matrix immediately generates.

Figure 15.1: A biographical research matrix in health and social care

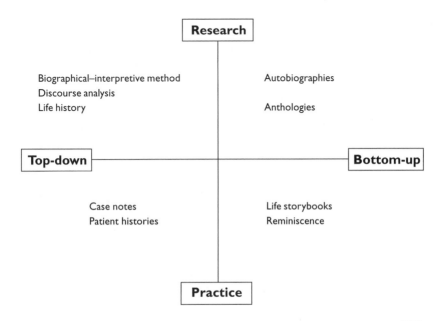

Research

The application of the matrix is not entirely straightforward. For example, the positions of top-down and bottom-up are contextually relative, so that describing a community-based group as 'bottom-up' may be questioned by those who are marginalised within a community, such as disabled or frail older people or refugees. Clearly, memberships and ownership can qualify the use of such labels. One way to position an example of biographical research might be to ask three questions:

- Who initiated the research and why?
- Who wrote it up and how?
- Who owns the outputs?

These debates have a lengthy history in feminist, oral history and learning disability research[2,] where questions of identification, representation, partisanship, partnership, ownership and essentialism have long been debated (see, for example, Roberts, 1981; Gluck and Patai, 1991; Wolf, 1996; Perks and Thomson, 1998; Atkinson and Walmsley, 1999; Hammersley, 2000; Mauthner et al, 2002). Each of the dichotomies placed at the ends of the axes presents opportunities for simplification and complexity. We argue that this is what makes the matrix both useful and attractive as a critical research aid. To elaborate this point, we now go on to illustrate this, drawing on examples from our own research.

Biography in top-down research

In this part of the matrix, we can place research approaches that use biography as source material for hypothesising, analysis and interpretation. The researcher sets out on his or her task with questions or hypotheses to test by reference to biography or life history. Alternatively, the researcher uses life histories to construct hypotheses or typologies. Thompson's (2000, pp 100-1) large oral history survey of Edwardian family life is a well-known example of such an approach. Looking at a much later period of family life, Bornat et al (1999) investigated the impact of family change on older family members. Although they consulted with older people initially and deliberately chose familiar words and language to describe their research, and although members of the team could empathise with interviewees, drawing on their own life histories to do so, these life-history interviews with a sample of 60 people were collected, analysed by the research team and then deposited in an academic archive. The process, then, was essentially top-down.

There is a whole range of approaches falling within this quadrant. Robert Edgerton's (1967) celebrated study of people discharged from a California institution for the 'mentally retarded' [sic] is one that has informed practice, albeit in a watered-down way. Through interviews with his subjects, Edgerton was able to develop a theory that proposed that survival after

---

deinstitutionalisation was largely determined by the person's success, or good fortune, in finding a benefactor to guide them through the vagaries of life on the outside[3]. One can see here how this finding has influenced practice such as citizen advocacy, widely seen as desirable if less widely practised in reality (Atkinson, 1999; Henderson and Pochin, 2001). Although dressed up, one could argue that the advocate is equivalent to Edgerton's benefactor in being on the side of the vulnerable person and willing to act as a guide and spokesperson. However committed, this is clearly 'top-down'. Edgerton initiated the process; he wrote the books; and he 'owns' the data (see Gerber, 1990 for a detailed critique, and alternative set of interpretations).

Biography in bottom-up research

While biography in top-down research casts the researcher as initiator, author and owner, the expert interpreter of other people's lives, in bottom-up approaches the person ideally speaks for him or herself. In Jan Walmsley's area of learning disability research, this approach has gained much credibility in the past two decades. Pioneered by Joey Deacon's celebrated autobiography, *Tongue tied* (1974), and ideologically buttressed by principles of self-advocacy in which people are enjoined to speak up for themselves, there is a considerable vogue for bottom-up approaches. The principal example we propose to use here is 'Mabel Cooper's life story' (Cooper, 1997).

Mabel, in her fifties, is a woman who spent much of her life in long-stay institutions for people with learning difficulties. Dorothy Atkinson, Mabel's partner in the enterprise of researching and writing her own life story, describes how the project was initiated:

> The idea itself predated my arrival on the scene by about 20 years, although a start had been made in the interim with the making of a tape for someone else's college project.

Mabel explains where the idea came from and how it took root:

> Hazel had asked me to do it because she wanted to do it for a college or something she was taking on, and I said, "OK, but will you put it on a tape recorder for me, and I will try to make a little book out of it, because there's a lot more to it than that on it". And because I'd already done the tape with Hazel I thought, well, if I find somebody else, I'll ask somebody to help me a bit more'. (Atkinson et al, 1997, p 7)

Mabel was the initiator, but because she does not read or write she needed help. Dorothy's arrival on the scene, looking for life-story material to feed into her teaching and research, enabled the project to take off. Going back to our three questions, we can interrogate the story thus:

- *Who wrote it, and how?* The answer to this question is complex. The physical act of writing was Dorothy's, using Mabel's taped words. Dorothy also edited the transcribed tape, taking care to involve Mabel in the process, and gain her approval.
- *Who owns it?* This is Mabel's life story. Dorothy's part in its construction is fully acknowledged by Mabel and is public knowledge. It has been explored in some depth (see Atkinson et al, 1997; Atkinson and Walmsley, 1999; Atkinson and Cooper, 2000). According to Dorothy, Mabel wanted Dorothy to put her name to it, an offer which Dorothy refused (Atkinson et al, 1997, p 9).

Here is an example, then, of bottom-up research, albeit aided by the skills of an experienced and well-respected researcher.

It is probably quite rare to find that research projects fall so neatly into these boxes. Indeed, one could argue that the use of Mabel's life story as an illustration here is in itself 'top down'. However, it is a way of categorising and making sense of a very diverse range of research in the area of biography (see Plummer, 2000).

Top-down practice

Top-down practice is pretty obvious. Most case notes and records fall into this category, although the 2000 Freedom of Information Act (The Stationery Office, 2000), which permits service users to gain access to their own records, may in time impact on their pure top-down nature. The parallels with research are not hard to find. The raw data come from the service user's biography, supplemented often by observations and evidence from other sources – psychological tests, input from professionals, friends, relatives, court reports, and so on. It is assembled and deployed usually for a particular purpose by someone with an official status. Rarely is the client invited to self-represent, although his or her words may be taken down and used again for quite a different purpose. Here, for example, is an example of records kept by a Mental Deficiency Committee about 'Dora', a woman detained under the 1913 Mental Deficiency Act. The Deputy Medical Officer of Health compiled the account in 1916:

> At the Court it was alleged that the girl was a menace to the troops as she had been sleeping with various soldiers in the neighbourhood and complaints had been made by the military to the police about her conduct....
>
> Her appearance is healthy but somewhat dull and heavy ... I am of the opinion that she has not got sufficient mental control to resist men who wish to assault her, but on the contrary her mental condition is such that she accepts these attentions from men, failing to appreciate the immorality of her conduct.

[Her mother reported] Dora had always been dull at school.... Three years ago the mother was sent for by the girl's mistress in domestic service as she had been behaving immorally with farm hands. Until her daughter was assaulted while in this situation she had exhibited no immoral tendencies, but from that time to the present she appears to have been immoral whenever the opportunity occurred.

Mr Tibby [stepfather] states that neither he nor his wife will receive the girl into their house as during the time she was living there she accused Mr Tibby of attempting immoral conduct with her.

In all probability she is not pregnant at the present time.

I regard the girl as a moral imbecile. (Names and source anonymised)

- *Who initiated it and why?* The Deputy Medical Officer of Health with the purpose of certifying Dora as a mental defective because of alleged wayward sexual behaviour and a complaint from an influential professional source.
- *Who wrote it and how?* The Medical Officer of Health, assembled from reports from other professionals and family, and tests he had administered.
- *Who owns it?* At the time, the Mental Deficiency Committee (not accessible to Dora or her family), now the County Record Office.

It is easy to castigate such records as the antithesis of empowerment. However, if we return for one moment to Mabel, there is a case to be made for them. Until she saw the top-down records kept on her as a person detained under the 1913 Mental Deficiency Act, Mabel did not know much about her past, except that which she could remember. Hurtful as they were in the harsh and unfair judgements made upon her by others, the records gave her some facts about her life that would otherwise have remained closed to her. From them, she was able to piece together her story and be empowered through knowing that her mother had abandoned her through no wish of her own (see Atkinson and Cooper, 2000).

It may seem perverse to select an example from almost a century ago. There are several reasons for this. The first is simply availability: because these records cite individual names (and often addresses) and relate to sensitive areas of people's lives, publicly archived records are generally unavailable within 80 years of their deposit. The second is that a historical example such as this highlights the assumptions made in compiling such reports in a stark way. Our language, and our thinking, has changed, making it easy to spot 'the official mind' at work. Third, although such practices seem alien to us today, there are legacies linked to the eugenic belief that certain people should not be encouraged to bear children. We may be more subtle these days, using abortion rather than institutionalisation, but some ideas and practices have not gone away. For these reasons, we felt this example was a useful illustration of the way top-down biographies can be used. Fourth, such an example might help us to be alert to our own prejudices and practice deficits today and to maintain a critical evaluation of biographical data generation and collection practices.

Indeed, the assumption that biographically informed practice can only empower and be used in supportive ways with service users is questioned in Chapter Sixteen of this volume. There, Riitta Kyllönen critically reviews the genesis and use of biographies of lone mothers by social workers in Venice.

Bottom-up practice

The importance of developing a positive sense of identity, especially where life experiences have been unpropitious or identity is compromised in institutional settings, has been increasingly recognised since the days Mabel was a hospital resident. The fact that she now has written her own life story is evidence of this changing climate. Children in care or adopted children, people with learning difficulties, older people in residential care, all are potentially enabled to gain or retain a sense of identity through biography (see, for example, Bornat, 1994; Ryan and Walker, 1993; Schweitzer, 1998; Stuart, 2002). Life-story books, reminiscence, photograph albums and precious possessions are means by which knowledge of a life is bolstered in more enlightened care settings. Training that involves exposure to worked-through biographies of typical care recipients has helped to strengthen claims for changed practice, awareness and more appropriate and sensitive service delivery (Pietrukowicz and Johnson, 1991; Bornat, 1994; Goldwasser and Auerbach, 1996; Bornat and Chamberlayne, 1999; Garland and Garland, 2001).

The extent to which such outputs can be located and pinned down as bottom-up practice remains an issue as we will now go on to illustrate with a worked-through example of a biographically based research project.

Moving around the matrix with an example

The project was an approach to grounding research and practice in a bottom-up framework, inclusive of patients and nursing staff (see Adams et al, 1996)[4]. With a brief summary of the project, we work through its rationale, different stages and outcomes, relating each in turn to points on the matrix with a view to determining its contribution to the empowerment of those involved.

The project took place on the continuing care wards of two NHS hospitals within the same health authority during 1993-94. Both hospitals were previously workhouses and were remembered as such by older members of the local population. These were wards that were then under threat from healthcare policies that were seeking to economise and rationalise bed use by older people. Eventually, most were to close, and the alternatives – beds in private nursing homes 'in the community' or targeted and heavily rationed domiciliary care – have become the norm (Glendinning et al, 2002)[5]. For the nursing and other staff employed there, this policy change put a question mark over their status and future professional lives that we were unable to ignore. With few exceptions, these were unqualified nursing staff who were conscious of their lowly position in the nursing hierarchy, a position compounded by the fact that they were nursing a group of people who were disregarded and marginal in relation to any notion of cure. Medically, the people occupying the beds were there because they were thought not able to 'improve'. For them, the idea of continuing care was one in which present difficulties loomed large and the future was hard to contemplate. Socially, the roles occupied by visitors and friends were restricted by the space and facilities offered in a hospital ward. Our aim was to find out how biography was used in nursing care and, through collaborative work, to offer the nursing staff, patients and their relatives a model for biographical practice that we felt would open up opportunities to enhance personal worth, agency, control and social confidence (Kitwood and Bredin, 1992) for everyone concerned.

We described our study as action research, using a 'technical collaborative' approach, meaning that we, the researchers, planned to test a specific intervention in a practice setting and with the help of practitioners to achieve the implementation of an innovation in clinical practice.

Working with the nursing staff, we began with baseline measurements, where consent had been given, of patients' levels of cognition and of depression. This was followed by observation on the wards, which at times was highly participative. Data from observation provided us with evidence of the extent to which biographical references contributed to normal daily interactions between nurses and patients. We then moved on to interview those able to talk about their past lives, taping and transcribing in each case. At this stage, collaboration with patients and their family members and friends became part of our process. Copies of the tapes and transcripts were given to patients or their relatives. Our planned next stage was to work with the nursing staff to produce a life storybook for each participant, using a cheap but attractively designed scrapbook. We wanted to be able to show that it was possible to produce a pleasing result that did not demand much in the way of resources. In the end, 11 of these were completed.

Such were the aims, methods and stages of the project. Using the matrix as a tool for evaluation of our empowerment quotient, how did we fare?

A point to make at the start of our evaluation is that what we are describing is a series of snapshots, beginning with the plan, going on through the process and then ending with the outcomes. Let us begin with the original plan. Mapping our plan onto the matrix, it seems that we occupied a place that is part way between research and practice on the vertical axis, perhaps nearer research. In order to minimise 'researcher effect', we chose not to tell the nurses at the outset what we were actually researching. We described our topic as 'communication' rather than reminiscence or biographical work. This perhaps skews our position on the horizontal axis more towards the top-down end. However, our aim from the outset was to engage with the patients in an interactive and collaborative way. Overall then, our research plan might be positioned somewhere in the top corner of the bottom right-hand quadrant of the matrix.

Complications arise as we move on to discuss the process. Unforeseen by us, the nurses proved less than enthusiastic about our project, despite welcoming interest from managers at ward and hospital levels. At the outset, we planned to include nurses in the production of the life storybooks and to reveal our interest in patients' life stories once the observation phase was past. This proved difficult, since our efforts met with resistance. With but one exception, nurses were 'too busy' to take part, even in partnership with our research assistant. Revising our approach, we decided to proceed by demonstrating the process ourselves. The life storybooks were completed with the help of patients, relatives, the local history library and other sources, and each was given to the patient or a relative. How does our process work out, mapped onto the matrix?

One thing that must immediately seem obvious is that the mapping will need to take into consideration the formal and informal interactions that determined and shaped our research process. Perhaps what we need is a more flexible structure, one that records the movement of our research as it succumbed to nurse resistance at one point and then re-emerged in a more collaborative mode at its point of completion, when the 11 life storybooks were in the possession of their originators. The matrix raises the question, in this case, of 'bottom-down for whom?'. Our aim was to contribute to improved nursing care, to extend nurses' knowledge of the lives of patients they were in daily contact with, and to collaborate with them in doing so. We met with resistance that we partly accounted for in terms of general dissatisfaction and concern about their own futures, but we were also forced to acknowledge that this resistance was also born of a professional pride in their particular caring work. This struggle over involvement means that our project moved up and down and to and fro on the two axes as the process unfolded. The nurses' personal and professional biographies were not officially part of our project but they, perhaps unwittingly, ensured that their practitioner life stories were a factor.

Despite this unforeseen development, the life storybooks were completed. Our sole partners in collaboration were the patients' relatives and friends. The life storybooks proved their worth on the ward. Despite the claim by several of the nurses that they were familiar with their patients' lives, new stories were forthcoming. It also became clear that, even when people were least able to contribute verbally, some degree of control and influence was being exerted in relation to the contents of the life storybooks. The bottom-up quality of a biographical approach to this particular piece of action research is perhaps confirmed. Perhaps, also, the very contested nature of the process pulls it down towards the practice end of the vertical axis. It was our intention to influence practice, and although the process had not developed as we had expected, the ownership of the project had clearly shifted, through struggle, over the weeks.

Finally, the outcomes: where would these be positioned on the matrix? In terms of tangible products, the life storybooks occupy the bottom right-hand quadrant. However, the effect on practice was much less obvious. My research notebook records a flickering interest among this hard-pressed group of nurses. One or two were able to make links between their own personal lives and the method, finding interest in some of the images and artefacts supplied by the local librarians. Others seemed to take pride in the patients' lives revealed to them in the life storybooks. However, unexpectedly to us, our presence in the hospital seemed to act as an encouragement to other groups of nurses, those who were strategically better placed to negotiate around the survival of their wards. Nurses on adjoining wards where rehabilitation was the focus were keenly taking on reminiscence work and given the resources and encouragement to do so. Similarly, staff who saw the future for themselves as a palliative care ward were equally keen to explore our approach to develop biography as part of their repertoire of care interventions. Yet again, our ability to predict or determine the direction of the work had not been entirely within our control. Here, perhaps, was confirmation that biographical research may indeed have empowering outcomes, if not always those that we intend.

The fact that it could be appropriated in this way is suggestive of both latent and explicit empowering qualities. Although our initial focus had been on outcomes relating to the quality of patient care, there were latent and unexpected outcomes for nursing staff, too. We scored more highly on the empowerment matrix than we had perhaps intended and not altogether in the ways or with the groups we had intended. Looking back, the matrix provides us with an object lesson in how to design and operate research in a practice terrain and how we researchers were certainly enlightened, if not ourselves disempowered.

Conclusion

How has use of the matrix helped in this review of our own biographical research? We suggest that the matrix has helped us to identify three aspects of biographical work in which empowerment is illuminated and perhaps elaborated as a process. First, in relation to time, the very fixed nature of the matrix illustrates how power and interests can shift as different biographies are brought into play and as the process of research shifts within the structures that define and determine practice. A research project has its own biography and the matrix helps us to map and check shifting empowerment balances during its lifetime.

Second, in considering the interests of stakeholders, ideas of research ownership and control may have to be redefined as perceptions of what is biographical in a project becomes more and less explicit, while different stakeholders shift in their understanding and appreciation of the biographical in their own and others' lives, Perhaps we need a multidimensional matrix in order to represent the interests and involvements of all the stakeholders in any project.

Finally, as a moderating influence on claims that biographical research and practice has consistently made as to an empowering role, the use of the matrix is 3a helpful caution, a restraint perhaps: a reminder that claims to speak for people, to 'give back' or to 'provide a voice' are only at one end of a continuum that also locks into professional interests, structural constraints and limits on resources. In the end, as others have pointed out (Buchanan and Middleton, 1994, p 68), biographical approaches can enlighten and change awareness; but can they change the conditions in which people live and work? We have yet to see.

Notes

[1] See Randall (2002) for a useful discussion and evaluation of the relationship between research and practice in relation to a specific project. Among his recommendations is the adoption of the metaphor of the bridge and a 'two-way traffic' between these different kinds of knowledge (Randall, 2002, p 120).

[2] This is not yet the case in UK disability research, however, where there is still resistance to the use of biographical accounts from activists and theorists who are committed to the social model of disability. Barnes, in a recent article (2003, p 10), argues for the inclusion of personal experience on the grounds that it is "empowering for some isolated disabled individuals" and that personal experience can "illustrate the social context in which the research was conducted". He also cites a 1966 source to suggest that "much of the writing by people with accredited impairments is 'either sentimental biography, or else preoccupied with the medical and practical details of a particular affliction'". He goes on to argue that "Social researchers have yet to devise adequate ways of collectivising experience" and that "experiential research alone has hitherto to yield any meaningful political or social policy outcomes". Perhaps the matrix will provide an opportunity to challenge such assumptions, enabling the social model and its proponents to value and engage with more subjectively framed experiences of impairment and a disabling society.

[3] The SOSTRIS project (see Chapter Two of this volume) used a similar 'emergent' approach, focusing on what lives can reveal about the nature of social transformation and how social policy might respond to that in order to bring it closer to life worlds and experience (with thanks to Prue Chamberlayne for suggesting this point).

[4] The project 'Models of biography and reminiscence in the nursing care of frail elderly people' was funded by the Open University Research Committee and run jointly by Dr Joanna Bornat, School of Health and Social Welfare, The Open University and John Adams of Sir Gordon Roberts College of Nursing and Midwifery, Kettering. The research assistant was Mary Prickett.

[5] The Royal Commission on Long-Term Care reported that 38% of long-term care beds had closed after 1983 during which time the number of beds in private nursing homes had increased by 900% (Sutherland, 1999, para 4.7). In absolute number terms, beds in long-stay geriatric and psycho-geriatric hospitals decreased from approximately 69,000 in 1985 to 33,000 in 2000, while beds in private and voluntary

sector nursing homes had increased from 38,000 in 1985 to 205,000 in 2000 (Laing and Buisson, quoted in Johnson, 2002).

References

Adams, J., Bornat, J. and Prickett, M. (1996) '"You wouldn't be interested in my life: I've done nothing"', in J. Phillips and B. Penhale (eds) *Reviewing care management for older people*, London: Jessica Kingsley, pp 102-15.

Atkinson, D. (1999) *Advocacy: A review*, York: Joseph Rowntree Foundation.

Atkinson, D. and Cooper, M. (2000) 'Parallel stories', in L. Brigham, D. Atkinson, D. Atkinson and J. Walmsley (eds) (1999) 'Using autobiographical approaches with people with learning difficulties', *Disability and Society* , vol 14, no 2, pp 203-16.

Atkinson, D. and Walmsley, J. (1999) 'Using autobiographical approaches with people with learning disabilities', *Disability and Society*, vol 14, no 2, pp 203-16.

Atkinson, D., Jackson, M. and Walmsley, J. (eds) (1997) *Forgotten lives*, Kidderminster: BILD.

Barnes, C. (2003) 'What a difference a decade makes: reflections on doing "emancipatory" disability research', *Disability and Society*, vol 18, no 1, pp 3-17.

Booth, T. and Booth, W. (1998) *Growing up with parents who have learning difficulties*, London: Routledge.

Bornat, J. (1989) 'Oral history as a social movement: reminiscence and older people', *Oral History*, vol 17, no 2, pp 16-20.

Bornat, J. (ed) (1994) *Reminiscence reviewed: Perspectives, evaluations, achievements*, Buckingham: Open University Press.

Bornat, J. (2001) 'Oral history and reminiscence: parallel universes or shared endeavour', *Ageing and Society*, vol 21, part 2, pp 219-41.

Bornat, J. (2002) 'Doing life history research', in A. Jamieson and C. Victor (eds) *Researching ageing and later life*, Buckingham: Open University Press.

Bornat, J. and Chamberlayne, P. (1999) 'Reminiscence in care settings: implications for training', *Education and Ageing*, vol 14, no 3, pp 277-95.

Bornat, J., Dimmock, B., Jones, D. and Peace, S. (1999) 'Stepfamilies and older people: evaluating the implications of family change for an ageing population', *Ageing and Society*, vol 19, part 2, pp 239-61.

Buchanan, K. and Middleton, D. (1994) 'Reminiscence reviewed: a discourse analytic perspective', in J. Bornat (ed) *Reminiscence reviewed: Perspectives, evaluations, achievements*, Buckingham: Open University Press.

Chamberlayne, P., Bornat, J. and Wengraf, T. (eds) (2000) *The turn to biographical methods in social science: Comparative issues and examples*, London: Routledge.

Chamberlayne, P., Rustin, M. and Wengraf, T. (eds) (2002) *Biography and social exclusion in Europe*, Bristol: The Policy Press.

Coleman, P. (2002) 'Doing case study research in psychology', in A. Jamieson and C.C. Victor (eds) *Researching ageing and later life*, Buckingham: Open University Press.

Cooper, M. (1997) 'Mabel Cooper's life story', in D. Atkinson, M. Jackson and J. Walmsley (eds) *Forgotten lives*, Kidderminster: BILD, pp 21-34.

Deacon, J. (1974) *Tongue tied*, London: National Society for Mentally Handicapped Adults and Children.

Edgerton, R.B. (1967) *The cloak of competence: Stigma in the lives of the retarded*, Berkeley, CA: University of California Press.

Frisch, M. (1990) *A shared authority: Essays on the craft and meaning of oral and public history*, Albany, NY: State University of New York.

Garland, J. and Garland, C. (2001) *Life review in health and social care: A practitioner's guide*, Hove: Brunner-Routledge.

Gerber, D. (1990) 'Listening to disabled people: the problem of voice and authority in R.B. Edgerton's "The cloak of competence"', *Disability, Handicap and Society*, vol 5, no 1, pp 3-23.

Glendinning, C., Coleman, A. and Rummery, K. (2002) 'Partnerships, performance and primary care: developing integrated services for older people in England', *Ageing and Society*, vol 22, part 2, pp 185-208.

Gluck, S.B. and Patai, D. (eds) (1991) *Women's words: The feminist practice of oral history*, London: Routledge.

Goldwasser, A. and Auerbach, S. (1996) 'Audience-based reminiscence therapy intervention: effects on the morale and attitudes of nursing home residents and staff', *Journal of Mental Health and Aging*, vol 2, no 2, pp 101-14.

Hammersley, M. (2000) *Taking sides in research: Essays on partisanship and bias*, London: Routledge.

Henderson, R. and Pochin, M. (2001) *A right result? Advocacy, justice and empowerment*, Bristol: The Policy Press.

Hirsch, K. (1998) 'Culture and disability: the role of oral history', in R. Perks and A. Thomson (eds) *The oral history reader*, pp 214-23.

Johnson, J. (2002) 'Taking care of later life: a matter of justice?', *British Journal of Social Work*, vol 32, pp 793-60.

Kitwood, T. and Bredin, K. (1992) 'Towards a theory of dementia care: personhood and well-being', *Ageing and Society*, vol 12, part 3, pp 269-87.

Mauthner, M., Birch, M., Jessop, J. and Miller, T. (eds) (2002) *Ethics in qualitative research*, London: Sage Publications.

Patai, D. (1991) 'US academics and third world women: is ethical research possible?', in S.B. Gluck and D. Patai (eds) *Women's words: The feminist practice of oral history*, London: Routledge.

Peace, S. (2002) 'The role of older people in research', in A. Jamieson and C. Victor (eds) *Researching ageing and later life*, Buckingham: Open University Press, pp 226-44.

Perks, R. and Thomson, A. (eds) (1998) *The oral history reader*, London: Routledge.

Pietrukowicz, M. and Johnson, M. (1991) 'Using life histories to individualize nursing home staff attitudes toward residents', *The Gerontologist*, vol 31, pp 102-06.

Plummer, K. (2000) *Documents of life 2*, London: Sage Publications.

Randall, J. (2002) '"The practice-research relationship": a case of ambivalent attachment?', *Journal of Social Work*, vol 2, no 1, pp 105-22.

Roberts, H. (ed) (1981) *Doing feminist research*, London: Routledge & Kegan Paul.

Ryan, T. and Walker, R. (1993) *Life story work*, London: British Agencies for Adoption and Fostering.

Schweitzer, P. (ed) (1998) *Reminiscence in dementia care*, London: Age Exchange.

Stuart, M. (2002) *Not quite sisters: Women with learning difficulties living in convent homes*, Kidderminster: BILD Publications.

Sutherland, S.R. (1999) *With respect to old age: Long term care – rights and responsibilities: a report*, Cm 4192-1, Royal Commission on Long-Term Care, London: The Stationery Office.

The Stationery Office (2000) *Freedom of Information Act, 2000 Chapter 36*, (www.hmso.gov.uk/acts/acts2000, accessed 14 February 2003).

Thompson, P. (2000) 'Projects', chapter six of *The voice of the past* (3rd edn), Oxford: Oxford University Press.

Walmsley, J. (1995) 'Life history interviews with people with learning difficulties', *Oral history*, vol 23, no 1, pp 71-7.

Webster, J.D. and Haight, B.K. (eds) (2002) *Critical advances in reminiscence work: From theory to application*, New York, NY: Springer.

Wolf, D.L. (ed) (1996) *Feminist dilemmas in fieldwork*, Boulder, CO: Westview Press.

SIXTEEN

'It's in the way that you use it': biography as a tool in professional social work

Riitta Kyllönen

How do social workers use biographies in designing social welfare intervention? How can biographies be useful in analyses of the ideological dimensions of welfare practices? These are questions that I will elucidate in this chapter. My discussion is based on a study that I conducted of how Venetian social welfare services interpret their lone mother recipients' needs and respond to them[1]. First, I locate social welfare services in the feminine subsystem of welfare programmes and discuss how the feminine subtext defines the status of its beneficiaries. I then go on to delineate the analytical framework adopted to examine discursive and ideological dimensions of welfare states through professional research narratives, as well as basic interpretive concepts.

The rest of the chapter is dedicated to answering the questions posed at the beginning of this chapter. In the study of the Venetian social welfare services, biographies surface insofar as they are the *tools* by which professional social workers define and reframe mothers' needs and claims, and shape the policy intervention. Professional constructions of biographies constitute normalising knowledge that is used to produce desired policy goals. From a biographical viewpoint, one of the policy outcomes of social welfare intervention is normalising welfare recipients' biographies.

Welfare dualism and its gender subtexts

Focusing on the duality of the US welfare system, Nancy Fraser (1989, p 149-51) differentiates between two major gender subtexts in welfare programmes that reflect the ideology of gender-specific 'separate spheres' of society at large, including its gender norms and assumptions. The duality model, to a varied extent, can be applied to other western welfare societies too, inasmuch as they are divided into two distinct spheres along gender lines.

On the one hand, there is the *masculine subsystem*, which is implicitly related to the primary labour market. On the other hand, there is the *feminine subsystem*, with an implicit link to the family/household. These two gender subtexts define the status of their welfare recipients differently as programmes have distinctive administrative identities. The beneficiaries of the feminine or family-based programmes are not individualised, but *familiarised*. They are often 'defective families', that is, families without a male breadwinner. The ideal-typical adult client is female, and she makes claims for benefits on the basis of her status as an unpaid domestic worker, or a mother-homemaker, but not as a paid worker in the labour market (a family-located identity).

The labour market-based masculine programmes – the most paradigmatic example of which is unemployment insurance – show different features. They are administered in a way that individualises rather than familiarises recipients. They are designed to compensate primary labour market effects such as the temporary displacement of a primary breadwinner. Their ideal-typical recipient is male, especially in societies where the female labour force participation rate is low. Finally, the recipient makes his claim on the basis of his identity as a paid worker – not as an unpaid domestic worker or parent (a labour market-located identity).

Feminine welfare programmes are further characterised by means tests. Recipients are subject to control and to an evaluative assessment before receiving services or maintenance allowances, which are financed from tax revenues. In contrast, the male benefits systems are considered to be individual rights to which recipients are entitled on the basis of their own prior contributions into trust funds. This subsystem is financed by social insurance schemes. In brief, the aspect of stigmatic surveillance and definition of needs is more extensive in the feminine subtext.

> Participants in the masculine subsystem are positioned as rights-bearing beneficiaries and purchasing consumers of services, thus as possessive individuals. Participants in the feminine subsystem, on the other hand, are positioned as dependent clients, or the negatives of possessive individuals. (Fraser, 1989, p 153)

This chapter takes the feminine subsystem as its focus. It deals with a group of women, lone mothers, who are welfare service recipients. In societies where many women remain outside the primary labour market, women's subsistence matters are to a great extent defined within the feminine needs-based subsystem, a paradigmatic example of which are social welfare services. Thus, the dualism of the welfare system has vast implications as to how social citizenship is unequally gendered.

Exploring ideological dimensions of welfare practices and programmes

Fraser (1989) has designed a framework to analyse the discursive and ideological dimensions of welfare practices and programmes, which she calls 'institutionalised patterns of interpretation'. Her idea is to interrogate a 'politics of needs interpretation' by unravelling the more or less implicit norms, assumptions and prerequisites that are constitutive of policies and welfare practices. The focus is on the active side of social processes, on how even the routine practices of social agents involve active construction, deconstruction and reconstruction of social meanings. Fraser suggests that analysing its mode of operation can best unravel the system's explicit norms and tacit assumptions.

> To see how welfare programs interpret women's needs, we must consider what benefits consist in. To see how programs position women as subjects, we need to examine administrative practices. (Fraser, 1989, p 151)

For Fraser (1989, p 153), the identities and needs that the social welfare system creates for its recipients are always interpreted identities and needs.

I have applied Fraser's framework in order to explore the ideological and subjective dimensions of welfare practices in the social welfare services of the city of Venice. The analysis of social workers' accounts of professional work processes with lone mother clients focused on the productive aspects of language; that is, "how talk about everyday life *constructs* the realities that are referenced" (Gubrium et al, 1994, p 4).

I set out to examine how social workers' representations of mothers' needs and social welfare intervention, while "meant to describe reality, in fact prescribe it" (Bourdieu, 1996, p 25). In this chapter, I discuss the issue of needs interpretation from a biographical vantage point. I believe that a biographical approach to the entire professional interaction process is particularly useful in unravelling the power and culture subtexts in the issue of need interpretation.

Moral career and interpretive biographies

In *Asylums* (1961), Erving Goffman introduced the concept of 'career' and, in particular, 'moral career', when analysing mental hospital inmates' trajectories. This elaborated career concept allows movement from personal (self) to public (signifying community); a passage from the inner aspects of career, such as self-image and experienced identity, to an official position, legal relations and way of life. In this second sense, a career is part of a public institution. Goffman is interested in career from the vantage point of its institutional and moral aspects. He defines the moral career of a person as consisting of a series of regular changes in the conception of 'selves', either him or herself or of others.

The uses of the concept of career and the biographical perspective are becoming more diffused in today's quantitative and qualitative policy analyses. These approaches are able to grasp the subjective dimensions of welfare processes in contrast to the top-down structural approach prevalent in comparative studies (for Italy, see Kazepov, 1995; Bosco, 1996; Kyllönen, 1999; Meo, 2000; Negri, 2002; Saraceno, 2002a, 2002b[2]).

For the Venetian study described here, I did not collect accounts about lone mothers on welfare as told by mothers themselves. The texts analysed, thus, are not autobiographical but instead biographical. The stories were formed through interpretive work by professional social workers. This is what Norman K. Denzin (1989) intends by the term 'interpretive biographies': social workers who create and signify lone mothers' biographies for professional purposes. The institutional vantage point is portrayed through professional social workers' eyes. By definition, biographical texts are always ideological statements that are elaborated from the perspective of the author. Hence, they reflect the specific (class, gender, and so on) interests and values linked to the author's social location (Denzin, 1989, p 18; see also Gubrium et al, 1994, pp 40-1).

The implication is that, when a biographer describes an individual's real life, she or he is in fact only creating that subject in the text. There is no direct access to the inner life of a person or to 'real' interacting subjects. What we can know is always filtered through language, signs and the signification process. When, in the texts, a seemingly factual, truth-like, image of a 'real' person is fashioned, it occurs only by obscuring how persons are shaped in texts (Denzin, 1989, pp 14, 21-2). In this chapter, I do not uncover lone mothers' 'real' biographies; rather, I explore how social workers represent lone mothers and consequently design a professional welfare intervention through their narratives.

Biographical texts thus presume an author or 'outside' observer who can record and make sense of the life in question (Denzin, 1989). As we will see, social workers present themselves as *knowing authors* who do not have doubts about their capacity to assess and judge lone mothers' 'real' inner lives, their motivations and intentions.

Although Venetian welfare services do collect some data on their beneficiaries' backgrounds and current situation, the information is not systematic, nor is it exposed or analysed to contribute to an overall body of knowledge about welfare recipients. In order to provide basic information about who the lone mothers are that receive benefits from the city of Venice social welfare services, a survey (Giullari, 2000) was conducted within a research project on lone mothers in Italy, of which also my study is part[3]. This background information was gathered with the help of social workers by going through lone mother welfare recipients' paper folders one by one.

Since lone mothers do not constitute a specific policy target in the welfare programme of the Veneto region, some social workers explicitly admitted that they had not been thinking before of lone mothers as a group. However, the survey data were collected before the qualitative interviews for my study were conducted, which provided social workers an opportunity to form a basic idea about lone mother beneficiaries in the Venetian social welfare services.

Producing knowledge is always a dialogical process, where the role of the researcher is crucial. I planned to interview social workers on the entire course of their professional interactions with lone mothers. This was in part because, as a foreign researcher, I did not feel all that familiar with the topic of the Italian welfare state. In part, the decision to explore the question thoroughly by discussing actual processes of welfare practices with social workers stemmed from my interest in the analysis of biographies and processes. I designed a question line that included questions about the whole process of professional

---

interaction: how and why lone mothers enter the welfare services; what happens when they arrive; how the intervention is moulded; and finally, how, when and where do lone mothers exit services, if ever? I believe that, as a stranger, I was allowed to ask 'silly questions' and social workers took my background into account by extensively opening culturally taken-for-granted aspects. A student member of the team whom I trained for the task conducted a couple of the interviews.

When analysing biographical texts about lone mothers on welfare, I discovered that social workers categorised mothers by their distinct biographical pathways and identities. For the analysis, I differentiate between lone mothers' *pre-client careers* on the one hand (Goffman, 1961), and *social assistance careers* on the other. The concept of pre-client career aims to identify social workers' views of the dynamics through which mothers seek welfare services. Social assistance careers describe how the welfare intervention and interaction with lone mothers are constituted and what the mothers' social destinies are. In the analysis, pre-client career acquires a significant role as it marks the entire professional relationship. However, to cite Goffman, it only has an impact insofar as coming to the welfare services demonstrates that lone mothers have behind them a pre-client career. Goffman (1969, p 115) claims that the vantage point from which an individual examines a past life is crucial for the career so formed. In fact, the entire course of pre-client career can be deducted from this reassessment. The social workers examined here construe moral judgements from their subject position of employed wives and mothers in middle-class, two-earner families[4] and as social work professionals inculcated in the moral values of autonomy (Payne, 1999).

The analysis will rely on the following concepts. *Turning point* (epiphany) refers to the notion that biographical texts are typically structured by significant turning-point events that become pivotal *meaning structures* that organise other activities in a person's life. The analysis seeks to explore how this incident comes to occupy a central place in a person's life by attempting to anchor the meanings of this event in larger cultural settings (Denzin, 1989, p 22).

In fact, social workers' constructions about how and why lone mothers seek help from welfare services do not just depict an ahistorical snapshot view, but take account of a longer temporal perspective and provide a richer, culturally and contextually sensitive representation of the processes. As in many biographical texts (for example, Denzin, 1989, p 18), social workers' stories start also with *family* (and with the linked work situation) in which they identify the *zero point* for lone mothers' social assistance careers. Actually, family appears as the 'natural' starting point for social assistance careers, since the principle of subsidiarity of the Italian welfare system assigns it the foremost responsibility in service provision for family members.

Composing pre-client careers

The Venetian social workers that were interviewed differentiate between two different types of pre-client careers for lone mothers on welfare. They elaborate distinct categories and judgements of the mothers' biographical identity and its moral quality (Payne, 1999), as well as mothers' needs and capacities for action.

The social workers' construction of the first category of mothers, *marginalised mothers*, is that of the traditional clients of welfare services. In their view, mothers have long-term problems that often are inherited from the parental family. Women as far back as three generations might have received assistance from the social services with daughters repeating their mothers' biographies.

From their vantage point, social workers see marginalised mothers' problems as originating in a specific *family culture* that they pejoratively name as the 'culture of dependency'. Mothers depend both on the family of origin and on welfare services. Social workers thus identify the zero point for lone mothers' social assistance careers in the socialisation and reproduction of this 'culture of marginalisation' from which lone mothers have no resources to exit. Although they recognise that the category is not homogeneous and that there are differences between mothers' cases, social workers see marginalised mothers as passive outcomes of their negatively labelled way of life, which would determine their actions and attitudes towards welfare services as well. For example, this Venetian social worker suggests that:

> usually those who in their turn have eventually had a difficult situation, with ... their own family and perhaps for years have been helped from the economic point above all. Some were inserted in summer colonies, services that were there principally, in that period. Then, how to say ... perhaps they are persons who already lived in council houses of the municipality. So, they have, how to say, maintained a bit of that mentality, that in any case the municipality has to give [laughter]. To give! The kind, to give a house, to give money, to give, to put the baby immediately in the day nursery, give her, and give her everything, perhaps even free of charge. (Venetian social worker)

Social workers' biographical constructions about marginalised mothers' pre-client careers are seemingly linear. There is only one unchangeable cultural meaning structure – dependency culture – across generations and no major turning points in the women's individual biographies except that the very event of becoming lone mothers often pushes women back to their parental family (if they had ever left it).

By contrast, the term *normal mothers* refers to a new type of social welfare client. Social workers identify a neat turning point in these mothers' pre-client careers: a contingent *family crisis*. Mainly separated and divorced, normal mothers would come from middle-class families where they tended to be orientated towards the domestic sphere. The pivotal meaning structure before marital disruption is that of wives and mothers who carried out free service work in families. These mothers, therefore, crystallise the ideal figure around which the Italian welfare state has been built and to which much care work is delegated. In social workers' accounts, marital breakdown abruptly changes the pivotal meaning structure. Social workers are concerned that, through separation, women lose those economic and relational resources that were tied to their ex-husbands' social position. Therefore, they portray separated mothers as suffering from marital crisis and with the need to reorganise their lives and to build up a new social identity. Thus, it is the canonical family orientation that makes normal mothers vulnerable. Social workers conceive these mothers as culturally 'normal' and have a hard time considering them as 'real' welfare service clients. They describe them as seeing welfare services as the last resort, as not knowing what to do, and as being ashamed of having to rely on stigmatising social services. They see these normal mothers as having a major capacity for action once the crisis is overcome. Again, a Venetian social worker explains:

> These women are more autonomous, they are more willing to stand on their own feet very often, or their families are far away and don't want to uproot their children from their environment. Perhaps such families have a greater respect for their children. It is really a *discourse of diversity of the cultural level* [italics added]. (Venetian social worker)

Shaping social assistance careers

As I have already mentioned, social workers use their constructions of lone mothers' pre-client careers as a resource in shaping professional welfare interventions. Uncovering social workers' accounts of mothers' pre-client careers and the linked rationale of why mothers would seek welfare services becomes a key to understanding how mothers are treated in the welfare services.

In this respect, it is illustrative to examine the subtexts of power and culture that underlie social workers' descriptions of lone mothers' interactions with welfare services. The issue is how professional power produces cultural definitions and what follows from these into determining social welfare interventions (cf Huttunen, 2002). While social workers see lone mothers' reactions to proposed welfare interventions as determined by their mothers' distinct subcultures, they also create and signify lone mothers' biographies and capacities for action from within their own cultural and professional vantage point, a factor that to varying degrees they seem to be conscious of. By presenting themselves as knowing authors, social workers at times tone down the culturally conditioned features of their own judgements.

Of utmost importance for the shape that lone mothers' social assistance careers take is the process whereby mothers' *needs* are subject to a rewriting process at the start of the professional interaction. Social workers claim that, when seeking out welfare services, normal mothers in particular would present a *masked need*, a request for tangible, material help, linked to their contingent difficulties (the search for a job, a house, a place in a nursery, at times also economic support). Alternatively, mothers simply ask for information about how to act in a difficult situation. Social workers, however, do not fall into the 'trap' of taking normal mothers expressed needs at face value.

> But the claim is one thing, the underlying [need] is always something different. The expressed [need] is, let's say very often of an economic kind. Ehm, underlying this there is a completely different problem, which is more complicated, of a social, psychological kind. Hence, usually people come here with a precise prefabricated claim – because it is a pondered claim, a form of contact, let's say. But, ehm, this usually masks also a different kind of problem. (Venetian social worker)

And again:

> Separated women with children are in difficult situations at the moment of separation because they have difficulty in finding a job, or the job is not enough to provide for the family and to pay the rent, I mean, these kinds of problems. And they arrive almost always at the [welfare] services with rather masked problems.
>
> Interviewer: In what sense 'masked'?
>
> In the sense that … they arrive asking for a job and not a different kind of help. I mean, only afterwards emerges a need of economic help, support for … children's education, in managing problems due to the separation. They cover the need with pretexts, I mean, there are needs, but they are not the real ones. (Venetian social worker)

Social workers make sense of normal mothers' *disguised access* by considering their previous social status and related values. In well-off families, normal mothers would be accustomed to considering their problems as private and would therefore have difficulty talking about them with professional helpers. Social workers find rationales for different approaches to welfare services in mothers' different subcultural traditions. The dependency culture of marginalised mothers, on the other hand, would have made them more accustomed to rely on social services. In turn, this would explain why marginalised mothers ultimately are more demanding, a feature which social workers strongly disapprove of.

Social workers identify the uncovering of normal mothers' *'real' need* as one of their first tasks. Building trust with mothers by alleviating their expressed material and economic problems is used as a tool for going beyond mothers' initial request. From the social welfare system's point of view, economic support appears above all as an instrument to reframe these mothers' original need.

The power subtext is evident in social workers' accounts: a profitable professional relationship can only be established insofar as mothers become 'capable' of managing the institutional interaction in social workers' terms. Mothers are expected to collaborate and accept the ways in which their needs are dealt with and the respective intervention. Social workers delineate the professional relationship as an exchange rather than disinterested help in economic need. They outline themselves as consciousness-raising agents whose aim is to build a deeper 'awareness' of the mothers' problems for them.

Needs are culturally and contextually constructed and discursively interpreted (Fraser, 1989, p 181). The term 'qualifying need' refers to how the institutional configuration of the welfare service structures the needs of welfare recipients (Kazepov, 1995). Although the law of the Veneto region defines welfare services as universal, in practice access to financial support occurs more selectively and is determined by a qualifying need. This means that one has to fit into traditional categories: elderly, handicapped, young people, and also 'adults in difficulties' or 'cases of discomfort'.

For marginalised mothers, the prerequisite of qualifying need does not present a specific problem. As we have seen, in the social workers' construction of their pre-client career, marginalised mothers do already have a problem of dependency and other problems that are eligible as qualifying needs ('cases of discomfort'). Social workers hence revalidate their earlier biographical construction as proof of marginalised mothers qualifying need. In social workers' creation of their biographical identity, normal mothers, in contrast, did not present a major qualifying claim at the point of entrance. Social workers, however, say that, when alleviated from their economic needs, some may start to talk about other immaterial problems, in this way spontaneously aligning themselves with the institutional definition of their 'true' need. Often the needs of other mothers are rewritten. Social workers make no attempts to tone down the use of professional power in this respect:

> After it surfaces, surfaces alongside their much more general claim, or at least we make surface also a psychological type of claim. In the meeting we uncover and, I would say, make them conscious of their solitude and of their need to be helped and supported. (Venetian social worker)

Creating a qualifying need is a discursive strategy that aims at pigeonholing mothers into categories, thereby giving them access to economic support. Social workers rewrite (normal) mothers' initial material-economic claims into a psychosocial or sometimes an educational frame: the overcoming of crisis, solitude, abandonment, vulnerability, or difficulties with children and in their education. They see such problems as more difficult and pressing but also only temporary, linked to the crisis of acute marital breakdown.

These reframed needs become the basis for professional social work. The institutional rewriting of mothers' needs in fact serves to fashion a specific type of professional intervention. For professional purposes, lone mothers are addressed as deep, complicated, selves (Rains, 1971) who mainly need something other than economic help. Economic support is considered to be short-term first aid, aimed at giving mothers time to recover from a crisis and to find a job. From this position, work on social problems becomes the centre of professional intervention: mothers need to be helped, and at times also corrected, with a more therapeutic approach. This hierarchy of preferential interventions is in line with Venetian regional law that aims to reduce the need for assistance by removing socioeconomic and psychological causes that can create situations of need and marginalisation. Social workers also consider work on social problems as the centre of their profession and an area where they have most discretion.

Thus, the aim of professional intervention becomes helping mothers to resolve their emotional and other problems and to take responsibility for their lives. Psychosocial support can be more long-lasting and is designed by networking with other helping institutions. Some support work is delegated to the private initiative of voluntary associations, a strategy that is also in line with the prescriptions of the regional law.

In the workfare type of social policy frame, social welfare intervention openly aims at rendering mothers 'autonomous' in the job market. However, the diverse profiles of professional interventions are fashioned for mothers according to different professional constructions of their biographical identities and capacities for action.

In this final section of the chapter, I look at how lone mothers react to needs and biographies shaped for them by professional social workers, and to the intervention proposed. While social workers deal with lone mothers as deep, complicated selves, normal mothers' and marginalised mothers' problems, in their view, are considered to be different and of diverse stability.

Normal mothers' social assistance careers may show initial difficulties due to their fear of social welfare services' propensity to control and stigmatise. Once social workers have alleviated their pressing economic problems and overcome their distrust, most normal mothers would spontaneously share the professionally imposed needs and the exchange basis of professional intervention. Indeed, in some cases, social workers say that they make mothers conscious of their 'real' needs. Aligning with the institutional definitions constitutes the turning point in normal mothers' social assistance careers. Thereafter, mothers agree on the direction their biographical destinies should take. Since little (if any) professional imposition is needed to fashion their normality biography as employed mothers, social workers regard work with normal mothers as relatively easy. They stress, however, that professional intervention is moulded in a way that takes into account mothers' different situations.

Marginalised mothers' reactions to professional intervention, in contrast, stem from their sub-culturally transmitted traditions of resistance (dependency culture). In the view of social workers, marginalised mothers tend to reject the institutional reconstructions of their 'real' needs and resist therapeutic initiatives while accepting material aid. The major difficulty in such professional interactions, therefore, is going beyond material help, as marginalised mothers often refuse to deal with their 'real' problems. Social workers interpret their unwillingness to collaborate as immaturity:

They pull back more when you try to talk about their problems. As if perhaps they wouldn't like to think of them very often, they take refuge behind other problems in order to not face them. (Venetian social worker)

When mothers continue to refuse to find a job and thus depend on welfare services, social workers may reduce or abolish economic benefit as a negative incentive to force mothers to take action and find a job. Biographical correction is then strongly imposed. Indeed, due to marginalised mothers' resistance, fashioning their biographical destinies becomes the very objective of the social welfare intervention and a neat turning point in marginalised mothers' social assistance careers:

If a kick on the bottom would help that person to become autonomous, at times we have to give that kick on the bottom. (Venetian social worker)

Biographies as normalising knowledge

This analysis of the subjective dimensions of professional welfare practice provides an example of how the feminine welfare subsystem expands its grip on welfare recipients' lives by rewriting their needs, even their biographies. Interpretation of people's needs is in itself a political stake (Fraser, 1989). Welfare programmes and practices act as a dominant power that legitimises itself by promoting values and beliefs that it finds congenial, and by denigrating ideas which are disruptive (Eagleton, 1991, p 23).

The professional rewriting of mothers' needs and the fashioning of their biographies in certain ways is ultimately determined by the workfare kind of policy framework. As Goffman (1969, p 101) says, the professional view of a person is important only insofar as this view changes his or her social destiny. Social workers interpret lone mothers' life situations and problems in terms of needs that necessitate a therapeutic kind of intervention. Producing and using lone mother recipients' biographies thus serves to fashion a specific social welfare intervention. Professional interaction with clients is the site where assumptions underlying the institutional welfare state configuration are translated into welfare policy outcomes and welfare recipients' biographical destinies.

Thus, social workers' biographical constructions constitute normalising knowledge, which subsequently serves the professional power of normalisation. From a biographical viewpoint, welfare programmes and professional practices in the Venetian social welfare services appear ultimately as strategies of normalisation. This is a practice of producing normal biographies. Professional biographical constructions of lone mothers are relatively stable, but they are explicitly fashioned to make changes in mothers' biographical destinies an outcome of the policy intervention.

Biographical categorisations of lone mothers' pre-client careers constitute the starting point for the professional work process. Based on these, social workers assess which policy measures and translation operations are needed to transform mothers' diverse pre-client careers into a normal biographical destiny. Different kinds of professional power are employed to deal with the diverse categorisations of lone mothers.

This workfare kind of policy framework rejects alternative biographical destinies for recipients on welfare. The issue is of importance for mothers of small children who already often lack a father figure after separation. As lone mothers in economic need cannot choose home making and mothering as their biographical destiny, even temporarily, children in one-parent 'defective families' have fewer rights for parental presence and affection than children who grow up in 'intact families'. Biographical normalisation techniques inscribed in the workings of the welfare state thus produce unequal life chances for different categories of individuals and families.

Welfare-to-work type policy frameworks that see recipients' job market participation as the ultimate policy goal create a peculiar paradox. While marginalised mothers 'possess' the very biographical and moral qualities needed to be pigeonholed into the category of needy welfare recipients, such qualities become dysfunctional for the very modes of operation and goals of welfare policy. Marginal mothers are thus constituted as 'Other' with regard to the working suppositions of social welfare policies. Normalising their biographies requires a considerable professional effort. Welfare services work best for normal mothers who are not even considered as actual clients of welfare services.

Although the professional practice of the Venetian welfare services shows some empowering features such as interventions tailored to encourage lone mothers' independence and initiative, they also exhibit repressive characteristics. Lone mothers' independent initiatives can only take one direction. What on the level of legislative and administrative norms appears to be an emphasis towards individualising interventions is in practice transformed into a more paternalistic rationale of finding 'individualised' means to create a single policy outcome. Recipients' alternative biographical narratives are rejected, or not heard. Only professional versions are authorised.

Notes

[1] See my analysis, Kyllönen (1999).

[2] See also Edgar and Doherty (2001) and Britton et al (2002).

[3] Progetto strategico CNR, 'Governance e sviluppo economico', research on 'Genere e diseguaglianze: Le donne sole ed i nuclei monogenitoriali a capofamiglia donna', coordinated by Franca Bimbi, University of Padova.

[4] In countries like the UK and Finland, many social workers are lone mothers themselves. However, there are no comparative studies on how this would impact on social workers' interaction with lone mothers, their biographical constructions and policy intervention designed for mothers.

References

Bosco, N. (1996) 'Le carriere degli assistiti tra biografie e politiche sociali: il caso Torinese', Consorzio inter-universitario di Milano-Torino-Pavia, PhD thesis.

Bourdieu, P. (1996) 'On the family as a realized category', *Theory, Culture and Society*, vol 13, no 3, pp 19-26.

Britton, L., Chatrik, B., Coles, B., Griag, G., Birand, P., Mumtaz, S., Burrows, R., Convery, P. and Hylton, C. (2002) *Missing conneXions: The career dynamics and welfare needs of black and minority ethnic young people at the margins*, Bristol/York: The Policy Press/Joseph Rowntree Foundation.

Denzin, N.K. (1989) *Interpretive biography*, London: Sage Publications.

Eagleton, T. (1991) *Ideology: An introduction*, London: Verso.

Edgar, B. and Doherty, J. (eds) (2001) *Women and homelessness in Europe: Pathways, services and experiences of using welfare services*, Bristol: The Policy Press.

Fraser, N. (1989) *Unruly practices: Power, discourse and gender in contemporary social theory*, Minneapolis: University of Minnesota Press.

Giullari, S. (2000) 'Madri sole, dipendenza e povertà. Il caso di Venezia', in F. Bimbi (ed) *Le madri sole: Metafore della famiglia ed esclusione sociale*, Rome: Roma, pp 165-82.

Goffman, E. (1961) *Asylums: Essays on the social situation of mental patients and other inmates*, Harmondsworth: Penguin.

Gubrium, J.F., Holstein, J.A. and Buckholdt, D.R. (1994) *Constructing the life course*, New York, NY: General Hall.

Huttunen, L. (2002) 'Valta, väkivalta ja kulttuuri', *Sosiologia*, vol 39, no 2, pp 125-9.

Kazepov, Y. (1995) 'Ai confini della cittadinanza: il ruolo delle istituzioni nei percorsi di esclusione a Stuttgart e Milano', *Polis*, no 9, pp 45-66.

Kyllönen, R. (1999) 'Interpreting the needs of lone mothers: a study of welfare services in Venice', *European Journal of Social Work*, vol 2, no 3, pp 270-87.

Meo, A. (2000) *Vite in bilico: Sociologia della reazione a eventi spiazzanti*, Naples: Liguori.

Negri, N. (ed) (2002) *Percorsi e ostacoli: Lo spazio della vulnerabilità sociale*, Torino: Trauben Edizioni.

Payne, M. (1999) 'The moral bases of social work', *European Journal of Social Work*, vol 2, issue 3, pp 247-58.

Rains, P. (1971) *Becoming an unwed mother: A sociological account*, Chicago, IL: Aldine-Atherton.

Saraceno, C. (ed) (2002a) *Commissione di indagine sull'esclusione sociale: Rapporto sulle politiche contro la povertà e l'esclusione sociale 1997-2001*, Rome: Carocci.

Saraceno, C. (ed) (2002b) *Social assistance dynamics in Europe: National and local poverty regimes*, Bristol: The Policy Press.

SEVENTEEN

Interpreting the needs of homeless men: interviewing in context

Karin Schlücker

Staff members of an advice centre for homeless men were seeking to improve the effectiveness of their service by investigating the 'needs' of service users, actual or potential[1]. I was approached by one of my students to see if I could help set up and conduct a project without incurring high financial cost, and so the study was initiated within the framework of a university training programme in qualitative research[2]. Exceptionally, the research was set up as a supervised students' project. In weekly meetings, students planned each step of their research design with their two lecturers and reflected on their experiences. I believe that some of the conclusions of this project have important implications for the policy and practice of contemporary welfare work.

This chapter focuses on one interview-based case study involving a young homeless man who will be referred to as Bernd. In particular, I discuss the specific interactions between interviewer and interviewee, exemplifying policy conclusions from the type of relationship that was established. These interactions reveal a need to talk about 'more intimate secrets' that Bernd could not present explicitly, raising questions about the 'need' for a facilitative and supportive context in which this could happen. The project indicated that the facilities available to frontline workers within the established welfare system do not necessarily meet the conditions in which such needs can be responded to effectively.

Interview context

Before data collection could begin, it was necessary to establish the framework of the research design. The students initially met with members of staff from the advice centre where they explored the character of the centre's work and its request for an analysis of the needs of its service users or potential service users. Following this meeting, detailed discussions were held between the supervisors and the students in which two main principles of research were established. First, we decided that the research was to be non-directive. We felt that it would not be beneficial to aim it specifically towards the question of needs, and that allowing homeless men – and informants in general – to talk more freely would allow them better to express their own point of view. We also wondered about the exact nature of the problems that had led the advice centre staff to ask for a research project: why did they send us 'to talk with' service users, as they put it, when they were talking with them everyday?[3]

Second, we decided to consider the project within a triangulated field of interrelationships, with three related groups as the cornerstones of the research proposal. The first group consisted of homeless men, who were service users or potential service users of the advice centre. The second group were the staff members of the advice centre, situated in that particular setting. The third group was the research team. Our position in the field and our relationships to each of the other two groups were not within the actual focus of the research, but our presence had to be taken into account and reflected on as an important contextual factor.

Within this field, we identified areas of potential research interest, both as a basis for selecting adequate instruments for data collection and as a focus during the analysis. The first area concerned the relationship between the advice centre and its service users. This included the interactions that establish the specific relationships of professional advice giving or counselling[4]. The second area concerned the biographies of both groups involved in such a relationship; that is, the advice givers and their (potential) clients, and how these might interfere with their immediate relationship. The third area we defined as the current experiences in both groups, especially their views of their own situation and relationships with any relevant others. The fourth area, finally, concerned each group's fears, wishes or ideas about the future, as revealed through their imagining of hypothetical situations and their fantasies.

Within this framework, half of the research team was engaged in collecting

Figure 17.1: The interview context: a triangulated field of interrelationships

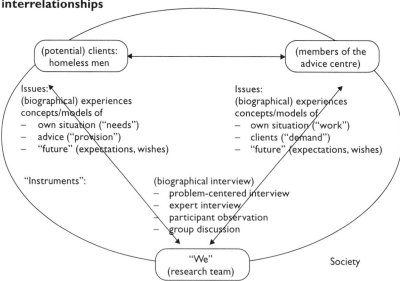

problem-centred interviews with individual homeless men who were clients or potential clients of our advice centre. The other students organised group discussions with homeless clients; they also interviewed members of the advice centre's staff, and did participant observation in the advice centre. The interviews with homeless men focused on the issue of advice giving and counselling and usually started with a question about the interviewee's experiences of being given advice. Although the interviews started with this initial question, it was intended that they should be as open and as respondent-guided as possible. All data collection was conducted during one week of field research. The students were asked to write field notes and reports and the research team met regularly for reflection and discussion.

Case study: the interview with Bernd

Bernd is a young man in his early twenties. At the time of our field research he was living in a hostel for homeless men. He was interviewed by one of our male students, Patrick Kraemer, who was also in his twenties[5]. During the interview both used the more informal German *Du* (you) instead of the more formal *Sie* (you).

A woman student first arranged the interview with Bernd. With Bernd's approval, Patrick then took it over. Patrick reported that they engaged in small talk, mostly about cars, prior to and after the recording. During these unrecorded periods, as throughout the recorded interview, Patrick disliked the manner in which Bernd handled the conversation. Patrick felt that Bernd affected a level of knowledge and ability he did not in fact possess and that Bernd's discourse was exaggerated and even dishonest. At times, Patrick felt he was being ridiculed: "How stupid does he think I am?", he wondered in his report. In the research team's first discussion of Patrick's interview experiences, Bernd reminded us of a young cock, ruffling his feathers to show off.

In dealing with the text of the transcribed interview, I want to concentrate first on the small stories told by Bernd. In contrast to his explanations, comments and asides, such stories are narratives in the more precise, linguistic sense. Modifying the suggestions of Brigitte Boothe (1993), I will analyse them as depictions of a social world. Such stories present characters as active protagonists, including the figure of the storyteller him or herself. These acting characters/protagonists are connected through their social relationships. Narratives are typically action-centred and follow a straightforward, chronological pattern.

In support of our first impression of Bernd 'showing off', the majority of Bernd's narratives are concerned with his achievements or what he would achieve if others did not interfere or gave him more opportunities. We found that Bernd's stories generally presented an asymmetrical relationship between Bernd as one protagonist and someone else as another protagonist. As an acting figure in his own stories, Bernd himself appears in two main ways, so that it is possible to divide the narratives into two main types.

A: Bernd competing with a superior

An example of this first category is a story in which Bernd impresses his employment officer with his "mile-long list" of jobs, as he puts it. The point of the story lies in its reversal of the status/power difference between them: in contrast to the assumptions of his employment officer as well as of his listener, he has not only been employed but he lists so many jobs that the officer's "eyes are falling out of his head". Triumphantly, Bernd presents himself as experienced and the employment officer as a little dense (however, should the listener doubt Bernd's point of view, then this impact is toned down so that the only impression is of Bernd showing off). Generally, in Bernd's narratives of this type, the relationship between himself and other characters is competitive. There are winners and losers, there are those whose words have the power to impress or to instruct, and those whose words are ineffectual and who often remain silent. They may be so impressed by the powerful figures that their 'eyes are falling out' of their heads.

B: Bernd as helper

In this category, all the relationships between Bernd and the other person are the opposite from those in the first category: here, Bernd helps others. As he says, commenting on his narratives: "If I can help, I gladly will". Within this category we found two further subgroups of 'helping'. In the first subcategory, Bernd helps someone who is in a higher social position, whereas in the second category he helps someone in a weaker position. Examples of both types of narrative follow.

Bernd helps someone in a 'higher' position. While discussing the pleasure he finds in arranging and decorating rooms, Bernd reveals a fantasy that he has entertained and treasures. As Bernd puts it, "A social worker comes to me in person and says: 'Bernd, listen, for some reason my office looks a little drab, have you any idea what to do about it?'" In the story, Bernd initially assumes a lower social position. This is indicated by Bernd's use of the German expression *höchst persönlich*, which is here translated as 'in person', referring to the social worker. Yet the social worker, in spite of his higher social status, asks Bernd for help in the same way as he would ask a colleague or a friend. Thus, the social worker in Bernd's story treats him as an equal. And Bernd presents himself as able to help someone of higher social status "by word and deed", as Bernd puts it in a comparable story.

Bernd helps someone in a 'weaker' position. Within the second subgroup, the relationship of social status and power is entirely reversed. In his fantasies of being a helper, we often find Bernd adopting the position of a social worker, advice giver, or counsellor. In fact, one of the most striking characteristics of Bernd's interviews is the frequency with which he slips into the position of a 'professional helper'. A good example is a sequence where Bernd is talking from a professional point of view, offering advice to a character that mirrors

Bernd's position as a client. The shift in positions (emphasised by italics) can be observed clearly:

> What *you* have to pay attention to, especially if there's a *client* comin' to *me*, is what age they are and so on and everything. *One* just has to set limits, if, now, a 20-year-old twit comes along, err, who wants to talk, well, about, err, more intimate secrets, *I've* gotta, got to treat it quite differently from if an 80-year-old comes and, maybe, she wants to talk about her dead husband or something.

An institutional career

Even though the student interviewers did not actively inquire into the clients' biographies, the biographical issue was always raised by the respondents. It was not unusual for them to introduce their past experiences even at the beginning of the interview. Whether briefly or in detail, they introduced their listeners to the life course of a homeless person, in order to assert their status as experts on 'advising homeless men'. This is the case with Bernd in this initial sequence:

> Patrick: I just mentioned that this is something about advice giving and counselling. Did you, somehow, ever have such experiences?

> Bernd: Ha! Well, I can tell any amount about that. So, let me see now, I've lived since about – what year is it now, '99 – for about four years I have not lived at home anymore, and I have, then, I have gone through, let me say, through several institutions. But, err, advice giving as such is only happening now.

Bernd shows himself to be highly familiar with the discourse of social care. Examples of this specialised vocabulary appear throughout the interview. In this initial sequence, he uses the specialised German expression 'to go through institutions' (*durch Einrichtungen gehen*)[6]. A little later, Bernd quite correctly uses the word *Sozialarbeiterschlüssel* to refer to the ratio of social workers to clients in institutional care. And, as we have noted, Bernd refers to 'clients' coming to see him. At the same time, however, he remains uncomfortable concerning more personal details. Briefly presenting his life course, he is vague about specific dates or timescales; he offers no reason for leaving or losing his home, and he offers no information about the different kinds of institutions he has 'gone through' after that. Throughout the whole interview, Bernd was ill at ease with biographical information, far more so than other respondents. However, at the end of the interview, he finally offered a radical summary of his life:

> I have actually spent all of my life – well, I was of no fixed abode for two
> months, and this is, now, a couple of years ago – really most of my life, in
> institutions like this one [referring to the hostel where the interview took
> place].

It seems likely that Bernd had spent many years as a user of welfare services –
if not almost all of his life, as he puts it finally. And we can gauge the effects of
Bernd's institutional career in the social world that unfolds in his narratives[7].
The stories are peopled with officials, social workers, 'shysters' and 'pigs':
characters all defined through the institutional framework. These figures are
always in a higher and more powerful position than Bernd, facing him in a
supportive and/or a controlling manner. Correspondingly, Bernd's strategies
to overcome his lower position in social relationships are crafted from his
experience of the institutional world. He can show himself helpful and
supportive to those weaker than him by adopting the guise of a social worker,
the role model he is most familiar with. He even can prove himself helpful to
those in higher positions. Or he can show himself competitive and challenging,
posing and ruffling his feathers like a young cock (as with his 'mile-long list' of
different jobs)[8]. This last strategy not only affects his narratives, but also his
reaction to the interviewer. He, too, confronts Bernd from a higher position,
protected by institutions and hegemonic discourses: by the university and
specialised knowledge.

The importance of 'talking'

The opening interview question asked Bernd about his experiences of being
counselled or being given advice. Even when he expanded his answer, after
the initial sequence, Bernd claimed a 'helper's position'. Meanwhile, he could
give advice, too, because: "I do have a small idea of it myself by now". Through
many examples, he reveals his long experience of a type of advice giving that
is mainly limited to an exchange of information, centred round 'administrative
problems'. Bernd tells us he has been informed about "what the housing
market looks like at the moment", and "of course everything about the official
channels I have to follow when I report as unemployed, when I have to go on
welfare" and "the right procedures: whether I go to the unemployment office
first, or whether I should go to the welfare department" and such like.

Bernd does not openly criticise this type of advice giving. From his point of
view, it is "to be judged positively in general". But the 'in general' reveals a
slight friction, and we can find other signs of an implicit critique. Bernd
repeatedly suggests that advisers should have more time for talk with their
clients. Indeed, wherever Bernd adopts the position of a social worker in his
narratives, the issue of 'talking' is central. Finally, in the last third of the interview
there is a very interesting development. Bernd starts to test the interviewer,
attempting to negotiate and establish exactly what sort of discourse is allowed

within the frame of the interview and what would be inappropriate. I will now go on to analyse this 'test' in more detail.

Following extensive complaints about his current social worker (a controlling figure), Bernd suggests a preferable alternative. Instead of an administrator, Bernd wants a 'confidant', someone he feels he could trust. Immediately after this, Bernd offers a surprising example of such a person: this might be a student volunteer in a day-care centre for homeless people, who was also a member of the research group. At first, Bernd's speech is stilted, searching for the right words, but he ends confidently, enthusing that he "somehow got the impression of being able to talk about all of my problems in her presence".

Our initial hypothetical interpretation was that Bernd was attempting to put to Patrick, the interviewer, a question that he could not directly voice. Such a question might be: 'You are in the same group – so perhaps you are one of her kind, too, someone to trust in?'. However, Patrick responds by reminding Bernd of the institutional framework of the research setting and as Bernd goes on praising this young woman, Patrick finally changes the subject:

Patrick (P): Well, I have to say that she is a member of our research project.

Bernd (B): I know.

P: Well, I wanted to mention that again.

B: I know. I have come to think of her as a nice person as well, and have learnt to value her as a nice person. I have grown fond of her, I think.

P: I understand … well, now I am quite at a loss. Shall we smoke a cigarette?

Four transcript pages later, Bernd returns to the example of this woman student. This time Patrick keeps to a short "yes, yes" – and Bernd goes on, introducing those "more intimate secrets" that he had previously only mentioned through the character in his narratives who mirrored his position as a client (the "20-year-old twit"). He talks about the love poems he writes, diary entries, and personal 'maxims' he finds to guide him. However, this intimacy is more than our inexperienced student researcher can deal with. Again Patrick changes the subject, and soon after this, he ends the interview.

Bernd's discourse raises significant questions, which we may now attempt to answer. What have we learnt about Bernd's experiences of being given advice? What is the more precise significance of his emphasis on 'talking'? And finally, how can we answer the advice centre's question: what are Bernd's 'needs'?

What Bernd appears to want from advisers and social workers, and what he feels he does not receive, he evidently cannot articulate easily or directly. We can understand why this is so. In directly admitting his wishes, Bernd would establish himself in precisely that passive and inferior position that he challenges by his strategies of helping or competing (whether they are realistic or not).

This is the reason for Bernd's reversing of positions in his narratives: Bernd is the social worker who would listen and "definitely" respond, as he puts it, if a client needed to "talk". At the same time, his own desire for a kind of informal discourse through which "more intimate secrets" could be expressed and discussed unfolds in the interaction of the interview (Argelander, 1970; Bosse and King, 1998). Bernd puts the interviewer in a position to listen to his 'intimate secrets', but only after testing the boundaries of the interview to see whether such discourse would be welcomed and allowed. Significantly, Bernd's desire to talk is even strong enough to overcome the barrier put up by the student's first negative reaction.

Conclusions for professional practice

In various ways, mainly dependent on life course experiences, the issue of talking played a consistently central role in every single one of our interviews with homeless men. We can conclude, therefore, and can so advise their advisers, social workers and counsellors, that they have clients and potential clients who are searching for a kind of discourse that is more intimate than a mere exchange of information and administrative advice. Furthermore, this need might well not be asked for directly or disclosed straightaway. If we examine Bernd's strategies of self-presentation in the interview, and his accounts of his self-presentation towards social workers and counsellors, we can suppose that someone like Bernd will succeed for a while in hiding or denying this need.

From the interview with Bernd, we can also draw some conclusions about the methods or requirements of implementation. First, to satisfy the wish for more intimate talk requires a degree of professional training in personal capacities that would enable advisers – like interviewers – to deal with such interaction. Second, it calls for an institutional framework in that more intimate talking is allowed[9]. This points to remedies on the service provider side, the advice centre and its staff. As I mentioned in the beginning, we consciously kept this 'other side' within the research design, following our initial question about why they sent us to talk with their clients when they were talking with them everyday. Did they themselves have a sense of missing a more intimate encounter in that they could meet the 'real' needs of their clients? And if they missed it, why? I want briefly to discuss two answers to such questions.

First, we found a gap between a concept of 'administrative' advice giving on the one hand, and the type of counselling (that in German language is called 'therapy') on the other, a gap that in the English language is represented by the difference between advice giving and counselling. The professional training of the practitioners and their accounts in the interviews seemed to reflect this gap[10]. For social workers in the role of advisers, the field of 'clinical counselling' seems to be something strange, explicitly ridiculed, and implicitly alarming. Recognising the concept of the client's biography might help to bridge such a gap. With each client, an advice-giving social worker must surely be aware, at some level, that he or she is dealing with the experiences of a whole life course even if the service user does not offer these experiences openly, as was the case with Bernd. Including this concept in life skills training, together with more open methods of facilitative talking, would allow advisers to understand the service users' experiences better and ultimately meet their individual needs more effectively. However, there should be no doubt – as is the case for both researchers and interviewers – that this requires a degree of organised and appropriate professional training.

Second, attention has to be paid to the institutional settings that facilitate or hinder more open and intimate talk. As Denzin and Lincoln (1998) pointed out, researchers cannot eliminate their own institutional position. The same is true of advisers and counsellors. A professional 'confidant' will still be a professional. As with research methods, we can identify conditions that facilitate or hinder talking. Current discourses on 'efficiency' tend to hinder such developments. It is difficult to see how more intimate talk could find a place alongside the criteria of efficiency that judge the success or failure of an advice centre and its professional practice solely by 'hard' statistical returns concerning the number of counselling appointments, the number housing allocations and so on. The aim of a more 'open' and 'respondent-guided' intimacy, when answering a 'need' for it, will not propel clients more rapidly into housing and employment. Why? Because talk, quite simply, needs time. Thus, institutional conditions, on the one hand, and more biographically informed work, on the other hand, necessarily clash. I fear that more would be required to change such infrastructures than the findings of this research project[11].

Finally, leaving aside the questions this project poses for professional practice, I want to conclude with a short comment on the concept of social exclusion. In our interviews, we found very obvious examples of exclusion. However, Bernd's case study suggests that the notions of exclusion and inclusion are not mutually exclusive and can be experienced simultaneously. Living in a shared room in his hostel for homeless men, without training or job perspectives and with at least one previous conviction, Bernd is certainly on the side of the excluded. Significantly, however, we find him included as well: in a network of institutions, in a structure of social status and relationships of power, and in forms of discourse (Foucault, 1977). In an analytical sense, therefore, Bernd is as included within this framework as is his social worker – even when he is in a different position. Further research should take notice of this *inclusion within the exclusion*.

Notes

[1] The advice centre was financed and managed by a partnership of established German welfare services. It employed a small number of trained social workers (both women and men) to work with adult homeless men (mostly white Germans aged between 18 and about 60). Working with other services, they mainly offered practical advice concerning housing and employment, financial support or a place in a 'de-tox' centre. This included "sometimes simply drinking a cup of coffee" with a client.

[2] This was in the Department of Social Science, J. W. Goethe University, Frankfurt-am-Main. Usually, this training programme has two parts (each with classes of two hours a week over a one-year period). The first introduces the student to the history, types and problems of methods. In the second, students participate in a formal research project run by their professor supervisors (for example, by conducting interviews).

[3] Weigand (1990) warns against straightforwardly following the explicit request of a commissioning organisation. Identifying the exact nature of the problem should be part of the research.

[4] In German, there is one noun (*Beratung*) for both advice giving and counselling. It is sharply distinguished from 'therapy' (*Therapie*), a noun that denotes more specifically therapeutic talk (although in English, this is also implied by *counselling*).

[5] I appreciate Patrick's permission to present his first interview experiences. I also want to thank all the participants in the research who gave their help and their experiences. I particularly want to thank all the student researchers and my colleague, Cornelia Rohe, for their dedicated work. What I present here is based on this collaborative work, although of course I take responsibility for every written word.

[6] The German noun *Einrichtungen* can refer to any type of welfare facility, from agencies for children to 'de-tox' centres.

[7] With Clemenz et al (1990) we can talk, too, of an 'administered biography'.

[8] This is possibly a typical male strategy. An analysis of the gender implications of Bernd's case, which could be very fruitful, exceeds the scope of this chapter.

[9] Pointing to the institutional setting of the research was the first of Patrick's strategies in resisting Bernd's 'test' on whether more intimate talk might be allowed. We should also not forget that standardised methods of data collection would preclude such talk a priori.

[10] The interviews with advice centre staff were arranged and conducted by a male student. Perhaps it was no accident that he only managed to talk with male staff, even though it was a mixed team.

[11] As if to emphasise this point, while our research team was composing the final report to give to the advice centre, we heard that it was to be closed. In the name of 'efficiency', frontline homelessness services in the local welfare system were being reorganised. We understood too late that the advice centre's request for research was also part of its fight for survival. At this point, the students' engagement in the project ended. Consequently, and because the project had already stretched the limits of our own institutional capacity (of two hours a week for a year), we were not able to reflect fully as a group on this development.

___

References

Argelander, H. (1970) *Das Erstinterview in der Psychotherapie*, Darmstadt: Wiss. Buchgesellschaft.

Boothe, B. (1993) *Der Patient als Erzähler in der Psychotherapie*, Göttingen: Vandenhoeck & Ruprecht.

Bosse, H. and King, V. (1998) 'Die Angst vor dem Fremden und die Sehnsucht nach dem Fremden in der Adoleszenz. Fallstudie einer Gruppe von Spätadoleszenten, interpretiert mit dem Ansatz psychoanalytisch-sozialwissenschaftlicher Hermeneutik und der Ethnohermeneutik', in H.D. König (ed) *Sozialpsychologie des Rechtsextremismus*, Frankfurt-am-Main: Suhrkamp, pp 216-56.

Clemenz, M., Combe, A., Beier, Ch., Lutzi, J. and Spangenberg, N. (1990) *Soziale Krise, Institutionen und Familiendynamik. Konfliktstrukturen und Chancen therapeutischer Arbeit mit Multiproblemfamilien*, Opladen: Westdeutscher Verlag.

Denzin, N.K. and Lincoln, Y.S. (1998) 'Introduction: Entering the field of qualitative research', in N.K. Denzin and Y.S. Lincoln (eds) *The landscape of qualitative research: Theories and issues. Handbook of qualitative research*, vol 1, Thousand Oaks, CA: Sage Publications, pp 1-34.

Foucault, M. (1977) *Die Ordnung des Diskurses: Inauguralvorlesung am Collège de France – 2 Dezember 1970*, Frankfurt-am-Main, Berlin and Wien: Ullstein.

Weigand, W. (1990) 'Die Analyse des Auftrags in der Teamsupervision und Organisationsberatung', in G. Fatzer and C.D. Eck (eds) *Supervision und Beratung: Ein Handbuch*, Köln: Ed. Humanist. Psychologie, pp 311-26.

Part Five:
Biographical resources in education and training

In quest of teachers' professional identity: the life story as a methodological tool

Marie-Françoise Chanfrault-Duchet

Applying the methodological tool of the life story, this chapter addresses the issue of the professional identity of teachers of French in secondary schools in France. I will explain this specific choice of issue and method by answering the reader's usual question, 'What position does the author speak from?'. This requires some background information on my own professional and intellectual development both as a researcher and academic.

As a researcher in scientific linguistics, I have worked for 20 years on the life story as a tool for collecting data within the framework of the social sciences. As an academic, I teach language and literary theory at a university, on the one hand, and on the other, French as a school subject as part of teacher training at an Academic School of Education, the Institut Universitaire de Formation des Maîtres (IUFM). Recently, the opportunity arose to supersede this divided situation: in 1999, the French Ministry of Education decided to specify and change the academic criteria for teacher training, and to develop research within this field.

This new approach, that was already intended with the creation of the Academic Schools of Education[1] in 1991 but not implemented[2], seeks to apply research findings and academic knowledge to teacher training. The challenge now is to utilise educational research and that of neighbouring disciplines to move away from the old tradition of training as the mere transmission of professional practice by experienced teachers to a new kind of scientifically based training that takes into account the issue of professional identity. In this context, I was able to 'import' my work on life stories into the field of training and to think through the issue of personal identity. For me this meant moving away from theorising the life story as a linguistic object to practising it as a methodological tool and integrating educational science in an interdisciplinary approach. This process has taken place within a research project set up by the School of Education. The project required that experienced teachers involved in training – that is, non-researchers – must be integrated in the research team[3].

Based on the research processes and initial findings of the project, this chapter focuses on the relevance of the life story as a research device in understanding professional identity. This specific issue raises a series of questions. How can we define 'professional identity'? How do teachers construct their professional identity in response to changes in practice? What are the links between personal and professional identity? To what extent can a life story be an effective methodological tool? Are my own types of analysis, using linguistic and literary theory to approach and process the life story as a text, relevant in this specific context? What do life stories tell us? How can the ethical and epistemological problems arising from the use of the life story in an open research team be resolved? What should be done with the data collected from the field of teacher training?

To attempt to answer these questions, I first sketch the main lines of argument concerning biographical methods and professional practice from the standpoint of professional identity, and outline the research context. I then review the methodological potential of the life story through the analysis of two life stories. In conclusion, I reflect on the possible effects and applications of the research process and findings to teacher training.

Teachers' professional identity and biographical methods

There remains in teacher training a temptation to extract 'teacher knowledge' from its context and to convert it into a transferable skill. This functionalist viewpoint, that conceives professional practice as 'expertise' (Schön, 1987), misses the core of the problem. Teachers involved, as defined by their professional identity, cannot understand professional practice without taking into account the meaning they attribute to it. In other words, professional practices must be understood in their context, including the singular ways in that the teacher, as a subject, shapes them and loads them with meaning. This point is all the more significant since teaching is a professional activity carried on in a 'face-to-face relation' (Goffman, 1973), in that the teacher is involved as a person. Professional identity cannot thus be viewed as a mere body of methods and techniques acquired during the training period. It has to be considered as the product of complex elaboration of a work-in-progress that involves the teacher's personal identity in relation to the education system and the act of teaching itself. It relates to:

- the aims and values of educational institutions;
- educational and pedagogic concepts;
- the community of teachers as a peer group;
- French as a school discipline (in content, methods, exercises and routines).

From the viewpoint of the ego, professional identity can be defined and understood as the crossroads between the social and personal self and, therefore, can be approached through biographical methods. Since these methods are based on narrative discourse, such an approach presupposes a link between identity and narration. Within this framework, the French philosopher Ricoeur's definition of identity holds. For Ricoeur (1985, 1990), 'identity' is the product of a narrative process, that, through the process of fictionalisation, fixes the evolution of the self through time and its permanency as a subject[4].

This position finds its echo within literary theory, in the definition of autobiography, proposed by Lejeune (1975), that can be reduced to the following equation:

I = author = narrator = hero of the narrative.

My definition of the life-story method results from my earlier research on the subject[5]. Rooted in an approach that articulates two theoretical and methodological frameworks – that is, pragmatic linguistics and literary text theory – it views the oral life story as a text. This position was developed in the 1980s before it became fashionable in the biographical field (Chanfrault-Duchet, 1984, 1985, 1986). The method focuses on the inaugural injunction 'Tell me your life story', that engages the informant as a narrator in a discursive process based on the narrative elaboration of the life experience as a whole. This contrasts with biographical interviews that lay stress on precise periods, facts or events within the course of his or her life (Chanfrault-Duchet, 1984, 1987, 1988), and with life history, that brings into play chronological organisation and thus turning points of an individual life path (Chanfrault-Duchet, 1987, 1994).

The narrative interaction at work in the life story brings into play a complex discursive system, organising the biographical data into a particular textual construction. This construction remains largely outside the conscious awareness of the narrator and must be brought out by the researcher by means of linguistic, narrative and literary deciphering processes.

On the basis of the shared knowledge of narrator and narratee, socio-cultural, symbolic representations are encoded into a singular narrative construction, conveying the singularity of the life experience of the self (Chanfrault-Duchet, 1984, 1987, 1988, 1990, 1991a, 1991b). In other words, the product of narrative interaction constitutes a system of meaning complete in itself; that is, a text. This definition requires textual analysis of the transcript in a process that integrates the oral features present on the tape and the paraverbal features registered in the field notes. Consequently, the researcher needs theoretical and methodological resources, that generally exceed his or her disciplinary competencies within the social sciences and call for an interdisciplinary approach combining pragmatic linguistics, narratology, discourse and textual analysis and literary theory[6]. As each life story is the unique product of a singular system of meaning, through processing the body of life stories beyond the similarity in their life paths, events and facts, practices, beliefs and values, the researcher can discover the individual meaning given by the narrator (as a subject) to his or her life experience.

Focusing on professional identity reshapes the genre of the life story. The inaugural injunction becomes: 'Tell me your professional life story'. This calls for the narrator to emphasise the professional dimension of the social self. If we consider identity as a construct that articulates different components of the self, the life story as a methodological tool should allow us, through the singular textual construction, to grasp the various devices social actors bring into play to resolve the tensions between personal and professional identity. Thus, the life story makes it possible to understand a teacher's professional identity from the standpoint of the global self; that is, to contextualise professional data in individual life experience.

On one level, the process of analysis concerns the interweaving of personal and professional identities in the narrative and, on a second level, the singularity of the subject as expressed within the textual ordering of the narrative. In order to conform to a scientific approach, that requires generalisation and going beyond the singularity of experience, the researcher has to elaborate the findings from the analysis by comparing the group of life stories and then theorising the results of the social research[7].

A specific research context

These general considerations have to be tailored to the research context. How does my research project redefine the methodological issues?

The research project I coordinate at the IUFM is concerned with professional identity among teachers of French in secondary schools within the wider context of changes in educational practice. It aims to describe current practice in reality, behind the institutional requirements, and to understand the identity crisis that has resulted from recent institutional changes brought about by:

- the introduction of an academic dimension to teacher education;
- the rationalisation and professionalisation of teaching;
- the redefinition of French as a school discipline now based on linguistic knowledge, instead of literature and humanities, and the introduction of new content, methods and exercises[8].

As these major changes in content and method were not adequately prepared for nationally through effective in-service training, teachers have been left in a distressed state. An article in *Le Monde* in March 2000 was entitled 'The "Rue de Grenelle" murders literature'[9]. In that year, the education minister was forced to resign. However, the political crisis has continued. In 2003 alone, there have been three months of strikes, formally over pensions, but actually over the general crisis in education, in that teachers of French are most affected.

In this particular context, the challenge of the project initiated by my institution, apart from applying the results to teacher training, is to identify the main features of teacher identity, as a means of sensitising institutional requirements. Its core issue concerns the relationship between teacher practices, professional biographies determined by generation, and professional identity in relation to French as a school discipline. To unravel this relationship, we must consider how professional and personal identity interacts.

The biographical approach currently represents a growing trend in this field. It was initiated in the 1980s by the use of life histories within the framework of ongoing training (Pineau and Jobert, 1989). In this specific context, although life histories are referred to as a methodological tool, they are not used as a data-gathering device for scientific purposes, but rather as a training tool. Trainees are invited to write out or tell their life history[10], then to analyse it, in dialogue with the trainers, to bring out their biographical development, and personal and professional potential, and thus draw up their own training project. In this model, autobiographical writing or telling is used as part of teacher education to encourage student teachers to identify how their own experience as pupils and students shaped their representations of teaching. Besides this use of biographical methods, a research use has recently emerged with a view to understanding professional training sociologically as a biographical process. This might help, for example, in comparing how student teachers assess their training course (Malet, 1998)[11].

However, approaches that emphasise either training or research separately do not offer a coherent framework for my project, since its specific institutional characteristics require that the academic research be articulated with research as a new training practice. In fact, the integration of field trainers in the research team raises a series of epistemological and educational questions. How can non-researchers participate in a research team? How can field teachers, as part-time trainers, study an object so close to their own everyday routines, to their own professional life? How can I combine being a researcher and, within an open research team, a trainer, using the research process as a training practice? Borrowing from educational research based on 'the ethnography of school' in the UK by Woods (1986) offers a coherent way of resolving these problems. In fact Woods, who works with 'mixed teams', goes beyond the old dichotomy in educational research between 'insiders' on the one hand (that is, field teachers), supposed by the researchers to be incapable of explaining educational practice epistemologically, and 'outsiders' on the other, researchers supposed by field teachers to be unable, because of their theoretical viewpoint, to account for the real experience of teaching practice. Ethnographic description of educational practice as rituals and rites taking their meaning from the cultural community created by the school as an institution allows the epistemological question of how to become a researcher while being so close to the research object to be side-stepped[12]. By treating the professional researchers as 'implied ethnographers', Woods started to use biographical methods[13] to grasp the viewpoints of the actors in the educational field.

Relying on these theoretical and methodological premises, it is then possible to consider the first stage of the research – *description* – as a first-level initiation in the research process. This can form the basis of training if the methods are scientifically based. Professional researchers, with the help of those trainers who wish to do a doctorate, can carry out the second stage: *theorisation*.

From the point of view of training, the dynamics of the life-story approach, rooted in biographical methods and thus discursive and textual outcomes, lies in the use of linguistic and literary theory that now forms the basic content of French as a school discipline. Consequently, the teachers and trainers have to update their academic knowledge and transfer it to the new context of research as opposed to teaching. This process makes them distinguish academic from school knowledge and thus question their own teaching practices.

On the basis of my previous work, I took charge of the life stories, collected first from the members of the research team – teachers and trainers who volunteered to tell their professional life stories with the express motivation of highlighting their own practices and professional identity – and then from 'standard' teachers in the field. I have now collected 10 life stories that I am still analysing. The first stage of the procedure aimed to outline the particular features of the professional life story, as actualised in teachers' narratives, by comparing an earlier body of women's life stories with this new body. As I mentioned earlier in this chapter, the genre is redefined by asking for the professional life story. The request places the emphasis on the professional sphere, relegating the personal sphere to a position of secondary importance and giving the narrative a specific form. In fact, the narrative does not begin with the narrator's birth, family and information about his or her background but with the beginning of his or her working life. This type of introduction leads, then, to a narrative that develops in loops with flashbacks and flashes forwards. The chronological dynamics, that lie beneath the surface of the narrative, have to be reconstructed within the analysis. In this way, the narrative reveals two life paths, the professional and the personal, that can develop harmoniously along parallel lines or interact or come into conflict with one another. It is within the framework of the relationship between these two paths and their dynamics that the narrator organises the biographical data into a singular narrative around his or her global identity. However, if the narrative produced is a real constructed narrative (rather than a chronology as in a life history), the narration is articulated with other types of discourse, depending on the teacher's professional discursive skills. In so far as teachers are inclined to use explanation and argument frequently in the classroom, these two modes of discourse tend to dominate the narration. So, the narrative is marked out by long sequences of explanation and argument[14] that interact with the system of meaning created within the narration. For French teachers, this approach takes the form of the 'dissertation' in the narrative, that, as a typical exercise within French as a school discipline, defines one of the bases of disciplinary identity.

The methodological potential of the life story

The force of the life story as a genre resides in the fact that it encodes, and thus condenses, a great deal of information in a global schema (the text), that articulates and organises it in order to produce meaning. However, as the textual system, that controls the construction of meaning, lies beneath the surface of the narration, the analysis must be capable of bringing it out. The questions are then: How can the analysis bring this system to the fore? How can the textual data be processed and applied within the research field; that is, to the teachers' identity?

Within the research project, the analysis proceeds through two stages. The first one consists of content analysis to bring out data about teaching practices and teacher careers, a point I shall not develop here. The second stage, that depends on the specific data from the life story as text, deals with a formal analysis that borrows its theoretical and methodological tools from the linguistic and literary field. The first aim is to draw out, behind the loops of the narrative surface, the two lines of life path, the personal and the professional, and their interrelationship; then to pick out the recurrent linguistic and textual features that define the outlines in the narrative of the singular system of meaning. Within this process, as the life story is an oral genre, careful attention must be paid to the oral and vocal features, as recorded on tape (Chanfrault-Duchet, 1994), and to the field notes, that provide the context of the interaction and that can thus throw light on the transcript. In this way, in keeping with the procedures that I have laid down (Chanfrault-Duchet, 1994), the analysis picks out the *key phrase* and the *key patterns*. The key phrase, as a refrain, expresses a stable relationship towards the society and the world in moral terms. Its regular recurrence throughout the narration represents the axes of the underlying system of meaning in the interaction. As for the key patterns, they transpose the stable relationship, expressed by the key phrase, into forms of behaviour. Functioning as narrative and textual schema, they are to be found beneath the surface of the narrative, within the anecdotes that dramatise the self and thus contribute to the fictionalisation of the biographical data, a process that presents the self as a character in the narrative. Indicating attitudes such as acceptance, resignation, refusal, compromise, negotiation and so on, the key patterns form a behavioural matrix that functions as a deciphering tool behind the diversity of situations and supports the coherence of the self in the face of change. So, the key phrase and the key patterns represent 'cells of meaning' that lead the analysis towards the singular system of meaning.

From the 10 life stories I collected for this research project, I shall draw on two that exemplify the methodological potential of the life story as a tool in social sciences, and allow us to test the relevance and the effectiveness of the type of analysis I am proposing. Within the limited space of this chapter, I can only give the main outlines of the analyses of the two narratives. Two secondary school French teachers, who also work part-time at the Academic School of Education and are part of the research team, produced them. Working with life histories and biographical interviews, they were eager to swap position from that of interviewer to that of interviewee and accept the risk of telling their professional life stories and facing the analysis – and thus interpretation – of their respective narratives[15].

René and Denise[16] belong to the same generation and present some similarities in their career paths. Their professional choice was not dictated by vocation but by their class position. Each discovered an interest in the profession while teaching. At first, they both failed the theoretical part of the teaching certificate, the *Certificat d'Aptitude au Professorat de l'Enseignement Secondaire* (CAPES)[17], but passed it on their second attempt the following year. If they take an interest in literature, it cannot be said that they are passionate about it. Denise confesses that she still finds it an effort to get into 'great' literature. As for René, he shows more interest in culture and humanities than in literature itself. However, they outline different life stories, revealing two different types of professional identity and two different personalities.

Denise was born in 1954. A Trotskyist militant in her student years, she married an Iranian immigrant and has four children. She passed an exam first to teach in technical school, then the CAPES (for secondary school) and finally the *Agrégation* (a competitive examination viewed in France as the crowning achievement for a secondary school teacher). She currently teaches in a *collège* (lower secondary school), that has a high immigrant intake and suffers from the violent conduct of students, a school where teachers generally do not want to teach but to that she is passionately committed.

René, born in 1946, passed the CAPES exam in 1972. He got married late to a teacher of French and has two children. After a short period in a *collège*, he has since taught in a *lycée* (upper school). In 1999, he moved from a town where he was deputy mayor in charge of schools, to an academic town, where he teaches in a school with a lower middle-class intake.

Each life story, in its singularity, brings into play formal features that mark out the system of meaning at work in the narrative. Among these features, oral and vocal signals assume an important role. They seek to make the listener attentive to the form of the narrative, thus constituting a specific entry to the underlying system of meaning beneath the narration.

Denise's narrative

What is striking about Denise's narrative, when heard on the tape, is the passionate tone of the narrator and the use of very colloquial language in contrast to the elevated style of the 'school French' expected of a highly qualified French language teacher. In fact, these linguistic features concentrate in vocal form the basis of the singular system of meaning at work in this narrative.

Denise's life path could be seen as a success story marked by social advance in that diplomas and promotion to higher positions constitute the turning points. However, this 'standard' interpretation would not account for the contradictions that Denise has had to face within a credible and coherent self in taking on a promotion that could be seen as disowning her class origins, a social position that does not tally with her political commitment and a profession that threatens her role as wife and mother to four children. The colloquial French that expresses her assumed social origins points to these tensions, whereas the passionate tone marks out Denise's will to present herself in the narrative as a subject with and above her contradictions. The oral and vocal features take charge of the conflicting but subsumed relationship between the professional and the personal spheres. In this narrative, the key phrase cannot be easily picked out because the refrain is kept within a complex enunciation device that weaves the various voices of the self: daughter, student, militant, wife, mother, woman, teacher, colleague, trainer into a coherent system. So the narrative progresses on the basis of an internal dialogue within that each voice gives meaning to the others in a movement that transcends different social roles on the one hand, and personal contradictions on the other. In this way, the narrator, who manages the polyphony in order to maintain the coherence of the self, develops the narration within temporal dynamics that proceed through the different periods, worlds and roles experienced, while simultaneously being kept at a distance by the different voices at work in the narrative. Within this device, the key phrase – "I am interested in that" – takes charge of the dynamics of the evolution of the self, providing an axis of coherence that articulates the personal and the professional spheres. The 'key patterns' tend to reproduce a behavioural pattern in that the subject refuses standard solutions and systematically chooses difficulty:

> When I asked the trade union how I could manage to get away from the Parisian suburb to go back to ★★★[18], they told me: 'Madame, with four children, you should stop working!' I laughed. They did not understand my motivations for teaching.

This pattern illustrates Denise's life choices as the wife of an Iranian, mother of four children, and teacher in a problem school. These axes are organised, within the system of meaning, in relation to a personal myth[19], life as an exploration, that deconstructs the social myth of teaching as a vocation. As a child, Denise wanted to become an ethnologist or a reporter; she is – as a woman, wife, mother and teacher – an explorer. This ordering axis is perceptible on the surface of the narrative through the regular recurrence of the metaphorical term 'tracks' (tracks to explore), that highlights the different types of school she has taught in, as well as her marriage to an immigrant (a choice that opens up another world, the world of strangers). Within this system of meaning, the unrealised vocations evoked at the beginning make sense at the end of the narration:

> I love my job in this *collège*, where nobody wants to teach. It is my field of exploration, my field of experience.

Thus, the course of her life appears organised in a narrative plot (see Ricoeur, 1985), that makes the subject the heroine of a sequence of new adventures in her different professional and personal worlds. Within the narrative system, the evolution of the self takes the form of a quest for tools to understand and master professional and personal situations. This quest is fulfilled in the narrative through the discovery of neurolinguistic programming (NLP), a technique of self-development that:

- provides a counterweight to Marxist ideology as an explanatory system;
- makes sense of the new methods in professional practice;
- applies to all spheres (personal, professional and social) and thus helps to maintain the coherence of the self.

However, NLP has another function in the narrative. It subsumes here both Christian and Marxist ideologies to provide an axiomatic foundation for the text. Through teaching, Denise works as a committed social actor for the salvation of the pupils, the transformation of the social world and for her own sake, her own 'salvation'. In her textual construction, Denise thus presents herself through a coded character, the hero of a novel who succeeds after a long quest in finding a balance in the end between the world, moral values and her self.

René's narrative

In René's case, when listening to his taped narrative one is struck by the constant use of standard 'school French', the fluency of his discourse and the odd mixture of neutral and emphatic tones. René speaks in a loud voice on the tape but at the same time he sounds as though he had not invested his own person in the interaction. In fact, the vocal features can be recognised as those of a well-run lesson in class. This form accounts for the absence of an individual self in the whole narrative.

René became aware of this absence the day after the recording. He telephoned me and said, "You only got the froth (*écume*). I only gave you the froth. We should go on". I like the metaphor 'froth', but do not pursue this further because the interest of René's narrative lies precisely in the defensiveness of the original discourse (see Cooper, Chapter Six of this volume).

In this narrative, the key phrase takes the form of an expression, "*alors voilà*" ("so there it is"), that punctuates the development and sounds like the recognition – and acceptance – of an established order. It leads, thus, to a key pattern that expresses conformity. At a first level of analysis, René's narrative appears to be an artificial story that reduces the quest for self to the account of 'How I became a part-time teacher at the School of Education', and presents the career path as the progressive achievement of promotion and social advancement. The subject is presented as a model teacher who follows carefully, or even anticipates, the changes in educational and institutional requirements, is highly thought-of by headmasters, and finally is selected by the inspectors to become a part-time lecturer in the School of Education. Thus, the narrative borrows its model from a form akin to the socialist–realist novel in that the heroic protagonist embodies the ideological and moral values of the institution through a life path that coincides with the career path mapped out by the Ministry of

Education. This model is marked out, on the surface of the narrative, by the use of the personal pronoun 'one', which when referring to the professional community, comes to supplant the 'I'. This device, that reshapes the narrative as a non-individualised 'narrative of practices' (Bertaux, 1976), imitates in its style of enunciation a 'dissertation', the typical written exercise of French as a school discipline. In fact, the narrative opens with a prologue that does not sketch the origins – as would be expected in an autobiographical discourse – but takes the form of an introduction to a dissertation:

> To speak about one's life as a teacher means – especially when one has many years of teaching behind one – to have a retrospective view of one's experience.

Thus, the narrative form is used here as a framework for a general account with autobiographical examples. This approach makes argument dominant in the narrative.

The system of meaning is then constructed so that the subject coincides with the model civil servant, exemplified by teaching French as a school discipline. This device resolves the tension between the professional and personal self through a form of identity that can be explained in relation to the 'ideological state apparatus' conceptualised by Althusser (1971), a system in that the subject fuses with the role assigned by the institution. René assumes this position all the more, since he gains symbolic gratification from recognition by the institution, that seems to fulfil his aspirations as an individual.

This ready-made discourse, reproducing coded contents and forms in that the singular subject is buried, requires closer analysis to bring out the cracks and gaps in the narrative behind the resistances. These are to be found, first of all, in the vocal features on the tape. Taking into account the supra-segmental signals – to use the linguistic terminology – the analysis of the oral account allows us to bring out micro-sequences that contrast with the overall narrative. In these sequences, the narrator abandons the 'institutional voice' and adopts a more personal one. He lowers the pitch, whispers and sometimes stammers, making the speech act a confession: "I feel nostalgic, when thinking about my activity as deputy mayor in charge of schools". These vocal features work together with socio-linguistic features – for example, the use of colloquial French, "If my practice doesn't evolve, I'm a dead man, I'll be fired. It'll be the end for me!" – and with the expression of emotions, perceptible through the voice, "When I began to teach ... [the voice falters] my father died of cancer. So I had to find an interest in teaching!".

These oral features that undermine the key phrase mark out on the surface level of the narration the existence of another system of meaning that the analysis has to draw out and relate to the dominant one. This process can be set in motion by selecting the sequences throughout the narrative marked out by the vocal signals mentioned earlier, and then by comparing their content, in terms of biographical data, with the key pattern – conformity – at work in the dominant ordering of the narrative. In this way, the analysis can draw out biographical facts and events that deconstruct the dominant system of meaning. In these micro-sequences, the narrator mentions when he first failed the exam, when he forgot to look for his results after the second attempt, the crisis he went through in his career after teaching for five years and finally his difficulties in integrating into an urban *lycée* after being in a rural setting. Therefore, behind the dominant ordering that structures the narrative on the basis of apparent conformity with the institutional model, the analysis of the secondary system of meaning points out the cracks in René's official, 'frothy' presentation of his *self*, and shows, behind the heroic protagonist, a problematic one. This raises the question of whether these two systems simply coexist in the narrative. Can we find a textual feature that tends to resolve the contradiction that they embody? A close analysis of the narrative leads us to note the recurrence of a metaphorical device that could help answer these questions. This metaphorical device is constructed around three terms: walls, door, and the verb to 'get out of'. I shall take a few examples:

> I became a teacher to *get out of my social situation*. It was not a vocation.

> As a teacher, you are always alone when *the door* is shut after the pupils.

> In recent years, one has opened the *school door* to pupils we did not have in class before.

> I have always tried to *get* French as a school subject, *out of* the classroom, beyond its *walls*: I used to take the pupils out to the theatre, to museums....

These recurrences make sense when related to a minor autobiographical anecdote in a rapidly recounted flashback:

> When I was a child, I used to play in a cupboard. I sat inside and wrote on the door with chalk. I played the schoolmaster with invisible children. I spoke to them; I made up lessons. My mother has kept the traces of the chalk on the door, as a keepsake of my childhood. She did not wipe the chalk off. One can still see it at home.

The relation between this anecdote and the recurrence of the image of walls, sketching closed worlds with doors that can open out, makes the metaphor the core of the narrative, a schema that organises all the phases of life, as well as the different selves.

According to Lakoff and Johnson (1983), personal metaphors play the central role in giving meaning to one's life experience. So what does René's metaphor mean in this context? As René's narrative is very complex, I shall only venture a hypothesis. Through this metaphor, the narrative poses the idea of closed worlds, that stand side by side, but that, for this subject, cannot be subsumed, as in Denise's narrative, to a single (albeit complex) world system. Thus, this metaphor tends to express René's difficulty in finding a balance between the different spheres of his self. As a result, when asked to tell his professional life story, he can only render the 'froth' of his institutional self and, concealing his deep contradictions, hint at his personal self. Within this framework the institutional self, that represents social advancement, remains confined within the school system as an 'ideological state apparatus' (Althusser, 1971), a dimension that veils the singular self. As for the personal myth of 'getting out of' the cupboard to teach real pupils (singular subjects), disclosing his real self, including his class origins, it cannot be achieved. René's identity remains split, having recently lost the fragile balance acquired during his short period as deputy mayor.

If Denise and René present some similarities in their life paths, their ways of resolving the tension between professional and personal identity, as presented in the singular system of meaning created by their narratives, differ. In Denise's narrative, professional and personal identities, as constituents of self, are mutually enriching, whereas in René's case, they remain separate and opposed. Both approaches spell trouble in terms of implementing a more biographised approach to education. Denise, by being so strongly identified with her student teachers, may lack the distance that is often necessary in difficult intersubjective situations. René's overemphasising of his professional identity suggests he too will remain remote from his students to help them to engage more personally with their academic and professional tasks. These positions, highlighted by the two narratives, raise questions concerning the criteria for the choice of the trainers in the Schools of Education in France. Chosen by the inspectors on the basis of their practice skills, René and Denise will have to do some work on their own representations of professional identity, on the basis of their life-story analysis, to be able to bring into play the new educational orientation; that is, to help teacher students to elaborate, during the practical year, their own professional identity.

Conclusion

The methodological potential of the life story is not only concerned with contextualising professional practice and thus the meaning given to professional experience. It is also concerned, as I hope I have shown through these two examples, with the complexity of the systems of meaning that account for the various complex ways of managing the professional and personal spheres within a singular self. Consequently, each narrative contributes both to enhancing and problematising the issue of professional identity. This means that the research process has to go through the results of the comparative analysis, elaborating a theory within a precise conceptual framework.

As regards my own research project, this process demands a significant number of life stories in order to be able to compare the cases studies on a scientific basis. It then requires finding a theoretical framework that would allow professional identity to be conceived as part of a global self. From this standpoint, the approach has to go beyond educational science, to embrace sociology, in order to integrate the concept of the social self and its relations with the singular subject. Dubet's (1994) 'sociology of experience', offers such an approach, insofar as he views social experience as the combination by the subject of three logics that govern action in the social sphere:

- *integration* (through the socialisation process);
- *strategic elaboration* (recognition of constraints, play and strategic manoeuvres organised by the individual within the system);
- *subjectivisation* (critical distancing of the subject from social norms and roles).

Transposed into the field of teacher identity, this theoretical approach allows us to grasp the three logics set by teaching norms and rules, teachers' coping strategies, and finally the singular subject, shaped by his or her history, options and aspirations. It is then in the singular combination of these three logics that teachers' professional identity can be studied as a component of the global self, available to us through analysis of the system of meaning at work expressed through narrative and textual means.

These considerations lead to reflection on the effects of the transfer of the research process and findings on teacher training. As the research project is still underway, I shall confine myself to a few remarks about the position of the institution and the attitudes of the trainers.

The research process cannot avoid the intentions of the commissioning institution and thus the institutional conception of professional identity and training that forms the implicit background to the project. If we refer to Dubet's theory (1994), professional identity, institutionally speaking, exclusively refers to the imperative of integration, the process of socialisation. Teachers' identity is thus considered as the result of two processes: internalisation of teaching methods and rules, and identification of the social role of the teacher with school norms (here the school discipline acts as a community). Training is thus defined as the basic framework for this dual process. This position, that stresses the social role, determined by the 'ideological state apparatus' (Althusser, 1971), obliterates the singular subject behind the social self, with its history, aspirations and values. Our preliminary results indicate that educational institutions have to take on board teachers' own individual identities as a component of professional identity.

This dimension highlights the identity crisis of teachers of French. The Ministry of Education modified French as a school discipline without taking into account the disciplinary identity of teachers, their personal investments and their own aspirations in education. It also suggests reasons for the chronic dissatisfaction of student teachers, who perceive their training course as an infantilising process.

The aim of the research is to improve the effectiveness of training and to throw light on the professional identity crisis of teachers of French. The questions raised by the initial results are: Will – and can – the education system take research findings into account that redefine the issue? Can it accept the new relationship between the professional and personal spheres and thus the end of teaching as a 'secular priesthood' (the old view, which remains a French republican myth)? These questions lead us to confront key institutional contradictions. The ministry stresses educational and teaching research on the one hand, and on the other hand aims to preserve its power over teachers as civil servants through such means as hierarchical management and an educational inspectorate.

The implications of the research methods and process for trainers can be considered on two levels: as the construction of linguistic and literary theory that forms the new basis of French as a school discipline, and as an aid to reflecting on their own training practice. Adherence to the scientific approach and the work on biographical methods within the research team led the trainers to adopt a new attitude towards academic knowledge. This knowledge, initially viewed as foreign and institutionally imposed, is now regarded, through its use as a tool for analysis, as a living force. As a result, apart from acquiring the academic knowledge now required for French as a school discipline, the trainers have come to adopt more critical distance within this field of knowledge. This allows them to transfer academic theories through appropriate elaboration to the content and methods of the school discipline. While the aims set out in this clause of the research contract have been achieved, the transformation of training practice is less certain. The research process has put the trainers in an uncertain position. It has raised questions about issues that they have suppressed until now. This has led them to rethink their own professional identity as trainers and to question their social role in the institution. Consequently, they are now trying tentatively to develop new training strategies that address teaching rules and norms and their dependency on inspectors. This entails superseding the image of the trainer as a model teacher conforming to an institutionally imposed social role, by an image of the trainer helping to bring the individual self into the school. By contrast, the old myth of teaching as a 'secular' vocation requires leaving the individual self to one side when at school. Trainers involved in the research team are challenged to go beyond these two positions, to be able to take a theoretical view of teachers' and trainers' identity as a construct. Such a perspective has to be brought into play in the long term, since it has the capacity to integrate psychological, sociological and educational theories; that is, to reflect on training, beyond a particular disciplinary practice (which was here the tradition), through a scientific, interdisciplinary approach.

Notes

[1] For information on the role of the IUFM in France, see Asher and Malet (1996).

[2] Two lobbies were active in counter-posing this trend: the teachers and their trades unions on the one hand, and the academic world on the other, both intending to

maintain the boundary in teacher training between theory (as the content of the academic curriculum) and practice (as the educational methods and professional techniques acquired in teaching through regulated training).

³ This clause in the research contract aims to introduce these non-academic trainers to research methodologies in order to give them an incentive to use scientific data and theories as training material for teachers.

⁴ The narrative of self is based on the assertion, 'Although I change, I remain "myself"'.

⁵ See Chanfrault-Duchet (1984, 1985, 1986, 1987, 1988, 1990, 1991a, 1991b, 1994, 2000a, 2000b, 2001).

⁶ My own theoretical and methodological background goes against the predominant French approach in these fields, defined by the founding texts – Kerbrat-Orecchioni (1980), Barthes (1977), Charaudeau (1983), Bakhtine (1984), Genette (1972), Lejeune (1975) – and their current development. Most researchers using the life-story method limit their approach to narratology. The specificity of what I propose lies in the use of a set of deciphering grids, that combines, beyond narratology, several fields (such as pragmatic linguistics, discursive and textual analysis).

⁷ One of the risks of biographical methods, that rely on the human richness of the collected data, is that they remain at the stage of presenting the findings of the analysis. The life story serves here as a tool, not an aim.

⁸ Teachers of French must now work within *séquences didactiques*, the organisation of teaching that follows a reasoned progression in the learning process. Integrating the scientific contributions of the past 30 years in the field of linguistic and literary theories, the discipline is now shaped by a linguistic definition of text. This evolution entails moving from a literary approach focused on authors and works to an approach that has its roots in semiotic analysis open to non-literary texts and even pictures. The framework for textual studies is no longer the French traditional exercise of textual exegesis – *explication de texte*, but methodical reading – *lecture méthodique*. Besides the *dissertation* (the old French writing exercise), a new exercise in creative writing is now prescribed: *l'écriture d'invention*.

⁹ The *Rue de Grenelle* refers to the French Ministry of Education.

¹⁰ "The life history is applied here as a means of questioning and constructing meaning, based on personal and temporal facts" (Pineau and Legrand, 1993, p 3).

¹¹ For current trends in biographical methods within education sciences in France, see Bliez and Mevel (1999).

[12] For the epistemological problems created by this situation, see Chanfrault-Duchet (2001).

[13] Mainly biographical interviews.

[14] On argument in life stories as a genre, see Chanfrault-Duchet (2000a).

[15] The research contract requires, on ethical grounds, that the analysis be submitted to the informant and crosschecked against his or her comments. To protect confidentiality, the personal data are coded and processed so that they can be used in the cases studies.

[16] I have changed the names for ethical reasons.

[17] The CAPES comprises two exams: theoretical and, after a year of teaching practice, practical.

[18] The education system is highly centralised in France; therefore, it is very difficult for a teacher, as a civil servant, to move from one region or town to another, in contrast to England where teachers are directly recruited by schools.

[19] On the role of personal myth in the life story, see Chanfrault-Duchet (1990).

References

Althusser, L. (1971) 'Ideology and ideological state apparatuses', *Lenin and philosophy and other essays* (translated by Ben Brewster), New York, NY: Monthly Review Press.

Asher, C. and Malet, R. (1996) 'The IUFM and initial teacher training in France. Socio-political issues and the cultural divide', *Journal of Education for Teaching, International Research and Pedagogy*, vol 22, no 3, pp 249-71.

Bakhtine, M. (1984) *Esthétique de la création verbale* (1st edn, Moscow, 1979), Paris: Gallimard.

Barthes, R. (1977) *Poétique du récit*, Paris: Seuil.

Bertaux, D. (1976) *Récits de vie ou récits de pratiques?*, Paris: rapport CORDES.

Bliez, Y. and Mevel, Y. (eds) (1999) *L'approche biographique en formation d'enseignants*, Spirale no 24, Lille: Publications de l'Université de Lille III.

Chanfrault-Duchet, M.-F. (1984) 'La litterature de témoignage en lange française: structures et formes linguistiques', Unpublished PhD, Université de Tours.

Chanfrault-Duchet, M.-F. (1985) 'Le pouvoir de la parole dans le récit de vie', Proceedings of the Vth International Congress of Oral History, Barcelona, pp 119-26.

Chanfrault-Duchet, M.-F. (1986) 'Life story and narrative strategies', XI ISA World Congress (RC: 38), New Delhi, unpublished.

Chanfrault-Duchet, M.-F. (1987) 'Le récit de vie, données ou texte?', *Cahiers de recherche sociologique*, Montréal: Université du Québec à Montréal, vol 5, no 2, pp 116-28.

Chanfrault-Duchet, M.-F. (1988) 'Le système interactionnel du récit de vie oral', *Sociétés*, vol 18, pp 26-31.

Chanfrault-Duchet, M.-F.(1990) 'Mytos y structuras narrativas en la historia de vida', *Historia y fuente oral*, vol 4, pp 11-21.

Chanfrault-Duchet, M.-F. (1991a) 'Oralité, choralité du récit de vie', in M.G. Margarito (ed) *Parole ai margini*, Torino: Tirrenia Stampatori, pp 129-56.

Chanfrault-Duchet, M.-F. (1991b) 'Narrative structures, social models and symbolic representations in the life story', in S. Gluck and D. Pataï (eds) *Womens' words*, New York, NY: Routledge, pp 77-92.

Chanfrault-Duchet, M.-F. (1994) 'Les refrains du récit de vie oral', *Rocznick-Etudes romanes*, Kracow: University of Kracow, vol 171, pp 41-9.

Chanfrault-Duchet, M.-F. (2000a) 'Dimension argumentative et refrains dans le récit de vie oral', *Cahiers de sociolinguistique*, no 5 ('Histoire de vie et dynamique langagière'), Rennes: Presses universitaires de Rennes, pp 137-49.

Chanfrault-Duchet, M.-F. (2000b) 'Textualisation of the self and gender identity in the life story', in T. Cosslett, C. Lury and P. Summerfield (eds) *Feminism and autobiography*, London: Routledge, pp 61-75.

Chanfrault-Duchet, M.-F. (2001) 'Analyse des pratiques: prolégomènes', in M. Marquillo-Larruy (ed) *Questions d'épistémologie en Didactique du Français*, Poitiers: Publications de l'Université de Poitiers, pp 261-6.

Charaudeau, P. (1983) *Langage et discours*, Paris: Hachette.

Cooper, A. (2000) 'The social subject in biographical interpretive method: emotional, mute, creative, divided', ISA Biography and Society conference, Biographical Methods and Professional Practice, London: Open University (see also Cooper, Chapter Six of this volume).

Dubet, F. (1994) *Sociologie de l'expérience,* Paris: Seuil.

Genette, G. (1972) *Figures III*, Paris: Seuil.

Goffman, E. (1973) *La mise en scène de la vie quotidienne* (1st edn), Paris: Minuit.

Kerbrat-Orecchioni, C. (1980) *L'énonciation. De la subjectivité dans le langage*, Paris: Colin.

Lakoff, G. and Johnson, M. (1983) *Metaphors we live by*, Chicago, IL: Chicago University Press.

Lejeune, P. (1975) *Le pacte autobiographique*, Paris: Seuil.

Malet, R. (1998) *L'identité en formation: Phénoménologie du devenir enseignant*, Paris: L'Harmattan.

Pineau, G. and Jobert, G. (1989) *Histoires de vie*, 2 vol, Paris: L'Harmattan.

Pineau, G. and Legrand, J.-L. (1993) *Les histoires de vie*, Paris: PUF.

Ricoeur, P. (1985) *Temps et récit III: Le temps raconté*, Paris: Seuil.

Ricoeur, P. (1990) *Soi-même comme un autre*, Paris: Seuil.

Schön, D. (1987) *Educating the reflexive practitioner*, London: Jossey–Bass.

Woods, P. (1986) *Inside schools: Ethnography in educational research*, London: Routledge & Kegan Paul.

NINETEEN

Narratives, community organisations and pedagogy

Rosemary Du Plessis, Jane Higgins and Belinda Mortlock

This chapter engages with three categories of narrative: stories about teaching a social research course; students' stories about their practice as researchers; and the stories of 42 women and men working for community organisations in a city in New Zealand. These stories emerge from a teaching programme in which final-year sociology students are involved in biographical research. Students write a life-story narrative drawn from multiple interviews with a single narrator, as well as a research journal, in which they offer an autobiographical account of their research process. They also submit an analytical essay; that is, a sociological commentary that locates the life-story narrative within its historical and social context.

This course draws on ideas about the significance of stories as strategies through which social selves are constituted. According to this account of stories, eloquently articulated in different ways by social analysts like Margaret Somers (1992, 1994), narratives are of ontological significance[1]: they are the practices through which people make sense of their lives, constitute their identities and know "what to do" (Somers, 1994, p 618). Life stories are relational: they are the product of interpersonal interactions in which stories about biographical 'episodes' are used to construct selves (Polkinghorne, 1988, p 21; Borland, 1991; Somers, 1994, p 616). They are conventional, drawing on established story tropes (Plummer, 1995), but also providing "a unique perspective on the intersection of the individual, the collectivity, the cultural and the social" (Laslett, 1999, p 392).

Like most teachers of research, we are also researchers who have asked people to tell us their life stories. Valuing and problematising stories are at the heart of our pedagogical and research practice. This chapter came out of a pedagogical exercise where we subjected ourselves to the challenges we posed for our students. Just as students were required to keep research journals that they later edited and submitted for assessment, so we kept our own journals while we taught this course. These journals and lively lunchtime conversations about lectures and tutorial discussions inform this chapter. The stories we offer about teaching this course are directed not at justifying and legitimating our practice, but at articulating its challenges.

Setting the context: biography, social practice and community organisations

We prepared for this course by asking specific community organisations whether they could provide the names of members who might be approached by students to participate in this project. Most of the groups we approached were involved in social interventions with respect to health, community safety and social care, education and community construction. We thought that their members would all have interesting stories to tell, stories that students could contextualise and interpret using a range of different theoretical and empirical sources. The resulting mix of participants included individuals from groups involved with the politics of health and caring work (AIDS Foundation, Youthline, Women's Refuge, Women for Sobriety, Child Helpline, Parents' Centre, Early Intervention Centre, Alzheimer's Society); globalisation and the environment (Trade Aid, Christchurch Environment Centre); poverty (Methodist Mission, Just Dollars); social justice and political education (Workers' Educational Association); and public access radio (Plains FM, Radio U). Other less overtly political organisations (for example, Guiding and Surf Lifesaving) were excellent sites for exploring gender and organisational change.

In deciding to make the community sector the focus of these projects, we knew that students were likely to encounter organisations undergoing considerable change, as well as individual narrators experiencing important challenges in terms of their work and their relationships within these organisations. Over the past 15 years, public sector reform has had a significant impact on the funding and work of many of the groups that were involved in this project (Boston et al, 1996). These reforms have encouraged the withdrawal of the state from the direct provision of most social services, and the contracting of these services to non-governmental organisations. The community sector in New Zealand, therefore, has become a significant provider of services (Higgins, 1997). The organisational implications of this for small third-sector groups have been considerable, not least in terms of their impact on the positioning and subjectivity of volunteers and professionals in these groups – the narrators in this project.

The life stories of individuals within voluntary sector organisations provided an opportunity to access facets of a changing context for the action of community groups. In their interviews and analytic essays, students were asked to explore what Somers (1994, p 625) would refer to as "the relational setting" of particular actors' social narratives. This involved attention to organisational dynamics, funding issues, gendered practices, policy directions and discourses of 'care', 'social justice', 'rights' and community 'responsibility'. This was also an opportunity for students to explore the ways in which lives are both constructed by individuals and shaped by institutions, dominant discourses and particular historical moments (Laslett, 1999, p 400).

Generating life stories

Students interviewed each narrator several times, transcribed audiotapes and wrote a narrative, usually in the third person, but sometimes in the first person. This narrative was checked by the narrator, edited in the light of their comments, and returned to them at the end of the course. Students received critical feedback from their supervisor on the first version of the biographies they produced. A number of them refined the narratives in the light of these comments. When asked about the skills they had acquired through doing the course, one student responded that they had learnt to "accept criticism and see it as improving the work"; others wrote about learning the value of 'silence', of listening and 'being quiet', rather than constantly posing questions. Many spoke in tutorials about the impact on them of listening to the interview tapes and reflecting on how they might have conducted the interview differently.

For some of the narrators, the project was an important opportunity to talk about their lives. Their interest was in constructing a self through telling a particular story. Our interest was in encouraging students to facilitate narratives about the "constellations of relationships" in which narrators were involved (Somers, 1994, p 616), particularly relationships within their organisation. For the most part, these interests gelled, but they did not always do so. Sometimes narrators were exceptionally committed to telling stories about how their organisation worked and how it had changed over time. Some narrators were very committed to making their organisation appear in the best possible light. Others used the research as an opportunity to look critically at aspects of their organisation or individuals within it.

This course was an attempt to combine the teaching of research methodology and theoretical analysis with ethical practice that provided narrators with an experience and a product of value to them. As members of the communities in which students were doing research, we also had an interest in meeting the needs of those participating in this research. Sometimes narrators' desires to use the project were at odds with our interest in ensuring that the tasks students did were appropriate for completing a tightly organised single-semester course. For example, some of the participants wanted to tell stories about their lives as gay men – their connections to the AIDS Foundation or other community initiatives were important, but their biographies could not be confined to their organisational 'selves'.

Compromises were reached about the focus of a number of the narratives. Sometimes an overview of key life events was constructed before discussing stories of work in a particular organisation. Sometimes work for the organisation was not a major focus of the narrative. These tensions illustrate the ways in which the pedagogical project we had designed did not always sit easily with the expectations of research participants who wanted to tell particular sorts of stories for their own reasons. They also illustrate the importance for many people of constructing 'ontological narrativity' – of being and becoming certain people through the telling of particular stories (Somers, 1994, pp 613-14). As students negotiated these tensions, they learned more about research ethics than they could gain from reading several textbooks and a lot about individuals' investment in the telling of certain stories.

The biographies: stories of community work

We interpreted 'life story' for this project as a personal story about some aspect of a narrator's life, not a comprehensive account of 'a life'. However, some of the narratives were inevitably life histories spanning many years. Rata's story begins with her discovery of alcohol as a 12-year-old in the late 1940s and ends with her involvement in a women-focused organisation addressing alcohol abuse. This is a classic story of challenge, struggle and overcoming, a story that follows some of the story tropes Ken Plummer (1995) has identified. Rata's narrative begins with the moment when, on a post-treatment 'high', she is encouraged to choose a new name for herself, a symbol of her hopes for a new life. It moves back and forward in time to explore how and why she became involved in Women for Sobriety. When she read her narrative for the first time, she thought that it read like someone else's addiction story, but on a second reading she realised that: "It really is MY STORY!". Rata's narrative is an account of how she lived with the stigma of being different, both as an alcoholic and as a lesbian, as well as a story about her involvement in a particular community group.

For a number of the narrators, there was an overlap between paid professional work and voluntary service to the community. Sometimes paid professionals were involved in 'gift work' and sometimes 'gift work' became paid work. These narratives disrupted any simple division between volunteers and paid workers. The part-time female staff involved in the Early Intervention Centre were paid professionals, but their investment in this work went well beyond their contractual obligations as professional workers. They were committed to early intervention services for children with Down's syndrome and other intellectual disabilities, and accepted relatively low rates of pay to advance this work. At times they even worked without pay when the trust employing them experienced a funding crisis. Their narratives illustrated the fragility of educational innovation outside the work of established organisations and the impact of government restructuring on the work of small local organisations.

Brian's story about the establishment of a community access radio station also illustrates the ways in which paid professional work and unpaid community work intersect. Brian had a varied career in broadcasting, publishing and community education before establishing a programme in broadcasting at the local polytechnic. The training course he founded was the catalyst for the access radio station. Brian had organised a frequency and a temporary license for students to practice real-time broadcasting for three weeks each year. In 1986, he booked six weeks' broadcasting time – the last three weeks would be devoted to community access radio. A group of students went out and found

30 community organisations to work with them on radio programmes. This was one of the highlights of Brian's involvement with community radio:

> I don't think I've ever been so thrilled as I was when we got that first broadcast to air. We did it against the odds, and it was phenomenally successful because of that.

Brian's narrative illustrates the intersection of professional and unpaid community involvement and the passions people bring to the overlap between them.

Volunteer work sometimes generated forms of paid professional practice. Jan, a teacher with young children, went along with her mother to a meeting for carers of those with Alzheimer's disease. Jan's father later died of Creutzfeldt-Jacob disease, but by that time she was involved in the Alzheimer's Society at both the local and the national level. Soon she became a local part-time paid resource officer and then the National Resource Officer for Alzheimer's New Zealand, a federation of local societies. She said this was like "being put on a roller coaster that I never got off until the day I resigned". Her story illustrates the challenges that many non-profit community organisations encounter when government organisations are continually in flux. The health system was being constantly reorganised in the 1980s and 1990s with significant implications for the operation of Alzheimer's New Zealand. According to Jan:

> You would just get someone in the Ministry [of Health] that you dealt with who knew the organisation, knew you, knew what you were about, knew the services you provided … and then you'd find there had been another restructure, and they had gone.… You would then have to start again from scratch building up networks and understanding in government bureaucracies.

Since narrators were contacted through organisations, they sometimes thought it was important to tell an organisational story, rather than a personal story about their involvement in this work. Janet's story was a story of organisational involvement that remained personal and specific while also recording the development of the Environment Centre in Christchurch. Her story begins with a detailed account of an international conference on the environment in Sweden that she attended in the early 1970s. She was "bowled away" by the opportunities for networking, and the "trumpeting from the podium of the ideas you'd hardly liked to whisper".

For a number of narrators, involvement in community organisations was a key source of friendship. Alice said that the friends she made as an adolescent and an adult involved in the Girl Guides were "friends for life". Lindsay, who has been involved in Surf Life Saving since the 1960s, spoke about the importance of the South Brighton Club as a place where "everyone can go down and socialise … when anything goes wrong in some people's lives … it is amazing … they come through". Allen also spoke about the friends he has made through involvement in this work. While united in their appreciation of the surfing club as a source of friendship, Lindsay and Allen were differently positioned in early 1960s when Allen, as club captain, was uneasy about women's membership at the time when Lindsay was a keen new recruit. In the end, Allen accepted the majority decision, dismissing his opposition now as "just male". He went on to coach women's teams and contribute at a national level to women's surf life saving. In 1974, he travelled to Sri Lanka as manager of the New Zealand women's team.

While narratives about involvement in the Women's Refuge, Trade Aid and the Methodist Mission were sometimes seen as providing most opportunity for political analysis, the narratives produced by those involved in the Girl Guides and Surf Life Saving often provided fascinating opportunities for critical analysis of gender dynamics, change over time in organisational forms, and the complex processes whereby gendered conventions are simultaneously constructed, reworked and transgressed. Students often learned most about doing research and sociological analysis when they were interviewing people whose political perspectives and organisational involvement were very different from their own. They reported on the challenges of this work in their research journals.

The journals: stories of research practice

As teachers, we wanted to facilitate question posing, listening, selectivity with respect to information, interpretation and theoretical analysis. The students often come into the course pleased to be doing something 'out in the community'. They want to 'represent' what is going on the world after reading 'a lot of theory' in their other courses. However, students are not just involved in the production of stories about others; at the core of the course are their autobiographical narratives.

Students' journals are an exercise in the construction of selves through stories (Somers, 1994, p 603). Through writing these accounts of their research practice, students have the opportunity to take on the identity of 'sociologists'. Their 'experience' as social researchers is constituted through the stories they tell about their relations with narrators, the challenges of transcription and editing, and the ethical issues associated with making sense of someone else's life. Our pedagogical practice is to facilitate these autobiographies as well as the biographies of their narrators' involvement in community organisations.

In their weekly research journals, students were expected to indicate connections between their own accounts of practice and their reading about biographical research, interviewing, story construction and issues of interpretation. Through this autobiographical work, and their interactions with research participants, many students experienced stories as contingent, relational and purposive. They became aware of the variety of stories they could tell about their practice as researchers. These intellectual autobiographies were not 'authentic' representations of 'what happened', but crafted narratives of sociological practice.

Students' initial expectations about what it means to be a social researcher gave rise to certain ideas about what they thought should be in the journals. More than one discussion in tutorials focused on the students' desires to write 'tidy' research journals that illustrated a model research process. These intentions were, to a certain extent, disrupted by a number of factors. Readings were chosen precisely to avoid a 'text book' approach to research practice and to encourage students to appreciate the contingent and dynamic nature of establishing research relationships and writing narratives[2]. The constraints of the process itself in terms of its relatively short time frame, the 4,000 word limit on the narratives and the busy lives of the narrators also required students to manage compromises throughout the research process, thereby creating quite specific and personal research experiences for each student. Inevitably, students found the process of 'doing research' and 'being researchers' to be more complex and challenging than they had initially thought.

Students reported considerable anxiety about when and how to make the initial approach by telephone. They wrote about making mistakes with computer technology and tape recorders; and they learnt what worked well or how they could do those things better next time. They also discovered that hearing, analysing, and writing about someone else's experiences does not happen without their own emotional responses. A young woman, whose narrator was involved in a Women's Refuge organisation, found it challenging to hear about abusive relationships that mirrored her own experiences. Another student wrote of her desire to hide her learning difficulties from her narrator as she felt disclosure may discredit her identity as a 'professional' researcher, and of the ethical dilemma she then had to resolve as she had signed a confidentiality form and could not ask anyone to proofread her work.

Most students found it relatively straightforward to grapple with, and write about, these practical and technical, ethical and relationship-building aspects of the research process. They were more reluctant to pursue the idea that, as researchers, they were not simply hearing and recording a story but were involved with their narrators in the co-construction of that story. Many were uncomfortable about acknowledging their own presence within the stories recorded. One observed that it was "difficult not to put myself into the story" as though this was a serious problem. This suggests that some students had trouble with Plummer's (1995, p 22) argument that:

> stories are never fixed but emerge out of a ceaselessly changing stream of interaction between producers and readers in shifting *contexts*.

To appreciate the force of this argument, students needed to abandon some firmly held ideas about social researchers as "data collecting instruments" (Ribbens, 1989, p 590) in favour of an understanding of themselves as 'data creating social beings'.

To help students to think along these lines, we encouraged them to reflect on aspects of the research relationship that they felt had impacted on the story they were told. These included aspects of 'social distance' (Ribbens, 1989; Cotterill, 1992) such as gender, age and professional status. For some students, the characteristics of 'distance' in their research relationship had a very direct impact on the final narrative. One student in her late teens who interviewed a mature woman with a university degree in a related discipline, recorded that this narrator had marked and edited her narrative in an authoritarian manner, and had, thereby, undermined the student's attempts to craft a 'professional' identity.

For most students, however, the impact on the narrative of such social characteristics was less direct. One student, who was pregnant, wrote of her feelings of discomfort while interviewing a woman associated with the Parents' Centre Organisation. She felt her pregnancy helped to engender rapport between them. However, the student personally disagreed with her narrator's philosophy on parenting, and felt uncomfortable about appearing to agree with her narrator in order to elicit her story. Not only had this student become acutely aware of the ways in which researchers construct themselves in order to gain and maintain rapport, but she wrote about her narrator's crafting of herself for a particular audience through her story about her involvement in the parenting organisation whose emphasis had changed from one of initial activism to one of support for working parents. In our requirements that the students write a social analysis of their narrative, this student had explored the complexities and challenges involved in maintaining the goals voluntary organisations are set up to achieve.

Some students did come to understand the narratives they had constructed as "a constant flow of joint actions" (Plummer, 1995, p 24), products of their interaction with narrators. One young woman introduced the narrative she had co-constructed with these words: "This story is Alice's; it is spoken by her; written like her; and presented for her". The student had begun the interview with assumptions that the Girl Guide movement had constrained young women in particular ways. Alice felt her involvement in guiding since the 1930s had opened up amazing opportunities for her. The student discussed how she became aware that Alice's story about this organisation was a way of representing of a particular kind of femininity, one that had been established as a key feature of the 'gendered culture' (James and Saville-Smith, 1994) existing in New Zealand. She wrote about her realisation that that her own life had been influenced by this 'gendered culture' in ways she had not considered before, and argued that analysing another's life story inevitably challenges researchers to subject their own lives to similar scrutiny.

Several students, therefore, did learn that their initial image of the social researcher needed to be reworked as they came to see themselves as (co-)creating data, rather than simply recording it. It is noteworthy that by writing the journals as diaries, week by week, rather than as final reflections at the end of

---

the course, this learning was made visible, both for us, as teachers, and for the students themselves.

Biographical methods and pedagogical practice: an assessment

What was the outcome of this attempt to generate different types of narratives of practice? Did students have the learning experiences we hoped to facilitate? How can we critically assess our practice as the teachers of social research, particularly in a context in which we are obviously invested in a narrative of pedagogical 'success'?

Students' research journals were probably the best assessment of the course, but quantitative and qualitative student evaluation forms also provided us with some answers to these questions. In the evaluations, students commented favourably on what they saw as 'the practical' aspects of the course – making contact with potential narrators, learning interviewing techniques, developing questions, learning to use different library resources, developing confidence in their interactions with others. Some students focused on the pleasure of using some of the sociological theory they had been exposed to in other courses. Someone wrote about the satisfaction of "being able to analyse your own work with your own ideas ... rather than just repeating theories from lectures". Others liked the way students were treated as researchers who were responsible for their own practice. Several students indicated that what they liked most about the course was "doing sociology rather than just studying sociology".

Students commented critically on the demands of multiple interviews, the physical challenges of transcription, the way their time was 'gobbled up' and the challenges of 'fitting in' with the timetable of their narrators. This may also reflect difficulties that students have in managing the heavy demands on their time in their final undergraduate year. Some students commented on doing a lot of reading, writing and transcribing that "you never use". A few students suggested that the readings we had set were "fairly heavy", had "too much jargon" and were "too feminist". One student suggested that a male teacher of the course would have provided "a bit of balance and a different approach". Others congratulated us on the inclusion of the work of feminist methodologists.

For some students, the research project was "a scary process to go through" for someone who was "just a beginner". One student suggested that narrators needed a safe way to say what it had been like to be interviewed. She indicated that, in face-to-face situations with students, narrators might have felt it was necessary to say:"Yes, it was great", when they might be critical of the experience and the product. Other comments indicate that, even at the end of the course, a number of students were still seeking a tidy research process, and were frustrated by aspects of the course that they saw as "inefficient" and unexpectedly time-consuming. These criticisms suggest that we were not wholly successful in conveying to students the essentially "messy" and contingent nature of social research.

Brian Pauling, who was interviewed about his part in the establishment of community access radio in Christchurch, had this to say about 'learning':

> Learning by its very definition is a dangerous activity. All learning is subversive and it's messy and it causes trauma. As you discover in the learning process, you sometimes get shocked, and you get afraid. All of those things are part of the human condition and they are part of access broadcasting. You've got to protect it, you've got to nurture it and allow that messiness to thrive. It's very much like a mushroom pit; it's got to have that fecundity in it to make it go. (Cruickshank, 2000, p 10)

Our practice as teachers of research is significantly indebted to the work of Charles Sedgwick, a colleague who pioneered life history teaching in our department (Sedgwick, 1988). He generated a course on qualitative research in the early 1980s with sufficient messy fecundity 'to make it go'. Participation in this course has sometimes caused 'trauma' and occasionally it has been 'scary'. It is challenging, even 'dangerous', because students are constituted not just as 'learners', but as those involved in professional practice. Some of them are uncomfortable about its 'messiness' and we as teachers have concerns about the unpredictability that is built into this project. On balance, we have opted to embrace this messiness and accept it as a condition for learning. However, embracing the things you cannot control entails a commitment to reflect on your practice. This chapter is our attempt to make our pedagogical practices more transparent, to open them to critical scrutiny and to indicate the significance of layers of personal narrative for the teaching of qualitative research.

Notes

[1] See Plummer (1983, 1995); Polkinghorne (1988); Davies and Harre (1990); Stanley (1992, 1993); Laslett (1999).

[2] On research relationships, see Mishler (1986); Ribbens (1989); Cotterill (1992); Armstrong (1994); Bishop (1996). On writing narratives, see Middleton (1993); Stanley (1993); Nespor and Barber (1995).

References

Armstrong, N. (1994) 'Sex, lives and audiotape', in L. Hill (ed) *Women's studies conference papers*, Raranaga Wahine, Auckland, May 1993, Auckland: WSA (NZ) Inc, pp 118-26.

Bishop, R. (1996) *Collaborative research stories: Whakawhanaungatanga*, Palmerston North: The Dunmore Press.

Borland, K. (1991) '"That's not what I said": interpretive conflict in oral narrative research', in S.B. Gluck and D. Patai (eds) *Women's words: The feminist practice of oral history*, New York, NY: Routledge, pp 63-75.

Boston, J., Martin, J., Pallot, J. and Walsh, P. (1996) *Public management: The New Zealand model*, Auckland: Oxford University Press.

Cotterill, P. (1992) 'Interviewing women: issues of friendship, vulnerability and power', *Women's Studies International Forum*, vol 15, nos 5/6, pp 593-606.

Cruickshank, C. (2000) 'Growing plains: Plains FM 96.9: A story of the growth and development of community access radio in Christchurch', narrated by Brian Pauling, Unpublished personal narrative, Department of Sociology and Anthropology, University of Canterbury (located in the Macmillan Brown Library Archive, University of Canterbury).

Davies, B. and Harre, R. (1990) 'Positioning: the discursive production of selves', *Journal for the Theory of Social Behaviour*, vol 20, no 1, March, pp 43-63.

Higgins, J. (1997) 'Transparency and trade offs in policy discourse: a case study of social service contracting', *Social Policy Journal of New Zealand*, vol 9, pp 1-15.

James, B. and Saville-Smith, K. (1994) *Gender, culture and power*, Auckland: Oxford University Press.

Laslett, B. (1999) 'Personal narratives as sociology', *Contemporary Sociology: A Journal of Reviews*, vol 28, no 4, July, pp 391-401.

Middleton, S. (1993) 'The politics of life-history research', *Educating feminists: Life histories and pedagogy*, New York, NY/London: Teachers' College Press, Columbia University.

Mishler, E.G. (1986) 'Meaning in context and the empowerment of respondents', *Research interviewing: Context and narrative*, Cambridge, MA/London: Harvard University Press.

Nespor, J. and Barber, L. (1995) 'Audience and the politics of narrative', in J.A. Hatch and R. Wisniewski (eds) *Life history and narrative*, London/Washington DC: The Falmer Press, Taylor and Francis Group, pp 49-62.

Plummer, K. (1983) *Documents of life: An introduction to the problems and literature of a humanistic method*, Sydney: George Allen & Unwin.

Plummer, K. (1995) *Telling sexual stories: Power, change and social worlds*, London/New York, NY: Routledge.

Polkinghorne, D. (1988) *Narrative knowing and the human sciences*, Albany, NY: SUNY Press.

Ribbens, J. (1989) 'Interviewing – an "unnatural situation"', *Women's Studies International Forum*, vol 12, no 6, pp 579-92.

Sedgwick, C. (1988) *'The helpless tail to the statistical kite': The life history: A method, with issues, troubles and a future* (1st edn 1980, 2nd edn 1983, 3rd edn 1988), Sociology Department, University of Canterbury, Working Paper no 1.

Somers, M. (1992) 'Narrativity, narrative identity, and social action: rethinking English working-class formation', *Social Science History*, vol 16, no 4, Winter, pp 591-630.

Somers, M. (1994) 'The narrative constitution of identity: a relational and network analysis', *Theory and Society*, vol 23, no 5, October, pp 605-49.

Stanley, L. (1992) *The auto/biographical 'I'*, Manchester/New York, NY: Manchester University Press.

Stanley, L. (1993) 'The knowing because experiencing subject: narratives, lives and autobiography', *Women's Studies International Quarterly*, vol 16, no 3, pp 205-15.

Student narratives referred to in this paper (Sociology Department, University of Canterbury):

Cruickshank, C. (2000) 'Growing plains: Plains FM 96.9 A story of the growth and development of community access radio in Christchurch', narrated by Brian Pauling.

Dann, A. (2000) 'A journey from addiction to sobriety', narrated by Rata Vivienne.

De Steiguer, J. (2000) 'Experiences of environmental activism', narrated by Janet Holm.

Fass, A. (2000) 'Gift worker in the WEA', narrated by Katherine Peet.

Forbes, D. (2000) 'Patricia Morrison's life story in relation to her involvement in the WEA', narrated by Patricia Morrison.

Jones, L. (2000) 'Struggling for equality against bigotry and ignorance', narrated by Ian Smith.

McKissock, M. (2000) 'Half a century with sand between my toes', narrated by Allen Lee.

Mann, V. (2000) 'My learning journey with the Alzheimer's Society', narrated by Jan Harrison.

Stephen, L. (2000) 'Lindsay Seddon: a dedicated lifelong member of Surf Life Saving New Zealand', narrated by Lindsay Seddon.

Taylor, L. (2000) 'The youthline experience', narrated by Jo Capstick.

Treacher, G. (2000) 'Adam Calje and his participation in the New Zealand AIDS Foundation', narrated by Adam Calje.

Wood, C. (2000) 'Guiding memories of Alice McElroy', narrated by Alice McElroy.

TWENTY

Doctors on an edge: a cultural psychology of learning and health

Linden West

This chapter derives from in-depth, longitudinal, collaborative and what is termed auto/biographical research among 25 general practitioners (GPs), or family physicians, working in demanding inner-city contexts, including inner London (West, 2001). The research focuses on the learning, role and wellbeing of such GPs during a time of changing roles and expectations, including within the management of healthcare in Britain, and a period of growing criticism over performance and levels of accountability. The serial killer Dr Harold Shipman has replaced, at least in part, the heroic Dr Kildare in the popular mind, and stories of doctors' mistakes far outweigh the triumphs (Smith, 2001)[1]. The inner city presents distinct challenges to doctors in a mounting crisis of social exclusion, escalating problems of mental health and growing alienation, as well as increasing inequalities in health and healthcare (Bardsley et al, 1998).

The research chronicles and theorises, using case study material and an interdisciplinary 'cultural psychology' (drawing on sociology, feminism and feminist psychoanalysis as well as the adult learning literature), the impact and meaning of social and cultural change among a diverse group of GPs. It focuses, too, on the role and nature of 'lifelong learning' in the management of change and professional development. It documents some of the doctors' doubts and anxieties about training as well as the biomedical model itself, in the face of problems that often seem more social and psychological than physical in nature. It explores the psychological distress and feelings of helplessness that can haunt a doctor, and the difficulties of dealing with this in a medical culture in which doctors are taught that they should know and cope. The stories at the heart of the chapter are of two doctors who, because of multiple identities and experiences of oppression, have felt on the margins of the profession. Such GPs – 'outsider-insiders' – raise radical questions about the health of medicine, its training and some epistemological assumptions about what doctors need to learn[2].

Self-directed learning

The starting point for the research was an evaluation of self-directed learning (SDL) groups for GPs in inner London. The groups were established in the early 1990s following concern over standards of care and the morale of many doctors. They were designed to give space to GPs to consider 'critical incidents' with selected patients that might be causing particular anxiety. These might include the unexpected death of a patient, or a doctor feeling muddled, inadequate and disturbed by a patient with emotional difficulties. The aim was to address the doctors' fears and anxieties in the role as well as to consider different management options and how particular forms of continuing professional education might be relevant. Each group consisted of about eight doctors, was confidential, and led by a skilled facilitator. The idea was to create a learning culture, rather than a blame culture, in which the GPs could be open about their work and 'failures' – without fear of criticism. The evaluation of the groups provided the basis for a more extended and in-depth study of how GPs manage their work and learn, in the context of a changing health service, and whole life histories. The research was to last four years, and involved six individual interviews, for most doctors, of upwards of two hours each. Transcripts and tapes were used to generate themes and consider their meaning and significance, dynamically and dialogically, over the four years.

Many of the GPs considered their initial training, especially its overly textbook approach and construction of illness as primarily physical and biological, often to be inadequate in the face of actual patients with multiple problems, rooted, as these frequently were, in the psychosocial pathologies of the inner city. While patients clearly want the most effective treatment available, based on the latest scientific evidence, it does not follow that most consultations require this. What is more often needed is a relationship in which patients can consider their 'dis-ease' within the totality of their lives, and explore the different options that might be available to them. What a number of these doctors understood – because of their own multiple identities and experiences of oppression – was the need for patients to tell a story and be listened to. They knew, experientially – because of their own gender, ethnicity or sexuality – what it was like to be silenced and misunderstood, as well as how damaging this could be.

Medical culture

General practitioners operate in a medical culture where specialist, hard, 'scientific' knowledge has traditionally been deified, while the softer skills of human communication and psychosocial medicine have often been disparaged, considered 'other', 'subjective', even 'woolly'. Such skills may continue to have marginal status in medical training, despite increased emphasis on communication and whole-person medicine (Sinclair, 1997; Salinsky and Sackin, 2000). Historically, of course, GPs are situated on the edge of the medical profession, at the interface between the 'scientific' claims of mainstream medicine, and the messy swamp of actual lives and uncertain symptoms (Schon, 1987). By the time a patient sees the specialist, a degree of clarification, a narrowing of possibilities will have occurred. General practitioners are, by definition, Jacks-of-all-trades, and general practice, as McWhinney (1996) notes, in its attempts to discover a distinct epistemological basis, fits uncomfortably in the highly scientific milieu of the medical school. In this and other respects, it is under constant pressure to become more 'scientific' as well as theoretical and quantitative[3].

The point here is that the epistemological basis of the profession is contested space. There is a long-established belief among many GPs that the skills and understanding required for much of their work has been neglected, and there is developing interest in more experiential, case study-based forms of learning, which include focusing on the doctor's feelings. These ideas build on older traditions, such as Balint groups, which employed psychoanalytic insights to enable doctors to consider the emotional dimensions of their work, including the transference and counter-transference aspects of the consultation. Disturbance often disturbs, as Michael Balint (1957), the distinguished psychoanalyst, once famously observed. Doctors have to learn to understand their own feelings and use these reflexively, not least to understand more of what may be happening within the patient; if, that is, they are remain open to the patient, rather than becoming emotionally withdrawn and defensive. However, such groups, including self-directed learning, remain a 'minority sport' among GPs as a whole (Elder, 2000). All of this can have serious consequences for the health of doctors, especially when combined with the growing 'blame' and litigious culture of healthcare in Britain, and the pressure of rising expectations.

However, the resistance on the part of many doctors to engage with the subjective aspects of their work also raises questions about dominant values within medical culture itself and the nature of professional socialisation. Many doctors find it hard to talk about their anxieties and perceived inadequacies, most of all mental health problems, partly for fear of what colleagues might think. Some male doctors in the research were enmeshed in a discourse of doctor as omnipotent and omniscient hero, partly as defence against fears of inadequacy and their own emotional difficulties. Particular doctors admitted to dispensing drugs far too promiscuously to ward off the demands of their patients (West, 2001). Whatever the causes, evidence of increasing unhappiness, stress, alcoholism and even suicide among doctors is mounting (Smith, 2001; West, 2001). This is a profession in which too many doctors are on the edge.

What is being suggested is that some of these problems are a consequence of the profession's own value base, which includes the dominant status of the intellectual model of medicine, grounded in the notion of bringing the natural sciences, 'objective' knowledge and a technical rationality to bear on people's health problems (Smith, 2001), to the neglect of other more subjective ways of knowing. Auto/biographical research, of the kind used in the present study, can illuminate more of what doctors, in reality, may need to know, including the place of self and emotional understanding, and greater psychosocial literacy, alongside the science.

Auto/biographical methods

There is, as noted elsewhere in this volume, a turn to biographical, life-history and/or narrative research methods across the social sciences. There is an attempt to illuminate the complex interplay of social structure and individual agency, or, in the present case, professional socialisation and personal health, formal and informal learning. The biographical imperative has switched attention to the personal, affecting the orientations of many disciplines but also their interrelations with each other (Chamberlayne et al, 2000). The personal, in these perspectives, is perceived to be deeply socio-cultural as well as political: individuals are both shaped by and also actively shape the cultural worlds they inhabit. There is also an interdisciplinary momentum at the core of the turn: people and their stories are not easily categorised according to particular disciplinary frames. Stories about learning, for instance, frequently defy definition as 'sociology', 'psychology' or 'education'. Biographical research, in these terms, is challenging the gaps between disciplines. Sociology, for instance, has traditionally lacked any convincing account of how the social, including learning, is translated into changes in inner life, and how this can be theorised. Mainstream psychology, on the other hand, tends towards an essentialism in which learning, for example, is conceived in individualistic and asocial ways, as in some theories of motivation (West, 1996). Biographical methods render new interdisciplinary conversations essential.

The term 'auto/biographical' requires explanation. It challenges the idea of the detached, objective biographer of others' lives, and the notion that a researcher's history, identity (including gendered, raced, classed and sexual dimensions) and power in the research encounter play little or no part in shaping the other's story; or ought not to, in the name of rigorous and objective science. Others, such as Liz Stanley, write, instead, of an 'intertextuality' at the core of biography, which has been suppressed in supposedly 'objective' accounts of others' lives. It is as if telling the story of someone else is a purely cerebral affair, disconnected from the academic and personal identity as well as discursive frames of the enquirer, and the dynamics of his/her relationship with the researched. This, of course, is part of preserving a kind of de facto claim for biography and life-history research as science: a process producing 'the truth,' and nothing but the truth about its subject (Stanley, 1992).

Michelle Fine (1992) insists that social scientists have persistently refused to interrogate how they create their stories. There has, at times, been a presumption, as in the natural sciences, that theories and methods neutralise personal and political influences:

> That we are human inventors of some questions and repressors of others, shapers of the very contexts we study, co-participants in our interviews, interpreters of others' stories and narrators of our own, becomes, in some strange way, irrelevant to the texts we publish as 'research'. (Fine, 1992, p 208)

Fine argues, instead, for the reflexive and self-reflexive potential of experience, in which the knower is part of the matrix of what is known, and where the researcher needs to ask her and himself in what way has she or he grown in, and shaped the processes and outcomes of research.

Attempts at such reflexivity have been central to my own work on adult learners struggling to recompose identities in conditions of pervasive uncertainty (West, 1996). Similarly, in asking questions of doctors about learning, identity and managing change, I realised I was asking related questions of myself. In hearing their stories of the psychosocial complexity of personal and professional development, and of what facilitates or inhibits growth, I was seeking to understand more of my own learning history and gendered identity, including my work as a psychotherapist. Around the role of a male therapist, for instance, in a profession discursively infused, over many decades, with the central importance of symbolically 'feminine' notions of the breast, feeding, good enough mothering and empathy (Sayers, 1995), I was asking questions too at a more personal level, at a time of change and uncertainty in my life and career. These included being a man socialised into a competitive individualism, and the damaging consequences for emotional wellbeing of the neglect of intimate life. I was questioning, like many men, the meaning and place of the 'masculine' and 'feminine' in various aspects of my life at a moment of challenge to essentialist accounts of gender. Men and masculinity have become an object of scrutiny, just as, historically, men have scrutinised everything else, albeit lacking awareness of the gendered nature of their interpretive frames (Samuels, 1993).

I came to share some of my experience, in the research, as relationships with particular doctors developed and they bared their souls to me. The dialogue, in these cases, focused increasingly on the relationship between learning, identity and the emotional aspects of being a doctor as well as a therapist. A profound reciprocity developed in some cases – a mutual openness, including interrogating the research process itself as well as a deep questioning of various concepts and their meaning – qualities often lacking in supposedly more 'objectivist' and rigorous research.

Two case studies: insiders and outsiders

I want to use two case studies to illustrate the relationship between objective and subjective forms of learning to be a doctor and how doctors need to learn on more of their own terms. Dr Aidene Croft [pseudonym], for instance, is an outsider and lesbian, who works in a difficult and impoverished part of London's East End. She is white but talks with a 'different' accent. She told me she experienced a major 'mental breakdown' in her career and, in the course of a year, phoned the British Medical Association Stressline and the Samaritans. She had felt over the edge as a doctor, unable to cope with patients and their disturbance. Some of the pain of her troubled life history was no doubt stirred up by interactions with particular patients: her own story included a mother who died when Aidene was four, difficult relationships with a succession of step-mothers, and a distant, emotionally withdrawn father. Becoming a doctor, she surmised, was part of an attempt to heal a fragile inner world.

She mentioned her sexual identity, from the outset, and that this fitted uneasily into the 'male' and predominantly heterosexual culture of medics. She was working as a single-handed practitioner when we first met, having left a group practice and suffered an emotional crisis. She had needed, most of all, she said, to find her own authenticity as a doctor. She felt torn between her feelings and living in the head as a doctor. Her life and work did not feel 'real':

> I was very much trying to connect the two…. I couldn't actually tolerate that level of incompatibility.

Aidene was sceptical of the gendered blindness of much conventional medicine. She worked in a women's hospital where the male doctors dismissed the notion of pre-menstrual tension. But "there wasn't an ovary in the room", she said. She was critical of her profession's neglect of mental health problems too, especially among minority ethnic communities.

She talked, early on in the research, about the relationship between aspects of her identity and interactions with particular patients:

> You know I think because if your sexuality is outside the normal experience of people's expectations of their doctor, it leads to identification with everybody from Greeks to Turks, black people, Irish people, you know what it's like to be an outsider, you know, to fudge around issues, to not quite explain, for people to instantly lose their curiosity or suddenly go quiet or whatever. All my experience is about being out of orb … you just know that there is that hesitation that people then rethink…. And I think it makes me more accepting of people. A lot of doctors find it terribly difficult to just accept people as they are without trying to change them into the wrong perception….

Aidene knew what it was like to feel lost in an alien culture, and to struggle to explain this to others. She was sensitive to the mental distress of many minority patients, and wanted to research mental health issues among different ethnic populations. She talked of how black and Irish people were over-represented in mental health services and quoted research indicating that rates of depression in various minority communities exceed those of the 'English'. Levels of schizophrenia were high, too, as were a range of anxiety states and personality disorders (Cochrane and Singh, 1989; Tilki, 1996).

A significant other

Aidene almost left medicine completely. She hated hospital medicine and its mores, including the very male, clubbish culture that often predominated. She found, she said, more humanity in general practice as she forged a strong relationship with a GP trainer:

> I had a wonderful trainer, very … astute, insightful, a really very, very nice man. And thought, "Yes, this is it. This is where it is at…. Feed me, feed me, this is a fascinating subject…." You could be very honest about your deficiencies in learning. I had done paediatrics and gynaey and house jobs. I knew sod all about dermatology … this was a really clever bloke. I mean clever, clever in a very wide sense. Within two or three weeks I was in there saying – "Jesus, I haven't a clue about dermatology, give me some pictures, skins, I had no experience of this kind of skin…." I had left home when I was 16 and was one of 11 children and suddenly here I was being given this – I had gone to boarding school…. And suddenly it was all – "Now what would you like? Where can we go?"… It just seemed incredibly generous and useful … he was somebody who respected people. I could learn from him that much more….

For the first time, she felt seen, valued and 'fed' in the medical world, as she did in her personal life with a new partner. It enabled her, alongside therapy, to understand more fully her own needs as well as those of her patients, and that she could be a doctor on more of her own terms. She learned to be realistic over what she could offer: she could not solve a housing crisis or the abusiveness of officialdom, although she might help. Nonetheless, she could listen, as she put it, "to, for and with" the patient's story. Empathic relationship and narrative-based practice were at the heart of effective healthcare.

New relationships – with colleagues and others – were at the core of her learning and professional growth, as they were in the narratives of many of these medics. Sean Courtney (1992), in reviewing processes of adult learning and change management, noted how frequently a significant other was essential to what he termed 'life spacing': that is, taking risks, experimenting, and managing personal transitions and crises. There were similar findings in my earlier research into men and women managing change, and using education, in communities undergoing major economic and social dislocations (West, 1996). What often seems critical to successful transitions is the sense of really being listened to and thus able to share – with a colleague, a teacher, a friend or therapist – uncertainties, doubts and feelings of failure in a non-judgemental and empathic relationship in which there is space and encouragement to think, and be open, without blame. Aidene's trainer listened and offered time, support and space for her to learn, during a period when she felt badly about herself as a doctor.

Feminist object relations theory helps explain some of these psychological processes. Individual development, in this view, is always and inevitably to be understood intersubjectively as 'inner' experience is shaped by a person's interaction with others, most obviously but not exclusively in earliest experience (Diamond, 1998). Psychological development is profoundly social as subjective life is forged in the relationships in which we are embedded and the wider scripts that inform them (Frosh, 1991; Schwartz, 1999). Feminist psychoanalysis, for example, in considering how intersubjective experience translates into intrasubjective life, frequently employs the metaphor of psyche as a cast of characters and dynamics in the social world that becomes internalised. Some people, 'out there', may injure or constrain us, and these dynamics come to characterise the inner drama too. However, casts of characters can change as new, more empathic others can enter the social stage and eventually become internalised, enabling us to develop a greater sense of legitimacy and existential hope. Such 'good objects' may be people whom we admire and can identify with: they may be friends, teachers and other learners. They mirror, in their actions and responses, new biographical possibilities for us (Sayers, 1995; West, 1996). A different philosophical way of seeing subjectivity characterises this view, compared, that is, to the conventional Cartesian separation of one person's inner space from another's, as though we are mere physical bodies completely distinct from one another. From an object relations perspective, human beings exist in a shared space of affective intercourse, and there is fundamental overlapping of each person in significant relationships. Such an intersubjective perspective on human development and learning, at all stages of life, is taking hold in developmental psychology, phenomenology as well as psychoanalysis (Diamond, 1998).

Our need for good objects may be strongest at times of frightening change, or of disturbance, when primitive feelings of anxiety – of feeling unloved and unlovable, or of being unable to cope, and of abandonment, for instance – are evoked. The disturbance of a patient, at such times, can deeply disturb a doctor, as can meaninglessness in a patient, which can pose basic questions of meaning in the doctor's life. At a wider professional level, some doctors, given the cultural psychology of medicine, can feel frightened and isolated in a sense of impotence and lost idealism that can stalk the consulting room, especially in the face of the despair in parts of the inner city. One psychiatrist has described how lost idealism can evoke states of denial in a doctor, as well as causing them to turn to drink, have affairs or play pointless power politics in a kind of emotional compensation (Bennet, 1998). Conversely, however, disturbing experience and anxiety can serve as a catalyst to new understandings of self, the patient, and the cultural psychology of the interaction.

Despising the mainstream

The case of Dr Daniel Cohen [pseudonym] illustrates how disturbance can be a means to growth. Like Aidene Croft, Daniel considered himself to be an outsider in medicine:

> I don't believe in what I think the mainstream believes in.... I am actually often appalled by the discourse, just appalled by ... the whole set of assumptions about the nature of reality, about the assumption of the doctor's

power and the assumption of sexist and racist ... ideas and ... the collusion around that.... I feel profoundly alienated by it, which is why I have so little to do with it.... Like mining a seam of gold called the medical fact ... from a pile of shit, which is the patient's sort of life ... a way of talking about ... patients as if the patient isn't there....

Daniel's crisis came eight years ago, over the amount of work and its endlessness. There were very few professions, he said, with such a workload in terms of volume or intensity. And there was no career development path for the GP; at the age of 37/38 you might 'look forward' to 20 years of struggling with the same sorts of issues, with few options or opportunities for career progression.

The personal and the professional

Being a doctor had forced Daniel to ask questions of himself, at many levels. There was no neat distinction between questions patients asked, like 'Who am I?' or 'Where do I come from?' or 'Why do I have the kind of problems that I think I have?' and those of the doctor. There was a seamless web connecting their story to his. Daniel used psychotherapy and experiential groups to reconsider aspects of his own family history and identity, in what he termed a process of narrative recovery and reappraisal. He was the child of refugees from Nazism, which led many like him into the caring professions. The desire to heal, he thought, was primarily directed at self. He was brought up, he said, with the experience of Nazism and fleeing persecution not being talked about at all and with the sense that his own suffering could never rival that of his parents. There was also a powerful imperative to succeed and never to rebel. He described himself as having been outwardly successful but inwardly distressed.

We shared and compared experiences of needing to perform for parents, and of being raised as males to succeed in highly competitive ways. We talked about the place of the feminine and masculine in the work of a doctor as well as in therapy, and the need, perhaps, for a kind of Jungian balance:

> I suppose a great deal of my job is masculine ... as we tried to start this interview it was interrupted by a phone call from hospital with information as to whether a patient did or did not carry a particular germ.... I have to deal with that.... The feminine side is that I am constantly striving to contain and manage those sorts of moments in order to create space for feminine types of experience [rather than] omnipotent theatre.... The feminine? Yes. Acceptance, tolerance, understandings of process rather than events and outcomes ... things that are fluid rather than chopped up and categorised. A sense of connection being more important than anything....

There was, he said, a great suspicion of subjectivity and emotional learning within a medical culture that often deified the objective and measurable. Yet, subjective learning and cultural literacy were at the very core of being a better GP. A Somali woman refugee came to mind as he talked:

> A mother and five children, father not in this country ... may have been killed in the war there.... Children with a huge range of problems from asthma to epilepsy.... Often just turning up out of the blue without an appointment.... And the anxiety and the sort of tension that arrives with that sort of situation are absolutely massive for a GP.... And I struggle to create situations where I can meet more of their needs really by putting an hour aside for them at a special time with an interpreter ... the mother of that family brought me a present for Christmas. Somebody had come over from Somalia with this and she brought it to me as a gift and I was immensely moved because it was a really strong symbol that we were providing ... a secure base ... and that she identified me as one white British person in authority who she can trust.... And we ended up having the most extraordinary conversation with the mother about Darwinian evolution in relation to why were her children getting asthma and eczema here when children didn't get it in Somalia and we talked about the way the immune system might be adapted for one environment but actually then is maladapted to another environment because the sort of ancestral immune system as it evolved is not to meet what it meets here....

He found himself, as he put it, having a grown-up conversation with this mother and she was transformed from being an exotic stereotype into an intelligent equal. This was part of a process of her becoming a person again, through being understood, empathically, by a significant other at a time of deep anxiety.

> That she could actually have what I would guess is her first conversation with somebody British which wasn't just about immediate needs, about housing or benefits, or prescriptions and that sort of stuff but actually recreate her as an equal adult.

In telling this story, he realised, for the first time, that he was making a connection between his own history and that of the Somali patient. There was profound auto/biography at the heart of the encounter. In his own family's narrative, a GP had acted as a bridge towards a new life for his parents and other relatives forced to flee war and persecution. There were differences, of course, in that his parents were central European Jews who actually chose to have a central European Jewish refugee for their GP. And yet, "I think it is in a way always coming back to the business of a personal search, actually trying to find out what life is about and what you should be making of it", both for the doctor and the patient.

Daniel, like Aidene, placed key relationships at the heart of learning to be a doctor: in his case involving two colleagues, a therapist, a personal partner and their young children. He understood himself, and his cultural roots, more deeply, which helped him develop professionally. General practitioners like him, he concluded, were situated between the truth discourse of the mainstream and the uncertainties and messiness of whole people and whole problems, including within themselves. A subversive synthesis was required, taking what was essential from the medical model but locating this within a person and narrative-focused practice in which doctors had to learn from within. The personal and professional were, for effective practice, all of a single piece.

The role of story

The research raised basic issues about the role of narrative in healthcare and in learning to be a doctor. Being able to tell one's whole story was at the heart of psychological health, for the doctor as well as her patient. Jeremy Holmes (1998) has noted that the word 'narrative' derives from '*gnathos*' or knowing. Making the unconscious conscious can be reformulated in terms of knowing and owning one's story. Narrative, he suggests, "turns experience into a story which can be temporal, coherent and has meaning" (p 228). It creates, potentially at least, links between past, present and future. Even the most painful material can be translated into symbolic form, which allows some detachment from what may be horrific experience. Freud argued for the therapeutic power of story and the importance of a narrative truth in 'the talking cure'.

However, storytelling, in healthcare and learning, among doctors as well as their patients is no easy process, surrounded as it often is by cultural constraints, defences and fear of what powerful others might think. We are 'storied' as well as storytellers. Doctors, like the rest of us, may simply reiterate the dominant narratives of their culture in ways doing injustice to their own experience and potential for learning. For instance, the narrative of doctor as objective scientist, engaged in the business of observing others and their problems and bringing the perspectives of natural science to bear is damagingly one-dimensional. Doctors like Aidene Croft and Daniel Cohen offer, via their stories, a rich and eclectic challenge to such a narrow, if still pervasive tale, that the profession tells itself.

Conclusion

A powerful case for a new paradigm of health and learning in medicine was made in these stories, one that connects head and heart, the socio-cultural and the personal, the science and the subjective, one person and another. The dominant paradigm within medicine has been of professional knowledge and technique derived from systematic, scientific enquiry. Such a story, however, has badly neglected the psychosocial, subjective, messy and indeterminate aspects of a doctor's work and has perpetuated a damaging split between psychological and physical medicine, the science from subjective insight. Despite claims that medicine is, at long last, encompassing multiple ways of knowing a world, the objective and arguably 'male' way – taking us into the real world and out of ourselves – remains dominant. The two stories at the heart of this chapter suggest that the capacity to learn from within lies at the heart of being both a more reflective, critically aware but also effective practitioner.

Notes

[1] Dr Harold Shipman, a Manchester GP, was convicted of murdering 15 of his patients and is suspected of being responsible for the deaths of hundreds more.

[2] The opportunistic sample of 25 doctors included many who felt on the margins of the profession, on the grounds, for instance, of ethnicity, gender and/or sexuality.

[3] The drive towards evidence-based medicine may be exacerbating the neglect of the more subjective aspects of clinical experience, in that evidence is often taken to mean statistically based definitions of risk and probability, derived from studies of large population samples.

References

Balint, M. (1957) *The doctor, his patient and illness*, London: Pitman.

Bardsley, M., Barker, M., Bhan, A., Farrow S., Gill, M. and Morgan, D. (1998) *Health of Londoners: A public health report for Londoners*, London: Kings Fund.

Bennet, G. (1998) 'The doctor's losses: ideals versus realities', *British Medical Journal*, vol 316, 18 April, pp 1238-40.

Chamberlayne, P., Bornat, J. and Wengraf, T. (eds) (2000) *The turn to biographical methods in social science: Comparative issues and examples*, London: Routledge.

Cochrane, R. and Singh, S. (1989) 'Mental health admission rates of immigrants in England: a comparison of 1971 and 1981', *Social Psychology and Psychiatric Epidemiology*, vol 24, pp 2-11.

Courtney, S. (1992) *Why adults learn*, London: Routledge.

Diamond, N. (1998) 'On Bowlby's legacy', in M. Marrone (ed) *Attachment and interaction*, London: Jessica Kingsley, pp 193-214.

Elder, A. (2000) 'Thoughts from the front line', Paper to the conference on 'Learning the Reality of Primary Care', March, London: Tavistock.

Evans, M. (1993) 'How the personal might be social', *Sociology*, vol 27, no 1, pp 5-14.

Fine, M. (1992) 'Passions, politics and power', in M. Fine (ed) *Disruptive voices: The possibilities of feminist research*, Ann Arbor, MI: Michigan University Press, pp 205-31.

Frosh, S. (1991) *Identity crisis, modernity, psychoanalysis and the self*, London: Macmillan.

Holmes, J. (1998) 'The changing aims of psychoanalytic psychotherapy: an integrative perspective', *International Journal of Psychoanalysis*, vol 79, pp 227-40.

McWhinney, I. (1996) 'The importance of being different; the William Pickles lecture', *British Journal of General Practice*, vol 46, pp 433-36.

Salinsky, J. and Sackin, P. (2000) *What are you feeling doctor?* Oxford: Radcliffe Medical Press.

Samuels, A. (1993) *The political psyche*, London: Routledge.

Sayers, J. (1995) *The man who never was: Freudian tales*, London: Chatto and Windus.

Schon, D. (1987) *Educating the reflective practitioner*, San Francisco, CA: Jossey-Bass.

Schwartz, J. (1999) *Cassandra's daughter: A history of psychoanalysis in Europe and America*, London: Allan Lane.

Seidler, V. (1994) *Unreasonable men: Masculinity and social theory*, London: Routledge.

Sinclair, S. (1997) *Making doctors*, Oxford: Berg.

Smith, R. (2001) 'Why are doctors so unhappy?', Editorials, *British Medical Journal*, vol 322, pp 1073-74.

Stanley, L. (1992) *The auto/biographical I*, Manchester: Manchester University Press.

Tilki, M. (1996) 'The health of the Irish in Britain', *Federation of Irish Studies Bulletin*, vol 9, pp 11-14.

West, L. (1996) *Beyond fragments, adults, motivation and higher education: A biographical analysis*, London: Taylor and Francis.

West, L. (2001) *Doctors on the edge: General practitioners, health and learning in the inner-city*, London: Free Association Books.

TWENTY ONE

Intercultural perspectives and professional practice in the university: what's new in Germany

Lena Inowlocki, Maria Teresa Herrera Vivar and Felicia Herrschaft

'Foreign' students at German universities

Attracting students from other countries and world regions has been an objective for German universities for some time, and more recent policies have facilitated the admission of foreign students. Their attendance is understood as contributing towards internationally recognised standards of education. It was always expected that graduates would act as multipliers upon their return to their countries of origin, although currently there is also a perceived need that for a competitive economy, highly qualified graduates should stay on in Germany to work. At the universities, new study courses and credit point systems have been established towards internationally comparable academic degrees. Intensive academic contacts have developed through student and lecturer exchange programmes funded by the European Commission. Through cooperation in international research projects, a new transnational academic landscape has emerged, at least among the EU and accession countries. And, as everywhere, students and lecturers have gained a more global understanding of subjects and issues through electronic media.

With these ongoing changes in perspective in German universities, there are also social changes in the composition of the student body. Very few lecturers are of foreign origin, but many students, at least in the western part of Germany, are either children of former 'guest workers' or other immigrant families, or have come from abroad to study. That there can be 'foreigners' born in Germany is a consequence of German citizenship laws, which until very recently have reserved German citizenship to those born of German descent.

In many ways, the attendance of students of 'foreign' background at German universities presents a new situation that has not yet been recognised in its potential for teaching and research practice and, possibly, its implications for social theory. In this chapter, we would like to describe some aspects of this situation and ask how social knowledge can emerge, as part of professional academic practice. Over the course of the last few years we have observed certain positive changes. Topics of migration have become more *generally* interesting, for students from varied immigrant and local backgrounds. 'Migration' does not automatically evoke a discourse on social problems but can rather lead to discussions of more general changes in society. We also noticed that students' (family) backgrounds are referred to more frequently and talked about more openly. This could be troubling in fact, if it intensified social identification and self-definition in ethnic terms. What seems new, however, is that such references tend to be more relational, in the sense of taking into account how the perspectives of others towards family and social background differ from and compare to one's own. Students seem to identify less in absolute terms with their own background, as the standard to evaluate and devaluate others by. Prolonged contact and interaction have created more of an interest in others as well as the knowledge, empathy and imagination to understand the position of others.

However, there is still political disagreement and social hostility to the fact that Germany has become an immigration society. It tends to be taken for granted that immigration brings social conflicts and problems and that 'integration' cannot be achieved. To 'integrate', immigrants are expected to fit into a given state and nature of society. That societies actually change through immigration is overlooked. Migrants sometimes pioneer these changes, but education and academic success are not part of what is generally associated with either immigrants or 'foreigners'. Low scores for school education in Germany, learning deficits and lack of achievement are commonly attributed to the percentage of children from immigrant families in school classes, rather than to exclusionary mechanisms in institutional set-ups and in teaching which actually concern *all* children from low-income families[1].

Probably as a consequence of the focus on problems of 'integration' in ongoing debates in politics, in the news media and in the social sciences, the achievements of high school and university students with an immigrant background are not widely recognised and rarely mentioned. On the one hand, this neglect is positive, in the way that the immigrant background of students *is not* an issue, in the sense that it has not been associated with problems. This might be an unforeseen outcome of the classic ideals of German universities, which emphasise educating autonomous personalities. In this respect there is more of a difference between high school and university education than in other European countries. While the conditions under which professors and students meet are usually far from ideal, teaching and studying in universities is still very different from school situations. In most schools there is an orientation towards deficits and compensatory measures and references to 'cultural differences' of students are quite common. In comparison, universities offer a more open environment in which important learning experiences can take place which go beyond, or can even transform, fixed notions of identity.

We focus in this chapter on some of the seen but unnoticed phenomena of academic education and their potential for the emergence of more equality

---

and reciprocity in social relationships. The university, and especially the social sciences, are potentially in a position to counter the hegemonic discourse on the 'foreignness' or backwardness of immigrants by recognising and pointing out, for example, the strong and dynamic link between immigration and educational motivation. Our aim is to explore the potential of intercultural perspectives in the professional practice of lecturers, and for students gaining such understanding in the process of becoming professionals.

It is certainly true that no one at the university – or for that matter anywhere – wants to be reminded of where he or she has come from, either in terms of upward social mobility from low-income populations, or country of origin. Instead, everybody has a right to dignity and equality of treatment, and can reasonably expect both, especially at university, where the pursuit of knowledge is valued. It is therefore important to explain why considering cultural difference or difference of origin can make sense for professional practice and how this can be possible without singling out individuals. In our view, biographical perspectives are an important part of such professional practice, in opening up an understanding for how individuals relate to their own history, in relation to the history of others[2]. We now go on to discuss some cases of relational biographical perspectives.

Education in an immigration society

In a brief overview we would first like to point out some specifics about the situation in Germany where the immigrant background of students is not discussed in the context of university education, but has for a long time been a concern in school education. An obvious reason for this could be that only since the 1990s has the younger generation in immigrant families come of age to study at university, and enrolment in larger numbers from this population is even more recent. Already in the 1970s, however, the background of children from immigrant families was a central issue in debates on school education and policy. The so-called 'foreigners' education' (*Ausländerpädagogik*) was based on culturalist assumptions that the social and educational problems of such children were tied to their difference in background and to their resulting cultural and identity conflicts. According to these assumptions, identity conflicts resulted from the difference between their culture of origin and the culture of the receiving country, in the sense that the children were 'torn', so to speak, between 'tradition' and 'modernity'. The problem was defined in theoretical terms with the concept of a 'basic cultural personality' (Schrader et al, 1976) from which it followed that once young children reached a certain age, their cultural identity was determined. Thus, immigration *after* such an early age would account for a lack of educational success and social integration, as well as for psychosocial problems. In this view, schools faced the difficult task of working against the disintegrating factors of immigration by compensating for the educational deficits of the children. At the same time, the children were to be prepared for their return back to their countries of origin. This took place in special language and preparatory classes that in many cases segregated the children from their German peers.

Educational practice moved away from deficit definitions at a time in the 1980s when it had become clear that immigrant families were 'here to stay'. A new perspective on immigration found expression with the concepts of an 'intercultural education' oriented towards dealing with 'cultural difference'. This difference was denoted in a positive sense since all cultures were to be equally valued. It corresponded with giving up the idea of preparing the children for the improbable 'return' to their parents' country of origin. Instead, they should learn to value their 'own' culture so they would be able to maintain it as members of a culturally plural, or 'multicultural' society. Such a society required everybody to learn how to practise tolerance and to respect cultural differences, of all children, their parents and teachers.

The presence of foreign children was now understood as culturally enriching and as a chance to create didactic learning situations. 'Intercultural education' was set against previous explanations of lack of educational success in terms of 'cultural' differences. But 'culture' was still understood as explanatory of social differences, even though now no longer in terms of pointing out deficits, but rather as a means of learning tolerance. A background of 'foreign culture' no longer functioned as a deficit factor, but was now considered of equal value. Students with a history of immigration, however, could still be perceived and addressed in a reductive way as being representatives of 'their culture'.

The situation of 'foreign' students at university

Against the backdrop of this discourse on culture and difference in school education, foreign students at the university are – so far – only mentioned in administrative categories. Since 1992, a distinction has been made concerning those who have been educated within the German school system (*Bildungsinländer*), but who are not German citizens. They could be resident children or even grandchildren of immigrant workers who arrived as early as 1960; yet they would still have only a foreign passport because of German citizenship regulations. Then there are high school graduates from other countries who come to Germany to study (*Bildungsausländer*). Some are also from families of labour migrants, but who finished high school in Turkey, for example.

Up until 1984, graduating from high school in Germany did not mean an equal chance for university admission for those without German citizenship. Identified as 'foreign' students by their passports, they had to compete with students from other countries for restricted subjects such as medicine or psychology, unlike German graduates who could apply for these subjects through a central distributive agency, and who were guaranteed a place to study sooner or later. They were thus treated as 'foreigners', to their disadvantage. The rationale for this treatment lay, as we pointed out, in seeing 'foreigners' as suffering from learning deficits. Even those who were born and lived in

Germany were not recognised as citizens, or even possibly future citizens of a society itself defined as non-immigrant.

Early in the 1970s, a quota of 6-8% had been set for foreign students at German universities. Under the old definition this quota was all but filled up with graduates from German high schools who held foreign passports and also those born in Germany, leaving little room for 'real' foreigners. The latter, however, were sought by the heads of universities, in the name of international orientation and the education of those who would return to their home countries and be leaders of economic and social development. Slowly, political support was gained for this position in the federal states, which have certain autonomy in education policies. In the federal state of Hesse, for example, which is also where Frankfurt is situated, the winter semester of 1987/88 was the first time graduates of German schools with foreign passports were treated equally with German students applying for a place to study.

For all of (former west) Germany, equal treatment was later provided only for children of work migrants from EU-countries and not for the largest groups, not for Turks, Yugoslavs and Iranians. Since 1991/92, all students who graduate from high school in Germany can apply for a study place through the central federal distribution agency, regardless of their passport. Since 1993/94, foreigners from EU countries with good knowledge of German have the same rights as German applicants.

This development in educational policy somewhat reflects debates on whether the younger generation of immigrant families are considered 'foreigners' or not, and on whether gaining admission to a German university can count as successful integration into German society. The shift in policies towards equality shows that the integration of foreign students – in any definition – at university seems to be the aim[3]. This implies that the labour migration of the 1960s and 1970s is retrospectively more and more understood in terms of immigration. It also extends the constitutional rights of freedom of choice of profession, place of work, and educational institution[4] to all of the resident population, regardless of their citizenship status.

In the most recent survey published by the German student organisation on students' social and economic situation there are separate overviews for students who came from other countries. For those who went to school in Germany, it is assumed that living and study conditions are the same as for students from German families (BBF, 2002a). It is noted, however, that students from immigrant families receive less financial support than their peers from German families, and depend more on part-time jobs. At the same time, they might face more difficulties in finding employment. They more often live with their parents than their German peers (47% compared with 21%), and this could mean that they have less room for themselves.

The most recent social survey shows a rise of students from abroad of 21.1% between 1997/98 and 2000/01 (BBF, 2002b). Of these, 39.6% came from so-called poor development countries[5], 29.4% from fast-developing countries and 26.2% from industrialised countries. The majority, 84%, came as 'free movers', that is, on their own initiative and not with an exchange programme or a stipend. These students who come from abroad generally study under more difficult conditions than their peers. They have more problems finding a place to live and a job; they have less income on average and less living space. There are restrictions concerning their permits of residence and work. Beyond these structural disadvantages, their previous academic achievements are not always recognised.

Foreign students encounter racist discrimination outside and within universities. According to a survey conducted by World University Service among foreign students at German universities between October 2000 and June 2001, about a quarter of the respondents mentioned open or subtle discrimination by lecturers, other students, or administrative personnel. The origin of students is often associated with prejudice against their academic abilities: "You're from Brazil? But that's where you dance the Samba and don't do any serious work!" (Jäger, 2002, p 102).

Foreignness and difference

We would like to focus briefly on the social psychological situation of 'foreign' students in German universities. 'Me-Images', that is, how others perceive us, can coincide and also differ from our own sense of self, the 'I'. 'Foreign' students, and this includes students from immigrant families raised in Germany, can find themselves confronted with strange 'Me-Images' of their cultural difference and 'otherness'. As members of social minorities, such students may furthermore not be included in and may even find themselves excluded from the 'generalised other', the collective representations of members of the university and the institution itself. These concepts of the Chicago social psychologist George Herbert Mead (1934/74) help explain how strange Me-Images can negatively affect processes of personal and social identity constitution.

To our knowledge, there is no research on university students that addresses these issues. Such research could, for example, ask how students position themselves in relation to a taken-for-granted discourse on the problems of migration and integration. With regard to schools, this has been the focus of a recent comparative study in four different European countries, which showed that adolescents situate themselves in relation to the political and educational discourse on immigration, citizenship and nationality in each country (Schiffauer et al, 2002). According to this study, the identity work of adolescents in immigrant families in Germany involves coming to terms with a discourse of taken-for-granted ideas about their cultural difference and strangeness, and also their non-membership in an imagined ethnic and cultural community.

How do students deal with strange Me-Images and with their non-inclusion or exclusion from collective representations of the university and other parts of society? In the following, we would like to describe our observations of students' personal and theoretical reflections on the discourse of foreignness and immigration. Our observations are not part of a systematic study but rather result from our experiences within the university as students and lecturers, as well as counsellors for foreign students.

Observations on processes of identity work

As we have already explained, many 'foreign' students belong to the so-called second or third generation immigrant families, due to the fact that German citizenship has been reserved until very recently to those born of German descent[6]. Then there are also those students who have come to Germany especially for their studies. In the following we use 'foreign' for all students of immigrant background whenever we discuss strange Me-Images.

As we have also said, the presence of 'foreign' students is a 'seen but unnoticed' social fact (Garfinkel, 1967). Theories and statements on immigration continue to perceive immigrant minorities as uneducated and therefore as a social problem within a modern, well-educated majority. Migration and minority groups in society are important topics and research areas in the social and educational sciences, especially concerning the consequences of migration for the second and third generation in immigrant families. The emphasis is regularly on problems, deficits and their possible compensation. Now such theories are taught in the same departments in which immigrant students, or students from immigrant families, are enrolled. This raises the question of how students and staff relate to these theories of immigration.

Our point is that such students should not be research objects in the sense of being a problem group, but rather that their perspectives and identity work within the university opens up new and different research perspectives. In the sociological literature, groups of foreign students are studied sometimes according to their country of origin (for example, Morocco), or how they deal with specific problems, such as identity and cultural conflicts, religious orientation, return or further stay. In such research, it is rarely asked how the paradoxical presence of students in the university from among this 'problem' population is even possible, much less how this reflects back on what is said and taught on these topics. Their contributions and especially their potential contribution towards understanding migration processes in the social and educational sciences have not yet been taken notice of. It can be objected that 'foreign' students should not be particularised and therefore not be made an object of inquiry in any sense. It can be argued, however, that it makes sense to introduce notions of biographical work and identity constitution to counter how *difference* is generally assumed and perceived.

Difference versus 'making strange'

'Difference' can be based on particularistic or universalistic notions of strangeness. In Emmanuel Levinas' (1992) concept of 'radical strangeness' difference is understood in a universalistic sense as a general characteristic of every one being *the other* – as an ethical obligation. In the perception of particularistic strangeness the other can be reduced to *being different* and categorised in terms of 'not belonging'. Awareness, or 'sensitivity to difference' would mean that the strangeness of the other is not the object of talk *about* the other but rather part of experiencing strangeness in meeting *with* the other (Liebsch, 1999, p 116). Such 'sensitivity to difference' would also critically consider the political and social terms of belonging and not identify difference according to taken-for-granted notions. Can communication and interaction be independent of such collective definitions of belonging? Consider, for example, a student saying: "When you are talking to me, remember that I am Black and forget it at the same time'. The desired space is where situated communication takes place, reflecting knowledge of one's own and of the other's situation without the identifying markers of 'belonging/not belonging'. But how is this possible?

Social science often proceeds by assigning properties to others that have to do with their background or origin, 'making them strange' or 'seeing them from above'. *Situated knowledge*, in contrast, as in Donna Haraway's (1991) feminist critique of knowledge at the university, would imply an awareness of the political and ethical basis of research. It is quite obvious, for example, that anything that concerns Islam or immigration from Turkey has a bad press, and not only in Germany. Still, many research projects continue to promote stereotypes and prejudice by the very questions they formulate, instead of working towards a shift in paradigm. In the following, we would like to show how situated knowledge could be an important part of academic professional practice.

Characteristics of professional practice

In our observations on professional practice, we refer to work by Fritz Schütze (1996) and Ulrich Oevermann (1996, 2001). Very briefly, what concerns us here in the context of teaching is that professional practice is characterised by the paradox of continuously making mistakes, failing, and reflecting. This is an inherent part of practice; only through awareness and reflection can systematic errors and mistakes be avoided or repaired (Schütze, 1996). Consequently, professional practice cannot rely on routines. Basically, routines are solutions that were developed previously in reacting to crisis situations. Unlike in engineering, in each personal and social crisis specific solutions have to be developed. Professionals in different fields, in health, mental health, legal matters, and those in a process of acquiring accumulated knowledge, are often reacting to severe crises that cannot be resolved by those who encounter them personally (Oevermann 1996, 2001). However, professionals who manage crises on behalf of others need to restore those individuals' autonomy as soon as possible.

The professional practice of academic teaching in the context of intercultural processes at the university fits well into this emergent discussion. According to Oevermann (1996, 2001), the working alliance between child and teacher that sustains crisis management depends on the structural curiosity of the child. University students are also curious about new experiences, and since learning about the world continues after adolescence this constitutes a basis for a working alliance between academic staff and students. Moreover, the acquisition of accumulated knowledge is hardly ever a smooth process. Acquiring scientific reasoning and methodical procedures changes a person's identity and is often accompanied by crises. In the following, some examples of crisis situations will be discussed, together with the possibilities they have opened up.

Some observations of how students encounter discourse on migration

In our seminars[7], we address different aspects of migration processes and of immigration to Germany. Topics range from biographical narrative accounts of migration to migration as a project of families and generations, to transformations of the practice and meaning of gender, religion and tradition, to socio-economic conditions and consequences of immigrant entrepreneurship, and to educational opportunities. Some teaching includes an introduction to qualitative interpretive research on these topics. All classes included students whose families had been immigrants, or who were immigrants themselves. In seminar discussions, in papers, theses and exams, as well as in tutorials, students talked about their own experience of migration, or the experience of family members in different ways. Of course students from German families also discuss issues of migration. We have noticed changes in how issues are raised and talked about among all students.

The topics we teach and the research styles of qualitative-interpretive methods, especially biographical analysis, probably create a setting in which students refer to subjective experience. Given the semi-public setting of university seminars, however, accounts of experience are rendered in more general terms as part of an argumentation since direct biographical accounts can be thought to lack legitimacy and can raise personal vulnerability. In tutorials, by contrast, students say more about what their own or their family's history of migration means to them in relating it to their research, writing and exam preparation. While institutional settings sustain such a division between what is told 'in public' and 'in private', more recently we have noticed a shift towards more interchange between the settings. Now we find that students raise aspects of migration and identity, for example, also in the classroom, in what we would describe as a non-identificatory and more *generalised* way. There has been a development towards more theoretical and personal sensitivity concerning migration processes that we would ascribe to the participation of students with an immigrant background in seminars that facilitate open interaction and communication. In the following examples, we retrace different kinds of student interventions we have noticed over the course of time, beginning with seminars held over the last eight years.

Stating the relevance of migration experience

In a seminar on 'Empirical Investigations in the Sociology of Music and Cultural Analysis' a student research team interviewed members of Hip Hop groups. One of the students found that language and background were important in specific ways for group members with an immigrant background. In her seminar presentation she explained how she discussed this with the two other students in her team who could not see the importance of the migration backgrounds of the artists, but would only consider how forms of music move from one place to another. From her own bi-national upbringing as well as through her work in a youth centre, she insisted that immigration experience mattered, that it was important to challenge taken-for-granted notions of 'identity' and 'culture', and that processes of social exclusion took place even in the Hip Hop scene. The research team resolved their crisis by dividing the thesis into different topics. But the tutors in this case included all participants of the seminar in the discussion of 'hidden' migration topics. In this way, the student's perceptiveness and awareness became extended to all other participants.

Transferring knowledge and experience of migration

In the course of a seminar on sociological concepts of tradition, a thesis was handed in on the formation of political traditions among youth from a North African background in French *banlieus*. Based on many documents, theoretically sound and well argued, this thesis had been authored, it seemed, by a student who had taken part in a European academic exchange programme and therefore knew the local situation as well as discussions in the literature. It then turned out that the student had never been to France. Instead, she came from a country in Latin America and had inferred her political experience and knowledge into the French situation. This was not treated critically, but the recognition of the student's achievement included acknowledging her ability to extrapolate from experience.

In the dominant discourse on migration, learning deficits of migrants are often stated in terms of their lack of local knowledge. In reality it is often the case that experiencing migration can lead to an understanding of structural similarities, through contrastive comparisons. Professional practice should acknowledge this and take advantage of the additional strengths it brings.

Creative attacks on stigmatising notions

A student came to the tutorial to discuss her final exams and mentioned that after finishing high school in Turkey she had come to Germany to study and join her family. She said that she noticed there was so much talk about 'honour' concerning Turkish migrants that she had questioned her mother and her neighbour on this topic, whether this might be something she had missed. Was 'honour' something she possibly lacked and had only become aware of in

Germany? In her written exam, in discussing the history of 'honour' concepts in Western societies, she tackled the way social science literature on 'honour' contributed to culturalist interpretations. In their professional practice, lecturers can learn from how students tackle taken-for-granted notions in everyday life *and* in the social sciences.

Taking the perspectives of others

Students sometimes choose topics for their research that reflect their family's migration experience. In several cases we noticed this had to do with being members of minority groups in, for example, Turkey. But in other cases students took a minority perspective that was different from their personal background. Thus, a student of Spanish background did his exam on the situation of Moroccan youth in the south of Spain, to study the specific relations between immigrants and majority in that context. Through such changes in standpoint, interesting and important aspects of modernisation and traditionality, and of minority status and migration, can be explored. Such imaginative work can arise especially when topics are not assigned, but rather developed out of the students' interests. Professional practice should enable students to pursue topics related to their specific experience.

Intervening in crisis situations

Crises arise, of course, in the context of referring to migration experience, as, for example, when students underestimate the impact of institutional settings. Thus, there was a discussion in a seminar on education about school problems among children of immigrant families. To counter mounting stereotypes and prejudice within the discipline on this topic, a student from an Italian immigrant family began telling about her own and her parents' experience, to explain that 'integration' can mean something different from taken-for-granted notions. In the situation of the seminar, her story had no effect on the dominant course the discussion took. It remained a single case in the sense of a personal exception to the rule. Instead of explaining the matter, as the student tried to do, she found she had to explain herself. What she said about herself became stigmatising information, in Erving Goffman's (1975) sense of a person becoming nailed down by her or his biography. In good professional practice, the lecturer would have intervened to move the discussion away from the personal experience of the student to a more general perspective.

Personal alienation under the impact of dominating discourse

Under pressure, as can be the case in exam situations, with no opportunity for critical discussion of hegemonic theories on migration, minority students sometimes refer to theories that focus heavily on personal deficits and social problems. While they are actually the living proof that there is more to migration than problems, this knowledge cannot always be used. In the case of one student, it can be said that his topic became strange to him[8]. For his final thesis, this particular student wanted to study the migration to Germany of members of a discriminated religious minority in Turkey. There was not much literature, but since his family belonged to this group, he thought he would be able to find out about cultural and religious traditions and how the group organised itself in Germany.

In the tutorial, the student took the opportunity to explore what this topic meant for him in a personal autobiographical sense, and also in more general terms what it meant to belong to 'a minority within a minority' in Germany. He talked about the ambiguities of enjoying more recognition in Germany than in Turkey but, at the same time, how much more easily he had learned Spanish and gained friends during an academic exchange, in contrast to the constant doubts and ambivalence of remaining a foreigner in Germany.

It turned out to be impossible for him to study his minority group. Instead, he focused on socialisation and integration of second generation immigrant worker families. When he handed in the first version of his thesis, his original perspective had become unrecognisable. In a personal crisis, dominant public perceptions of migration as the source of conflicts and problems can become overwhelming and so he reached a resigned conclusion on the impossibility of integration. Professional intervention offered a critique of his argumentation, which he could use in re-working his thesis. At the same time, during tutorials, he returned to his original quest and talked about what he had found out about the group his family belonged to.

This example, together with the previous ones, shows that talking about and exploring one's background is not straightforward, particularly as a member of a minority group. The ways in which one's biography and family history are different raise pressures to constantly explain oneself. Without open communication with others, and under the constraints of strange Me-Images, it can be very difficult to develop one's own biographical process of exploration and reflection.

What's new?

Over the past few years, we have observed changes in how immigration has become a topic in university teaching. It seems that more students with an immigrant background now choose topics concerning their family history. Discussing different aspects, such as work migration, passages from rural to urban life, and the transmission and transformation of values between the generations, adds new dimensions to social theory on migration. But interestingly, there are also more students now from a German background who draw on their family history to work towards more general concepts of family and social processes. One student, for example, presented a paper with many visual documents of her family who had been living in the same farm in a German village for many generations. It seems that discussions of different local and migration contexts had prompted her interest in the conditions of remaining settled. There is thus a natural laboratory taking place in the seminar situation, similar to a student workshop in which research cases are interpreted and discussed in a contrastive comparative way, both of which build and elaborate general theories of family processes.

The fact that students now more frequently adopt perspectives beyond their particular background is important for tackling issues of a seemingly taken-for-granted character. Thus, a student presentation of research on urban Turkish families led to a discussion of types of families and a remark by a (German) student that it did not make sense to talk about 'the Turkish family' which is otherwise a common sense notion in social science research. Another student who had transferred from a university in eastern Germany gave a paper on right extremist youth groups. The discussion proceeded to more general aspects of the transition of the former German Democratic Republic to becoming a part of the Federal Republic of Germany. Students then referred to earlier discussions of migration processes, which made it possible to recognise transition difficulties involved in the German unification process, most of which have been glossed over and seem already forgotten. In another seminar in this series, research on Turkish youth in Germany was being presented, in which young men talked about village life and their grandmothers, when one young woman student commented how this reminded her of her own – German – grandmother.

In recent years, a turn to Islamic religion by the younger generation in immigrant families has been noted. This has become especially visible through women students who mark their specific Islamic practice of observance by covering their hair and body. It is widely debated whether this assertion of difference signifies turning away from Western societies or, on the contrary, expresses the quest for an individual, reflexive, positioning within society as a part of modernisation processes. What we have observed leads us to support the latter. We have also found, however, that in many teaching and tutorial situations students who observe Islam do not argue out their religious convictions when it comes to social issues. In the few cases when they choose a specific topic that has to do with Islam, such as family law, it is discussed in sociological terms. While many students with an Islamic background are explicitly secular, some study fundamentalist group membership. One student from a Turkish background gave an impressive paper on young women turning to religion in which similarities became clear between Islamic, Jewish and Christian forms of new orthodoxy.

Certainly, students who observe Islamic religion do not speak more in terms of group or collective membership than other students. However, the presence and contributions of students from different backgrounds sometimes change the ways in which certain sociological topics are discussed such as family, adolescence, modernity, and traditionality. It is remarkable that in these discussions, a shift takes place in the usual awareness contexts of identifying conflicts, for example, between generations in families as caused by immigration, or of identifying traditional ways of life with non-western societies. A professional practice of teaching can enable interactions that de-emphasise identifying one another in terms of origin. This can free individual potential to take the perspective of others and can turn the university into a more inclusive generalised other, as a shared and participatory social undertaking. Indeed, we would underline the importance of interactions that take place in the university, between students, and students and lecturers. Sometimes a seminar can generate model situations, and students who later become schoolteachers might be able to transfer their own experiences of such situations into their own teaching practice.

Changes in perspective can be related to reflexive biographical insights and, at the same time, indicate ongoing transformations of collective identities. As Fritz Schütze points out in a related context, "Active participation in social worlds and social arenas is indispensable for arriving at democratic political equality at the level of the nation state as well as at the level of trans-national communities" (Schütze, 2002, pp 5-6). Especially important in his view is the biographical work of comparing the expectations of various generalised others with whom the individual has come to terms in the course of his/her social life, and the biographical work of transgressing the demarcation lines of tradition-based milieus and of ethnic we-groups via all sorts of 'intercultural' communication.

Intercultural interaction processes further biographical work and also the crossing of habitual boundaries. To conclude, we summarise our ideas on how professional practice can support intercultural processes in the university.

Conclusion

First of all, we want to emphasise again that topics concerning 'foreign background' are not conducive to intercultural communication *by themselves*. It can be stigmatising when students (have to) become speakers for their own we-group. The recognition of individuals depends on their non-identification with particular groups.

Second, it is important to understand that educational processes are connected with biographical knowledge, which can be acquired outside of and beyond conventionally expected channels. It can be significant how parents who did not have the opportunity to go to university or even attend elementary school explain to their children how they gained access to their own occupations, or how they experienced their project of migration. Many students from migrant worker families relate their educational effort and aspirations to their parents' endurance and quest of a better life[9].

Finally, an interest in one's background, religion, history, culture and traditions is commonly interpreted as turning away from modern society and as a sign that integration has failed. A task for teaching and research in the social sciences would be to make the exploration of one's background *generally* 'familiar', for all students, in recognition that it may provide the basis for the exploration of theoretical issues.

Against making some backgrounds stranger than others and characterising minority members and their concerns as fundamentally 'different', it is important to show that biographical work invariably extends to one's family background and that it is not at all in opposition to modernity but rather generates it. The university is a good place to do this.

Note

Earlier papers on this topic were presented by the first author in cooperation with the second author at a biographical research conference in Halle, February 2000, and by the first and third author in the session on 'Comparative Social Research' at the International Conference on Methodological Problems of Biographical Research, University of Kassel, May 2001. For discussing these presentations, we would like to thank Ursula Apitzsch, Roswitha Breckner and Regina Kreide.

Notes

[1] PISA 2000, the Programme for International Student Assessment initiated by the Organisation for Economic Co-operation and Development (OECD), found a relatively low level of overall literary and mathematical performance among school children in Germany, and a stronger relationship between social background and student performance than in any of the other participating countries.

[2] Biographical perspectives are carefully taken account of in biographical analysis, a research approach aimed at understanding how individual lives are part of, and at the same time relate in different ways to, given states of society. For historical and recent developments of this approach, see Apitzsch and Inowlocki (2000), for an overview and different examples of 'doing' biographical analysis (Apitzsch and Inowlocki, 2000).

[3] In the winter semester of 2000/01, 187,027 foreign students were enrolled at German universities, 10.4% of all students. Most of these had obtained their qualification to study in other countries. Of the 3.4% who graduated from German high schools, 58% were the younger generation of families who had migrated as contract ('guest') workers, 13% from neighbouring EU countries, and the others in many cases from areas of political conflict (such as 6% from Iran). Newer figures show that during 2001, 206,100 foreign students were enrolled, and 13,800 successfully completed their studies.

[4] "All Germans have the right to freely choose profession, place of work and educational institution", German Basic Law, Article 12 I (*Alle Deutschen haben das Recht, Beruf, Arbeitsplatz und Bildungsstätte frei zu wählen* GG, Art. 12 I)

[5] In this terminology, 'poor development' countries refer to poorer and less industrialised countries than those considered as 'fast-developing'.

[6] Since 1 January, 2000 every child born to legal migrant residents is entitled to German nationality and registered with two nationalities. But between the ages of 18 and 23, a decision for one nationality has to be made.

[7] At the Department of Social Sciences, J.W. Goethe-University, Frankfurt-am-Main. Some of the seminars involved cooperation with Professor Dr Ursula Apitzsch.

[8] In Gerhard Riemann's study of biographical accounts of psychiatric patients, he described how their own biographies became strange to them through their being processed as institutional 'cases' (Riemann, 1987).

[9] Similarly, Catherine Delcroix describes how young students learned from their father, who drove a heavy goods vehicle and had six children (the first four girls): "He has taken each of his daughters, from the age of 8 years upwards, with him as he drives around France. In this way, the girls get to go with their father several times a year and are able to discover the towns and historical monuments of France". The comments of two of the girls show how their father "has opened the door to future career options for his daughters. They also show how he has been able to give them an idea of the world through his own experiences of migration and work, and to enable them to be critical" (Delcroix, 2000, p 182).

References

Apitzsch, U. and Inowlocki, L. (2000) 'Biographical analysis: a "German" school?', in P. Chamberlayne, J. Bornat and T. Wengraf (eds) *The biographical turn in social science: Comparative issues and example*, London: Routledge, pp 53-70.

BBF (Bundesministerium für Bildung und Forschung) (ed) (2002a) *Die wirtschaftliche und soziale Lage der Studierenden in der Bundesrepublik Deutschland 2000*, Ergebnisse der 16, Bonn: Sozialerhebung des Deutschen Studentenwerks durchgeführt durch HIS Hochschulinformationssystem.

BBF (ed) (2002b) *Internationalisierung des Studiums – Ausländische Studierende in Deutschland – Deutsche Studierende im Ausland*, Ergebnisse der 16, Bonn: Sozialerhebung des Deutschen Studentenwerks durchgeführt durch HIS Hochschulinformationssystem.

Delcroix, C. (2000) 'The transmission of life stories from ethnic minority fathers to their children', in J. Attias-Donfut (ed) *The myth of generational conflict*, London: Routledge, pp 174-89.

FQS – Forum Qualitative Sozialforschung 4(3) 2003 (Forum: Qualitative Social Research), http://www.qualitative-research.net/fqs/fqs.htm

Garfinkel, H. (1967) *Studies in ethnomethodology*, Englewood Cliffs, NJ: Prentice Hall.

Goffman, E. (1975) *Stigma: Über Techniken der Bewältigung beschädigter Identität*, Frankfurt-am-Main: Suhrkamp.

Haraway, D. (1991) *Simians, cyborgs, and women: The reinvention of nature*, London: Free Association Books.

Jäger, T. (2002) 'Diskriminierungserfahrungen ausländischer Studierender in Deutschland: Die Hochschule als Spiegelbild der Gesellschaft – Ergebnisse einer Umfrage des WUS', *Auszeit* 44, vol 39, no 3/4, Wiesbaden, pp 96-112.

Levinas, E. (1992) *Jenseits des Seins oder anders als Sein geschieht*, Freiburg: Alber.

Liebsch, B. (1999) 'Politische Differenzsensibilität und ethische Differenzvergessenheit', *Babylon*, vol 19, pp 79-105.

Mead, G.H. (1934/74) *Mind, self and society: From the standpoint of a social behaviourist*, Chicago, IL: University of Chicago Press.

Oevermann, U. (1996) 'Theoretische Skizze einer revidierten Theorie professionalisierten Handelns', in A. Combe and W. Helsper (eds) *Pädagogische Professionalität. Untersuchungen zum Typus pädagogischen Handelns*, Frankfurt-am-Main: Suhrkamp, pp 70-128.

Oevermann, U. (2001) 'A revised theoretical model of professionalisation', unpublished manuscript.

Schiffauer, W., Baumann, G., Kastoryano, R. and Vertovec, S. (eds) (2002) *Staat – Schule – Ethnizität. Politische Sozialisation von Immigrantenkindern in vier europäischen Ländern*, Münster: Waxmann.

Schrader, A., Nickles, B. and Griese, H. (1976) *Die Zweite Generation. Sozialisation und Akkulturation ausländischer Kinder in der Bundesrepublik*, Kronberg: Athenäum.

Schütze, F. (1996) 'Organisationszwänge und hoheitsstaatliche Rahmenbedingungen im Sozialwesen: Ihre Auswirkungen auf die Paradoxien professionellen Handelns', in A. Combe and W. Helsper (eds) *Pädagogische Professionalität. Untersuchungen zum Typus pädagogischen Handelns*, Frankfurt-am-Main: Suhrkamp, pp 183-275.

Schütze, F. (2002) 'A basic theoretical approach on a research project on European identity', unpublished manuscript.

Index

A

Abbott, Andrew 46
abductive reasoning 53*n*
abuse *see* male violence
accountability: negative effects 5-6, 8
action and individual 19-20
activity routes in caring 22
advocacy 224-5
agency
  and biographical methods in health
    care 169-70
  and structure 24
AIDS *see* HIV/AIDS
Aldrich, H.E. 74, 75
Alheit, Peter 24-5, 28, 60-1
alienation effect 31
Almaliach, D. 109
Althusser, L. 275
analysis
  case study analysis 32*n*
  levels 2
    cross-level analysis 8-9
    in-depth 140
  sequential analysis 44-5, 52-3*n*
  see also biographical interpretive
    method; textual analysis
Andrews, Molly 195-6, 199
anorexia nervosa 212-13
Anthias, Floya 42-3
anxiety
  general practitioners 300, 301, 303-4
  role in male violence 152, 159
Apitzsch, Ursula 61
appropriation systems 24-5
Arendt, Hannah 19-20
arts-based approaches 27
Atkinson, Dorothy 225-6
audit culture 5-6, 8, 27
auto/biographical methods 302-3
  and male subjectivity 158
autonomous choice: state repression
  132-9
autopoiesis 24-5, 61

B

Bakhtin, Mikhail 129*n*
Bakhtine, M. 280*n*
'balancing position' in Russian jobs 118
Balint, Michael 169, 301

Balint groups 301
Balzer, H. 115
Bar-On, D. 106, 188
Barnes, C. 232*n*
Barthes, R. 280*n*
Bateson, Gregory 93-4, 98-9
bathing: 'social bath' 214
Baumann, Zygmunt 19
Begin, Menachem 106
behaviourist view of entrepreneurs 74-5
Bhabha, Homi 195
biographical co-construction 11
biographical embeddedness 57-68
biographical interpretive method 2, 32*n*
  lone mothers in Venice 239-49
  needs of homeless men 251-61
  and race and ethnicity 208
  social subject in 93-9
biographical methods
  auto/biographical methods 302-3
  effective applications 6-7
  range of 2
  skills and training 29-31
  user groups 6
  see institutional cultures
biographical resources 9
  education and training 11-12, 59,
    61-3, 64, 67, 68
  see therapy
biographical work: use of term 32*n*
biographicity 24, 25, 28, 60-1
biological terms 24
Bion, Wilfred 96-7
body
  racialised identity 206-7
  and resistance 209-17
Bolton, G. 30
Bonacich, E. 41
Boothe, Brigitte 253
Bordo, S. 215
Bornat, Joanna 168, 169, 170, 224
bottom-up practice 228
bottom-up research 223, 225-6, 229-31
Bourdieu, Pierre 58
Brain, J. 210-11
Britain
  openness to biographical methods 20
  policy on domestic violence 149-60
  Polish community interviews 197-200
  professionalism in 3, 4-7

training in biographical methods 29
Bude, Heinz 52*n*
Bury, Michael 166
Butler, R. 6

C

Caisse Nationale d'Allocations Familiales
    27-8
'canonical' identity work 138-9
capital 58-9, 80
careers concept 239
caring
    'Cultures of Care' project 21-2, 24
    need for biographical work 22
Carpenter, Belinda 169
case study analysis 32*n*
Cavarero, A. 31
Chamberlayne, P. 193
    'Cultures of Care' project 21-2, 24
    SOSTRIS project 22-3, 24, 27, 232*n*
Charaudeau, P. 280*n*
Chicago school of sociology 2, 46
Chinese entrepreneurs 76
citizen advocacy 225
citizenship 3, 19
    denizen status 47, 51-2
    German citizenship laws 313, 316-17
    immigrants to Greece 87
civil servants 115
class resources 58, 59
cognitive-behavioural programmes for
    violent men 150-1
collective group analysis 188-9
    workshop experience 31
collective memory: Holocaust survivors
    101-2, 106
Collier, R. 151
commissioned care management 5
communication systems in Russia 117
community-based teaching in New
    Zealand 12, 285-94
conditional translation 194, 196-7, 200
'confined' identity work 137-8
continental welfare model 41
continuing care in NHS 228-31
Cooper, A. 5-6, 196
Cooper, Mabel 225-6, 227, 228
coping strategies
    life-course regime East Germany
    135-9
    new entrepreneurs 48-9, 64-6, 68
Courtney, Sean 305
creativity 93, 97-8

crime: narratives of fear 25-6
cross-language research: translation
    issues 193-200
cross-level analysis 8-9
cultural capital 159
cultural imperialism of English language
    194-5
cultural psychology of learning and
    health 299-310
culture of dependency 242
'culture of guilt' 26
'Cultures of Care' project 21-2, 24
Curran, Chris 26

D

Dartington, T. 6
databases: health biographies 172-3
Dausien, B. 24-5, 28
Deacon, Joey 225
defence mechanisms 26
defended subjects
    and *anorexia nervosa* 213
    and male violence 152-8
    see Hollway, Wendy
Delcroix, Catherine 328*n*
denizen status 47, 51-2
Denmark: TSER project 57-8, 77-88
Denzin, Norman K. 240, 259
dependency cultures 242
dialogic relationship in Dostoevsky
    129*n*
difference: foreign students in Germany
    319-20
disability research: biographical methods
    232*n*
'discursive' identity work 136
disempowerment trajectories 11
'disenchantment' 136
disguised access 244
doctors
    biographical resources in training 12
    cultural psychology of learning
    299-310
domestic violence *see* male violence
Dostoevsky, Fyodor 129*n*
dreaming 97-8
Dubet, F. 278
Duluth domestic violence model 149,
    150
Durkheim, Emile 85

E

East Germany
  caring cultures 22
  managers 10, 131-45
    state control of life-course decisions
      132-9, 142-3
    transformation research 140-4
  research on 140-4, 195-6
economic necessity 143
'economic redundancy' 39, 47
Edgerton, Robert 224-5
education and training 29-31
  biographical resources 11-12, 59, 61-3,
    64, 67, 68
  community-based research in New
    Zealand 285-94
  foreign students in Germany 313-28
  'foreigners' education' in Germany
    314, 315-16
  health training in biographical
    methods 173-4
  self-directed learning for GPs 299-300
  state control of 132-3
  see also teachers
ego: monolithic representation 102
Elwert, Georg 52*n*
embeddedness *see* biographical
  embeddedness; mixed embeddedness
embodied resistance 209-17
emotional distancing 26
emotionality 9-10, 93, 95-6, 97
empowerment 2, 5
  biography as empowering practice
    221-33
  disempowerment trajectories 11
  user as consumer 7, 8
English language: cultural imperialism
  194-5
entrepreneurial capacity 57, 58-9
entrepreneurship
  research limitations 73-4
  self-employment of migrants 39-68
  biographical embeddedness 57-68
  coping strategies 48-9, 64-6, 68
  and gender 9, 40, 42-53, 65-7, 82-7
  as innovation 73-88
  self-employment schemes 57-8
epiphany 207
Erikson, E. 6
Esping-Andersen, G. 41
ethics of interviewing 10-11, 181-9,
  291-2

textual analysis reveals more than
  narrator intended 152, 185, 186-8
'ethnic economies' 39, 40-3
  definition 42
  resources for ethnic business 58-9
  women's role 42-3, 52
ethnic minorities
  entrepreneurship 9, 39-88
  healthcare and race 205-17
  students in Germany 12, 313-28
  see also migrants; race
ethnic networks 76
'ethnic succession' theory 76
Europe
  biographical methods and social policy
    19-34
  female self-employment study 43-52
evidence-based systems 5
  conflict with biographical methods 25,
    170
  domestic violence policy 149, 150
experience: as entrepreneurial resource
  60-1

F

family cultures 242
fear
  fear of crime narratives 25-6
  fear of dying defence mechanisms 26
feminine welfare subsystem 237-49
feminism
  agency and prostitutes' biographies
    169-70
  domestic violence 149-60
  object relations theory 305-6
  'fictional-critical writing' 30-1
Fine, Michelle 302-3
Finerman, Ruthbeth 168
France
  biography in institutional context
    27-8
  formal and informal social sphere 20
  teachers' professional identity 11-12,
    265-81
  training in biographical methods 29
Fraser, Nancy 237-9
Free Association Narrative Interview
  Method 152
Freedom of Information Act (2000) 226
freelance professional practice 9
French, R. 6
Freud, Sigmund 63, 93, 97, 98, 309
Froggett, L. 3, 5

G

Garfinkel, H. 140
Gartner, William 73
gender
  and identity 11
  in psychotherapy 303
  self-employment of migrant women 9,
    40, 42-53, 65-7, 82-7
  subjectivity and male violence 151,
    152-8
  welfare dualism 237-8
general practitioners: cultural
  psychology of learning 299-310
generation agendas 144
Genette, G. 280*n*
genocide: psychoanalytical
  conceptualisation 102
Germany
  biography in institutional context 28
  caring cultures 22
  hermeneutics 20
  homeless men interviews 251-61
  institutional contexts 26
  migrants
    citizenship constraints 313, 316-17
    discourse on migration experience
      321-4
    educational achievement 314, 315-16
    self-employment 39-53, 57-68
    and structural opportunity model
      76-7
    as university students 12, 313-28
    professionalism in 3-4, 7-8
    training in biographical methods 29
    see also East Germany; Holocaust
      survivors
gerontology 6, 24
ghost writers 193-200
Giddens, A. 25, 98
Gilbert, G.M. 111*n*
Glade, William B. 75
Godard, Barbara 194
Goffman, Erving 33*n*, 141, 239, 241,
  247, 323
Gonzalez, L. 167
GPs: cultural psychology of learning
  299-310
Granovetter, M. 40-1
Greenhalgh, Tricia 169
grounded theory 44, 62
group analysis 188-9
  workshop experience 31
Gubrium, J. 6

guilt
  culture of 26
  East German insulation 138
  Holocaust survivors 104
Gunaratnam, Y. 6

H

Hammersley, M. 222
Hanses, A. 24, 25, 28
Haraway, Donna 320
healthcare
  cultural psychology of learning
    299-310
  empowerment through biographical
    methods 221-33
  health studies 165-75
    applications of biographical methods
      166-8
    databases 172-3
    difficulties of using biographical
      methods 169-70
    interdisciplinary dialogue 170-1
    therapeutic interventions 171-2
    training in biographical methods
      173-4
  and race 205-8, 211-17
Hearn, Jeff 151, 157
Hegel, G.W.F. 63
Helling, I. 189*n*
hermeneutics 2, 20
heuristic concepts in transformation
  research 142-4
Hillmann, F. 51
HIV/AIDS: biographical methods 165,
  167, 168, 171
Hoerning, Erika 60
Hogarth, S. 165
Hollway, Wendy 25, 152, 157, 158-9,
  216
  fear of crime narratives 25-6
Holmes, Jeremy 309
Holocaust 10, 32*n*
Holocaust survivors 101-11
  control group studies 104-5
  criteria for first generation survivors
    106
  emotional survivors 103-4
  fuzzy boundaries for second and third
    generation survivors 106
  legal definitions 103, 104
  scales of suffering 107-10, 307
home-based caring 21-2
homelessness 11

biographical acuity of homeless 23-4
needs of homeless men 251-61
professionals' defence mechanisms
  26-7
training of workers 29
Honneth, Axel 63
Hughes, Everett C. 3, 46, 48
human capital 58, 80
Hunter, K.M. 169
Hurwitz, Brian 169

I

identity
  empowerment through biographical
    methods 228
  identity work with East German
    managers 135-9
  'Me-Images' of foreign students 318-
    19
  sexual identity and professional
    practice 303-4
  teachers' professional identity in
    France 11-12, 265-81
  see also gender
illegal migrants 52*n*
immigrant communities *see* migrants;
  Polish community in Britain
indescribability 102
individual *see* subjectivity
innovative ethnic entrepreneurship
  73-88
institutional cultures: biographical
  methods 26-8
'insulation' 137-8
intercultural interaction in Germany
  316, 326
interpretation
  revealing more than narrator intended
    152, 185, 186-8
  see also biographical interpretive
    method; needs interpretation; textual
    analysis
'interpretive biographies' 240
  see also biographical interpretive
    method
interpreters *see* translation
intersubjectivity 3, 4, 10, 25
intertextuality 302
interviews
  ethical aspects 10-11, 181-9, 291-2
  revealing more than narrator
    intended 152, 185, 186-8
  narrative work

homeless men 251-61
open narrative interviews 32*n*
research students' experiences 291-3
translation issues 197-200
Israel: Holocaust survivors 101-11

J

Jackson, David 158
Jefferson, T. 25, 152, 157, 158-9, 159-60,
  216
  fear of crime narratives 25-6
Jews
  as entrepreneurs 76
  Holocaust survivors 101-11
Johnson, M. 276
journals 285, 290-3
'just world' hypothesis 108

K

Katko, Tamar 103-4, 108, 109
Kerbrat-Orecchioni, C. 280*n*
Keren, N. 109
Killick, John 166
King, A.: 'Cultures of Care' project
  21-2, 24
Kivinen 115
Klein, Melanie 152, 157
Kloosterman, R. 41-2
Knowles, C. 207
'known past' 126, 128
Kolchar, 111*n*
Kosovo: war trauma counsellors 93,
  95-6
Kupferberg, F. 77-8

L

Labour governments 5
  see also New Labour
Lakoff, G. 276
language
  analysis of life histories 272-7
  inadequacy for Holocaust survivors
    102
  translation issues 193-200
Lauret, Maria 194-5
learning disability: biographical methods
  224, 225-6
Lejeune, P. 267, 280*n*
less-demanded knowledge 152, 157-8
Levinas, Emmanuel 102, 319
Lewis, G. 6

life histories 2, 5, 6, 7
  community-based research in New
    Zealand 288-90
  empowerment through 221-33
  of health practitioners 166, 230, 303-9
  interview ethics 181-9, 291-2
  research students' experience of 291-3
  teachers' professional identity 265-81
  see also narrative work
life-course regime in East Germany
    132-9, 142-3
  coping strategies 135-9
Light, I. 58-9
Lincoln, Y.S. 259
lone mothers 32*n*
  in Venice 11, 237-49
Lorenz, Walter 20
Lupton, Deborah 167
Lyth, Menzies 26

M

macro-sociological reasoning 140
McWhinney, I. 300-1
male violence 10, 149-60
  cognitive-behavioural programmes
    150-1
  defended subjects 152-60
  in immigrant stories 209
management
  East German managers 10, 131-45
  managerial styles in Russia 116, 117,
    120-1, 124-5
managerialism 4, 5
marginalised groups
  biographical methods 23-4, 33*n*
  general practitioners 299, 303-9
  lone mothers in Venice 242, 244, 245,
    246-7, 248
  see also migrants
Marks, L. 165
Martinez, M.A. 74
masculine welfare subsystem 237, 238
masculinity
  in doctor's work 307, 309-10
  in psychosocial biography of violence
    151, 152-60
masked needs 243-4
'masking' 138-9
Maurer-Hein, R. 28, 29
'Me-Images' of foreign students 318-19
Mead, George Herbert 63, 318
meaning structures 241
medical culture 300-1

memory
  collective memory of Holocaust
    survivors 101-2, 106
  screen memory 137
Mental Deficiency Act (1913) 226, 227
Mental Deficiency Committee records
    226-7
Merton, Robert 81, 82, 87
Meshcherinka, Elena 129*n*
Messerschmidt, James 151, 157
metaphor 276-7
migrants
  foreign students in Germany 313-28
    educational achievement 314, 315-16
    migration discourse 321-4
  in healthcare context in Britain
    208-17
  illegal migrants 52*n*
  self-employment 39-53, 57-68
    biographical embeddedness 57-68
    entrepreneurship as innovation 73-88
    motivation for 75, 76, 78-80, 84-7
    of women 9, 40, 42-53, 65-7, 82-7
Mills, C. Wright 23
minorities *see* ethnic minorities; women
'mixed embeddedness' 40-3
Monde, Le 20, 268
Monk, Gerald 172
monolithic representation of the ego
    102
moral careers: lone mothers in Venice
    239-47
'moral degeneracy' 226-7
moral rethinking 87
Morokvasic, Mirjana 43, 51
motivation
  for ethnic entrepreneurship 75, 76,
    78-80, 84-7
  social recognition 63, 65-6, 67-8, 79
  unlived lives 36, 61, 62, 64-5, 67-8
  job motivation in Russia 117, 122-3,
    125-6
  as migrant resource 61-8
Murard, N. 25-6

N

narrative 2, 131
  ethics of interviews 181-9, 291-2
  for GPs' mental wellbeing 309
  interviews with homeless men 253-5
  marginalised groups 24
  narrative biographical 179
  narratology 265

subjective constructions 25-6
therapeutic effects 171-2, 183, 309
see also biographical methods; life
histories
National Practitioners' Network 149
see also RESPECT
National Service Framework for Older
People 29
National Sound Archive: health studies
166, 171
Nazis
perpetrators of Holocaust 109-10
psychiatric diagnoses 111*n*
needs interpretation
homeless men 251-61
lone mothers in Venice 239-49
neo-American welfare model 41
neoliberalism 4, 5, 8
Neuberger, J. 207
neurolinguistic programming (NLP)
274
New Labour
policy on domestic violence 149-60
policy on homelessness 27
new professionalism 9, 50
New Zealand: community-based
teaching 12, 285-94
Nittel, Dieter 3
normal mothers 242-3, 244, 245, 246
nurses: cooperation with biographical
project 229-31

O

object relations theory 305-6
Oevermann, Ulrich 3, 4, 46, 48, 52-3*n*,
320-1
older people
biographical methods in continuing
care 228-31
oral histories 24
and health care 166-7, 168, 171
psychology of old age 6
'social bath' 214
ontology of human subject 96-7, 285,
287
open narrative interviewing 32*n*
opportunity structures 9
entrepreneurship model 74-7, 86, 88
oral history tradition 2, 5, 6, 7, 24
health applications 166-7, 168, 171,
172-3

organisational structures: Russian
transformation 115-29
outward-oriented caring 21, 22

P

participation 2, 5, 6
Patai, Daphne 223
Pauling, Brian 294
Peace, S. 223
Peirce, C.S. 53*n*
Pence, Ellen 149
person-centred social work 26, 27
personal fate 144
personal support for carers 22
Plummer, Ken 6, 288, 291
Polanyi, Karl 40
Polish community in Britain 197-200
political correctness 6
Popay, Jenny 168
postmodernism 166
post-traumatic stress disorder 106
power relations
disempowerment trajectories 11
in health care 165
life-course regime in East Germany
132-9, 142-3
in public and private sector
employment in Russia 117, 119-20,
121-2, 124-5
'social bath' 214
pre-client careers of lone mothers in
Venice 241-3, 247-8
precarious work: migrant self-
employment 41-2
private sector employment
in Britain 115
in Russia 115-29
private sphere *see* public/private spheres
processing people 133, 139-40
professionalism/professional practice
1-8, 46-7
in Britain 3, 4-7
challenges to 7, 8
characteristics 320-1
defence mechanisms 26-7
in Germany 3-4, 7-8
identity of teachers in France 11-12,
265-81
new professionalism 9, 50
professional histories 166
self-awareness 10-11
and sexual identity 303-4
skills and training 29-31

state control
   in East Germany 132-45
   in Russia 115-16, 123-5, 127-8
Prosser, J. 213
prostitution: biographical methods 165,
   167, 169
'protective touch' 214-15
'proximity': French interpretation 20
Prussian bureaucrats 128-9*n*
psychoanalytical approaches
   Balint groups 301
   feminist psychoanalysis 305-6
   Holocaust survivors and suffering
      101-11
   trauma and emotionality 93-9
   violent men as defended subjects
      152-60
psychodynamic approaches 2, 5-6, 25,
   26
   Holocaust survivors 103-7
psychology
   cultural psychology of learning and
      health 299-310
   of old age 6
public sector employment
   in France 115
   in Russia 115-29
public/private spheres: caring 21-2

Q

qualifying needs 245

R

race
   and healthcare practices 205-17
   and identity 11
   see also ethnic minorities
racism 209-10, 318
Randall, J. 232*n*
Rath, J. 41-2
reconstructive social pedagogy 26
'redemptive heroism' 108-9
regulatory culture 5-6, 8, 27
relational settings 12
resistance: embodied resistance 209-17
RESPECT 149
Rhineland welfare model 41
Ricoeur, P. 267
Riemann, Gerhard 3, 328*n*
risk
   aversion of ethnic entrepreneurs 82-4

and biographical method in health
   167
risk society: SOSTRIS project 22-3
Roer, D 28, 29
Rosenberg, H. 123, 128-9*n*
Rosenthal, G. 183, 188
Royal Commission on Long-Term Care
   232*n*
Russia: public and private sector
   employment 10, 115-29
Rustin, M. 25

S

Sabras 108-9
Salamon, Alice 20
Sassen, S. 41
Schumpeter, Joseph 74
Schütze, Fritz 3-4, 61, 145*n*, 320, 326
screen memory 137
Sedgwick, Charles 294
Selah, O. 106
self-advocacy 225
self-awareness of professionals 10-11
self-directed learning for GPs 299-300
self-employment of migrants 39-53
   biographical embeddedness 57-68
   entrepreneurship 73-88
   and gender 9, 40, 42-53, 65-7, 82-7
   resources for 58-68
SEM project *see* self-employment of
   migrants
semantic codes 143
separate spheres 21-2
sequential analysis 44-5, 52-3*n*
service users
   as consumers 7
   participation 2, 5, 6
sexual identity 303-4
shared cultures in caring 22
Shipman, Harold 299
Simon, Sherry 196
Simpson, P. 6
situated knowledge 320
skills *see* education and training
Smith, Graham 168, 169
social assistance careers of lone mothers
   in Venice 241
social background: life-course regime in
   East Germany 144
'social bath' 214
social capital 58-9, 60, 80
social change *see* social transformation;
   transformation research

social citizenship 51-2
social difference 205, 216
social exclusion
  and biographical methods 23, 26-7
  health inequalities 168
  see also marginalised groups; SOSTRIS
    project
social interactionism 26, 33*n*
social pedagogy 20
social policy: European comparative
  review 19-34
social recognition
  as motive for migrant entrepreneurs
    63, 65-6, 67-8, 79
  in Soviet professions 116
social strategy 98
social subject 93-9
social transformation 2, 10
  coping with risk society 23
social workers
  biographical constructions of lone
    mothers in Venice 237-49
  needs of homeless men 251-61
  skills and training 29
  see also professional practice
'sociopoiesis' 24-5
somatic experiences 205, 213, 216
Somers, Margaret 168, 285, 286
SOSTRIS project 22-3, 24, 27, 232*n*
  workshop experience 31
Sowell, T. 76
Spanò, A. 28
Spivak, Gayatri 193, 195, 196, 199
Stanley, Jo 172
Stanley, Liz 194, 302
state control of professional life
  East Germany 132-45
  Russia 115-16, 123-5, 127-8
Steedman, Carolyn 31
Steinert, Heinz 52*n*
structural hermeneutics 2
'structural opportunity model' 74-6, 86,
  88
  German migrants 76-7
structural text analysis 182, 186-8
structuration theory 98
structure and agency 24
subjectivity 9-10
  and male violence 151, 152-8
  in social theory 19-20, 23-6
  see also intersubjectivity; ontology of
    human subject; psychodynamic
    approaches
'surplus population' 39

'suspension of belief' 10, 142
syllogism 53*n*
symbolic interactionism 2, 46
systems of power *see* power relations
systems theory 24, 33*n*

T

teachers
  professional identity in France 11-12,
    265-81
  research journals 285
textual analysis
  ethics of revealing more than narrator
    intended 152, 185, 186-8
  life story narratives 267-8, 270-7
  mediated biographies 240
textuality 118, 129*n*
therapy: narrative work as 171-2, 183,
  309
Thompson, P. 167, 224
Thomsen, M.N. 77-8
Thomson, Al 173
To Reflect and Trust group 109-10
top-down practice 226-8
top-down research 222-3, 224-5, 229
touch in healthcare 214-15
training *see* education and training
trajectories
  control of 61
  disempowerment trajectories 11
  see turning points
transformation economies *see* East
  Germany; Russia
transformation research 140-5
translation 193-200
  politics of 193, 194-7
trauma 63, 95-6, 97, 98, 102
  see also Holocaust survivors
TSER project *see* self-employment of
  migrants; SEM and SOSTRIS
  projects
turning points 241
  see epiphany
Twigg, J. 214

U

undiscussability 102
unemployment: self-employment
  schemes 57-8
universal translation 194
universities: foreign students in
  Germany 12, 313-28

'unknown future' 126, 128
unlived lives 9, 24
  as motivation for self-employment 36,
    61, 62, 64-5, 67-8
user participation 2, 5, 6

V

'vacancy-chain businesses' 41-2
Velvet Revolution 134, 135
Venice: biographical methods and lone
    mothers 11, 237-49
violent men *see* male violence
Vobruba, Georg 28
vocational cultures 143
voluntary sector in New Zealand 286,
    288-9

W

Waldinger, R. 41, 75
Walker, Robert 33*n*
Walmsley, Jan 166, 225
war trauma counsellors in Kosovo 93,
    95-6
Warner, S. 211
Weigand, W. 260*n*
Weizsäcker, Victor von 61
welfare systems
  gender dualism 237-8
  models and self-employment 41-2, 51
  role of biographical methods 19
  see also healthcare; social workers
Wengraf, T. 196
Whiteford, L. 167
Willis, Paul 158
Winslade, John 172
Winter, R. 30-1
women
  self-employment 9, 40, 42-53, 65-7,
    82-7
  see also gender; male violence
Women's Units 149-50
Woods, P. 269
work traditions 143
workshop experience 31
Wright Mills, C. 23

Z

zero point 241